27 April 2013
Oldfields Spirit Night

To Alyssa —

Hope you enjoy
the flying changes in

Flying Change

these pages!

[signature]

Flying Change

A Year of Racing and Family and Steeplechasing

PATRICK SMITHWICK

Chesapeake
BOOK COMPANY

BALTIMORE, MARYLAND
2012

Library of Congress Cataloging-in-Publication Data

Smithwick, Patrick, 1951-
Flying change : a year of racing and family and steeplechasing / Patrick Smithwick.
p. cm.
ISBN 978-0-9823049-4-5 (alk. paper)
1. Smithwick, Patrick, 1951- 2. Jockeys--United States--Biography. 3. Steeplechasing--United States. I. Title.
 SF336.S623S64 2012
798.40092--dc23
[B]
                   2012001236

Manufactured in the United States of America. The paper used in this publication meets the minimum requirements of the American National Standard for Information Sciences Permanence of Paper for Printed Library Materials ANSI Z39.48-1984.

Available wherever fine books are sold. Distributed by Alan C. Hood & Co., Inc., P.O. Box 775, Chambersburg, PA 17201 (Phone: 717-267-0867; Toll-free Fax for orders, 888-844-9433; www.hoodbooks.com.)

For Ansley,

And our children—

Eliza, Andrew and Paddy

Contents

Everyman

YOU DON'T KNOW ME unless you've read a book by the name of *Racing My Father*. That book was written mostly when I was younger, and I told the truth, mainly. For propriety's sake—or was it for the sake of my children, or of my wife, or of the people about whom I was writing?—I toned it down a bit. Maybe I did this to make it all believable.

There was more drinking than I described, more vodka and bourbon poured into black coffee in the early morning hours, and there was more carousing, more men and women seducing each other, whether at the bar of the Brass Rail at Delaware Park, at a booth at Sperry's in Saratoga Springs or at a table at Esposito's outside the back gates of Belmont Park, but I discovered that people didn't believe the real thing. They thought I was telling "stretchers." So, I toned it down, even about the horses, especially the rogues—the ones that want to bite and kick you, run off with you, that act like they would run right through the outside rail by the three-eighths pole at Pimlico Racetrack, through the ten-foot-high chain-link fence topped with a roll of razor-sharp concertina wire, and end up flipped over on Northern Parkway. Readers of early drafts couldn't understand why we all lived that way then, what we did to straighten out those rogues—as well as ourselves—and what happened to those who didn't straighten out.

That book was about my father, A. P. "Paddy" Smithwick, a legendary and much-loved steeplechase jockey, a member of the National Museum of Racing's Hall of Fame. *Racing My Father* focused on my youth and my relationship with my father—a father, a youth and a relationship that I loved. Pop died when I was twenty-one. Six years later, I became a father. After the birth of the first of our three children, A. P. "Paddy" Smithwick III, I strove to carve out an upbringing for my children that they would love, taking the best of what I learned from my father, mother and grandmothers, and putting it into action. Our life as a family of five was proceeding along these lines when I decided to undertake a quest that many believed was directly opposed to being a responsible father: to return to a passion of my childhood.

The memoir of that quest, *Flying Change*, is in no way meant to depict the protagonist—myself—as a great rider or heroic figure. This is in contrast to *Racing My Father*, in which my father is shown in action and discussed by friends, colleagues, and writers as a charismatic figure and as the greatest steeplechase rider of all time. *Flying Change* happens to be about the one subject that I know better than anyone else except my wife Ansley, and she's busy enough raising three children, tending her gardens, keeping track of me, teaching French, and running the academic program of a boarding school three hundred and sixty-five days a year without writing a book on her husband's adventures. So I wrote it. And in it, I have tried to show the physicality, the sensuality, the love of the horse on one hand and the lure of the racetrack on the other. It was my aim to inspire the reader from any background, any continent, any age—especially the mid-life reader—to , as Jake Barnes says about bullfighters in Ernest Hemingway's *The Sun Also Rises*, "live life all the way up."

Flying Change is a close-up account, a narrative of an Everyman who makes a sudden one-hundred-and-eighty-degree life change. Then, while attempting to keep his family, love and professional life intact—with the psychological odds stacked against him, his wife and mother disapproving of his new goal, naysayers deriding his decision and thirsting for schadenfreude, kibitzers criticizing his every move—goes for it while making plenty of mistakes, errors and wrong decisions along the way.

If only we could gallop and school those horses again, lose those pounds again, ride those races again, listen to those directions from a childhood friend who is the country's best steeplechase trainer and from an uncle who was steeplechasing's greatest Hunt Cup rider, again, well then, we certainly would have . . . but life's not like that, race riding's not like that.

You get *one* time at bat, and while you're up there, you get *one* swing. You can't analyze that swing, critique it, redesign it and then do it over just so gracefully, perfectly, powerfully, even if writing—with its propensity for being edited, revised, polished, honed, rewritten—*is* like that. And so, I keep riding. I keep writing.

PART ONE

To Far-off Shrines

When April with his showers sweet

The drought of March has pierced to the root,

And bathed every vein in such liquor,

From whose virtue is engendered the flower; . . .

Then people long to go on pilgrimages . . .

To far-off shrines, known in sundry lands;

And especially, from every shire's end

Of England, to Canterbury they wend,

The holy blessed martyr to seek,

Who helped them, when they were sick.

— Geoffrey Chaucer, *Canterbury Tales*

CHAPTER 1

Call Me Ishmael

There are twenty-two fences in the four-mile Maryland Hunt Cup, the toughest timber race in the world, held the last weekend of April. The first fence is a black four-foot, four-board fence. There are a dozen panels. You jump it after starting at the bottom of a hill. It sets up nicely. Often, a group of horses jumps it together. Sometimes riders do not pay enough attention to the first. They let the horses get in too close and the horses unnecessarily hit the top board, which is thick and of oak and will not break.

"In the air," says Uncle Mikey, seated on the top rail three days before the running of the race, "You need to be looking at the next fence." He holds up his right hand — mottled, sun-seared, palm permanently blue-black from being caught in a loop-tightening shank as he was dragged across a field by a colt — points at the second fence, "maybe even pulling a little on the left rein, Sonny-Boy, so that the second you land you take the straightest and shortest route."

We climb down and walk through the thick grass. He is hunched over and we are poking along but if a pretty girl were to show up, our pace would quicken and his posture would stiffen. He stops, looks up. "Don't wander off this way like some amateur bug boy and lose three lengths," he asserts, catching his breath and waving his cane toward the big hill from where in his heyday tens of thousands of mint julep-sipping spectators — the men in three-piece suits topped off with fedoras, the women in long dresses and floppy straw hats — used to cheer him on as year after year he put on a show winning six out of the twelve Hunt Cups in which he rode. From under the sharply tilted visor of his Irish wool cap, from

3

under his thick gray eyebrows, his dark brown eyes squint in a way that reminds me of my father, his brother, and he says, "You might need those three lengths at the wire."

⌇

J ULY 1998. WE HAD A CABIN in the Adirondacks in the midst of a small summer camp for teenagers on Saranac Lake. We were having a blissful time. The whole family was together. It was Utopia. We were at Camp Forestcraft for a week, and then we'd go to Saratoga Springs to stand in the winner's circle, no matter who won, and present the trophy in honor of my father, A. P. "Paddy" Smithwick—the legendary steeple-chase jockey, the grandfather my children never met—after his memorial race. I was forty-seven years old. Or, six months past the age of my father at his death. Unexplored territory. On my own. I was at an age my father never reached.

Late one afternoon, I was sitting on round cannon-sized river rocks, piles and piles of them at the bottom of what, if nobody had been there, I would have called a stunningly beautiful series of high waterfalls. Yet, we were close to the main road, and the whole entourage of waterfall daredev-ils and groupies was present: the over-twenty-one-year-old men smoking cigarettes and drinking beer, their bellies and love handles bulging over the empty belt loops of their cutoff blue jeans; their pale, smoking and wine-cooler-drinking girlfriends in tank tops and cutoffs; the teenagers in their still-gaunt frames climbing nimbly up to the highest leaping point, climbing easily, freely, quickly; the over-twenty men, with their muscle and added padding looking invulnerable, knowledgeable, professional, climb-ing to the perfect spot where they had climbed a thousand times before and showing their comrades as well as the younger set that they could still do it. It was all there, the cussing, the daring, the yelling, the swaggering, the smoking, the drinking, the littering, the broken glass. Over the years, I had been to many of these waterfalls where my sons Paddy and Andrew were always lured by the local daredevils into leaping off cliffs and out of trees and across rocks, and I did not view these cascades as picturesquely as one would otherwise.

This day I had felt creaky as I crawled upwards over slippery and jagged rocks in bare feet to watch Andrew, fourteen, leap from a four-story rock promontory into a pool of water, and to watch others leap off a six-story ledge—out, out, if they were going to make it, out past the rocky edge, but away from the smooth, deadly rock on their right, and yet not too far out, not too close to the other side where the water was shallow and they might break a leg or two. They had to hit the six-foot-wide bull's-eye. Three weeks ago, by missing this target, a young man had lost his life.

I used to leap. A couple of years earlier in North Carolina, cajoled and teased by Andrew and Paddy, and their Uncle Graham, I had leaped off rocks into pools and had bounced down Bust-Your-Butt Falls, even after hearing someone had drowned there that summer. But now, I had neither the light carefree touch of the supple, skinny teenagers on the rock face, nor the experienced professional look with the added muscle and padding of the twenty-plus-year-olds. I was closer to being an old goat in a gaunt teenage body, a fifty-year-old novice who was out of his league, climbing where there was not one person over the age of twenty-five. Unlike the ten or so males and five or six females huddled together smoking and drinking above, I was being awaited by my wife and daughter with the other children and families down below the falls beside the large natural pool with water so clear that swimming underwater you could see each uniquely shaped and colored pebble on the bottom and you could distinguish the red and blue and yellow swatches on the individual scales of each fish swimming past. I did not go to the cliff to jump off. I was saying goodbye to cliff jumping; this was the first time in my life I had made this sort of concession to age. I sat on the edge of the cliff. Andrew stood tall, storklike, on the promontory across the pool. He grinned at me.

I nodded and smiled back.

He waved.

I waved back.

"Come on over Dad," he hollered.

I shook my head and yelled, "No thanks."

He stepped forward, swung his arms behind him, and then his knees flexed and his arms shot forward and he was flying through the air, mouth wide open releasing a primal scream, arms and legs spinning and wheeling around as if he were trying to catch hold of something. He slammed into the water, making an explosive splash, and then stayed under . . . , stayed under . . . , stayed under . . . , and finally shot up out of the surface gasping and blinking and grinning victoriously.

I crawled stiffly down the rocks, jagged on my cold feet. Swam, retreating, across the pool, back to Ansley and Eliza. Andrew was climbing up to the outcropping of the four-story rock again. Paddy, nineteen, was off with a group of elite campers on a three-day mountain-climbing expedition. I was reminded of a prior experience, a similar feeling, but I couldn't recall it. I had been through this before. Déjà vu. I crawled along, thinking of trips I'd taken with the kids and then it came to me, the ski trip to Canada last spring. Down a narrow, steep, icy, concave slope the boys had flown, their paths intertwining, lacing in and out of each other. And there I'd been at the top: cold, fatigued, leaning on my poles, recouping my strength, looking down at them. I'd been happy and fulfilled that they—whom I had taught to ski—could do this, and I'd known that soon after I pushed off I'd feel the red-hot burning in my thighs. My days were numbered keeping up with these two. How the hell was I going to get down this steep, tube-like slope, especially with these old secondhand racing skis that were long and straight and stiff as hell, hard to handle in tight, tricky spots. "Come *on* Dad. You can do it!" the boys had yelled. The adrenalin, the old war cry—it was still there, it rose up in me, filled my chest. I'd pushed off. I'd gotten in a good rhythm. I had to keep it, hold this rhythm. Bam, bam, bam, I'd made the turns. Back and forth, back and forth. I'd show these young-bloods who's an old geezer. Thighs burning, aching. Then, I'd gotten late on a turn. I made it to the edge of the tube, whipped around and started heading to the other side going too fast now, tips of skis pointed too much down the hill now, weight too far back. I jammed my edges into the snow, uplifted to make the turn, crossed the tips of my skis, and fell, rolled, skidded, a whirligig of poles and skis and arms and legs, the rest of the way down the chute. "Are you all right Dad? Are you OK?" they'd asked, patting the snow off me. "Yes, yes, I'm fine," I'd said, standing up, pulling myself together, hurting a little here and there, feeling like the most pathetic of old farts. They held back the rest of the way down the mountain. At the bottom I asked if they wanted to go in for a hot chocolate. "No, Dad!" Andrew said, leaning back, pushing powerfully with his poles, and skating off with his big brother toward the lift. Into the lodge I'd hobbled, looking for my wife and eight-year-old daughter.

At the waterfall, Eliza was in front of me, doing something photogenic. Making something. She's always creating, forming, drawing, painting, pulling beads onto tiny wires, cutting paper characters, collecting stones and shells, designing a rug for her doll house by coloring patterns on a sheet of paper. I awkwardly crawled across the rocks to my satchel, pulled out my nineteen-year-old Vivitar with the screw-mount lens that we'd bought when Paddy was born. Had a good seat but was too close to my subject. Didn't want to distract Eliza by moving. Leaned back to get a better shot, certain there was a rock behind me that my back would touch and that would then support me. I leaned and kept going. Back I went, camera in right hand. I was falling backwards to my right. I couldn't put my hand out. I felt foolish. I was falling—the drop well below the height of my rump—my right elbow catching, smashing against a pumpkin-sized rock and my lower back, my kidneys, taking the rest of the fall. My head— luckily there was no rock for my head to crack against.

"Are you all right Sweetheart? Are you all right?" Ansley asked.

A woman in her twenties sat four arm lengths from me. Half an hour ago, she'd been in the same spot while a local man in his forties watched his young daughter swim and discussed the danger of the waterfalls with me, told me of the death at these falls he'd witnessed a few weeks earlier. We'd spoken disparagingly of the youths climbing up the precipices and leaping off. And now here I was, foolish and creaky, brittle and out of place, stunned, like a turtle—or a cockroach—on its back, my feet above my head. At first, I just lay there. Then, like Kafka's Gregor in *The Meta-morphosis*, I wiggled and struggled to get up, knowing I was lucky not to have been knocked out. My lower back and kidneys felt as if Muhammad Ali had used them as a punching bag. The point of my elbow stung. Each time I moved my arm an electric shock started in the elbow and sizzled up to the tips of my fingers.

I wanted to leave. If I were to put myself on the line, let it be on a horse, live flesh. Let my legs be wrapped around a fellow living being with a soft, smooth, bay or gray or chestnut coat, a moving, jigging, snorting body, a galloping, racing, flying animal. Let me sail through the air on an animal that can respond to my directions and let his or her legs be moving, be galloping, be suspended in flight over the turf, and leave these stones— unforgiving, uncaring, unchanging—to others.

That night I had a horse dream with both sisters in it: I am on Ben Nevis, winner of both the Maryland Hunt Cup and the English Grand National with Charlie Fenwick in the tack. I am riding him for Charlie, schooling cross-country. He's jumping well. I am preparing to ride him in the Hunt Cup. He's a shoo-in. He jumps easily, smoothly, gracefully around the Elkridge-Harford racecourse. He feels powerful between my legs. Charlie and other Fenwicks, including my first wife, Carol, are around. We are all happy. My sister Sal is with me, on a gray pony. She is following me and I am watching out for what we jump. I awaken, wonder why the hell I am having this dream here in the Adirondacks, why I always dream of horses when on vacation. Back to sleep.

Now I am on Florida Law, a big, rangy gray horse trained by Tom Voss. I'm out foxhunting over by Atlanta Hall, the Voss farm. We are galloping across the "finish line field" of the Elkridge-Harford racecourse. Mimi, Tom's wife, yells, "Go on Patrick!" wanting me to push Florida, to get him fit for the races. Sister Sue Sue is with me on a small, dark brown pony; we are kids now and I am watching out for her. I want to release Florida, let him gallop over these fences with the other horses but I hold back, won-dering if Sue Sue's pony can handle fences this high.

I feel comfortable, confident and at ease on Florida, whom I have hunted for years but there is some sort of mix-up on the hunting clothes. And I have one of these new-fangled stirrups where the cross-piece is on a swivel and I don't like it at all. It is on my right leather. Then I'm cooling Florida out in Tom's indoor track, walking beside him and losing my clothes. Suddenly, I have no shoes on. I am barefoot, walking alongside this huge gray—almost white—horse with big feet that have steel shoes nailed to them. I am not concerned. Florida is a close friend and he will not step on my feet. Tom has walked off, is joking around, and won't help. Dickie Small, a fellow Gilman student, is there, in a boyhood way. I ask him to help. Then I dream I am back at Gilman School, as a student— comfortable, safe and happy.

I lie there giving myself the choice between riding Florida or Ben Nevis. I add up their ages, Florida, thirteen, Ben Nevis, over twenty. It is funny. Nothing serious.

AWAKENING IN OUR CABIN at Camp Forestcraft, I remembered that Eliza was up the hill, having spent the night with her new friend, Andrea, and Paddy was still off with a group of hardy boys and girls on the mountain-climbing trip. Extremely hardy—most of the boys were preparing for a wrestling camp. Each time they reached the top of a mountain (they were climbing three or four a day, climbing them fast, trying to set a Forestcraft record) they'd knock off forty-six push-ups, one for each of the High Peaks, all of which they were going to climb. Paddy, my first son, my father's namesake, my partner for so many years, an extension of my body, of my soul for all of his early years, now seemed to be perpetually gone: off at college, off camping with the big shots, off at parties, off on dates, off playing lacrosse. It was Ansley, Andrew and I today.

We grabbed a stack of sandwiches the Forestcraft cook made us after he'd served up a breakfast of oatmeal with yogurt, nuts, raisins and peaches, and scrambled eggs, sausage and toast. Ansley neatly packed water jugs and the sandwiches in a backpack and was ready to leave for a hike right away. I made myself unpopular by going off to the boathouse, writing for an hour and jumping in the lake. Upon returning, I fussed around taking too long, looking for the right clothes, checking the camera, checking the film canister, finding my book on trees, while Ansley watched, stared, and commented. Finally, we loaded ourselves into the Volvo and headed for Ampersand Mountain. Andrew was by himself, or, solely with us, depending on your point of view. No Eliza on one side; no Paddy on the other. No fighting and elbowing and arguing over space. Yet, this didn't pick him up at all; it brought him down: Eliza was "with a friend having a ball," and Paddy had been OK'd to go on a "real mountain-climbing trip" and was off "having fun" with all his new friends. Andrew, the middle child, was stuck in the middle again. He was with his boring parents. And he had not been chosen to go on the hiking trip; in fact, he'd been told by the assistant head of the camp—now definitely *not* a favorite of mine—that he could not go. Sitting in the back seat, Andrew did his depressed thing: he leaned over and went to sleep.

I was looking forward to the easy climb up Ampersand, just the three of us. Eliza had gotten bored and tired on some earlier hikes, and I'd had to carry her. The kids at camp had told us this wasn't a tough climb; in fact, they said Eliza could handle it. Since the climb wasn't steep or rocky, I'd left behind the 1950s, heavy-duty, thick-soled hiking boots I'd bought a decade ago in a consignment shop.

After we'd driven for ten minutes, Andrew started humming. He began muttering some lyrics. He used the tune to frame his own lyrics; he was be-bopping along, with an occasional squelch from Ansley to pipe down. I was enjoying it.

We parked—he was out and it was Andrew Unleashed. Ansley and I laughed as he composed the quick-rhyming song and went into a rap rhythm with it. We started up the path. Ah, much easier than yesterday's climb, such a gradual incline. Andrew be-bopped along, his limber, lanky legs eating up the path. He dashed ahead, finding walking staffs, talking nonstop, rapping, singing, telling stories, asking questions: Andrew Freed. Ansley and I laughed and strolled, free and easy and happy.

The path steepened. Ansley had been right, as usual, this time about leaving immediately after breakfast. We'd gotten a late start, I realized, as

I saw more and more hikers funneling down the mountain, but I certainly didn't draw attention to this revelation. I commenced to sweat, to feel my chest expand and contract with every breath. No matter how far I expanded my chest, my lungs were not getting enough oxygen. I concentrated on lifting one leg and setting it down, then lifting the other and setting it down. Andrew zigzagged back and forth, bounding twenty or thirty yards ahead, and then posing, leaning against a tree, waiting. Nonchalant, he philosophized and directed us on what path to take. Looking out over the canopy of trees toward Saranac Lake, he delivered reports on the beauty of what he could see from his high perch while I focused on maneuvering over the gnarly roots and sharp rocks in the dirt gully.

Ansley marched upwards, stopping to examine trees and ferns and flowers, and to give their names and species. I stopped beside her, stared at the tree leaf, flower or fern she was discussing, and tried to memorize its name and characteristics. I had a journal and an aged, mouse-chewed paperback on trees in my satchel. To prepare for this trip, I had been reveling in yet another reading of my green, leather-bound copy of *Walden*. While packing, I had decided that, Thoreau-like, I would study and take notes on trees during our hikes. I had sandwiched half a dozen tree leaves from other climbs between the pages of the journal. In the evenings, by our fire, I had written down the date and place of collection, and notes on each leaf.

This was a beginning. The Adirondacks were my Walden Pond. This was a turning away from the world of horses. I could study the Adirondacks; the mountains would launch me into new non-horse interests and subjects to write about.

The Vivitar, heavy compared to the new plastic cameras, hung from my shoulders. I kneeled, set the f-stop and aperture opening, focused, and snapped a shot of Andrew standing majestically, like Moses, staff in hand, on a boulder.

The path became a rut, an eroded vertical ditch. It was wide, three to six feet, not a blade of grass in it. Dirt and roots and sharp rocks. Straight up in places, a scar ripped through the timber line. There was no breeze. The air was heavy, hot, humid. My eyes were on the terrain before me.

Having a difficult time breathing, I proceeded slowly, behind Andrew, in front of Ansley. What the hell had those kids at Forestcraft meant by "an easy climb." I stopped and listened as Ansley pointed out the Latin name of a fern—she was into ferns—its common name, its characteristics and soon the genus and species and characteristics were whirling around in my mind and I could not distinguish one from the other.

Andrew leapt ahead. Light and graceful as a bird, his thin frame flew from rock to rock, sped up the steep inclines, glided up and over and around the eerily protruding roots.

What was going on here? I had been running a few miles every day. I had been swimming and bicycling. I should be far fitter than this upstart but my more muscled legs were plodding along while those great blue heron legs of his sprung up the mountain as if buoyed by wings from boulder to tree trunk to precariously outreaching root.

The top was sheer rock, rounded, windswept. The wind blew and the view of lakes and mountain forests—the full 360-degree expanse—was majestic. The sun warmed our backs and dried our shirts. We sat out of the wind on the leeward side of an outcropping and ate our sandwiches, resting our legs and looking out over thousands of acres of mountains and lakes.

We stood up and walked around the rock. A hiker in all the best gear, including a new, sleek, state-of-the-art pair of hiking boots, lined his wife up, with Saranac Lake in the background, to photograph her. I volunteered to photograph them both. He unzipped his "fanny pack," pulled out a compact camera and handed it to me. It felt useless, like a plastic toy in my hands. I took a couple of shots of the grinning couple, each leaning on a pair of shiny, ski pole-like walking staffs, as if they were about to push off and schuss down the mountain but had forgotten to snap on their skis. I then handed the man my Vivitar. He gently laid his walking staffs on the hard rock without scratching their metallic surface. They were strange looking—toward the bottom where the basket to keep the pole from sliding into the snow should be, there were spring-loaded shock absorbers.

Our photographer looked about my age and I felt a commonality—he would know how to adjust the settings. Andrew, Ansley and I posed where the couple had stood. Our photographer squinted through the viewfinder, then lowered the camera, his eyebrows knotted in a puzzled expression. I trotted over to him, pointed the camera toward Ansley and Andrew, checked the shutter speed, focused on Ansley's nose, and ran back. Lord, I must be even older than he if he can't use this simple camera. I felt as if an ally had deserted me. Andrew laughed and joked to his mother about ". . . Dad's old-fashioned camera, something you see in the black-and-white movies."

Going down, Andrew shot ahead. He skied down, *wedelned* down. As soon as the slope steepened, my quadriceps strained on every step. Andrew leapt here and there. He found Ansley and me walking sticks, told us we should buy a couple of walking staffs like the couple had. "That would be a ridiculous waste of money," I announced, though I was concerned about taking pressure off my knees, especially the right one which I had broken as a teenager in a motorcycle accident. I worked around this knee, setting the left leg down first to absorb the shock. The thigh muscles pulled against me. I used two staffs like ski poles but I didn't hop or jump like Andrew. This worked well at first. I put more and more of my weight onto the staffs. Suddenly, it felt as if my right elbow had been shocked with a cow prod. A sizzling, electrical current ran through it, down my arm and into my little finger, and I remembered the previous day's fall on the rocks. I stopped putting as much weight on the right staff and I even imagined how the shock absorbers on the poles of the perfect hiking couple would be useful at this point. Then I stepped awkwardly on a rock and my left foot, in just the running shoe, twisted, this the same foot I had sprained last spring training to ride in the Wild Goose Chase.

I could feel a sharpness in the right knee. An ache in the left foot. I didn't want to exacerbate either further. I especially wanted my knee in good shape for further hiking, and for galloping at Saratoga. Horses. They were in the back of my mind. I imagined heading down this path on a horse, my legs like those of Confederate Colonel John S. Mosby's, gracefully, naturally, wrapped around the rib cage of my mount as I led my band of Raiders behind Union lines. Both thighs burned as I leaned back into the mountain. My elbow was zapped with the electric shock when I relied

too much on the right pole. I gingerly picked my way, stepping down two-
or three-foot inclines, my eyes on the gully, the roots, the rocks. We were
deep in this scar on the mountain proceeding through the stagnant air.
Ansley marched ahead. Andrew flew down, leaping from one side of the
gully to the other.

I gave in to my role of the old guy lagging behind. This was Andrew's
first foray out into the lead. He was calling back, "You OK Dad? Come on,
this part's not so steep."

BACK AT THE CAMP, after dinner, I stepped into a canoe and paddled along
the shore of Gilpin Bay, up to the point and back. I felt strong, able. I returned and found Andrew lying around in the cabin.

"Andrew, come on, let's canoe around the lake."

"No, I'm good."

"Come on, it's beautiful out. The sun's setting."

"No thanks. I'm fine here."

At this point, I did something all the child psychologists, and my wife,
and my sisters—but perhaps not my mother—would berate me for, but
too bad, they weren't around. I casually stepped behind Andrew as if I
were looking for some clothing, grabbed his strong, wiry right arm with
both my hands, twisted it up behind his back, marched him down the path
through the woods to the boathouse and forced him into the canoe. Out we
paddled, past the point, on a two-hour trip around the Girl Scout camp,
which had its own special thirty-acre island. We paddled quietly, staying
down low, spying on the hundreds of girls wandering around the wooded
island in little groups. The energy level on the island gradually picked up.
The girls were running down paths and in and out of their cabins, doors
slamming behind them, laughing and calling to each other. Forty yards
off the shore of the island, we quietly paddled, watching the girls filter
through the trees to a clearing near the southern tip of the island where
there was a campfire. They bustled and laughed and called to each other
as we paddled, and then as the sun dipped below the tree line, all we could
see was the glow of a bonfire.

For a minute, they were quiet. We listened to the dipping of our paddles, the *swush* of the paddle beneath the surface, and the *plash* of the paddle pulling out. We fell into a rhythm, our paddles dipping into the water and pulling out, as one. We listened to the *pat-pat-pat* of the bow making its way through the ripples, and we heard and felt the hollow-echoes caused by the ripples reverberating through the body of the canoe. And then, the dipping in and splashing out was overwhelmed by the rising swell of young voices united choir-like, their singing flowing out over the water to us like a fresh breeze. Andrew was mesmerized. I was too.

Returning, Andrew grew tired. I let him rest and paddled on my own, the J-stroke gradually coming back to me, my shoulders feeling it. Andrew lost his sense of direction and I tested him on it, with the moon and the stars and the island and the lights of the boathouses ahead. I taught him how to get his bearings on the water by lining up three points and felt back in my role of knowing our direction and being able to handle the physical stress—of welcoming it, taking it on, for my sons, for my daughter, for my wife, for my family.

THE NEXT MORNING, I wanted to get back on the water. It was cold and blustery. Looked like it would rain. No one would want to hike today. But look at that breeze. Ansley and I had lived on the Eastern Shore of Maryland when we'd first gotten married, and I had worked for two years as a waterman on the Chesapeake Bay, dredging for oysters on the skipjack fleet, the only working-sailing fleet in North America, and crewing on a crab boat. In the Adirondacks, I had been eying the many boats both inside and outside the Forestcraft boathouse.

You walked down a wooded path from our cabin out onto the dock with the boathouse on your right, Saranac Lake directly before you. The boathouse was wood-shingled and barn-sized, two stories with a gabled roof. There were two big slips inside and above the slips, a high-ceilinged, capacious, pine-paneled room housing two worn Ping-Pong tables. I loved rising early in our cabin, perking a pot of coffee in the old, dented aluminum percolator, jumping naked into the frigid lake, toweling off and then

sipping a mug of the strong, gritty, black coffee as I wrote in my journal on the Ping-Pong table in the mist-softened rays of the sun, and then,
on a fresh legal pad, worked on the latest chapter of a book on my father
while the waves I'd stirred lapped against the dock below and the boats
and their riggings knocked and jangled against their moorings. Outside
this big room, a balcony hung out over the water. On hot afternoons, the
campers and my sons climbed up on the railing of the balcony and dived
and jumped and cannonaded into the lake. One afternoon, Eliza jumped
off the balcony. And then, I had too.

A flotilla of all types of boats clung to the walls of the building. Above
the rowboat and the old motor launch jostling restlessly in their slips, long
Indian war canoes swung from block and tackle. Exquisitely made Adirondack guide boats—long, sleek, light, rowing vessels—hung from the
back of the building. I had set *Walden* aside one evening and picked up a
paperback from our cabin bookshelf, *The Adirondack Letters of George
Washington Sears*. Sears loved lightweight canoes. He thought they were
the answer to most of humanity's woes and that they were far superior to
the Adirondack guide boat. Nessmuck, the pen name he used in the 1880s,
became my literary inspirer as well as a guide to the waterways of the Adirondacks. Nessmuck and Henry David both carved paragraphs as lean as
their bodies and were Spartan when it came to the necessities of life, such
as sleep and food. Neither wrote a word about that other necessity for most
of us males that is somewhat more difficult to wrap up in a blanket and
toss in the bow of a canoe.

Day after day, I was taunted by a fourteen-foot Sunfish bobbing at the
dock. It was a lightweight boat with a fully covered hull except for a small
cockpit where one or two people could brace their feet while holding the
tiller and the sheet (line) to the mainsail. Just the thought of taking it out
brought to mind the sailing I had loved when Ansley and I were first married and lived on the Miles River on the Eastern Shore. I would slap on my
Caliente—my first helmet, which Pop had bought for me and in which I, as
a teenager, had won my first race at Saratoga as an eighteen-year-old on
a rogue named Tote'm Home—climb aboard our old heavy Starfish, push

the deep-reaching centerboard down through its well, clip in the extra-long rudder (both of which I'd built of strong black walnut in these un-usual dimensions so that I could sail in high winds and high waves without capsizing), and let it fly with frightening power and speed in the fall and spring storms coming off the Chesapeake Bay.

FINALLY, IN THE LATE MORNING, Andrew and I marched down to the boathouse. I hadn't rigged a sailboat in fifteen years. We pulled down a mast, and sail and spars, from a high rack. We found a rudder, a tiller and a centerboard. Andrew had never sailed. He helped out while I scrambled around on the deck of the Sunfish. Kidding me, and yet showing some anxiety, he asked every imaginable question about sailing as he watched me recall, at what to him was an agonizingly slow pace, how to rig the boat. Finally, we had the boom in its setting, the centerboard lying by its well, and the rudder lying above its cleats.

I pushed the boat out of the shallow water and we hopped aboard. We struggled a few moments—the boat tippy and unstable with neither the sail up nor the centerboard down. Then, I set the rudder in its cleats, pushed the centerboard down through its well. Andrew hoisted the sail. He sat forward in the cockpit. I handed him the mainsail sheet, the line that regulates the angle of the sail, while I took the tiller. Magically, the sail caught the breeze, we had balance and stability, and the hull cut quietly through the water, headed out of Gilpin Bay.

With Andrew holding the sheet and controlling the angle of the sail, we headed up into the wind. We began to tack: sail northeast, then angle into the wind and over to the other side, duck, come about, the boom swinging over our heads; sail northwest, then angle into the wind and over to the other side, duck, come about, the boom swinging over our heads.

We were out in the open, Andrew laughing and joking and in wonder, his side warm against mine. We lost air, going through the gap formed by Eagle Island, home of the Girl Scout camp, to the east, and the peninsula to the west, but soon we were beating into a wide-open section of Upper Saranac Lake. The wind picked up. The sheet was taut in Andrew's hand, turning his fingers blue. I showed him how to cleat if off and then to lean back, using his whole body, as the boat heeled over.

"Whoa Dad! Whoa Dad! Are you sure you know what you're doing?" The waves smacked against the bow billowing spray over Andrew. We laughed and laughed. On leaving the cabin, I'd grabbed my well-worn Old-fields School sweatshirt and a frayed and faded blue jean jacket, intending to wear both, and told him to grab something too, but it was warm on land and he couldn't see the point. I'd made this mistake once before, the first time I'd boarded a skipjack, for an overnight trip up the Chesapeake Bay, and I'd never do it again. Andrew was in shorts, T-shirt and my jacket. I was in blue jeans, T-shirt and sweatshirt, a favorite, won early the morning of the Maryland Hunt Cup at the Oldfields Alumnae Weekend 5K, during which many of my former students asked why I wasn't race riding that afternoon instead of foot-racing that morning.

We looked toward the southwest. A broad swath of ripples was speeding across the water toward us. "Do you know what those are?" I asked Andrew.

"What?"

"Those ripples. You see them?"

They were really moving now, covering an area the size of a baseball diamond.

"Yes," he said. We were tacking to the northeast and he had to twist around to see them.

"Teddy Rouse, an old friend of mine, used to call them *greenies.*"

"You mean like a green horse?" he asked.

I was surprised by his quickness. "Yes."

They hit. The sail caught the first gust, the boat heeled over and Andrew was yelling, "Dad, Dad, Dad!" and gripping the mainsail sheet as tightly as if his life depended on it. I was laughing and leaning back and then within a split second the tip of the sail was dragging in the water, the hull was on its side, and it looked like we might be taking a swim. I grabbed the sheet out of Andrew's hand, released it, and instantly we were upright. A blitzkrieg of questions, a blast of inquiries, poured from Andrew.

Up into the wind we continued, tacking one direction, coming about, tacking the other, Andrew moving across the deck and ducking under the boom smoothly now, taking the spray each time we came about. My hands and feet were blue and numb and I was loving it. We had a system, we were a team. We picked out a boathouse on a far shore and headed for it. Over and over, beating into the wind, we came about, Andrew ducking and scrambling across the deck as the boom swung over his head.

It was just the two of us and we were having the time of our lives. This was a goal of mine modeled after the sipping coffee and riding and driving and eating and conversing with my father, just the two of us, when I was Andrew's age. In fact, Andrew was now the same age I had been when I'd spent my first summer galloping racehorses at Belmont Park with Pop and had driven him at 80 mph down the Garden State Parkway to Monmouth Park, where he had a fall in a steeplechase race that changed the lives of everyone in our family.

ANDREW SHIVERING, we headed in. We ran before the wind and surfed the waves, no tacking now, no splashing. We glided like a huge swan back to our bay and executed a perfect landing at the dock. Andrew and I dismantled the rigging, hung the sail to dry, put away the rudder and tiller, and tied the boat to its buoy. Knees unbending—reminding me of walking stiff-legged from the barn to the house, my legs numb and cold and molded to the shape of my pony, Queenie, after fox-hunting all day with my mother—Andrew and I scuttled up to the cabin.

The coals in the woodstove were still glowing. Andrew filled the stove with logs of pine and maple from a stack outside the door. We stripped off our cold, wet clothes. I jumped in the bed in the middle of the room and pulled up the covers. Andrew bustled around by the stove, then, holding a steaming mug of hot chocolate, and with a wool blanket over his shoulders, pulled a chair up to the open-faced woodstove, the logs blazing.

I watched in disbelief as he sipped the hot chocolate. "Andrew," I said, "in the future when this sort of occasion arises, you might consider asking the person you're with if he or she would also like a hot chocolate."

"Oh—I thought you just drank coffee—that you'd want coffee . . ."

I let it go.

It could've been the nineteenth century. The eighteenth century. The seventeenth. My son and I and a fire and warmth in the middle of a chilly Adirondacks afternoon after we'd been out together in the wind and the cold and the waves. I told Andrew stories of my days working as a waterman on the Chesapeake Bay, when, enervated by the white-collar world, I had quit my cushy job as a feature writer and photographer for a newspaper immediately after marrying Ansley, and like Ishmael, gone off to work on the water.

For a split second, I saw myself up on a light-bay stakes winner called Epilogue walking down the stretch at Pimlico, in the shadowy light of 5:40 a.m., trainer R. W. "Dickie" Small—back from a tour in Viet Nam as a Green Beret—alongside on his pony, trying to calm Epilogue. Urged on by his three ponytailed galloping girls on other horses around us, Dickie peppered "Professor Smithwick" with literary questions, including, "What's the first sentence of Moby Dick?" But now, I wasn't on Epilogue jigging and dancing and rooting along the outside rail of Pimlico, I wasn't in a classroom at a school, I was here, alone, in a cabin with my son. "Call me Ishmael!" I sang out, as I had twenty years earlier, heels down and calves squeezing against Epilogue's sides.

Andrew raised a quizzical eyebrow, squinted slightly and tilted his forehead forward, maintaining a straight-lipped expression. "Who's Ishmael?" he asked. I was shocked by how he looked as if he were doing an imitation of the expression my father made when concentrating. I stared at him. Eerily, his face, lit only on one side by the flickering light of the flames, lost its three-dimensionality, and I studied it as if it were a one-dimensional painting. In his eyes, or was it something just under his skin, under the thin glaze of undulating paint, I could see he was thinking that I might have just gone off the deep end but that as the dutiful son he would be polite and stick it out.

Looking Andrew in the eye, I attempted to recite the following sentence from the first page of *Moby Dick*:

Whenever I find myself growing grim about the mouth; whenever it is a damp, drizzly November in my soul; whenever I find myself involuntarily pausing before coffin warehouses and bringing up the rear of every funeral I meet; and especially whenever my hypos get such an upper hand of me, that it requires a strong moral principle to prevent me from deliberately stepping into the street, and methodically knocking people's hats off—then, I account it high time to get to sea as soon as I can.

I EXPLAINED TO ANDREW how, fed up with the squabbling and office politics of the newspaper office, I had headed out to sea, and how many another time, under similar circumstances, I had waved goodbye to safe, steady employment at newspapers, private schools, colleges, and magazines, and headed for the racetrack with the music of this one sentence winding its way through the passages of my mind.

The fire crackling, the drizzle drumming on the roof, Andrew stood up, blanket over his shoulders. I watched him walk to the refrigerator and get out a quart of milk. He poured milk into a pot. He turned on the old but bright white gas stove. I stared at the blue-red flames flickering and hissing under the pot. My eyelids closed, the bed felt as if it were rocking in the waves. I drifted off.

"Dad, Dad," I heard. "Dad." It was a whisper. I was confused. I was not sailing the boat. I was in bed and there was a hand gently rubbing my shoulder and then Andrew was handing me a steaming hot chocolate in a heavy, thick-sided, white porcelain mug.

Chapter 2

Babylon Revisited

The second fence of the Hunt Cup would be a good-sized fence in any other race but in this one, and especially with the third coming up, the riders barely give it a look. You have to remember not to do that. It is a post-and-rail with plenty of panels and for years, until a tornado took them down, it was framed by trees on either side and was a favorite of photographers. At this point in the race throughout the thirties, forties, fifties, and sixties the horses had not formed a line, one behind the other, or fallen into a pattern of a twosome in front jumping head-and-head, and a pack of three behind, and a few lengths back, other horses jostling for position. Instead, the horses were fanned out horizontally as they approached the fence, the riders leaning back, trying to settle them, and they jumped it together, a wave of horses and riders flying four feet off the ground. You jump it on an angle and head straight for the crossing over Tufton Avenue, on the other side of which is the third fence. "This is the one that's in the old photos," Uncle Mikey says, climbing over. He stops, glares into my eyes. "Have you ever seen those photos? You see where they're jumping this fence?" He points in disgust to the outside panels. "Look where we are right now, look at the third — you want to be right here, one of these three panels, in line to cross Tufton and jump the third." He climbs down, picks up his cane, looks up toward the crossing, and we march across the field to the big gate leading to where the mulch will be spread across the road.

Upon our arrival in Saratoga Springs, New York, in the late afternoon of an August day, I pull on my running shoes and shorts and T-shirt, head out, up Lake Avenue, toward the old cinder track around which I used to train. I jog up the sidewalk, thinking I will also run around by Pepper's Market and look for the rented house of my childhood friend—"partner" we used to call one another—Tom Voss. I lengthen my stride heading up the sidewalk, past the capacious clapboard houses, feeling a rhythm, the sweat beginning to break, the stiffness from the drive down from the Adirondacks easing out of my pores (all five of us, the entire family, packed into our thirteen-year-old gray Volvo station wagon, two plastic "bubbles" stuffed with bags tied to the roof rack, three bikes hanging off the stern). I accelerate through the gate and into the East Side Rec Area looking forward to getting off the concrete and onto the cinder track which will have the nice slide-give each time a foot strikes.

Onto the playing fields. Boys in full football armor, fishbowl helmets and puffed up shoulder pads making them look as if they might tip over. The coaches—big men. Dedicated fathers younger than I, with waistlines steadily expanding, standing in front of lines and lines of nine, ten, eleven-year-olds. Talking. Explaining. Tossing passes. Showing blocks. Giving. And parents, eased back, out of the arena and on the sidelines for life, in the twilight, watching, sipping cold, brightly colored—orange, blue, yellow—sports drinks out of plastic bottles.

I'm jogging easy. Over to the old cinder oval. The track is no longer a running track—it is smooth as ice, glistening, hard, black. There is only one runner on it. It looks tough on the knees. No slide-give when a foot strikes. The football field inside is green and lush. The stands to the baseball field over to the southeast are empty and quiet and reach lonesomely for the sky and the sky looms vast and violet and streaked with wisps of red. The field is a flat green space, an oasis, in the middle of the now fenced-in track.

I enter through a gate, hope no one orders me out, cross the track, open up my stride and start running around the field, and the other runner is jogging along around the steel-black track with his earphones on, wires attached to a gadget at his hip, and I am traveling back in time in concentric circles jogging on the grass inside the track, which is inside the three-foot-high chain-link fence that in turn is inside the seven-foot chain-link fence around the rec fields, which are inside the city lines of Saratoga Springs.

It is hard to believe that I am the same A. P. Smithwick, Jr. who, thirty years earlier, in a rubber sweat suit and layers of clothes jogged around this track when it was cinders. Here I am now: married, with three children; have written books, edited newspapers, taught too many English classes, worked on newspapers and magazines as a reporter and photographer, worked on the Chesapeake Bay as a dredge hand on a skipjack, a culler for a hand-tonger, a deckhand for a crab-potter; tended bars; galloped count-less racehorses; and I am jogging around this same field on which I used to do sprints and push-ups and sit-ups and the damn duck-walk when I was losing weight to ride races for my father. It's been twenty-five years since my father died, and I am in Saratoga to inhale the life of the racetrack, to see old friends, to celebrate my father's life and present the trophy to the winning jockey of the A. P. Smithwick Memorial Handicap. Yes, I had been watching my weight all the previous week in the Adirondacks. Yes, I had been out running at dusk to be fit and loose and light, to arise at dawn and to ride.

Around and around, four times, one mile. Into the center. Standing, I extend my arms and swivel my torso to the left, swing back to the right, back and forth. I extend my right leg, stretch the hamstrings, hook my fist under my left elbow, pull hard and twist to the left, feeling the sin-ews of muscle in my legs, waist, shoulders and neck straining, stretching. Then the other side. Spread legs farther apart, let torso fall forward and hands hang down, fingers in the grass. Slowly rise up, arms reaching out. Continue past standing-up-straight position and lean back. I picture a for-mer Oldfields student, an athletic beauty who once during a scrimmage smacked me in the face with a backswing of her field hockey stick as I chased her down the field. She is stretching before practice, bending far-ther and farther back until her fingers touch the grass and she flattens the palms of her hands on the ground, forming a perfect bridge. I lean back, hands dangling three feet from the tips of the blades of grass.

Sensing something coming, seeing something out of my upside-down peripheral vision moving fast around the track, I gradually raise myself up and watch a young woman in skin-tight black lycra that reveals every curve of her body—the cupping of her breasts, the narrowing of her waist, the expanding of her hips, the tightening of her flattened pelvis—hands held behind her back, glide beautifully, quietly, doing graceful cross-overs, around the turn of the track past the goal posts. I'm dizzy; it's like I am on a huge green flying carpet whirling through the blue sky. Feeling old-fashioned in crumpled shorts, cotton Gilman School T-shirt, and battered running shoes—no lycra, no roller blades, no earphones—I lean forward. My leg muscles loosen; my fingers sink into the grass. Then, up and moving again, taking short steps at first, through the playground, past a bulbous, fat-upholstered teenager practicing his skateboarding techniques in a fenced-off, child-sized, skateboarding area, past the future football champs, the parents elbowed back on the bank, through the gate, over to Lake Avenue. I think of those years of reducing and of always seeing, especially when exercising, people or billboards of people doing the opposite: boys and girls drinking fizzing Cokes out of wet, chilled bottles; young men laughingly popping open brown bottles of Budweiser, the sudsy foam exploding out of the tops; kids eating cheeseburgers and French fries; tennis players uptilting bottles of Gatorade.

Tom's wife Mimi had said over the telephone they could walk from their house to Peppers, the tiny, one-room grocery store where you can get the best sandwiches, melons, and steaks in town. I cross Lake Avenue and jog down a side street behind Peppers, the houses small and unpretentious, see an SUV with plenty of dirt on it. Can't be Tom's. . . . I look closer. Maryland tags. Then I see the Voss racing colors, yellow with a black cross-sash, on a sticker on the front bumper.

Jog over. Interrupt steeplechase jockey Jonathan Kiser and assistant trainer Todd Wyatt having a smokefest in the glassed-in porch. See Elizabeth, Tom and Mimi's teenage daughter, tall, lithe, intimidatingly beautiful. She pulls herself up off a couch where she's been watching television, flings her long blond hair behind her shoulders. I ask about the horses Tom is training. They're not doing too well, she says. Ask about her brother, my godson, Sam. Would he be coming up for the A. P. Smithwick? She laughs at the thought. "He's fly-fishing in Wyoming." Find out the location of Tom and Mimi's house.

I run back across Lake, down to East Avenue. Sweating heavily, I jog up a long, new, asphalt driveway. I hear some talking behind a modern two-story house, all sharp angles and big plate-glass windows, and jog around the expansive lawn. There is Mimi, tall and slender, with thick, healthy auburn hair, standing on the low-slung deck, wearing a loose-fitting cocktail dress, and, as usual, looking . . . sensual. She is talking to a man and a woman, two of Tom's owners. It's a married couple, the wife in a tight red dress that shows off her slim waist and ample, tanned and freckled breasts, the broad-shouldered husband in a tie and jacket. They are both laughing, cigarette in one hand, drink in the other. "Patrick!" Mimi calls out. She opens her arms and gives me a hug and a kiss. The owners laugh and joke with me. "Are you pulling weight? Do you have a ride tomorrow? You look light. Why don't you get a ride in the A. P. Smithwick?"

Twenty feet away from the deck, away from Mimi and the owners, collapsed on the lawn, is Tom. He is about my . . . length. He used to be my height, five foot eleven and a half, or actually taller, but in recent years he has shrunk an inch and, though his weight goes up and down, it is down now due to his recently acquired addiction to late-afternoon workouts at health clubs combined with yet another return to the lure of tobacco and nicotine. He is lying on his side, chin propped up by one elbow, beaten baseball cap advertising a feed company perched on his head, visor down low, chestnut hair protruding from the sides and extending out of the back of his cap, down and over his shirt collar. He is wearing battered tennis shoes, blue jeans that are too tight and are ripped at the top-inside corner of both rear pockets, and a washed-out, sun-bleached, blue polo shirt with a rip running along the seam from one shoulder to the turned up and frayed collar. A red bandana hangs out of the right-rear pocket of his jeans. His arms, face and neck are sunburned. His initials, "THV"—how egocentric—are amateurishly tattooed in faded blue-black ink across one well-muscled forearm. "Hep," a groom of my father's, performed that work of art when Tom and I were sixteen, growing up like brothers and galloping horses for my father. I turned down the opportunity.

Tom lies in the grass, off, away from us, not looking up, manipulating his "itcher." Ever since we were kids and used to ride together on our ponies, Pepper and Queenie, he has taken dollar bills, often mine, crumpled them into hard, pointed arrowhead shapes, and in moments of meditation, scratched—with short, barely perceptible movements—his arms, hands and face with them.

He uses his itcher without saying a word and then lays his head on an arm. A door slams shut and two puffy Norwich terriers skitter across the deck, leap off the steps, and jump all over him. We laugh. He covers his face with an arm to keep the terriers from licking him and his cap falls off revealing a monk's pancake of white.

"Trainer," I say, "what time should I be at the barn?"

He looks up, quizzically. His eyelids are puffy; he has droopy Michael Caine eyelids. He squints, Scrooge-like, in my direction, as if he's just noticed that I am there and is wondering who the hell I am. Don't I realize I am being a pain in the ass disturbing his one moment of peace during the day? I brace for his bark. He looks me directly in the eye, turns back to fend off the terriers, sighs, and says, barely above a whisper, "Six thirty." I know he arrives at the barn at 6:15, the riders at 6:00, the grooms at 5:30 and one groom feeds each horse two quarts of oats at 4:30. He is giving me a break. I'll be arriving when they're getting the tack on the first set.

Back at a lope to the narrow, towering yellow house on the corner of Lake and Ludlow Streets. It belongs to John Rockwell, "Rocky," my sister Susan's boyfriend, and a native of Saratoga. He's renting us a few rooms for almost nothing. I briefly join in the family hubbub—Andrew, Paddy, Ansley, Susan, Rocky, sister Sal up from Miami—and begin to cool down. Eliza wants to see the terriers. I peel off my soaked T-shirt, pull on my sweatshirt, the fresh hollowed-out scent of Saranac Lake rising up from it.

Out we go. She on her new purple bike. Me on foot, pushing the envelope but legs still feeling good. I teach her how to ride down the sidewalk, how to stop, get off the bike, look both ways and cross the street. I teach her to stay to the right of pedestrians. I love it. I run. I am in the present. She pedals ahead of me. This is life. This is great. It is August in Saratoga. Eliza is eight. My daughter, my daughter, my only daughter. She flies down the Voss's driveway. I jog along behind, breaking back into a good sweat. She plays with the two Norwich terriers, Otis and Pip (named by Mimi after Otis Redding and Gladys Night and the Pips). She loves them. How she wants a little dog! I have just gotten her a pony, Chim Chim, and now she wants a little dog. "I need something I can hold, something small," she says.

Up at 5:30. Seems bright out. Traffic is active, noisy. Especially compared to the early-morning, damp-shadowy quiet of the Adirondack camp. Racetrackers whoosh by the house. I'd put ground beans and water in the coffee machine the night before. I'd set out on a straight-backed wooden chair: my favorite blue jeans for riding, the freshly washed denim clean and crisp; a pair of elastic leggings to keep my calves from being rubbed; my father's leather belt with the silver western buckle, given to him by Tom's father, Eddie, before I was born; and a folded $20 bill in the change pocket of the jeans ($20 is the equivalent of "change" in Saratoga Springs during the racing season). At the foot of the chair I'd set my polished dark brown Kroops, zip-up over the ankle paddock boots, custom-made fifteen years ago when I had returned for a two-year stint of galloping racehorses for trainer Dickie Small. Dickie's right-hand man—hot-walker, night watchman and philosopher Charles Turner—had traced my feet on a sheet of paper and ordered the boots specially tapered to fit my high instep. These boots are made of high-quality leather on the outside, and, in contrast to most boots nowadays, they are lined with another, thin layer of leather on the inside. I'd just had them resoled, with a full leather sole, and they slid in and, most importantly, out of a pair of stirrups just right.

I sit at the head of the dinner table, ready to go. Streamlined. No brief-case. No upcoming car pool. In the quiet, sip my coffee. 5:45 . . . 5:55 . . . 6:00 . . . Clear-headed. No hangover. Alone but peaceful. Alone but not lonely. So many mornings I sat with my father like this. It seems like yes-terday. Coffee and pulling on leggings and lacing and zipping up boots. No rushing. Gentle talking. Respect for the other's slipping gradually out of the private world of sleep.

I think of Susan and Sal above sleeping. Mom is also upstairs—but not sleeping. She made the trip up from Maryland yesterday with her favorite driving companion, Wiggles, a cocker spaniel who loves her. I'd driven up for the race many a year with Mom. She is the best traveler I know. She never complains. She trusts my driving implicitly, never second-guessing. She remains still and quiet when an emergency flares up, such as a few years ago when an empty heavy equipment trailer be-hind a truck broke away and spun out of control across the New York State Thruway and into our lane. She gritted her teeth as I jammed on the brakes and yanked the steering wheel—the trailer careening past our front bumper and off into the median strip. She remained calm when I floored the accelerator to avoid the tractor-trailer bearing down on us from behind. She's been like this all my life—giving me her support, no matter what sort of jam I've gotten into. She knows the most direct route to wherever we're going, the exact number of miles, and she times us. She never has to stop to go to the bathroom or to eat. She can spot a state trooper—"John Law"—a mile away and doesn't mind being the lookout. When she gets in the car, she wants to do one thing: get to the destination by the quickest and most direct route. She does draw the line at an old technique of my Uncle Mikey's. Hitting 80, 85, 90 miles per hour, having just finished work at the farm and rushing to get to the races at Belmont, or Monmouth, or Delaware Park an hour before post time, Mikey used to make Speedy Kiniel, his top groom, sit in the suicide seat and, as if that wasn't bad enough, lean out the window with a pair of binoculars to his eyes, periscope-like, and scan the horizon for radar traps and state troopers.

I'd heard Mom moving around in her bedroom when I was tiptoeing out of mine. She is a light sleeper, especially when away from the farm, which is not very often.

I had quietly opened her door and stepped into her room. "You all right?" I'd asked. "Want to go to the track?"

"No thanks," she'd said in a muffled voice over the whir of her fan. "Not this morning." She paused. "Say hi to Tommy and have a good time riding." I was relieved and happy she had arrived. She was my ally. She knew her way around the track; only she fully appreciated and celebrated this annual Smithwick pilgrimage to Saratoga, to racing and steeplechasing and gambling and drinking and laughing and living on the edge. She knew why I arose at 5:30 on my vacation to gallop horses in this draining heat.

Wearing my exercise helmet, I ride my bike down Caroline Street to the East Side Rec Area, right on Granger Avenue, left on Fifth Avenue to the "Annex:" a fifteen-acre compound half a mile west of the main track, containing two long barns, each having thirty stalls on a side, where most of the steeplechase trainers have been stabled since I used to "walk hots" there as a child. There are also two turn-out paddocks, two bunk houses for the grooms, and a four-acre area on a hillside, half used for grazing horses and half taken up by a dirt ring where riders jog and warm up their horses before heading out to the track.

I pedal through the gate of the tall picket fence along Fifth Avenue and step off. Pushing the bike and looking up at horses with their riders aboard, I have the feeling of being shortened, too close to the ground, each of my strides covering an unimpressive distance.

Leaning into the handlebars, I walk to where Tom was stabled last time I was up, a few years ago. I feel a racing of the heart. These aren't his horses. These aren't his grooms and riders. These aren't his colors. The number "007" is garishly painted on the stall doors. What is going on? Double-o-Seven? James Bond? I feel out of place/time. An anachronism. I ask a groom where Tom Voss is stabled, steer the bike, the gears making the satisfying *tick . . . tick . . . tick . . .* sound of childhood, around two barns and a pond-sized mud puddle, and there are Tom's horses, there are his riders, Jonathan and Kiwana; his grooms, Fernando, Ernesto and Armando; and his daughter, Elizabeth. Assistant trainer Todd Wyatt ducks out of a stall. "Hey jock! Good to see you this morning." He walks up grinning, shakes my hand.

UP ON A HORSE. Stand in irons to get the weight off his back. Walk around dirt ring. Ease myself into saddle. With left hand, curl left flap of lightweight exercise saddle upward, undo girth buckle attached to six-inch elastic band, pull up on billet, tightening girth, reset buckle, undo other girth buckle attached to another elastic band, pull up on billet, push prong of the buckle into hole of billet. Pull helmet chinstrap across, buckle it. Keeping toe in stirrup, pull right knee out away from saddle, let stirrup leather down a few holes. Pull left knee away, let leather down. Stand in irons to see if they feel fairly, though not completely, even. Due to years of galloping on racetracks, and always galloping to the left, I ride slightly acey-ducey, as do all American flat-racing jockeys, with my right stirrup a "hole or two"—an inch or two—shorter than my left. When galloping fast around the turn of a racetrack, a horse leans in, like a motorcycle, and the jock must lean in with him. By having the "outside," or right stirrup, shorter than the "inside" stirrup, the rider feels evenly balanced as he flies around a banked turn.

Tom is on Mickey Free, the "pony," actually a retired Thoroughbred who a decade ago won the A. P. Smithwick in a stunning, heart-wrenching finish right out of the movies. Tom is riding long, his legs stretched out. Jonathan and Elizabeth are each on a horse, irons jacked up short, helmets on.

We walk out to the paddock behind the two long, narrow stables. Todd Wyatt is on foot. He's neatly dressed in khakis and a long-sleeve Oxford shirt, clean baseball cap over dark hair, folded bandana in back pocket. His expression is serious, focused. I sometimes kid him that with his square-jawed, dark-eyed good looks, he might've made the wrong career choice. I know he'd rather be riding and that I may be taking his mount. Along with Tom, he quietly studies each horse as we jog around the dirt ring.

Our horses "sound" and moving well, we head out to Oklahoma, the one-mile training track. I check the length of my stirrup leathers. Leave them long, compared to the other riders out here, yet short compared to how I'm used to riding at home. My knees are bent at a 45-degree angle, not at the 30-degree angle of many of the smaller riders. I'm just under six feet, 159 and a half pounds, down from my usual 165 since riding in the Wild Goose Chase, a fun race for old-timers in which Tom and I had ridden last spring the week before the Maryland Hunt Cup. Most of the exercise riders on the track are five feet to five nine and weigh 115 to 135 pounds, though they always claim to be lighter.

Horses are coming and going, passing through the half-dozen gaps in the heavy, white outside rail of Oklahoma, the most well known training track in the world. It's all here, just the same, unchanged. A big man on a horse, a trainer, riding western, walks up the tree-lined path toward us, leading a jigging horse with a "galloping girl" in the tack, her black hair swinging out of the back of her helmet, brushing back and forth across her shoulder blades, her chin strap unbuckled. She's sheathed in tight, black stretch jeans and a type of sweat-wicking, sleeveless body shirt now favored by female and male riders at the track because they don't become soggy beneath the protective vests. She must not be taking this horse to the track and thus has jettisoned the vest. Her breasts jostle to the rhythm of the horse's movements while her legs, hips and rear-end remain still. As the horse dances and tosses its head, she is steady, sitting up straight in the saddle with an arch in her back and her "seat" doesn't change a micro-meter: her legs and groin muscles are squeezing firmly inwards against the saddle, against the sides of her horse, her buttocks tight against the leather. "That trainer reminds me of the one at Delaware Park . . . what was his name . . . who rode western and who always had the good-looking exercise girls? He was dragged to death early one morning," I say to Tom. That'd been twenty-five years ago. The trainer had been "ponying a horse"—leading one horse while riding another—around the track early, in the dark, before the outriders set up, before the ambulance crew was at their station, before you're allowed on the track. He'd had a fall, his foot had gotten caught in the stirrup, and his horse had run off, dragging him.

"Del Carroll," Tom says. "That's his son."

Around the track I go. Feel OK, but not as "tied-on" as I'd like to be.

Second set, I get on Teb's Bend. Teb is by Whatever For, whom I used to gallop for Tom years ago, and whom Tom still says I broke down breezing at the Elkridge-Harford Club. He claims I galloped too fast early in the breeze around the sharp turn that rises steeply and breaks away from you, before you reach the uphill straightaway where you can let them gallop on full speed. Teb is out of Buper's Rose, whom I'd also ridden often. Buper is the dam of Mickey Free. Teb, Buper and Mickey are all wonderful horses with excellent conformation and great attitudes and are owned by Mimi.

Back at the barn, a bit of confusion. Too many riders? I don't want to be in the way. "Looks like I'll be heading out," I say to Tom.

He points to Brigade of Guards. "You can get on Brigade if you want."

I play it back in my mind, "You can get on Brigade if you want," look at Tom and say, "Yes, I'll get on Brigade."

Brigade is broad-shouldered, barrel-chested, muscular, with well-rounded hindquarters. He is not the play-around type. He stands in the back corner of his stall, looking through the wire mesh opening into the next stall, to his friend, a gray horse, Versus. Brigade is a dark bay with a splash of white on his face. He has one speed and that speed is full steam ahead from the moment the flag is dropped. "Take the lead," as Pop used to say, "and improve your position."

When you step into Brigade's stall to tack him up, he doesn't pleasantly walk up to you, as Rolling Rock, a horse of my father's, and then, years later, Epilogue used to do. He doesn't nudge you, rub his face against you, accept a pat or two. And when you turn to pick up your tack, he doesn't pull your bandana out of your right rear pocket, then stand there playfully, waiting for you to scold him, pull it out of his mouth and give him a rub between the eyes. No, Brigade pins his ears back as you enter, bares his teeth. He teases you, tries to nip you in the arm, in the butt. He grabs the throatlatch of the bridle or the crosspiece of the figure-eight, and chews on it. You feel like giving him a swat across the mouth but you don't. This is the horse that is running in the $50,000 A. P. Smithwick Memorial Handicap, the reason we Smithwicks have made the pilgrimage here, and you will do everything you can over the next five days to help him prepare to win it.

For the first mile of galloping around Oklahoma, Brigade tries to get his head up, to force my hands up so he can raise his mouth and shake his head and swing his neck and shoulders back and forth. I will have none of that. I keep my hands down on his withers.

Two miles, we gallop the first day. Two miles and a sixteenth the second day, two miles and a quarter the third. My legs do well. It's the kind of fitness that would be required if you were riding a bike fast, with no seat, and were forced to stand up in the pedals but keep your rear end down, your head up, and your back straight, parallel to the ground, while knowing that the bike might try to stop or duck out or sprint off at any moment. You keep your center of gravity low in preparation for any of these maneuvers. Instead of holding the handlebars, you are gripping a set of reins. With an almost imperceptible tightening/bending of the wrist or the slightest change of grip, the horse will change his path and speed. The farther you go, the harder the reins pull.

I concentrate on my hands. Don't take his bait. Don't take a hold. Stay relaxed. Keep the hands low. Keep the long hold on the reins. Tom is taking extra care with these legs. I see from the spots of hair singed off his front legs that Brigade has been "fired," hot pins poked into his lower legs, and "blistered," a turpentine-based concoction painted onto his tendons, both treatments given to increase circulation in his tendons, and I don't want to be standing up high in the irons, like a water skier, swinging on him, and having him throw his head and fling his legs in a way that would enable him to hurt himself.

My job is to steady him. The pressure is on my shoulders and triceps, which are pulling my outstretched arms toward my groin, and on my stomach muscles. I am communicating to Brigade that this is a cinch. I can gallop him like an old fox-hunter, my hands balancing above his withers just in front of the pommel of the saddle.

I have to concentrate the first few days. I can't be looking up, glancing at the rail, yelling out, "Good morning Jimmy" to Jimmy Murphy or "Hey Billy" to one-time jumping rider Billy Turner, or "Scotty, got a mount?" to Scotty Schulhoffer, Pop's great friend and a Hall of Fame trainer. I can't be saluting riders I don't know with "Lovely day"—the greeting I most remember, made by a grinning Snake Frock, king of the Maryland freelance riders, sitting tight on horses sidling off the track and clattering onto the asphalt all winter at Pimlico, in the snow, in the sleet, in the rain, and, finally, on breezy sunny May mornings, coming up to the Preakness. I don't glance over to where I know Mimi and Todd are watching from the trainers' stand near the rail. I keep my ass low, back straight and head up.

Walking back to the Annex, Tom takes a long route. We pass trainers who were my father's best friends. They all recognize Brigade, and they ask, "Little Paddy, are you riding that horse on Thursday?"

One thing is completely new: the requirement of protective vests. I continually forget to wear one. Each morning, Todd patiently asks me, "Hey jock, where's your flak jacket?" I have a hard time finding one that fits. I borrow Kiwana's, Jonathan's, Todd's, and they are like girdles, too tight around the chest. I let them out, loosening the ties that run up the sides.

On the second day, dripping sweat after galloping just one horse, I have a moment of doubt. If I strain this much galloping one horse maybe I should hang it up. Beads of sweat plop from my face, from the edges of my helmet, only the second I've ever had, also a Caliente, given to me by Dickie Small during my stint galloping for him at Pimlico and Fort Erie, Canada back when I turned thirty-three and my track colleagues all called me "old-timer." I look at Elizabeth and Jonathan and Kiwana beside me: no sweat.

By the fourth day, the day before the race, the feel is returning. The legs are limber. Riding short feels better. I am more at one with the horse's movements, in particular when he or she leaps sideways. Sticking tight to the horse during these feints, spooks and plunges is the toughest part of riding once you pass the half-century mark, explained Bob Witham, close friend, one-time steeplechase jockey, while galloping "upsides" at Tom's last spring. The strength and ability of my groin and inner-thigh muscles to squeeze inwards and keep me in the tack during these acrobatics is returning.

CHAPTER 3

An Old-Timey Gimmick

At four foot ten, the third fence is one of the biggest on the course. Each panel consists of not just three rails, as are most post-and-rail fences, not just four rails, as are a few high post-and-rail fences, but of five thick black rails. We're thinking about this fence as we walk from the second, up a slight incline, to a steel gate. We climb up on the gate. Mikey takes a deep breath, and sits on top of the gate, maintaining perfect balance — his butt on the top pole, his feet on the pole below — as a lithe teenager would. He looks across Tufton Avenue, toward the third.

We step down off the gate, walk across the asphalt road where you gallop over the blanket of mulch, pick up speed going down into a dip which flattens out and then, if everything is going all right, you feel like you're in a chute and you're being drawn in straight and fast as if by a magnet to the one panel you've picked out, perhaps the one on the far right beside the flag. This is it, all or nothing. The horses are fresh. They are pulling. You let your horse roll on into that fence, spectators lining both sides of it. You sweep in a wave of horses and riders into the fence and then you are in the air — breathtakingly high — for an impossibly long time. There are a few more legs that bang against the top rail than at most fences and the riders sit farther back and the spectators hold their breath longer than at any other fence. If no one falls, the crowd heaves a collective sigh. In the old days, the third fence was nicknamed "the Union Memorial," after the renowned Baltimore hospital where riders who "hit the deck," as Uncle Mikey calls it, were taken for X rays and treatment. When I was seventeen, I hit the deck there on a filly called Moonlore and most witnesses thought that my time was up.

37

"You and Florida ought to jump this one well," Mikey says, one arm stretched out straight from his shoulder, hand gripping the top rail. "He's used to crowds and all the commotion here won't bother either of you. Still," he looks me in the eye, takes his hand off the top rail, puts his fists close together as if he is holding a pair of reins, "he's a spooky horse; you've got to keep him on the bit, watch out for the other horses. They might stop, run out, fall — anything can happen here. You pick your panel, go straight for it, and stay out of trouble."

EACH MORNING I SIP my coffee alone at the long dining room table and look at two classic, black-and-white, framed montages of Pop on the walls. Each consists of three photographs. In one series he is on King Commander, flying over the last fence, whip cocked, feet outstretched in front of him, rear end off the saddle, headed for the wire. This is a big fence, a five-foot brush fence, a type not used anymore in the United States. In the second photo, another horizontal set beneath the shot of the last fence, Pop is low in the saddle, riding for the wire, ten lengths in front of the second horse. In the third photo, he is in the winner's circle, relaxed, sitting on King Commander with the groom holding the bridle by the bit, and the trainer, M. G. Walsh, standing by the horse's head. Pop is not victoriously grinning; he does not look the least bit excited; his body is relaxed on the horse. He is letting down; he is part of the horse; and he looks into the camera with a this-is-just-another-day's-work expression, and a hint of let's-get-this-photo-business-over-with.

In the second montage, he is again in three shots. One shows him suspended high in the air over a water jump. He has cleared the brush fence and is sitting back, that relaxed expression on his face, continuing in flight over the five-foot-wide expanse of water. The still rectangle of water looks like a long mirror reflecting and creating an inverted and crystalline-clear image of horse and rider soaring through the puffy cumulus clouds. Another shot shows him racing a horse down the stretch and beating him by a neck. In the third shot, he is sitting relaxed on the horse, Sun Shower, in the winner's circle. Sipping my coffee, I look over these photos. The dates on the photos: 1952, 1953. I was one; I was two.

Each morning when I get on Brigade, I think of my father. I have left the hardiness of the Adirondack Mountains and the peace of Saranac Lake to others. Elizabeth, Todd, Jonathan and I hack our horses through Horse Haven, the stable area inside the "pony track," which is actually the original site of Saratoga Racetrack. I see Pop's old friends. More memories return. We often pass Barn 50 where as teenagers Tom and I worked for Pop, and Tanza and Emmett and Jack the Indian and Mike the Englishman were all there. It was on the Horse Haven track in 1966, while Pop lay paralyzed for the month of August in the New York hospital, that trainer Evan Jackson and steeplechase jockey Tommy Walsh taught me how to ride with my stirrups short like a flat jock's. Evan and Tommy soon had me galloping a long-backed, easy-going, lanky, low-headed chestnut around Oklahoma. His name was Lake Delaware and I learned that he was owned by the great Yankee pitcher Whitey Ford. I felt flattered that Tommy often came out, leaned on the rail, and watched me gallop Lake Delaware two miles with a loose rein. Once or twice, Whitey was there leaning on the rail with his million-dollar arm, watching. I found out later that Tommy never wanted to gallop Lake Delaware because he had bad legs, carried himself with his head low, and when training on the dirt, was constantly on the verge of tripping and turning ass-over-tin-cups. I didn't know this, and thus, I jacked up my stirrups, as Evan and Tommy directed, and galloped him his two miles just fine. After I hopped to the ground, Tommy, standing next to Evan, would commend me on how well the horse had gone. When Evan stepped away, Tommy would hold his hands up as if they were gripping a set of reins, look me in the eye, and assert in that muffled way of his, barely moving his lips, "Now tomorrow Little Paddy, for Christ's sake, take a hold of that sonovabitch's head." I had no idea what he meant but I always nodded yes. At this time, Tommy was winding up his red-hot blaze of a riding career and wasn't interested in the mundane work to be done around the barn. On my first morning of work,

Tommy and I sat on buckets, beside one another. We each held sharp-bladed knives, and Tommy showed me how to quickly and efficiently slice thick carrots into small pieces to be put in with the horses' feed. I thought this was wonderful, working side by side with the great Tommy Walsh. To top it off, he then set up our two sets of tack for cleaning. We carried a "horse," a portable wooden rack for the saddles, out of the tack room, and we hung the bridles from a bridle-hook swinging from a screw eye in the lintel of the tack room door frame, and cleaned and soaped the bridles and saddles. Tommy asked questions about my love life, gave me pointers, and I looked forward to this communion with him every morning. We then got out two rakes and he showed me how to level and rake the dirt walking ring with the long-handled, stiff, four-foot-wide aluminum rake, and how to rake up the bits of straw and hay, and the droppings, around the barn with the light, springy rake, so that the area outside our stalls was the neatest looking in the Annex. Thyben's tack truck pulled up outside of the barns. We walked over to it and Tommy ordered a new, lightweight pair of zip-up riding boots for me, just like his own. "Those ones your father got you are all right for the farm but not for the track," he told me. The driver asked about payment for the boots and Tommy said, "Put it on Evan's bill." The next morning, when it was time to cut the carrots and clean the tack and rake the walking ring, Tommy had to rush off to "the office" to make some important phone calls. Oh well, I thought, standing there in my new lightweight galloping boots, surveying all the work to be done, we'd be cutting the carrots, raking the ring, and cleaning the tack together the next morning. But the following morning, again, he had to leave to make some important phone calls. And the next. Evan chewed him out for leaving so early, and cussed and muttered under his breath, but this had no effect. I remained there at the barn after we had gotten all the horses out and Evan was nervously pacing around, telling the grooms how to put the bandages on better, feeling the horses' legs, making "to do" lists, asking veterinarians to look at ankles and tendons and sesamoids and splints and knees and then telling the vets they didn't know what the hell they were talking about, and scrutinizing, critically eyeing, watching everything I did, "Now

Little Paddy, didn't your father ever teach you how to . . . ," grabbing the sponge or rake or knife or whatever I was holding out of my hand and in his hyper-energetic way, showing me how I could do it better. One morning, when Evan began cussing under his breath about Tommy leaving early, I piped up, volunteering the information that Tommy had gone to his office. "Goddam, Little Paddy, your father isn't raising you to be a gullible fool, is he?" He grabbed the rake out of my hand. We walked fast to his car. Leaving the sandy parking spot, he peeled out. Then, we were parked in front of Scotty's Paddock, a bar and restaurant just outside the front gates to the track. "Go on," said Evan. "Go on in and see if you know anyone in the office." I got out of the car, walked into Scotty's, and there Tommy was leaning against the bar with two other riders as the bartender set down a fresh round of screwdrivers.

MORE THAN TWENTY-FIVE YEARS have passed since I left the track and riding as my chief means of income. I have been back for one- and two-year stints but they were temporary measures, quick stopgap solutions. They were a means to an end: ride in the morning so I could write in the afternoon.

There was the year of galloping and schooling horses for Jill and Bobby Davis at Delaware Park; Monmouth Park, New Jersey; and Camden, South Carolina; the year of galloping for Dickie Small at Pimlico and Timonium Racetracks in Maryland, and at Fort Erie, Canada; the two-year period of freelance riding, getting on twenty-one a day, starting in the morning at Pimlico and then continuing at Corbett and Taylor's Purchase Farms north of Baltimore. There were the multiple six-month stints of galloping for Tom on Atlanta Hall Farm. And then there was the summer following my breakup with Carol, when my Aunt Dot Smithwick offered me the opportunity to work as a tutor and au pair for her old roommate at Vassar, Jacqueline Kennedy Onassis, on a yacht while sailing around the Mediterranean. Instead, I started a novel about the racetrack and for research I took an immature, eighteen-year-old girl who had the longest legs and the blackest hair and the tannest skin first to Rockingham Park, to visit Tom and Mimi and gallop Tom's horses, and then to Saratoga to stay at a house rented by J. B. Secor and Bob Witham and work as a freelance rider. At the time, I thought that the writing, the riding, and the romancing was of urgent importance and that an opportunity such as yachting around the Mediterranean with the Kennedy clan would present itself again. But it was mainly the horses, the wanting to return to horses, to get the racing world in my bones, and to write that novel, my *Portrait of a Writer as a Young Rider*, that caused me to sacrifice this chance of a lifetime.

EACH MORNING at 5:30 I step sideways—the Achilles tendons tight from riding—down the long, steep and narrow stairway of Rocky's house, gripping the banister, and leaning lightly, because of the shocks still coming up through the elbow. In the kitchen, push the button on the coffee machine. Back up the stairs, pull on jeans, polo shirt; brush teeth. Down. Coffee, toast. In the moment. Pull on leggings, feel them slide over my calves. Step into boots, zip them up, feel the leather tighten around instep and ankle. This is the quiet time.

Time to reflect. Time and space to myself. The circular movement of the minute hand on the clock above the stove slows. I can hear the ticking. It slows.

No car key needed. No wallet. Pop's western belt snug around my hips. Helmet hanging in Tom's tack room.

No briefcase stuffed with rough drafts to edit, papers to grade, bills to pay.

No newspaper overflowing with news to keep up with.

No manuscripts to drop off at the post office.

No checks to deposit in the bank.

No car pool.

No traffic.

No rush.

I stand. Grab dark blue Gilman School baseball cap, slap it on. Walk to bike. Pedal a mile to the Annex, savoring the feel of my leg muscles warming up, loosening. Step off bike, steer it into barn area, lean it against fence. Walk to tack room, prepared to ride. Each morning when I get on Brigade, as Jonathan and Elizabeth and Kiwana and I walk our horses out of the Annex and prepare to cross Fifth Avenue, headed for the Oklahoma training track, we pass the last barn in which I worked full time for Pop, the last barn in which Pop trained at Saratoga, the year Wild Amber won over hurdles here, my last win. It was 1972 and we had Bel Sheba, who in later years was bred to Alydar and foaled Alysheba, who won the Kentucky Derby and the Preakness in 1987, and who as a four-year-old was Horse of the Year, Champion Handicap Horse of the Year, set new track records at Belmont Park and the Meadowlands, and won the Breeders Cup Classic and the Santa Anita Handicap, among others, making him the all-time leader in earnings until Cigar topped the mark in 1996. The flashy Robyn Smith, who later quit riding and married Fred Astaire, rode Bel Sheba in the afternoon, and sometimes Pop had her breeze Bel Sheba in the mornings. I galloped Bel Sheba and the reporters came out to watch. She was the smoothest mover I'd ever ridden. I was reading the *New York Times* after work every morning and Hemingway's *Death in the Afternoon* during the long afternoons, and studying, in training for Johns Hopkins University in the fall, preparing to head out of the horse business while my wife of a few months, Carol, who earlier hadn't liked the track, was falling in love with it.

That fall, I left riding races to concentrate on my studies. In January of 1973, I stopped galloping in the morning before classes and doubled my course load so I could graduate on time. In May, Mom and Pop attended my graduation. We had a bright, sunny, cheerful, laughter-imbued, champagne-sipping lunch afterwards, Pop teasing me, "Professor Smithwick," about my high-powered future in the world of journalism. He had been losing weight all spring, had been in and out of the hospital, and had finally been operated on for lung cancer. He was starting chemotherapy. That August, Pop was inducted into the Racing Hall of Fame. He was too weak to make the trip to Saratoga. I flew up from Cambridge, Maryland, where I was editor of the *Dorchester News*, and accepted the award for him. After the ceremony, I was so drained and so determined to get back to my newspaper that I turned down an invitation to spend a day at the races with Robyn Smith and her new husband, Fred Astaire.

Over Thanksgiving, Pop died of cancer.

MORNINGS AT SARATOGA, I feel closer to Pop. Who to tell? Who to share this with? Late one morning, Tom is on Mickey Free, one-time winner of the A. P. Smithwick, and I am on Brigade, one-time winner of the A. P. Smithwick. We are hacking through the barn area of Horse Haven when we bump into ex-jumping rider Pat Myer. Tall, neat, slim as ever, Irish wool cap pulled low over his eyes, he follows us for half a mile on foot, talking about race riding, asking how I was doing and telling me stories of my father. "He was my idol. He was my absolute idol. All I wanted in life was to be just like him," Pat says, walking alongside me, looking up into my eyes, having to step quickly to keep up.

One day to go. I'm walking Brigade out of the barn area. A tent is set up and a cook in a chef's hat is flamboyantly flipping pancakes and breaking eggs into pans. People are seated at tables, eating and talking. The announcer on a loudspeaker drones on about something and then I hear ". . . the A. P. Smithwick Handicap today . . ." and I am A. P. Smithwick, Jr. It feels like it was yesterday that Pop and I were in that barn, on that shedrow, fifty yards away and, laughing and joking, he was giving me a leg up onto Wild Amber and I was going out to Oklahoma, Pop, Carol and our silky terrier Aaron, walking along behind me.

It wells up inside and I feel I might lose it but I cannot at this moment. I stand in the irons, squeeze with my legs, set Brigade to jogging around the dirt ring. Around and around. I post, up and down, up and down, with each stride. I focus on getting on the correct diagonal, a show-ring maneuver no one on the racetrack cares about, posting down with each back-stride of Brigade's outside shoulder and then lifting up and sending my weight forward at the exact moment his inside hind leg is coming forward, thus "aiding" him as he turns and bends to the left. I concentrate on the rhythm of Brigade beneath me, making him a part of me, letting this cadence—my metronome—settle, calm, focus me.

The chef flips pancakes. A photographer steps out of the tent, video camera on shoulder, and films us. The announcer drones on. Two bales of straw and a hurdle are set up in the middle of the ring. Tom asks me to walk Brigade up and take a look at the hurdle, which is actually just the roll of a hurdle, three feet high, made of foam padding covered by a thick green canvas sheet. A full hurdle nowadays has a long, narrow, unforgiving, steel box behind the roll, into which is stuffed branches of plastic "brush."

I walk Brigade up to the roll. He is standing at an odd angle and not paying attention. I pull him out, circle him and walk up to it again. Still, he is flat-footed. Tom and Todd confer. They decide not to jump the hurdle now. Out to gallop we go.

Once on the training track of Oklahoma, following Tom's orders, I "drop" Brigade's head, take a relaxed grip of the reins and let him gallop right along for a mile. I walk him back to the trotting ring. The tent is filled with people. Ansley is there; this is unusual and makes me feel good. Jonathan Sheppard, who has trained the winner of the A. P. Smithwick many a time, is on a "pony," a retired racehorse, and is directing a young woman on a chestnut filly to pop the filly over the bales and then the roll of the hurdle. I follow Sheppard's chestnut into the hurdle at a canter. I squeeze with my legs, urge Brigade to take a hold of the bit. Nearing the hurdle, I don't let my butt hit the saddle. Brigade hesitates and I squeeze and he gives me a big one, kicks off, rocketing over the hurdle. I land in my stirrups, no rear-end hitting the saddle, and it feels like I am setting a jet-fighter down on a runway, carefully decreasing the forward thrust of the engines, and that with just one miscalculated flick of a finger the engines will roar and I'll have to lift the nose of the jet and steer it off into thin air as it suddenly and uncontrollably picks up speed.

Return to the barn. On the winner.

Ansley walks back to Tom's barn. I hop off Brigade, hang up my tack and walk out to the tent with her. The chef makes me a deep-yellow cheese omelet with green peppers. I pour a glass of rich, pulpy orange juice. Ansley makes a cup of coffee and butters a bagel. We sit at a table. I've been on four horses. I've gotten plenty of exercise and will run later today and,

I must remember, I am not reducing. No one is going to pull out a set of scales and ask me to step onto them. Still, I am experiencing a Pavlovian reaction: I feel as though I am soon to ride a race. I feel as though I have a few pounds to lose, I should not be eating, I should be in the hot box. But I know that I can eat. Breakfast never tasted better. The sharp cheddar cheese that would never be allowed when reducing. The crisp slices of green pepper. It is seldom that I am able to share a moment like this, from the world of horses, with Ansley.

A few tables away is a group of adults with a cute little boy—freckles, sandy-blond hair. They are either owners who haven't been around the track much or over-dressed racing fans. Relieved and clearheaded, delighting in experiencing no vestiges of a hangover, having just gotten off the next winner of the A. P. Smithwick, I joke about this boy. "Sweetheart, now look at that poor boy, you know his parents dragged him out of bed, made him put on that outfit. Look at that hair. . . ." It is combed, oiled, has the neatest part you've ever seen and is scooped upwards and back in a 1950s wave. Ansley, seated beside me, looks up into my eyes, giving me a scowl and purses her lips into a *shush*. Pretending to have misunderstood this expression, I lean over, surprising her, and kiss those pursed lips. I pull back. Her dark blue eyes flash and I prepare for a frown but instead she stares knowingly, womanly, into my eyes—she's in a blue V-neck T-shirt that accentuates the intense blue of her eyes and shows off the broadness of her shoulders tapering down to a narrow waist—and then looks down to her mug of coffee. She takes a sip, pushes her chair back and walks to the coffee table. Her hair is up, revealing the long lines of her slender neck. The jeans are snug, the pockets winking at me as she steps away, just as they did years ago the night I met her at Hollins College when she turned away toward a rumbling washing machine, dropped ice cubes into a glass, picked up a bottle of Scotch, slowly poured the whiskey over the vibrating ice, handed it to me, and then, as now, I started to think of ways to get away, to be alone with her.

THAT NIGHT, AT DINNER at Sperry's, an old racetrack watering hole and restaurant, Susan, Sal, and I are discussing our childhood with each other and with my old race riding buddy and Johns Hopkins classmate Kip Elser. Rocky, owner of Sperry's, is waiting on us and intermittently joining in the conversation, but is quick to become very busy when things heat up. Susan and Sal are healers, reformers—they have both gone into professions where they analyze people's problems, offer solutions, and focus on directly helping people, easing people's troubles, making this a better world. They are serious about this. This is their mission. There's not much room for humor. If Kip and I retell a story of a prank we played on a newcomer to the racetrack thirty years earlier, all in the room but Sal and Susan will laugh. They might not even "get" what is funny; the main thing they want to know is if that newcomer was all right afterwards. What did he do? How did he recuperate? What is he doing now? Did this inflict psychological damage that would affect him the rest of his life? Good Lord.

Sal is thin, lightly built, fair-skinned, with a classic, sharply delineated face. She exudes high energy, and if she is not on the move, looks as though she is about to be. Of all of us, she looks the most like Mom and has Mom's flare, spontaneous energy and occasional fiery temperament. Sal is an acupuncturist, and a birthing nurse who specializes in difficult births.

Susan isn't as tall as Sal, is more solidly built, has darker skin, and has a round, mysterious face that, combined with thick black hair to her waist, used to drive boys and young men wild while she either pretended not to notice, or actually did not notice—I never could tell which it was. Of all of us, she looks the most like our father. She loves to be calm and still, to let others do the hustling and bustling, and to go for marathon swims and walks, both by herself and with others. Susan is a therapist and health/energy guru who specializes in working with families that are experiencing violence.

These two are dissecting our upbringing at the dinner table, and the result is not a positive one. We have always differed on this subject. Ansley is listening to us go back and forth. I am trying to explain, without arguing, the enchantment of going to the track with Pop as a youth, the

old-world wonder of a child going to work with his father every morning. I struggle to get it right for them. I have a difficult time formulating
the sentences that will articulate the concept hovering out of my grasp. I
am frustrated it is even necessary to explain what seems self-evident to
me. They are giving me the you-are-a-bit-nutty look. Elser interjects in
his snappy, succinct, make-the-point and get-it-over-with way: "Not to
mention what it would be like to wake up every morning and go to work
with someone that every single person you met absolutely loved." That
was it. I would've had a hard time saying that to them. But that was it. I
don't know if it sunk in. They were negative about our childhood, and as
I was to learn, negative about the racetrack and even about parts of their
relationship with our father.

They never had those quiet mornings with Pop, the calm before the
action, sitting at a breakfast table at 4:30 a.m. in Maryland, or the early
mornings in racetrack cafeterias, or in racetrack tack rooms, or in coffee
shops outside of racetracks—especially the Greek coffee shop in Elmont,
Long Island, not far from the back gates to Belmont Park. An easing into
the morning. Pop lighting a cigarette, sipping his coffee, studying the
Morning Telegraph, the smoke slowly spiraling upwards. There were almost no women on the track in those days, and you never saw a girl.

As THE MORNINGS tick by, I begin to feel as though I am going to ride this
horse in the A. P. Smithwick Memorial. Twenty-five years have passed
since I last rode a race at Saratoga. A long time. But in a haunting, somewhat depressing way, it seems the flash of a second. Settling horses down
by riding them around the stable areas of Oklahoma and the main track,
I am shocked that some old friends, ex-riders, trainers, grooms, do not
recognize me at first. Aged face, gray hair? Could they see the gray with the
helmet on? Short hair? Along with Andrew and Eliza, I'd gotten a short
summer haircut before we left for the Adirondacks, which made my face
look sharper, more angular.

The time away from the track—the people, the degrees, the writing,
the students—what do these years mean as I sit on a jigging and bucking

horse heading onto a racetrack alongside a 20-year-old jockey whose sole interest in life is riding races and raising hell, a 17-year-old daughter of a best friend who is deciding where to go to college, and a 30-year-old galloping girl (the only human who Tom will allow to cut his hair) who says she is getting too old to continue exercising horses.

I am on vacation. What kind of a nut am I? Who else on vacation would get up at 5:30 every morning, go to the steamy barn and gallop horses in this sticky weather? I could be sleeping late and putting the early-morning moves on my wife. I could be arising with my wife and children and sisters, sitting around the breakfast table drinking coffee and joking with them. I could be getting to know my sisters better.

What is a man to do at this age? Most men get heavy, drink, develop a paunch, work out occasionally at a health club, play golf. They don't jump up on a three-year-old racehorse that is fueled and trained to the point where he is about to explode with nervous energy unless he is allowed to bust out of the gate, drop down on the rail, lower his head, and let the turbos roar, let them scream, those finely tuned and pampered and prayed-over legs fully extending themselves, faster and faster, digging in, taking more pressure, on the fine red line of disaster, pushing the rpms up, up, into the danger zone until he is under the wire, and the tension is released, and he slows to a gallop, a canter, a trot. Most older horsemen give twenty-year-old jocks leg-ups onto these horses and they ride a pony to the track and they hold a stopwatch in their hands. They sit comfortably on the pony and watch the horse and the rider and the hand on the stopwatch and the poles flash by, and at the wire, they punch in the clock.

The theory is that your athletic talents plummet after forty. But look at the great Willie Shoemaker, who rode races until he was sixty, and then, after he'd stopped riding and was training, had a drink at a bar after work, rolled his truck in a freak accident, was paralyzed, and only lived for a few more years. This after he'd ridden thousands and thousands of races. Look at George Foreman whipping boxers half his age. Look at Jimmy Connors and that great, inspiring run he made at the U.S. Open. How about Irv Naylor, in his sixties, scuba diving in the summer, skiing in the winter, riding races in the spring, and having a ball, kicking ass—winning the Wild Goose Chase last spring.

All the winter before, I'd been hunting Florida Law for Tom, and I'd thought about trying to get the ride on him for the spring races, but I didn't push it. As the races approached, I was torn, yet again wishing I were participating, and then one afternoon I met a friend for lunch, during which I decided to end all thoughts of race riding. After the lunch, I stopped by a coffee shop on the way back to work, had a mug, and wrote up a resolution saying goodbye to any race-riding ambitions, so long to all the associated problems: worrying about losing weight, how I'd do, what people would think, what my employer would think, how Ansley would react, how my children would react, how to get fit, how to keep up with the writing schedule, what could happen out there.

In black ink on a yellow legal pad I said good night to horses and good morning to dedicating myself to writing about a wide range of subjects that would "broaden my outlook," expand my "range of knowledge" and improve my writing by "pushing and stretching it to the limit." Pleased with myself, I returned, long-striding and walking tall, to my office at Gilman School. I sat at my desk and picked up a WHILE YOU WERE OUT pink slip: "Call Charlie Fenwick."

Charlie, a Gilman alumnus, class of 1966—five-time winner of the Maryland Hunt Cup, one-time winner of the English Grand National—was the chairman of the school's $6.5 million Centennial Campaign. I had written the history of the school and now Charlie was raising the money. Strange that two country boys from horsey backgrounds were the ones chosen to do this work. As director of publications and public relations, I thought Charlie probably had a story idea or a plan he wanted to bounce off me. But in my gut there was a tightness, a foreboding, an inkling that he was calling about something to do with racing, and something that would test my afternoon resolution. I set the document finalizing my self-imposed ostracism from the riding life and my dedication to the writing life on the desk before me and dialed Charlie's number.

"Patrick," he said, and then harrumphed, clearing his throat, getting ready to fire out his short-clipped phrases. "Good to talk to you. I think I've got a job for you. You're perfect for it. Patrick, could you come out to my place after work next week one day?"

This is the way he is, leaving things businesslike but mysterious, especially when he wants to engage you in a project. If I said "yes," he would then say, "OK, see you such and such a day at such and such a time," and that would be the end of the conversation.

"Well, sure," I said, "but could you tell me what this is about?"

"Patrick, you know this is the centennial of the Grand National?"

"Yes," I said, stretching the truth.

"We're thinking of having a reunion race, a race for old-timers to celebrate the anniversary. Anyone who rode in the Grand National 25 years ago would be eligible.

"Patrick, it could be great. . . . You're just the man to help plan it. . . . Can't you see some of these guys. . . . Gene Weymouth, Kingdon Gould, Dougy Small, Buzzy Hannum, Johnny Fisher, Russel Jones. . . . We've got Wild Goose Ale to sponsor the race. . . . Could you come out to my place next Tuesday at six for a brain-storming session?"

I had a whirling-sinking sensation of being whipped around and around, down a vortex, and then being buffeted, slapped with the exact sequence of events and emotions—the offer of a ride in a race, my immediate acceptance, my soaring excitement—that I had just sworn I'd never experience again.

— Yes, I could go to the meeting. . . .

— Yes, I might want to ride in it. . . .

— Yes, I could help recruit others to ride. . . .

— Yes, I thought Tom Voss would want to do it. . . .

— Yes, that was an ingenious idea to have Wild Goose Ale sponsor the race.

Within a five-minute period I'd gone from driving my life absolutely and irrevocably in one direction, to spinning the wheel one hundred and eighty degrees, and steering in the opposite direction.

Soon I was back galloping at Tom's on the weekends, both of us galloping now. Tom was using the race as an inducement to spur on his weight-loss program. He began increasing the intensity of his workouts, eating less, and dropping the pounds.

On the first Saturday morning of galloping, I was up on a pokey horse, and I was carrying a stick. Tom had told me I would need it. Jonathan and I were jogging down to the start of an uphill breeze when he looked over at my hands. I had a rubber band wrapped around the stick and my middle finger stuck through it, an old trick Pop had taught me.

"What's that?" Jonathan asked.

"What's what?" I replied.

"What do you have on your finger?"

"That's a rubber band. I have my finger stuck through it."

"Why?"

"So I won't drop it." There is that flash of a second when a rider, at the end of a race, twirls his stick, changing from holding it down along the horse's shoulder and being able to tap or slap the shoulder, to holding it up across his withers like a baton and being able to reach back and really crack him across the rump with it. At that split second a rider sometimes loses his stick. "It helps. You ought to try it."

Staring straight ahead, standing in the irons, Jonathan asserted, "I don't need to resort to some old-timey gimmick to hold my whip. I'm a professional and professionals don't drop their sticks."

CHAPTER 4

In a Delirium of

Competition and Pain and Joy

Walking across a flat stretch toward the fourth, Mikey stops half-way. He takes a breath, exhales. "Now you go in a straight line for the inside panel. See it Young-Blood?" He takes another breath and restarts our march. "You don't wander, you don't drift off to the right like a Green Spring Valley boy we all know used to do because his grandfather told him that when he was a kid there was a groundhog hole in the middle of the field."

Your horse is settled. You gallop straight, headed with confidence for the inside panel. It is four feet high with thick rails. You time it so your horse jumps it in stride without slowing and in the air you pull slightly on the left rein, setting up for the fifth.

T HE MORNING OF THE A. P. Smithwick Memorial there are all sorts of peo-ple stopping by the barn, loitering around, bringing us boxes of do-nuts and cups of coffee, sitting outside the tack room reading the *Racing Form* and the *Pink Sheet*, walking their dogs, getting in the way—all trying to get a piece of Tom. We've gotten two sets out, and it's getting hot, hot and humid. There is no breeze. Every horse has a fan propped up outside his stall, blasting hot air through the stall door.

Tom's not saying much. He's focused—totally focused and quiet, and this has the rest of us, especially Jonathan, quieter than usual.

53

Todd walks to the porta-pad, a portable, circular paddock consisting of wire mesh panels, six feet high. He catches a big, strong-shouldered, thick-necked bay, leads him out, puts him in a stall, "Come on jock," he says, as if I should've known I was getting on this horse, "You've got another mount."

I grab my tack, step around the vibrating, whirring fan, set the saddle, pads and bridle on the runner, a rubber-sheathed chain stretching from screw eye to screw eye across the stall door. "Hold him a minute, would you please?" Todd is down low in the deep straw of the stall, balancing on the balls of his feet. He gently runs his hand down one leg, then the other, both of them big-boned and looking like they've been many a fast mile. "Could you hand me the polos?" he says. I pick up two sets of dark-blue polo bandages, each rolled tightly into a hard tube, hand him one. He sets the end of the six-inch-wide bandage against the inside of the horse's ankle, wraps it around the ankle, at first angling up one turn, then angling down, forming an X pattern, and finally spiraling upward to just below the knee. There, he pulls the strip of Velcro across the bandage, securing it. To be sure the bandage doesn't come loose and unwind—you see this on the track, a horse galloping along, a bandage unraveling and then dangerously flopping around, longer and longer, between the horse's legs until it finally comes off—he sticks a safety pin through the bandage at the top. He rises halfway, takes a step under the horse's neck and is down on the balls of his feet again. I hand him the other polo. Whipping it from one hand to the other, he wraps the leg in seconds. He stands up. "OK, you got him now jock?"

"Yes."

I start tacking up. I don't know this horse well, don't even know his name. I call him "the Sprinter" because I know that his forte is running short races on the flat. He likes to bust out of the gate and go full-tilt, five-eighths of a mile, around one turn. Last spring, I'd galloped him around Tom's indoor track when I was getting fit to ride in the Wild Goose. The horse had been stabled in one of the eight stalls inside the perimeter of the indoor track. Louis Bosley and Jonathan were stationed up at the Indoor (others were down at the Pretty Boy Barn, the Bank Barn, and the Charles Town Barn). If I had time before school to get on a few, I'd call the barn at 6:00 sharp. Jonathan would answer. He'd be rushing, trying to get the stalls mucked out before they started galloping. He'd pick up the phone, breathless, and say, in a rising, hopeful tone, playing on an expression of my Uncle Mikey's, "Old-Blood?"

"Yeah," I'd say, "Be there at six thirty."

"We'll have your big horse tacked up."

When I arrived, Jonathan would be leading Sprinter around the dirt ring inside the perimeter of the indoor track. I'd walk alongside the horse, Jonathan would lean down, grab my leg as we walked and give me a leg up. The first turn or two of galloping around the one-sixth of a mile track, Sprinter would lunge forward and throw his head. I'd let him open up his stride, move on and finally he would relax and gallop nicely, switching to the correct inside lead and leaning his whole body in, each time we approached the sharp turns. I'd let the reins out longer and he'd put his head down and take a good hold of the bit. I kept my heels down and my rump low and was vigilant in being prepared for any of his antics. If he saw the simplest change in the pattern the harrow had made in the dirt when Tom worked on the track the night before, or if a bird flew out in front of us and banged into one of the window panes, or if a breeze buffeted the side of the track causing the old wood frame to rattle, he could stick in his toes and stop on a dime or duck to either side with lightning-fast reactions. After I galloped Sprinter, I'd hop off and Jonathan would pull out another horse. "That's good Old-Blood. You're doing great with him. Goes like a lady's hunter for you," he'd say.

IN THE STIFLING AIR of the Saratoga stall, I have Sprinter tacked up and am ready to go out when I see Tom bust through the pack of dogs and hangers-on outside the tack room like a running back coming through the line of scrimmage. He strides up the shedrow, an old set of black blinkers in his hand. He's wearing a dirty baseball cap, the brim rubbed raw and frayed, a polo shirt, once blue now sun-bleached to purple, and worn jeans. He's squinting, staring into my eyes, and grinning, a crumpled Pall Mall (what my father smoked) hanging off a lip. There's a sparkle in his eye and I know well the meaning of this mischievous, focused expression: he's pleased about a change in training procedure he's made, about an out-of-the-box idea he's concocted, something that should make the horse perform better but may put more pressure on the rider. As he nears, I am shocked, even knowing him as well as I do, at seeing close-up the sweaty, uneven stubble on his face. Here we are in the big time. The best horses, best riders, best trainers in the world are on the grounds of Saratoga for six straight weeks. All sorts of rich and famous and glamorous types hovering around. And he looks the same as on a hot summer morning on Atlanta Hall Farm when he's had several long and tough days back-to-back, that is: unshaven, sweaty, dirty, and focused totally on his horses.

He takes the cigarette out of his mouth and flicks it in a puddle. The Pall Mall hits the water, burned end first, and bobs there, like a buoy, wedged between horse droppings. "Hold on," he says, standing outside the stall. He reaches up, slips the openings in the top of the blinkers over the horse's ears, pulls the nylon fabric down so the leather half-cups are just outside each eye, blocking the horse's peripheral vision. He tests the two thin leather straps, attempting to pull them around the jaw, but they are set far too short to make it around this horse's wide head.

Patiently, he takes the blinkers off and lengthens the straps. I'm standing in the stall, holding Sprinter, who is leaning heavily and forcefully against the webbing, and who is watching two horses, with Elizabeth and Kiwana in the tack, walking around the ring. He paws, wanting to get out of the stall to these other two. He digs up the straw, reaching the dirt, pushes like a bull against the webbing.

Lengthening the straps, pulling the circular openings of the blinkers over the horse's ears, Tom is clearly happy to be actually doing something with a horse and not down by the tack room holding a press conference with the gaggle of owners and old friends and a gambler wanting a tip and the sycophants that gravitate to him, and now, add to the list: the National

Steeplechase Association handicapper, with his daughter, as well as a reporter/photographer for the *Steeplechase Times.*

A prospective owner—been one for five years now—walks by with his wife and children, all looking like they are on their way to the country club. They progress down the long line of stalls to the tack room where the patriarch opens up his *Racing Form.* His kids and the daughter of the NSA handicapper pat and spoil and cluck to and *ooh* and *aah* over Mickey Free, who is leaning on the webbing, soaking up all the attention. The patriarch starts discussing the weights for the A. P. Smithwick. This is not a good topic at the moment. Tom believes the handicapper put too much weight on Brigade, and the prospective owner has no idea that the man standing outside Mickey Free's stall *is* the handicapper who is sending Brigade to the start with 156 pounds, only four short of 160.

The prospective owner, his wife, children and friends drift toward Tom and me. Tom releases a soft, oh-well sigh. "Finish this," he says, and then walks down the line of stalls, straight past the would-be owner and his eye-catching wife, her long, fit, darkly tanned legs scissoring out of a short white tennis skirt. Without saying a word, Tom walks to Mickey's stall where a little girl is rubbing Mickey between his eyes. He reaches into his pocket, pulls out something. Must be a peppermint. He unwraps it and hands it to the little girl. He bends down, shows her how to hold her hand out flat. She stands stiffly, her hand outstretched, and Mickey gently, as if teaching her how to do this, nuzzles the palm of her hand with his soft muzzle and whiskers. She laughs and shakes all over as Mickey tickles her. Mickey nibbles the mint off her hand. Tom says something to the girl, pulls Mickey out of the stall, reaches down, picks the girl up and gently sets her in his saddle. He begins to lead her around the ring. Mickey probably looks better than any horse in the barn. He has a finely shaped, black Arabian-like head, and a perfectly proportioned, compact body. Though, Tom does give him too many treats and he does have a belly. The phone in the tack room rings. Tom hands Mickey to Jonathan and ducks into the tack room. He steps out, calls, in a mock-formal tone, "Patrick Smithwick. Telephone. Long distance."

I jog down to the tack room and pick up the receiver. "Pa-pa-patrick. . . ." It's Bob Witham, knew my father well. He spends August on Atlanta Hall Farm galloping all morning then weed-whacking and fussing around all afternoon. He lives in the main house and runs the show, throwing a few great dinner parties. Every morning around this time he calls and checks in with Tom. "Pa-pa-patrick, how are you?"

"Feeling good Bob. Yourself?"

"Same as ever. Listen Patrick, you've been galloping Brigade?"

"Yes, I have."

"How's he going?"

"Good, really good."

"Too bad the handicapper is a fu-fucking idiot."

"Ha!" I laugh. Bob is so proper and formal that it is always funny when he cusses. "Yes, he is," I say, looking out the doorway at the so-called "fucking idiot" but unable to say anything about him.

"Well, I hope Br-Br-Brigade wins it today, Patrick. I hope he wins it, for your sake, and for Tom's. Your old man would like that." He laughs.

"He sure would," I said, picturing Pop, seeing his full face in my imagination as clearly as can be, thinking about him for the first time that morning as a man of flesh and blood.

"Give my best to Ansley and your sisters."

"I will. Talk to you soon Bob."

BACK IN SPRINTER'S STALL, I'm having a hard time loosening the hard and cracked leather straps of the blinkers when the prospective owner and wife descend on me. I look out of the stall: Tom is on Mickey, ready to go. Jonathan, Elizabeth, and Kiwana are on their horses, ready to go. Suddenly I'm late, holding up the works.

The questions come fast and furious: What does Tom think about the weights? How is Brigade going? Why has he only run once all year? Is it really possible for him to be fit enough without having a racetrack work listed in the *Racing Form*? Will he go to the front? Who is this I'm getting on? A flat horse? Tom trains flat horses?

I cannot think straight and I have the blinkers on sideways—it looks like Harpo Marx put them on. Todd sees my predicament. He walks over, steps through the group outside the stall, and professionally, unhurriedly, steadily, in no time flat, has the blinkers on correctly. The group walks away. Todd unsnaps the runner and the webbing, frowns. "This horse has never had blinkers on," he states flatly.

"I didn't think so."

He shakes his head. "Another new idea of Tom's." Yes, it was true; Tom often has new ideas, and he doesn't mind experimenting with them, even at the last minute. "Jock, he's going to pull."

"I hear you. Thanks Todd."

Tom, on Mickey, walks past us. "Come on," he snaps. "Get on that horse. This isn't fucking pony club," and walks on.

On other mornings, say on the farm, I might react, explaining how it was his great idea of pulling out a set of blinkers last used by Mrs. Bedford herself (founder of the Pony Club, to which both Tom and I belonged for a very short time as kids) that was holding us up, or, if Todd had been under the gun already, he might clench his jaw and reply, "If you want blinkers on the horse, we've got to get them on right." After either of these rebuttals, Tom would chuckle, pleased that someone had challenged him, take a drag of his Pall Mall, and ride off, the tension dissipated.

But on this morning, Todd grits his teeth, pulls the horse out, and I disregard the remark. Todd gives me a leg up, which is unusual in the Voss stable, and then he doesn't drop the reins and turn you loose the second your rear end hits the saddle. He walks us around the dirt ring as I tighten the girth, adjust my stirrups and tie a knot in the reins, all of which takes me longer than the average galloping boy. He looks up, "Tied on jock?"

"Yes."

"OK," he says. "Don't let him get away from you."

I look at him questioningly.

"He's in the day after tomorrow," Todd says, "and this'll be his first gallop on the main track."

"All right," I say, thinking: the main track, blinkers and the main track and he's running in two days. He's going to be tough to hold and this must be what Tom wants.

I catch up. We walk quietly the whole way over, no one saying much. Trainers nod to Tom as we pass them leaning on the outside rail of Oklahoma, standing outside their barns, walking back from the training track to their barn. We stop, let the horses idle outside the barn of Leo O'Brien, a successful New York trainer who got his start in this country riding jumpers for Pop and Mikey. Tom wheels and deals with Leo, buying flat horses from him and turning them into jumpers. In fact, he'd gotten Florida Law through Leo. I'd been the first to ride him the day he arrived at Atlanta Hall. Leo walks out grinning, directly to me, looks me in the eye, shakes my hand, asks in his cheerful Irish lilt about my mother and sisters. I think back on the first running of the A. P. Smithwick Memorial, a lifetime ago, and remember presenting the trophy to Leo, the winning jockey. Leaving Leo's barn, I ask Tom, "How's Michael?" Tom gives me that taken-by-surprise expression of his, and, to give himself time, asks, "What?" I repeat the question. "As good as can be expected," he says. "He's one of the leading trainers over there, year after year." I'd ridden races with both O'Briens. Michael, the younger brother, was more extroverted and talkative than the quiet Leo. His riding career in the states was taking off when he had a fall in a hurdle race that left him in a wheel chair. We pass Jimmy Murphy, leading a horse and rider to the track. Jimmy, one of Pop's best friends back when they were riding races together, lets his horse continue to the track, turns and walks alongside Tom and me, asking what I've been writing. We pass Billy Turner, another ex-jumping rider—trainer of the great Seattle Slew, the only undefeated horse to ever win the triple crown. Billy is high-energy, excited to see us, asks how Mom and my sisters are doing. Tom is picking out this route so I can see all these friends of my father's.

I have my irons jacked up shorter than usual, preparing for this big horse to pull, and look over at Jonathan in disbelief, wondering how he can actually ride that short. Like a posse setting out on a mission, we ride past Oklahoma training track, through Horse Haven, across Union Avenue, past the big wrought-iron gate posts through which the gamblers and spectators and families will be pouring that afternoon. We walk quietly down the dark dirt path with a white board fence on either side, in and out of the dappled shadows of the trees. Racing fans are already setting up coolers of iced beer and sandwiches, slapping down their *Racing Forms* and *Pink Sheets* on picnic tables, unfolding plastic chairs beneath the damp shade of the trees.

A Pinkerton holds up a few cars as we pass through the wide gate outside the entrance to the jocks' room. The chain-link fence behind us, the long, low-slung building holding pari-mutuel betting windows to our left, we are walking along the path where, in a few hours, racehorses on their way to run will be parading past thousands of fans, families, and Thoroughbred aficionados who will study every detail of conformation and breeding and every subtle nuance of the way the horses carry themselves. They'll examine the gloss of each horse's coat, check to see if he has broken out in a nervous sweat, or if his legs are wrapped in bandages that may be hiding old injuries. The horses will be jigging and dancing past the families, Mom, Dad and one child on foot, the other in a baby walker, Mom in a tank top, her stomach lapping over the elastic band of her shorts as seated outside the jocks' room in the shade, she pushes the stroller back and forth, back and forth. Dad will be buying his son a hot dog and Coke, himself a beer and a hot dog, and getting scolded by his wife for allowing their son to spill ketchup on his clean white shirt, and then, unnerved by his wife's scolding—*isn't this supposed to be a relaxing afternoon at the races*—watching as the foam of his just-poured beer billows onto his hot dog bun, causing the mustard to run and the bun to flatten and his shoulders to slump, his unopened, unread, unmarked program in his back pocket.

The dancing, nervous two-year-olds and the calm, professional older horses will be parading past the laughing and happily T-shirted, pot-bellied men in their thirties on vacation with opened, earmarked and notation-scrawled *Racing Forms* in their left hands, large paper cups of beer in their right, and wives and children at home. The four-legged beauties bred for men to bet on and to root and holler and urge down the stretch will be strolling, some languid and long-legged, others wide-eyed and skin-twitching, a few—fillies with raised tails flicking back and forth, colts with phalluses tumescent and swinging—raucous and lascivious, past the clusters of gamblers.

The real New York City gamblers will be there: men in ample, loose-fitting suits, four or five in a group, in their sixties, having driven up from the Big Apple in a long wide-seated Cadillac, cigar smoke spiraling out of the driver's window—old friends since childhood, here again on their annual pilgrimage to "the Spa," frequent visitors to Belmont Park, always the four or five together. No wives, no kids, just the boys and their combined knowledge that comes from three decades of following the ponies and their combined inexperience in the early years of soaring success at the windows one day followed by flaming failure the next and now their steady flow of successful bets maintained by studying the *Racing Form*, the *Pink Sheet*, the cheat sheets, by keeping up-to-date with the tactics, techniques and methodologies of the major trainers. The totality of these factors will come into play as they decide how to invest in these animals who to them are the sparkling, gem-like embodiments of statistics, each four-legged beauty a storehouse of synthesized stats created, filed, printed, computed, analyzed for one purpose: to predict how this horse will run on this day against these other horses. The stats they gather will give them the hard facts: how many races won, what distance they were won over, what type of race, what type of conditions—muddy track, hard fast track, grass—how fast they breezed last time, what the trainer's winning percentages were here last year, who is riding the horse, what percentage of his rides are ending up in the winner's circle. Finally, if you throw these stats of each horse, trainer and rider in a feed tub together, how do they match up?

How does this colt, whose sire is all speed, match up against this gelding, whose sire is all staying power and endurance, and how is the track today? It is not muddy and slow, it should be average today . . . but for some reason the breezes this morning at five-eighths of a mile when the four had breakfast by the wire were slower than usual and the times in the first few races were a second or two off and so maybe today's track does not favor the colt by the speed sire. And how will this older jock who is starting to occasionally take "the married man's route" do against this young hot bug boy who loves "to thread the needle" and who carries less weight because he's still an apprentice?

The horses are led by their proud grooms, among the lowest paid workers on the track and yet the ones who spend the most time with these eye-flashing grays and long-necked bays and soapy-chested chestnuts. The procession will continue down the fence-lined path, the Thoroughbreds and their grooms passing the quartet of gamblers from the Big Apple, the lifelong friends and lovers of not only Saratoga, but also Belmont Park and Aqueduct and the Meadowlands, and of Finger Lakes, and way back, of Rockingham Park and Atlantic City. To this foursome, these animals are *betting interests*, not individual live beings with personality traits, athletic eccentricities, hearts, and nervous quirks; they are not youths who have left their friends back at the barn, who were led away from the gentle galloping girl whom they felt calm around and who stops by their stalls every afternoon to give them a carrot, whisper lovingly to them, caress them behind their ears, stroke them rhythmically and hypnotically down their long, cylindrical necks; they are not adolescents with creases of fear rippling up their spines and a new sensation of claustrophobia pressing in on them as this herd of humans squeezes in closer, creating a gauntlet through which they have to walk, not allowed to react as nature has trained them over two thousand years: to take flight or to fight back, to snort, stamp their front feet, and throw up their heads, to rock forward on their front legs and let loose a blast with their hind legs that would kill any wolf or lion, or human. These two-year-olds are not teenage prodigies who could with a snap of the head, knock the groom leading them off the path, or rear and break away. The chestnut with the long, shiny mane, the bay with a checkered pattern curried onto his rump, the wild gray, her eyes wide-open, her neck in a lather—to the foursome from the Big Apple, each of these horses is a betting interest, and there is nothing wrong with that, for without their love of gambling, there is no track. They are what keep the owners, trainers, jockeys, galloping girls, and grooms in operation.

Our foursome pays close attention to the five-year-old colts, geldings

and mares who have been down this path many a time, who've been training two weeks at the Spa, galloping easy around and around Oklahoma,
being held back, forced to gallop slowly, forced to "breeze" in control—
three-eighths of a mile at a brisk pace on Oklahoma one week, five-eighths
of a mile at a good clip on the main track the next—and then to pull up
quickly after passing under the wire. They've been cooped up in the narrow stalls all day watching the perpetual caravan walk, drive, bicycle and
ride by. Each morning, they've gotten a little fitter, more on edge, until
they cannot wait to explode out of the gate, to break strong and straight as
a rocket, to run as God created them to run, to cut loose, to come around
that last turn in a flight of flying manes and pounding hooves and yelling jocks and streaming-jetting-stinging dirt and show those others who
is boss as they were brought up to do in the big fields of bluegrass back
on the farm in Kentucky. They are craving to dig down into the rich dark
dirt track, to switch to the outside lead, pull to the outside away from the
shotgun blasts of sand and dirt stinging them in the eyes, in the nostrils,
to pull out into the clear air, onto the freshly harrowed dirt with the clean
long furrows stretching to the wire, and to allow every vitamin fed into
their system, every protein-infused quart of oats and sweet feed they've
consumed, all the nutrition from the hay and the clover and the alfalfa the
trainer had so carefully picked out, to allow the culmination of hundreds
of years of carefully planned, meticulously carried out, painstakingly, ob-
sessively orchestrated matchmaking accomplished in pine-paneled offices
in Kentucky over a shot of Jack Daniels with millions of dollars at stake,
in boardrooms in New York and London and Dubai over cross-country
and trans-Atlantic phone calls, in tack rooms on the backsides of Churchill
Downs, Pimlico Racetrack, Belmont Park Racetrack, to finally allow the result of all these efforts to be tested. Fed up with conserving, with behaving,
they are ready to inhale the oxygen through their nostrils with the force of
air funneling into the jet engines of a fighter plane, to let it soar-twirl with
every chest-stretching, lung-expanding, heart-pumping stride in a vortex
of God's clean pure energy down the turbine of their outstretched necks
and into the bellows of their lungs and then into the engine itself, that

which is the most important of all, without which a horse, no matter what his breeding, what his training, what his conformation, is nothing, to let that oxygen explode into the heart and the heart to pump it throughout the long sleek perfectly-tapered neck, torso, rump and legs that want to fly, to take off, to be released from gravity, to kick into high gear, a higher gear, the highest gear, and go all-out in a delirium of competition and pain and joy for the wire.

Chapter 5

Into the Hurly-Burly

The ground is low lying after the fourth fence and if there has been any rain the going becomes boggy. Riders slow their horses as they turn to the left, and then straighten to jump the fifth, a nice four-foot post and rail at the foot of a gradually rising hill. It is a "line" fence — part of the actual paddock fence — and jumping it seems as natural as jumping out of a field on a run out hunting. "You might be tempted to relax going into this fence," says Mikey, standing in front of it. "It looks like something you'd jump in a junior hunter class, doesn't it?" He looks at the fence as if he is embarrassed by it. "But you've got to be thinking one fence ahead here. You've got to be setting yourself up for the sixth. You know, make sure you're not stuck behind a bad jumper, or on the right of a horse that jumps to the right. Going into the sixth you don't want to be worrying about the others." Upon landing after the fifth, you head for an orange pylon, knowing that once you make a sharp turn to the left around that pylon, you'll be galloping into one of the biggest fences on the course.

⤠

WE WALK ALONG the path toward the paddock. It is the morning of the A. P. Smithwick. This is it. No horses are coming toward us. Tom, on Mickey, is beside me, Kiwana and Jonathan and Elizabeth behind us. Tom has timed it so we'll arrive as the track reopens after being harrowed. We reach the paddock—it's twice the size of a show ring. A white-railed fence extends around its perimeter, with the dark-dirt ring inside the fence. The paddock is vacant. It's like walking into a theater where you know Peter O'Toole, Katharine Hepburn, Richard Burton and Elizabeth Taylor will strut and act and love and fight that night but now the stage is bare without the panoply of owners and trainers and jockeys and horses milling around, each groom leading his perfectly manicured horse to a tree with his number posted on it and then walking the horse on a narrow dirt path around and around the tree, trying to settle him before the valets in their gray outfits, holding the jockeys' tack, and the jockeys in their colorful silks with helmets jauntily perched on their heads and chin straps dangling walk lightly with assured athletic grace onto the stage. Each trainer—most in sports jackets or suits—motions for the groom to stand his or her horse inside the circle by the tree, and the groom leads the horse in, stands directly in front of the horse, jiggles the shank to relax him while the trainer lightly runs his hand, once, twice, down the delicate back of his horse before he and the valet set the pads, number cloth and featherweight saddle onto this smooth, sleek, flinching fuselage.

Elizabeth and Kiwana are on young horses who have never been to the main track. They're jigging and fussing and staring wide-eyed at every new thing they see. Tom is "paddocking" them. He tells Elizabeth and Kiwana to walk them for five minutes around the paddock, then hack back to Oklahoma, and jog around once backwards.

Jonathan and I walk around the paddock a couple of times. My horse's neck is in a lather. The rubber-sheathed reins have a little age on them and the reins are smooth, slippery. I reach back, pull a faded red bandana out of my right rear pocket—how do people make it through the day without having a bandana or two ready for use?—slap it on the rein under my right hand and feel my grip become more secure.

Tom is relaxed on Mickey. He is riding the exact same length he always has, which is about two holes, or two inches, shorter (or more racetrack-like) than what is considered proper foxhunting or show ring length. He is by the gate that leads out under the clubhouse to the main track. An older man in a suit walks up, leans on the rail, and starts talking to Tom. Jonathan and I circle around again. Tom is talking to the man but he is also doing something with his arm. Without looking up at us, he is waving us over, signaling that it is time to head for the track.

The three of us walk down the chute across the path where thousands of spectators, entering from the clubhouse gate, will be crossing in just a few hours.

"Patrick," Tom says in his clipped, early-morning business tone. "Patrick," he says again, not waiting for me to answer, "you go off first. Jog him back to the quarter pole, turn, and gallop twice under the wire. Jonathan, you follow."

"OK, jog down the stretch to the quarter pole," I say, as if to myself, but really to repeat it back and ensure I have it right. "Turn around, gallop twice under the wire, and pull up. . . . Go past the chute and then pull up?" The chute to the starting gate is around the turn. If you gallop past it, and then pull up, you add an eighth of a mile.

"Yes," he answers, sighing, as if it were the biggest effort, "and then walk back to this gap."

We walk under the clubhouse and out onto the track where the bugler will play as the horses for the A. P. Smithwick Memorial file out this afternoon and then the announcer will call out "the horses are on the track." In my mind's ear I hear the great Fred Capesella announce, "the *horses* / are *on* /the *track*," in perfect iambic trimeter. I am hearing Capesella, I am seeing the bugler with his trumpet by the entrance gate to the track and I am listening to the notes which always send tingles up my spine, whether as a kid with my old friend Mike White thirty-five years ago, both of us lying on our backs, fishing poles by our sides, down by the Yaddo pond half a mile away, or up on Wild Amber headed out to ride in a hurdle race.

We're on the track. I take a left. Sprinter immediately begins to jog without me giving him any signal to do so, feeling like one of Pop's old cars with the rpms set high so that the second you take your foot off the brake the car shoots out from under you. The track is beautiful. It is inviting. The dirt surface has just been harrowed and watered, and the dirt lies in parallel and even rows with no hoof marks, no clumps, no droppings. It's like being at the top of a mountain in the early morning, standing in skis, looking down at the fresh powder having fallen the night before and preparing to push off. I stand in the irons, lean back against the reins and let Sprinter trot along the outside rail. I'm thinking about an old friend who is the speaker at Breakfasts at Saratoga, and yes, there she is—fit and youthful and snappily dressed—facing slightly away from me, explaining something to her tables of listeners. I almost call out her name but decide not to interrupt her talk, and besides, I am getting down to business on this horse. She is now a successful racetrack commentator, and for years I've wanted to go to her Breakfast at Saratoga, to surprise her and have a good chat, hear about her life, but I have never done it. Instead, in the early morning, I've always been on one of these horses of Tom's while she, who had hung up her tack, was doing something far more practical, making good money talking about what she knew and loved.

I jog Sprinter quietly for a quarter of a mile, up to the head of the stretch. Horses are entering the track from its many gaps. I pull up to a walk, turn Sprinter toward the inside rail, make him stand. "OK?" I call back to Jonathan, who also stands his horse up. "All set, Old-Blood."

I ease Sprinter off, keeping my hands down. We gallop easily down the wide stretch, the empty grandstand—consisting of timber beams and wood planking and built on a scale relative to the human and to the horse— looming long, low-slung and historic on the right. It is open to fresh air; there is no wall of glass and steel beams partitioning off the spectators, disjoining them from the horses and riders. During the prerace post pa- rade in the afternoons, you can smell the lather between the horses' hind legs, the nostril-clearing scent of the droppings, the freshly saddle-soaped leather of the tack; you can hear the jangle of the polished bit of the bridle and the slapping of the reins and the quick, light hoof-pats on the powdery surface.

At the sixteenth pole, I hear my old friend over the loud speaker, "And that's Patrick Smithwick up here to present the trophy for his father's me- morial race this afternoon. He's helping out trainer Tom Voss who is run- ning the favorite in the A. P. Smithwick today. . . ." A horse charges down the stretch and under the wire on my inside. Sprinter throws his head up and lunges a stride or two. I keep my hands down, lower my butt, and steer him in and out of horses who are pulling up—going from a gallop to a canter to a trot and angling to the outside rail—as we pick up speed going around the clubhouse turn.

Around the turn, past the starting gate chute, headed down the backstretch and I still have my hands down. I slow Sprinter. He leans into the bit. I lean back against him, in control. Out of the corner of my eye, I spot Scotty Schulhoffer leaning on the rail. I nod to him, one of my father's greatest friends and the most kind and gentle man ever to be inducted into the Hall of Fame.

I hear horses coming up on my inside. A rolling, thundering chaos of hooves gaining on me fast. The jangling of steel bits, the slapping of reins against necks and boots against saddle flaps. Men yelling. Sprinter's head shoots up. I lean back. We pick up speed. The three horses are alongside us, two in front, one behind. The jock behind and on the outside is pushing and trying to get his horse up with the others, cussing and yelling at the riders in front to wait up. He reaches back and cracks his horse on the rump with his stick and now they are alongside me. This is embarrassing. I can remember this feeling so well. It immediately returns. They are *working*—going full tilt—but they are stuck alongside me, the exercise riders pushing their horses and this damn Sprinter is taking these huge, powerful strides and keeping up with them while I am standing straight up in the irons looking like a farm boy galloping his first tough horse. There's no finessing Sprinter. He wants to go with this trio. He's dying to cut loose and show these guys who's boss. I have no doubt he could do it if I so much as relaxed my grip for a fifth of a second. They start to pull away from us and Sprinter digs in, fighting me, wanting to be released. He is strengthening, I am weakening. I feel like I am about to lose him. How mortifying this would be. How dangerous this could be. What would he be like going full tilt? Would I be able to control him? To steer him? Would I be forced, in order to get past the other horses now crowding onto the track, to pull him over on the rail where he would think I placed him to *work*.

Halfway around the turn, I lean back with one final recall of strength and run the bit back and forth through his mouth, and they go on without us. Their hooves blast a stream of the wet, gravelly dirt into my face, across my chest. I duck down.

I am not fit for riding a puller. To gallop a puller, more than your legs have to be fit; your hands, arms and back have to be strong and used to this position and able to maintain it. My legs are in good shape. I am gripping, squeezing the reins as hard as I can but my right arm—Sprinter is pulling to the left, trying to get down on the rail—is going numb. My fingers are outstretched, about to give out. I pull the arm to my side and lock my elbow against my rib cage, trying to take pressure off the arm.

We gallop down the stretch. I'm no pretty picture. Sprinter has his head down and is pulling relentlessly against me. With every surging stride he's trying to break away. My hands are like clamps on the reins. I am ordering them to grip, to stay strong, but I don't know how long they can hold on. I remember this feeling of having to stay calm when you are about to lose control as if I had just experienced it on one of my father's horses the day before: It could be Limbo, black, gigantic, incredibly long-striding, who would throw his head high before trying to take off; or it could be Wadsworth, a chestnut who liked to gallop with his nose inches from the ground, gradually pick up speed, his nose skimming the dirt of the track, until your feet were "up on the dashboard," up on his shoulders, and you were leaning back with all your strength and all you could do was feel those shoulder muscles powering themselves faster and faster, wrenching a notch looser from your control with every stride. Or it could be Arnold W., who would leap and plunge, and duck and spook, the entire time around, as if he were playing, and suddenly, after one plunge, he would land with his legs churning, burning up the track, and you couldn't believe the speed at which you were going. Pop would be standing by the rail and when the horse would give that one fraction more of a surge, my arms would give out and I'd have no choice but to release the reins and resign myself to letting him kick into high speed for a quarter of a mile, three-eighths of a mile, while feeling the laser stares of the riders on other horses, the trainers leaning on the rail, and Pop. I'd be boiling over with failure, feeling with each passing and irretrievable second more and more of a flop, a weakling—a race car driver whose car has gone into a spin, a quarterback who watches as his pass spirals blissfully, perfectly, toward the moving target and then is snatched out of the air by a defending linebacker.

The red bandana is flapping under my right hand. We pass my friend the stylish announcer on the right as she speaks to her gathering. I don't as much as glance at her standing there—she who would instantly see the precariousness of my situation. Nor do I look at the Bloody Mary–sipping, eggs Benedict-eating spectators watching Sprinter and me and having no idea of what is happening.

We're under the wire. Time to pull up. There's a confusing hurly-burly of horses in front of us. Some are on the outside rail jogging back to the clubhouse gap, some easing up from their gallops and pulling across the track toward the outside rail, some starting off on gallops and having to go closer than normal to the inside rail. We have to lace through the crowd. I'm pulling hard with all of my body. He is not responding. My legs are shot. My back is worn out. I see Peter Pugh, one-time jumping rider, now a successful trainer, riding western on a pony, cantering along, going my direction. I think about calling out and asking him to "catch me," to gallop up alongside me, grab a rein, and ease me up. But I don't.

Standing up straight in the stirrups, I lean back as hard as I can. We slow to a canter, a trot, a jog. I feel balanced, feel like an extension of this big, long-striding horse. Not an extension, rather a part of the horse, able to predict every movement. We've made it.

It is 8:45 a.m. My coworkers at Gilman would be arriving at the parking lot, a few minutes late, walking to the Alumni Building, setting down their pocketbooks and laptops and lunch bags, fussing around, going to the lady's room, getting a cup of coffee or tea, making instant oatmeal in the microwave and sitting down at their desks. Several were at the beach, where, they told me, they never even thought about getting out of bed before 10:00 a.m. The concept does occur to me: Why am I out here doing this? I try to come up with a rationalization but have no success. Instead, my mind leaps back to something Mikey had said ten days ago after we'd had him over for dinner with Mom to kick off our trip to Saratoga for Pop's race.

MIKEY HAD EATEN enough for three people. He apologized over and over for accidentally slamming into my car from behind in February and giving me whiplash. We were sitting in the living room, Mikey asking Paddy, Andrew and Eliza about their schools, and telling childhood stories about Mom and Pop, when I asked if he wanted another glass of white wine.

"What'd you say, Sonny-Boy?" He'd lost his hearing aid again.

"How about another glass of wine?" I asked, more loudly.

He was slumped down in a big easy chair. His soft brown eyes, that the women so loved, looked up over his scratched and cloudy five-dollar reading glasses, into my eyes. He shook his head, "Couldn't do it. Couldn't do it."

Mom was getting fidgety. She stood up, said under her breath, "Come on Patrick. Walk me to the car."

Mikey pushed up out of his chair and stood, hunched over, looking at Mom. "Hey Good-Looking, where do you think you're going?"

Mom laughed. "I'm going home," she said at a high decibel level.

Mikey walked over to Mom, shuffling a little, put his arm through hers, and started chuckling. "Now listen you wild good-looking thing. Why don't you just come home with me tonight?"

"Oh Mikey!" Mom pulled her arm away from his. "Come on Patrick."

Mikey looked at Paddy and Andrew. "This was the best-riding, best-looking, wildest girl in the Green Spring Valley. Everybody was after her. I had the biggest crush on her but your father got her. . . ."

"Grandfather," I said, walking out with Mom. "That was their grandfather."

"Grandfather," Mikey said, grinning mischievously at Mom over his reading glasses and not paying any attention to this correction

I walked Mom to her car, her big yellow lab Willie jumping around in the back seat. Mom didn't plan on anyone bothering her. Often, she drove with Becky, the rottweiler, and Wiggles, the cocker spaniel, also along. At home, the three were the first line of defense. The second, since Pop died, was the twenty-gauge shotgun behind the kitchen door.

Soon, I was driving Mikey down the Manor Road back to his farm in Hydes. It'd been hot as hell all day, but it hadn't made much difference to me: I'd been coolly ensconced in my office at Gilman. We had the Volvo's windows open and Mikey told me how he loved the smell and feel of the cool evening air after a hot day—Could I smell the honeysuckle? "You know, the heat must've gotten to me," he added. "My eyes are aching a little."

"What time did you get up this morning?" I asked, certain he would say five-thirty, the time he usually called me on Saturday or Sunday to check on how I was doing.

"Four," he said.

"Four o'clock?"

"Well, Alex," he said, speaking of his female companion of twenty years, "got up at three-thirty to feed and let me sleep in until four. We took a set up to the club and walked the hounds. They go out at six before it gets hot."

"Could you take a rest after you walked the hounds?" I knew he'd been having dizzy spells. Alex had told me she'd talked him into going inside for a couple of hours during the hottest part of the day.

"No Sonny-Boy," he said, as if I'd just made the most ridiculous remark. "As soon as we got back from the club, we had to take two to Pimlico, and then, when we got back to the farm, we still had a bunch to get out."

"How'd you get to Pimlico?"

"Took the van." He glanced over at me to see if I at least appeared to be sane, after now having asked two crazy questions.

I wondered if he traveled in the air-conditioned cab or in the back with the horses.

"Went in the back with the horse. He's a nervous shipper," he said, looking straight out the window. "We brought two actually, one to give the other company."

I pictured Mikey bouncing around in the back of the van, patting the skittish horse, chanting, "Whoa-a-a-a- boy, whoa-a-a-a, that'a boy," as the van roared down the Jones Falls Expressway toward Pimlico and the straw and dust whirled in the scorching air pounding in from the open windows. The horse finally calm, I imagined Mikey, the visor of his Irish wool cap pulled low, leaning dangerously on the door, his hands gripping the vertical steel bars of the window, and looking out at the traffic. The people in their cars would glance up at this old-timer—a down-and-out hot walker or groom, they'd think, feeling sorry for him—as the seventy-year-old Hall of Fame trainer savored the van ride and planned exactly what the horse would do that morning.

"How many did you get on today?" I asked, thinking about the heat.

"What'd you say?"

"How many did you get on today?"

"Oh, five or six, if you count being the pony-boy at the track."

Picturing the waves of heat rising off the track at 8:30, I glanced at Mikey, comfortably seated, peering out over his cloudy glasses. I was thinking of asking him one more question but I didn't really want to hear the answer.

Without any prompting, looking straight ahead, Mikey stated, "The horse that's about ready to run is a little rank, might throw his head up and try to take off. So, I got on the other one and galloped around once alongside the rank horse—you know, I was just being the pony boy—before he breezed."

On the radio all day the disc jockeys had been warning of a heat-humidity index of over 100, an emergency alert, the air quality abysmal, telling senior citizens to stay inside in air conditioning. News shows for several days had been recounting stories of senior citizens in row houses in Baltimore found dead lying on beds in front of fans with still blades and air conditioners with quiet motors, their electricity cut off due to non-payment of bills.

"Got on the donkey too," he added. "Petunia. Rode her bareback. Ride bareback at least once every day." He looked over at me. "Good for your riding, Young-Blood. Got to do it."

I envisioned Mikey, the idol of so many, happily jogging up the stone-dust driveway to the top paddock on Petunia at noon with the heat index at over 100 and everyone else in the state of Maryland sealed away indoors, fans whirring, air-conditioners blasting, shades down.

"Why the hell do you make yourself get up and walk the hounds when it's so early and the days are so hot?" I asked.

He stared ahead, peering out the window. "I suppose I've gotten accustomed to it," he said. We drove along, the honeysuckled air flowing through the windows, and I thought about that.

I PULL SPRINTER UP, walk a few steps, turn him around and start back. Jonathan jogs up alongside us. I relax, don't tell this young virtuoso that I was on the verge of being run off with, breaking this horse down, tearing around the turn, careening into anyone who got in our way. Oh Lord, how I would've felt defeated, disgraced, and Tom, approaching on Mickey Free, would not have said a word. I knew from past experience he wouldn't have even made eye contact. He'd just look into the horse's eyes and make this disappointed frown and shake his head as if he had just seen the most pathetic sight. Then he'd pat the horse and show all kinds of sympathy for this animal who had put me through the ringer, look down over the horse's legs, unsnap the blinkers, pull them off, mutter "Jesus Christ" and walk on. But the horse hadn't gotten away from me. He'd had a strong gallop without having to breeze. We had been on the edge of disaster and had dodged it. This was something, this was an accomplishment. Furthermore, the horse should be perfectly prepared for his race in two days.

"You had him Young-Blood, you had him," Jonathan says, revising the not-so-flattering "Old-Blood."

He looks me in the eye. I'm huffing and puffing, trying to hide it. "Why aren't you riding this afternoon?" he asks.

"What do you mean?"

"I mean that not too many of us could've gotten that horse around here . . ."

"Well, thank you."

"Tom knew exactly what that horse was going to do, and he only tried those blinkers on him because you'd be riding him. Why aren't you riding races?"

"I don't know. . . ." Suddenly, I cannot remember. Why aren't I? What have I been doing? "I had other things I wanted to do." And what are they? I look out at the track. We are around the clubhouse turn and headed toward the gap. Two horses are racing head-and-head down the stretch toward the wire. One a broad-shouldered chestnut, the other a lithe and graceful bay. At the sixteenth pole, the riders in bright red and bright green helmets are timing it perfectly so that they will go under the wire together. Others are galloping their horses in the middle of the track. Behind us, a group of riders is joking and laughing. The chestnut and the bay fly under the wire in unison. Their riders ease up out of their tucks, let the reins slide through their fingers.

"Ha," Jonathan said, "You've been writing, you've been chasing your kids around. Here you've been up hiking in the mountains, stop by Saratoga and first day you can gallop these horses with one hand."

I look over. He has those irons jacked up impossibly high, like a flat rider. His horse is jigging side to side. A rider, having no control over his horse, is cantering sideways toward us on the outside rail; he yells out a few cuss words in Spanish and cracks his horse with a whip. Jonathan's horse spooks, shooting out into the middle of the track. Jonathan maintains his seat, doesn't lose one ounce of balance, steers the horse back to me and continues talking.

Tom, on Mickey, meets us at the gap. He's grinning. I walk Sprinter up to Mickey. Tom turns Mickey, and we walk off the gap and under the clubhouse, Sprinter rubbing his head against Mickey's shoulder and Tom's leg. Tom reaches over his mane and rubs and pats Sprinter on the neck. "That-a-boy, that-a-boy," he repeats softly as he unbuckles the snaps and pulls off the blinkers. Jonathan rides up on the other side of Mickey, and his horse rubs his head hard against Tom's left leg. Tom maintains his patience. He's in the moment. He's not concerned about the race in the afternoon or the weights given for the race or the myriad of questions asked by his owners. He's calming Jonathan's horse so he can unbuckle the strap to the figure-eight and pull off the tongue-tie. Quietly, without talking, we walk back, down the tree-lined path outside the grandstand, across Union Avenue, through Horse Haven, alongside the outside rail of Oklahoma, across Caroline Street to the Annex, watching the grooms, hotwalkers, galloping boys, and trainers at work, feeling the rhythm of the horse's stride come up between our legs and become a part of our bodies, inhaling the sharp, sun-sweetened air, smelling the hay, the manure, the clover, the sweat of our horses.

CHAPTER 6

A Day at the Races

Mikey picks up the pace as he steps down off the fifth and we head up a slight grade. His eye is on the orange pylon placed on a deep-set rock up ahead. There's a brightness to his step. We reach the pylon. He stands, turns, looks back. "You land over the fifth and head straight for this pylon," he says, slapping it with his cane. He turns, faces the ground rising up to the sixth fence, takes a few breaths. "Then, you turn sharp, pick a panel and ride into it like you're on an open jumper in the show ring." We start walking the thirty yards to the fence. Mikey is headed straight for the inside panel, by far the highest panel, just to the right of the red flag. "Some riders drift up the hill to jump one of those lower panels," he says with disdain, waving his cane in the direction of the lower, more inviting panels. We reach the fence. We're standing in a dip in front of the fence. The top rail is big and thick and at eye level. "I like to jump it right here," he says, standing straight, forgetting that he will never again ride in the Hunt Cup, sounding as if he will be asking Pine Pep to stand off at this fence in just a few days. He reaches up, above his shoulder, and grips the top rail of the highest panel of the biggest fence on the course. "If you cut that turn at the pylon sharp and jump it right here, Young-Blood, you can gain three lengths on the rest of the field."

﹥

AUGUST 6, SARATOGA SPRINGS. It is a late race, the ninth; after galloping for Tom in the morning there is no rush. Back at the house, everyone has plans. Going against the grain, I say I'll stay there, take a nap. Mom also stays.

I read the *Racing Form*, read the *Steeplechase Times*, fall asleep. I get up and go for a jog. I start off in Congress Park, then head into the town, toward the track. I pass a house where fifteen years ago Tom had rented a room. We'd both flown in from Fort Erie, Canada—where I was galloping for Dickie Small, and Tom was training a string of ten flat horses—for the A. P. Smithwick. We were taking showers, getting ready to go to the races and had a rare quiet moment. We talked about the upcoming A. P. Smithwick, my father, the chance Tom's horse had of running well, his jockey, and then I asked him why he had asked me to ride a big gray horse of his in a timber race at Arlington Park, Chicago, earlier that summer, the day of the Budweiser Million. I hadn't ridden a race in a long time. The horse was rank, would go to the front and burn himself out early, and his riders seemed helpless to prevent this from happening. "Because you're the only one who could rate him," Tom whispered. "You're the only one who knows how to do it."

BACK AT ROCKY'S, everyone has returned from their trips to pools and lakes and tennis courts: Ansley, Paddy, Andrew, and Eliza; Susan's boys—Colin and McLean. We are showering, shaving, bumping into each other in the bathroom and halls. I become the ironing man—ironing shirts for Colin and McLean, lending McLean a jacket and Colin a tie. Mom is dressed and sitting in the dining room looking over the *Racing Form* I had given her, calmly waiting for us. Finally, all but one of us is dressed and ready. We are heading out the back door for the cars when Susan, in shorts and T-shirt, arrives back from a twenty-mile round-trip bike ride to Lake Desolation, where she's gone for her daily hour-plus swim. "Pat, have you had a peaceful morning of writing?" she asks. It is typical. It is predictable. She is like a kid who does not like this race detracting attention from her. But I had been determined to remain free of her, to not allow her to weigh me down and make us late. I'd heard it all before, countless other times, trying to get to this race on time: "Oh Pat, could you go pick up so and so on the way?" "We'll be in plenty of time. Patrick is just such a *control* freak."

Over the years I've learned I can tell how the week will progress by how it goes when Susan and I first meet up. One year, when Ansley and I drove up by ourselves, we met Susan and Sal in the late afternoon out at Andy's—Susan's ex-husband's—where Ansley and I were going to stay while Andy and his wife were away. It was sunny with a nice breeze. I had been cooped up in the car, focused on making good time, for over six hours, and I was celebrating being outside, being at Saratoga, being with my sisters and wife, by walking, checking out the fields and woods surrounding the house, breathing in the fresh air. Standing on a knoll overlooking the pond behind the house—perhaps not as far away or hidden as I might have been—I began to take a long, relaxing leak.

"Pat! Don't do that. Don't go in one spot. You'll kill the grass."

I flipped out, lost my temper, said some things I shouldn't have said, and that set the tone for the rest of the day, all three women now united against me, as well as for the week.

Another time—the year Andrew turned eighteen, just before he joined the Marines, and Tom won the A. P. Smithwick with a horse I often galloped and schooled called Anofferyoucantrefuse—Andrew and I excitedly pulled up in front of Susan's house and, having made excellent time that Mom would have approved of, victoriously walked in. Susan and a few friends were standing in the small kitchen.

"Shhh!" she said, "you're waking everyone up walking on your heels like that."

This was at 5:30 p.m. and I was dying of thirst, ready for a cold beer. It ended up that McLean had just gone upstairs to get away from everyone, though Susan had told him he should "take a nap." She turned to her friends. "Patrick gets up early in the morning to go to the track, walks on his heels with his riding boots on, and wakes everyone up."

She moved closer to Andrew, put her hand up on his shoulders. "Now Andrew," she said, grinning and looking him in the eye, "needs to get plenty of sleep while he's here. Maybe he needs to take a little nap right now like McLean's doing."

She had hit a sore subject. "No," I said. "Andrew does not need a nap. He just slept the entire way up in the car." I had thought that Andrew would help with the driving and we'd have some great father-son conversations, but he, as Paddy also used to do before a long drive, had pulled a late one the night before.

"Oh Pat, now don't think you're going to come up here and be telling Andrew what to do."

"Well actually," I said loudly, more loudly than I intended, her friends stepping back—it was already starting, they were perceiving me as the male-chauvinistic, coffee-and-alcohol imbibing, meat-eating, selfish, non-spiritual, non-granola eating, non-meditating, non-yoga practicing throwback to the 1950s—"I am up here with Andrew and I *am* going to be telling him what to do."

"Now, Pat," Susan said, grinning and looking around at me, at Andrew, at her friends, "Andrew can sleep late every morning and we'll take some nice, long walks."

Andrew was swiveling his head back and forth as if at a tennis match.

"No," I barked. "Andrew is going to be getting up early and coming to work with me, learning about the horse business."

"I'm not sure if that's really what Andrew wants to do. Is that what you want to do Andrew?"

"Susan, Andrew is going to be my sidekick up here. He is my bodyguard. He is my partner and we are going to the barn together in the morning, to the races together in the afternoon and to the sales together at night."

"We'll see. We'll see," she said, surveying the jury like a lawyer. "It looks to me like he might need some long walks, some good naps and some late-afternoon swims. I don't know if it's good for him to be hanging around all those racetrack people."

The guests were backing out of the kitchen. I let them slip by. Andrew was opening the refrigerator, only to find shelves stuffed with piles of cellophane bags of powdery, dusty health concoctions, and jars and jars of muddy-looking stuff.

"Susan, the whole reason we came up here is to be around 'those racetrack people.' Remember, Mikey is coming up. We're taking him to the Hall of Fame inductions and then to the Hall of Fame luncheon." She smiled at me, nodding up and down, not showing a flicker of interest, and so that week continued.

ALL THIS WEEK SUSAN had acted as if the race itself were nothing more than an intrusion into her life. I had told her I'd been galloping the favorite, Brigade of Guards. She could stop by in the morning and watch him go. Rocky had bicycled over and helped clean the tack. Ansley came by. Sal visited the barn. Susan refused. In fact, one evening, she and Ansley were discussing walking to the barn the next morning, and at the conclusion of the discussion, she said, "Or, we could go bird-watching."

This is one of the only years since the inception of the race that my great friend Hank Slauson hasn't come, bringing along his three children—the same age as ours—and doing everything in his power to support me and to honor my father while keeping me up too late in Saratoga dives, freeing my spirit, inspiring me to laugh and live in the moment, to shed all concerns about fulfilling the expectations of upper crust society or responding to the hoity-toity and sycophantic behavior of someone at a stuffy cocktail party. "Or, we could go bird-watching," I would quote to Hank, our elbows on a brass rail at the bar, and we'd have a good laugh.

I push on. Everybody but Mom is giving me orders. I'm sweating. Mom, Ansley, Eliza, Andrew, Paddy and I file into the Volvo, Colin following with the rest in his car. More orders are given regarding the air conditioner, where to go, where to park. "Quiet," I snap, the word exploding from me automatically and more loudly than I intended, coming from my days in the classroom.

With no sticker or badge empowering me, and knowing Colin is right behind us, I drive in the gate, past line after line of cars parked on the grass, and following my instincts, duck the car past a Pinkerton or two as if I know exactly where I'm going. I squeeze the Volvo, grateful for its long, narrow shape, between a tree trunk and a portable wooden "horse" set there to prevent anyone from entering, and park. Colin follows. I feel good about getting us all onto the grounds with some élan. Mom criticizes the parking spot. This is unusual. Too far away, she says. The Pinkerton gives us a funny look and pulls another wooden "horse" across the space through which we have just passed.

We hop out of the air-conditioning into the wall of heat and humidity and start walking down the road along the ten-foot chain-link fence. Beads of sweat drip down my sides. I walk beside Eliza, leaning down to talk privately to her, trying to persuade her to present the trophy with me.

A stinging pain, as if a miniature post-hole digger with a red-hot tip has just been cranked up, begins in my right temple in its precise and favorite dime-sized spot. Since experiencing the whiplash from the car accident on the night of my father's birthday last winter, I had endured excruciating headaches, brought on by noise, tension, or bright light—try teaching a class of seventeen tenth-grade boys without any noise or tension— throughout the spring, and now these headaches would still desultorily (*desultor*—I taught my students—a circus rider who leaps from one horse to the next!) creep up on me. I try to keep it low-key. I tell the woman in the will-call booth that the National Steeplechase Association has left us a dozen passes.

Standing beside me, Mom says, "No Patrick, why do you have to be so stubborn? The New York Racing Association is leaving the passes." Our group is squeezing up behind me in a bottleneck, listening to every word.

Trial by jury. Guilty until proven innocent. The woman finds our passes. I hand them out. One by one, each of us puts our hand on the counter, has it stamped, and walks through the narrow turnstile.

Over the years, this—going to Pop's race with my extended family— has on occasion developed into a frustrating and draining experience. The day of the race Susan usually makes things difficult, either by getting there late, or by having her boys, when they were little, dressed in something Mom would disapprove of, or by disagreeing with whatever plan we have for presenting the trophy. Just a few summers ago, I had been presenting the trophy with my boys, and at the last minute, Susan, standing outside the winner's circle, had awkwardly, for all of us, shooed her boys into the area. Why she always makes a big deal about her boys presenting the trophy, and yet at the same time downplays the race and the day, is just another enigmatic thorn in the side of my mission: to immerse myself for a few days in the world of Thoroughbred racing and to honor my father and pass on his legacy to my children and nephews.

Once inside the gates, I breathe a sigh of relief. I'd brought Ansley, Paddy, Andrew and Eliza to the races on two other afternoons, so they know the routine. McLean and Colin are experienced racegoers and gamblers; I would not be fielding questions from them. In fact, the night before, feeling a little ornery and knowing my upcoming remark was not something Susan wanted to hear, I had complimented Susan on McLean's manners and helpfulness at the track, *and* for his uncanny ability, utilizing the full gamut of statistical permutations modern-day betting offers, to pick winners, to parlay his winnings back in an intelligent and controlled manner, and to increase the Shanley/Smithwick family fortune. She then took my remark as a karate black belt does a flying attack. Using my aggressive forward-thrusting energy, she verbally stepped aside, grabbed my arm and flipped me on my back by calmly making the pronouncement, "Betting at the tracks should be eliminated; it is really not good for anyone," so that instead of my remark heating her up, her remark infuriated me with its display of ignorance about how tracks finance themselves and where the money for purses originates, not to mention why most people even go to the race. Or, was it really ignorance? Perhaps the ignorance was feigned, a tactical move?

We walk up the old wooden steps, near where I had earlier in the day ridden Sprinter under the clubhouse and onto the track. Into the clubhouse— we walk toward our boxes. I bump into an old girlfriend, Cathy, really just an old friend who liked to flirt with me. "Wish you could've been a little pushier," she'd told me earlier that spring at a party in honor of the great steeplechase jockey, Joe Aitcheson. "You could've broken my maiden." I knew perfectly well who had broken her maiden; it was Uncle Mikey, and she was the first of a long line of girlfriends/woman jockeys. But Mikey's prowess with young women was not what got him into the Hall of Fame: it was his ability to communicate with the horse—his natural, instinctual and deep pool of ancestral knowledge of the horse passed down to him and his brother by their Irish father. It was his gift in being able to strengthen a horse's "heart," a horse's desire to win; and it was his talent, combined with his relentless and disciplined work ethic, to teach a horse to jump, and then to have the horse win and win and win, most of the time with my father in the tack.

I watch a race with Cathy and another friend, Beth (a member of the Bosley clan who can gallop across a field standing on a horse's back), and I think about the upcoming trophy presentation. My immediate family hadn't been to Saratoga for a few years. This year was my turn to choose the presenters, and my choice was Eliza and I. Eliza had never presented it. The day before at the races, whenever a trophy was presented, I had pointed out to Eliza what was happening and informed her that she would be doing the same on the day of her grandfather's race. She had held back, and on this day, walking from the parked car, she'd said she only wanted to do it if Paddy and Andrew were with her.

I had felt it would be too country-fairish to have four of us in the winner's circle but when I ask Beth and Cathy for their opinion, they go to the other extreme, saying I should definitely include all three kids: it shows the family's support of the race, the history, the following, the continuity; it is great PR for steeplechasing, shows we care.

The sixth is over. Two more races to go. Heading back to our two boxes filled with Smithwicks and Shanleys, I feel alone. How the hell can anyone feel alone in a clubhouse with thousands of spectators crammed into "boxes"—each box six feet long and four feet deep, holding five rickety wooden chairs—and his entire family within arm's reach?

I feel alone with Pop—or is it lonely without Pop—and with my desire for Brigade to win this race. I am holding my breath. It's how I feel when I rise early to write and have been thinking about the writing and want to keep a clear head. If I come across someone en route to my desk, anyone except Eliza, Andrew, or Paddy—who are, after all, a part of me—I do not engage. I am off. I do not want to lose my focus.

We have plenty of time. I slow down. Back and forth, from the paddock to the boxes, we walk. The kids place some bets. Our ante on the day rises as we discover that every betting ticket has "A. P. Smithwick" written on it. The day grows in stature. It is "A. P. Smithwick Day" at Saratoga Springs.

Mom is nervous but having fun. I don't know where Susan is. Sal is taking pictures of us all. She walks up close to me, looks into my eyes and asks, "Patrick, how are you feeling? You look a little a tense." She steps behind me, into the aisle way behind the boxes, gives me a soothing neck and upper back rub, and the red-tip of the miniature post hole digger that was beginning to burrow into my temple pulls back, withdraws. Since the accident, I'd been to a chiropractor for the whiplash and a neurologist about the migraines, and was soon, on Sal's advice, to begin weekly sessions with an acupuncturist, the only successful treatment. In contrast, the morning after the accident—in which Mikey's air bag had gone off, he'd had a concussion and had totaled his car after ramming into mine—I dialed Mikey's house planning to ask how he was feeling, to tell him he'd better take it easy. (I was staying home from work for the day.) No answer. I called the barn. It was 6:30 and the thermostat outside our kitchen window read twenty-eight degrees. "He's out on a horse," said one of his girls.

As Sal massages, I look down over the rows of boxes, to the best box in the entire clubhouse, the box on the lowest tier, closest to the track and right on the finish line, the box that belonged to the half-century icon of racing, Alfred Vanderbilt, owner of the great Native Dancer, one-time owner of Sagamore Farms, and there, seated in the box chatting away with Alfred Vanderbilt, is Susan, with Rocky beside her.

Eliza and the boys know their way around and are having a good time. McLean is betting and winning and organizing the gambling for the whole crew. Colin is laughing and joking and in wonder—cash in one hand, betting tickets in the other—at the miracle of making money by doing nothing more than stepping up to a window, laying down a few dollar bills, and calling out a number. Paddy is high-stepping and fully into the honor and glory of the day. Leading his sister and younger brother and nephews, he is walking into the paddock where the horses are being tacked up for the fourth race when a Pinkerton stops him. "You can't go in," the Pinkerton asserts, "unless you're associated with a horse in this race or with the A. P. Smithwick."

Paddy looks him in the eye. "I *am* A. P. Smithwick."

The Pinkerton takes a step back and asks for identification.

Paddy shows him his license. "Alfred Patrick Smithwick III."

"Excuse me, Mr. Smithwick," says the Pinkerton. He does a half-bow and gestures for Paddy and the rest to proceed through the gate.

How I wish Paddy could have known his grandfather. Paddy loves all the racetrack business, was born with a feel for it.

As soon as the eighth is over, it wells up inside me. My father's presence comes up out of the creaky, worn floor boards as I walk across them carrying his heavy binoculars on my shoulders and a program in my jacket pocket, as he used to do. Disconnected from everyone, I walk down the stairway, one step at a time, focusing on placing the ball of one foot in the concave dip of the step, and then setting the ball of the other foot in the concave dip of the next step—as I had concentrated the day before when jogging Brigade, up down, up down, posting one stride at a time— past the counter where the binoculars are rented on the left, past the betting windows over to the right, into the smoke and smell of cigarettes and cigars, gamblers milling around, some lining up to collect their money, others marking up their programs and *Racing Forms* and studying the odds board. I walk past men gathering in huddles—exactly where Mike White and I used to meet Elmer Delmer, the bookie, to have him place our bets—and looking up at the replay of the last race on one of the many televisions. Near the entrance to the clubhouse, on the far left, is the bar where Pop and I would relax, Pop sipping a beer and I a screwdriver, after we'd run a horse on the flat. Pop would know the bartender and we'd talk to him and to each other.

Pop's presence presses on me and the gravity of the day increases: my father's name, my name, my son's name on every betting ticket, the horses soon to be entering the paddock in his honor, then the riders, the trainers, the owners, the gamblers all watching, and finally my children and I presenting the trophy. Down the stairs, out onto the asphalt. Holding myself together, not wanting to smack into the oncoming wave of fans and friends of my father in the paddock, I stride around the long way, past the jocks' room. Follow the horses into the paddock. Maintain my focus on Brigade.

THEY TACK UP in the paddock. They file out onto the track.

We walk back in a stream of people toward the clubhouse. On the ground floor, the boys and Eliza gather. They look up at the odds board, down at their programs. Susan is waiting for them, laughing as she listens to a very talkative, English ex-jump-jock who in our youth had ridden some races for Pop and had had a terrible crush on Susan. Paddy and Andrew confer. Paddy heads for a betting window. McLean heads for a window. He turns around, comes back, double checks with Colin and Eliza, and strides purposefully for the window to place their bet. Susan watches with a disapproving forced grin combined with raised eyebrows, as if she is witnessing, and just this one time overlooking, the immoral execution of a white-collar crime. Sal, Mom and I head up the steps.

The bugler plays, sending ripples up my spine.

I'm in the box, binoculars pressed to my eye sockets.

The horses are lined up at the start.

Susan steps into the box, sits directly behind me.

The flag is up.

False start.

Back they go into the infield.

Mill around. Mill around.

In a line.

Onto the turf course.

They turn.

The starter holds the red flag high.

They walk forward.

The starter drops his arm.

They're off. This is it!

First fence. The pack is together.

Second fence, directly in front of us, Brigade in the lead, pulling away. He stands off an entire stride early—a whispery gasp wafts through the clubhouse and ripples through the thousands in the grandstand and down on the rail—takes a huge jump, Jonathan sitting perfectly with him, and jets cleanly over the hurdle, gaining two lengths on the horses behind him.

Around the clubhouse turn. Brigade in front. "Whoa boy," I'm saying. "Whoa boy," I'm saying under my breath.

"Dad? Dad? Is that bad Dad? Is that a bad thing for him to be in front now?" asks Andrew.

Susan flatly replies, "They never win when they start in front like that."

"He's OK, Andrew. He's going nicely."

Down the backside, over three.

Jumping well.

Jonathan is sitting still, in his perch, his preferred seat, with his butt higher than his head. I secretly wished he'd learn to lengthen his hold, stand up slightly, get the horse to relax. Rate the horse. Let him go to the front and then gallop along without fighting the rider, saving his reserves of energy for the drive to the finish. Jonathan's hands, that's what he needs to work on. The art of riding. The subtle part. The part most people can't see. He is a natural; he has all the nerve in the world; he rides with strength and with conviction, but what he doesn't realize is that he has the potential of becoming even better, developing into a more well-rounded rider, a sophisticated rider.

They're going well.

Brigade galloping along easily in front.

Around the far turn for the first time. Next time around that turn they will be driving for the finish. How well I remember that turn, that drive for the finish, the reality of it, all or nothing: it was everything.

Down the stretch at a long-striding gallop. Over the two hurdles directly in front of the clubhouse. Under the wire. They've been a mile and a sixteenth. They have exactly one mile to go. They pass by us, Brigade four lengths in front, on cruise control, not one wasted movement.

Around the clubhouse turn.

On the inside saving ground, Jonathan still hasn't moved, hasn't asked Brigade to run; he's in his low stance and riding patiently. You could set a glass of water on his back, as old-timers say, and it wouldn't spill a drop.

They're starting to come to him now.

Down the backside.

They're bunched and just behind Brigade going over the last down the backside.

And now, this is it. They start driving. Sticks are raised, but not Jonathan's. A good sign. He's being patient. He's waiting. Not making his move too early. They are picking up speed around the far turn. One more hurdle to go, Brigade running well in front.

One horse is moving fast, passing horses, coming up on the outside. It's the one carrying only 140 pounds. He's coming up on the outside. It's time for Jonathan to pick up the stick, crack Brigade a couple of good ones before heading into this last fence, but there is no sign of him using the stick. The oncoming horse and Brigade jump the last fence head-and-head. They're side-by-side. It's Jonathan Sheppard's horse. It's Romantic, carrying only 140 pounds versus our 156.

They're head-and-head, neck-and-neck, and it's Romantic by a nose, ahead a nose.

But now Brigade has shifted gears, is up alongside, has made up that nose, is ahead. What heart. What guts. Spotting the other horse sixteen pounds. Having led all the way. Brigade ahead by a nose. But his surge fizzles.

Romantic is ahead on the nod and his jockey cracks him hard with the whip across his rump, and then cracks him again.

Brigade is ahead on the nod.

Romantic is ahead on the nod by a whisker.

Brigade ahead.

Romantic ahead.

The nod will determine it, the nod will determine the finish, I hope. I hope this but don't in my bones believe it, for even where I am sitting, past the finish with a distorted point of view of the wire, I can tell Romantic has the momentum. Romantic's jockey is whipping and driving and Romantic is responding, accelerating. Jonathan is on the inside and looks strangely quiet, he's down low and he's not whipping and what is going on? I hold my breath.

We should be on our way to present the trophy. Who won? Some deserters in our group have gone over to the other side, backed their Brigade bets with bets on Sheppard's horse, very smart, but I don't need to hear their cheering or what the odds are on their long shot to win. The New York Racing Association woman is here. She has been so wonderful, especially to Mom, over the years of this race. We've got to go. It's on the toteboard and it's not Brigade. Who is the rider? We're presenting the trophy and I don't know who the rider is.

"Come on Eliza, I'll hold you."

"No Dad, no."

The boys and I head down. I don't understand the finish. Something was strange. Why was Jonathan so still? We're walking down through the boxes, down the stairs, to the winner's circle. Ansley asserts, "I saw him drop his stick."

"No," I tell her, being the big shot know-it-all, "he must've just switched hands," thinking he was on the inside and must've switched from the right to the left hand so he could swing the whip more freely without striking the other horse. And then, remembering a phrasing of Jonathan's, the words popping back into my mind—"I'm a professional and professionals don't drop their sticks"—I see my hands gripping a set of reins and feel the tightness of a rubber band around my finger and hear the edge of another phrase, "old-timey gimmick," and I have a sliver, a shard, a splinter of doubt.

At the presentation, Paddy, Andrew and I are there. I'm not doing a good job of including them. I am out of it. Standoffish. In shock. The jockey is Blythe Miller. The jockey is a very pretty young woman. I think this is a first. The sisters will be happy. Where is Eliza? This would be perfect. I look around but can't find her. Blythe rode one hell of a good finish. I approach her, wondering if I should kiss her on the cheek, or shake her hand, but I don't get a chance to do either. I want my sons to shake her hand. An official pulls me over to the side to hold one handle of the big trophy. I do shake hands with this cute freckly little boy, the owners' son, I assume, who looks familiar. I hear no loudspeaker announcing our names. This is what, I realize, had provided the impact in the past. This was the announcement the race-caller made to everyone in the grandstand and the clubhouse and to everyone in heaven and hell, and to posterity. And I can't hear it. I lose track of where Andrew and Paddy are and feel badly about not putting them more front and center for the photo.

After the photos have been taken, the NYRA woman asks us back to the Trustee Room to have some champagne. Guided by two Pinkertons, most of us—the owners of the winner, Jonathan Sheppard, Paddy, Andrew and I—are being herded back through the thicket of racegoers. Then I hear Ansley's voice. I hear her calling, "Patrick." It sounds harsh. She almost never calls me *Patrick*. I hesitate. The Pinkertons, Jonathan Sheppard and his group of owners are disappearing into the crowd ahead of me. I ask Paddy to see what she wants. There I am in the middle. I don't remember exactly where this room is. I could find it but I couldn't succinctly explain how to get there. Andrew is saying—"Dad, Mom wants you. Dad, Mom wants you." I slow. Paddy, Andrew, Colin and McLean are bunched up around me. How can I go back? They won't know how to get to the room. We'll be all discombobulated. The Pinkertons are out of sight. What could she want? I have to decide. I march on toward where our group disappeared.

Into the room. Cool. Champagne. A long table set up with cheese and crackers and perfectly shaped pyramids of cut fruit. An elderly, gentlemanly waiter with a thick Italian accent walks around the congested room with a tray of tall fluted glasses filled with fizzing champagne. He is there every year and does a great job and I don't even know his name. I only see him here, in this room, once every year or two, and yet I dread the afternoon we barge into this cool, tastefully designed room and he is not here with the tray of champagne-filled glasses. I had wondered if this would be awkward, my two-month and counting break from drinking, but it's no problem. I filch a couple of glasses of champagne for the boys and order fizzy water for myself. The race is on the overhead television. We watch it together. They all cheer and ride out the finish and pat each other on the back. And then it comes on again, and again, and again. Susan, Ansley, Sal, Mom, McLean, Colin, everyone finds us in the room. I catch hell for leaving them. I am tired of catching hell. Ansley has verified it. Jonathan dropped his stick. It's not sporting to be saying that the reason Romantic won is because of something the jockey on the other horse did. I don't talk about it. They are all talking about it. What I'm thinking is: rate that horse. One hundred fifty-six pounds. Rate him, relax him.

The boy who was in the winner's circle with us: Ansley points out that he is the same boy who was in the tent the day before. I had joked about the perfect part in his hair, the slicked back 1950s look of his fore-lock, and here he is with us now, the victor, the winner. His parents own Romantic. I am shocked at how Brigade's not winning is getting to me. After all, he'd run a great race, and Tom had gotten him fit and strong enough to run two and 1/16 miles in front, start to finish, without "work-ing" him, without "breezing" him, without letting him gallop full blast for 5/8 or 3/4 of a mile. Instead, to save those old legs, he'd gotten him to the race on long, strong, steady gallops. It was an admirable feat of horsemanship. Or really, more like the fine, precise, and intuitive work of an artist pushing his medium, day after day, to the limit, until on the last day, the last stroke is applied, the last piece of stone is chipped away, and if anything else is done, the painting will be ruined, the sculpture will crumble.

WE WALK THROUGH the racetrack parking lot, and across Union Avenue to the Racing Museum for the NSA post-race cocktail party. Everyone is talk-ing about the stick. Yes, it might have made a difference. Thinking of the rubber band trick, I envision Jonathan and me, back on Atlanta Hall Farm, jogging our horses down a hill, and I hear not his words but the tone of his youthful disdain for such a play-it-safe tactic.

I pass Tom on the way. "Yes, he dropped it!" he snaps. "He asked me if I'd go out on the course and get it. I told him I was going to find it and then I was going to come back and take his temperature with it."

More important than the stick, I believe, is the rating of this horse. If my father had been on Brigade, he could have settled him, like the Shoe used to do in the Belmont, and that would have been worth more than just a nose. Of course, that's why the race is called the A. P. Smithwick.

I try to make Tom feel better by relating a worthless platitude or two to him along the lines of "You can't win 'em all." He answers, "Yeah, well, maybe he would've won if your fat ass hadn't been galloping him all week." Oh boy, that's the way he is sometimes.

And here I am, having worked my tail off to earn degrees from three universities, the education my father never had, having dedicated myself since college to learning and practicing the art of writing, having sacrificed time on weekends, vacations, evenings with my wife and children to write, having pushed my endurance to the limit by rising in the pre-dawn hours to apply pen to paper before going to my too-many different jobs, having finally gotten the career moving forward, and I am wondering, flirting with the idea: Could I have rated that horse? Could I come back here at the age of 50, and like in the old horse movies, win my father's race. Or, more probably, could I return to riding races, if not here, wherever, perhaps in a timber race where the weights are heavier. But why would I, a teacher who listens with interest and empathy to the problems of students both young and adult and then dispenses well-balanced advice, want to do such a crazy thing?

I could be learning to kayak, preparing to take the family on a backpacking trip, furthering my knowledge of sailing and passing this on to my children. Training for a triathlon with Paddy: that was an option, we're always swimming, running, and bicycling anyway. I could be bicycle racing. Learning a martial art with Andrew. Taking up yoga with Ansley. Learning dressage, something quiet and peaceful and artistic—dance on a horse—with Eliza.

Spending more time teaching Eliza to ride!

Devoting more energy to writing, furthering my career. That's what I should be doing.

At twenty, I thought the craving would be gone by the time I was twenty-five. At twenty-five, I was certain that by the age of thirty, maturity and sagacity would have set in and the yearning to ride races would have evaporated, floated off like the fading memory of a dream as one rises out of bed, like the swirling ribbon of smoke from one of Pop's Pall Malls.

How depressed I was on my thirtieth birthday. How low I felt. I was not the leading rider of the country as my father had been. I was not the leading *anything*.

When I turned thirty-three, what did I do but quit the nicest teaching job I ever had, go back to galloping horses, lose fifteen pounds, and before I knew it I was flying to Chicago to ride a horse for Tom in a timber race at Arlington Park on the day of the Budweiser Million. There I was in the jock's room with Lester Piggott, a childhood idol, Chris McCarron, and Willie Shoemaker, the best flat riders on the planet. After the Chicago experience, I knew that was it. Hung it up for good. Not interested. Bored with it. Could care less. Back to teaching, raising my children, doing everything I could for my boys, and stealing any extra time, free time, unscheduled time, to bicycle up the railroad path along Gunpowder Falls to the former Monkton Hotel, march up the three flights of narrow stairs to my rented garret—no telephone, no fax machine, no visitors—sit on the wooden chair before my grandmother's old table, black pen and a long yellow legal pad before me, and then walk, trot, gallop, breeze the pen down the fresh-harrowed lines of the pad.

Upon passing forty-six and a half—Pop's age when he died—I wondered, could I still do it? My fixation on this number, 46 and 1/2, seemed silly, arbitrary, irrational. Yet, there it was. I felt liberated. I was past the age of my father at his death. I hadn't realized until I passed this number that on approaching it, I'd been nervous, holding my breath, wanting to live through it, break through it—feeling there was something that would try to stop me—and continue on the other side.

These were extra years. As the short story writer Raymond Carver said about the years given him after he stopped drinking, these were the gravy.

CHAPTER 7

Alone

Upon landing, after making it over the sixth, you feel a sense of release. Early on, if your horse had been wound up and the runners were packed tightly going into the fences, all sorts of unforeseen events could have occurred. But now, you are in the race and you have three fences coming up, each parallel to the other, each equidistant from the other, all of them good sized but none of them huge. It is the only straight stretch on the course; the edge of the woods is up the hill on your right and the thousands of spectators are off to your left, half a mile away on the hill on the far side of the finish line. You are out here on your own, away from the spectators and stewards and trainers and know-it-alls and friends and wife and children. The course rises before you so that for a few seconds you can't see the seventh fence but you know where to aim, how to follow the mowing lines in the grass. You gallop up the rise and then down. "Don't fall asleep going along here, don't drift up the hill. Stay on this straight line," Mikey says. "Ride your horse into this fence. Many a rider hasn't paid attention to this one, has let his horse chip in, and lost two or three lengths. Do like your old man used to do: use your stick, tap your horse on the shoulder." He grips his cane as if it were a whip and snaps his wrist. "Let him know you're there." He raises his mottled hands up beside each other. "Run the bit through his mouth once or twice," he says, pulling on one imaginary rein and then the other, picking up his pace, lengthening his stride, riding Pine Pep into the seventh fence of the Maryland Hunt Cup, daring anyone to go along with him.

I HELD ON throughout the week as if riding an invisible bucking bronco while I talked and chatted with others. I tried to be steady and quiet on the outside while inside the storm raged, the questions came out rapid-fire, and I wondered if I could do it, ride a race. Or, could I change my life-style so I could at least be more involved with horses, to be outside more, and to have more time to write?

Riding. Galloping horses. Schooling Tom's new horse "SOS"—Soaring Over Seattle—over hurdles, going full blast. What the hell. I loved it. And the thought of not riding each morning, of leaving the track—that, I didn't like at all.

Yet, didn't I remember why I originally quit the horse world? I was go-ing to sit Hemingway-like in cafes on the Left Bank and write novels and pen articles that would inspire people, make them cry, laugh, hold their breath. I wanted to write the perfectly structured short story, to carve the most sensuous and aesthetically pleasing poem.

I was free. I had to remember I was free. I had no obligation to ride races. No one knew I was contemplating these thoughts. Though, actually, when I galloped it usually did come up—"Hey Little Paddy, you going to pick up any rides this week"—and there was the Wild Goose Chase. People did ask if it made me feel like doing it again, and after the race, Tommy Smith, one of the greatest timber riders of all time, winner of the English Grand National and second only to Uncle Mikey in Hunt Cup wins, rushed up to me and said, "You looked good out there Patrick. Not like some-one who has been away a long time. I was watching you, and your form was good throughout the race." If steeplechasing was the kind of sport one could do when older, why not do it? I'd just finished reading *Into Thin Air*, about an expedition up Mt. Everest. Why not live life to the hilt? I'd been captivated by the nerve and fitness and bravery, the drive, of the mountain climbers. I'd been itching to do something like that myself. Defy danger, disregard the odds, and do it. But I had no money for an expedition to climb Everest and I had no desire to freeze my ass off or to die on Mt. Ever-est. So, why not ride? Look at Irv Naylor.

The equivalent for me of climbing Mt. Everest would be to ride in the Maryland Hunt Cup, the Everest of timber races, the steepest climb, the most unattainable—and yet possible—athletic feat I could imagine. To get fit and to train to jump those gigantic fences at race pace after not having ridden in a Maryland timber race for thirty years—that would be my tackling of Everest. And why would I want to do such a thing? The standard reply from a mountain climber was, "Because it's there." And then, there was a remark made by one of my Gilman teachers that had stuck with me. Last winter, after working out in the Gilman weight lifting room, I had waxed poetic to history teacher, coach and iconoclast Nick Schloeder about the interesting and motivating quotations hanging from the walls. He'd said, "There's a difference between reading them and doing them."

ON THURSDAY, I said goodbye to Saratoga. At the barn, I wanted closure. I wanted to walk around and shake hands with everybody and wish them good luck and hightail it out of there, what I had done hundreds of times on leaving the track, leaving racing outfits, leaving horses. Instead, I just said "So long" to Tom and Todd, explaining that we needed to pack and head down the road. (I never use the word 'goodbye.' "Never say 'goodbye,'" Pop once told me. "Just say 'So long for now.'") We wouldn't be leaving on Friday but it might be good to sleep late one morning, and be with the family—sisters, nephews, wife, children, the works. I planned to get the bubbles up on the Volvo's roof Friday afternoon, throw the largest bags into the bubbles, lash the bikes to the rack, and leave at 5:30 Saturday morning. Mom had already taken off. She hates to hang around.

I tried to sleep late Friday. Got up, by myself, fixed some coffee, loitered. Felt that at any moment the adults would arise and my day would start with talking and chattering and going off in this or that direction without at first experiencing the peace and quiet and soul-affirming moments of sipping my coffee, lacing my boots, feeling the time pass slowly. I woke the kids but couldn't get them up to do anything. The adults arose. I was criticized by Susan for not allowing the kids to get all of their necessary sleep for developing strong bones and intelligent minds. I was criticized by both sisters for drinking a mug of coffee. It took forever for us to get going. I made another pot of coffee and drank too much. I longed for the peace and simplicity and immediacy and quiet of being in the tack.

THAT EVENING Susan took off for a long walk while we were getting ready for dinner. Ansley, Sal, and John did the preparations. Kip and his daughter Taylor, Eliza's age, came over and Kip and I had some good laughs watching the girls play and set up their own table. I was the gofer, carrying tables and chairs outside. Kip made a tray of hors d'oeuvres. Paddy and Christopher, Kip's son, stopped by. They'd stayed late at the races. Christopher only had time to say hello and rush to the sales, where he would work until 10:30. Paddy was on his way to Sperry's to bus tables for Rocky. Later, Paddy and Christopher planned to meet up and hit the town. Christopher—lightly built, dark haired, high energy, upbeat, skilled soccer player—was following in his dad's footsteps learning the horse business from the sales end of it. He loved the sales, loved Saratoga, and loved staying up late at night with his crew of close friends. Kip applied no pressure but was delighted to have his son around for a full month learning the family business. It was time to look at colleges, and Kip and I were both urging Christopher to check out our alma mater, Johns Hopkins. I would live to regret this decision.

Sal had asked me earlier in the day if I were going to call Andy, Susan's ex-husband, and I'd been feeling guilty about not doing so. Andy—one of my best friends back when he was married to Susan—was on my mind. It would be pathetic to be in Saratoga and not see him. Usually we went for a few runs together, laughed and carried-on. He was a passionate writer and runner. However, our communication had fizzled since he had remarried.

After dinner, McLean—tall, lanky, easygoing—sauntered into the dining room and talked to Susan about a golf game he was organizing with his father.

"Were you just talking to Andy?" I asked.

"Yeah."

"Give him a call back, would you please?" He called him right there, in the dining room—I was not doing this surreptitiously—and handed me the phone.

"How're you doing?" I asked.

"Great," Andy said, instantly recognizing my voice. "How's your trip been?"

"Good. You doing much tomorrow morning?"

"No, not much."

"Stop by Tom's barn, if you feel like it."

"What time?"

"I get there at 6:30. You can come by whenever you want, though the track's closed for harrowing between 8:00 and 8:30."

"All right. I was thinking about taking Katelin out in the morning anyway. See you there."

We hung up. Ah, that's the way to do things. So simple. I stretched out my legs and savored it. For thirty seconds.

Then all hell broke loose. Susan was irritated that I would be going to the track on Sal's last morning before she flew back to Miami. She had thought I would be there at the house. I had too, until I talked to Andy and on the spur of the moment told him to meet me at the track. I certainly hadn't made the decision with any malevolent intent. I didn't think anyone would even notice. Usually, by the time I bicycled back from the track—stopping at Pepper's on the way to get a melon, and maybe some eggs, bread and a paper—everyone was just getting up. As far as I was concerned, my one morning there at the house had been a flop. There was also tension about going to see my "ex-brother-in-law."

— Why'd I have to go?

— Why'd I call Andy?

— Hadn't I been to the track enough?

It was late. Midnight. We moved to the living room "to talk." I now had the cold hard fact before me that I would soon be arising at 5:30 a.m. to get on Thoroughbreds trained to go as fast as God will permit them and not always cooperative in using this speed and energy and power as directed by the rider. I was no longer eighteen. I could no longer drink through the night, hop in a car with Tom and drive 90 mph down the highway, arrive at the barn without having had any sleep, slosh down a scalding-hot cup of black coffee and get a leg up on my first horse. Sitting quietly, slumping down into a sway-backed sofa, acting as if I were paying attention to the controversy swirling around me, I laughed to myself, thinking back to the last night at Saratoga Tom and I had spent when as sixteen-year-olds we'd been galloping for Pop. We had my car, my grandmother Smithwick's old Corvair, in which we had both learned to drive, speeding it through the fields at Hydes. It was our last night at the Spa and we were driving back to the house Mom had rented, via sidewalks. As we bumped along a concrete sidewalk at 2:00 a.m., a police officer, separated from us by the curb and a line of majestic trees, attempted to "pull us over." We out-ran him until he headed us off at the end of the block where the car wouldn't fit between two trees, one on either side of the sidewalk. We came up with all kinds of excuses, informing him we were very important to the nation's Thoroughbred racing industry, and that we would be leaving first thing in the morning for Maryland. "OK boys," he said in a lowered voice. "You be out of town by sunup. I don't want to see you or this car in Saratoga again this year. Out of town by sunup! You got that?"

The ferocity of that officer years ago was nothing compared to that of my sisters in this moment. First Sal chewed Susan and me out for being "so fucking stubborn."

Then Susan was making me out to be a selfish egocentric, for not remaining at the house on the morning of Sal's last moments in Saratoga, not to mention that it was now obvious that I would much rather be with Andy than with her. In fact, she said, throughout their entire marriage I always preferred to be with Andy.

And here I was, not drinking. I was not drinking—good thing—and yet I was feeling the rage rise up in me, the Irish temper. And then it broke. Resentment, anger, bile poured out.

— Why were they this way about the track?

— Here their father was in the Hall of Fame, a legend. Didn't Kip explain it the other night at Sperry's: "Why wouldn't anyone enjoy a child-hood where he went to the track every morning with someone everyone on the track loved?"

— They didn't know anything about the track.

— They made no effort whatsoever to understand it.

— Looking at Susan, I lectured that she had never taught her children anything about steeplechasing, about racing, or about their grandfather.

— She'd never come to the barn. Here I, A. P. Smithwick, Jr., had been galloping the favorite of the A. P. Smithwick Memorial every morning, and when I'd asked her to stop by, her response had been, "We could stop by, or, we could go bird watching."

— Ansley had come over and had a great time the morning of the National Steeplechase Association breakfast. Mom had walked around the Annex visiting old friends.

— Rocky had bicycled over, with no prodding, had helped clean tack and had further spoiled Mickey Free, brushing him off and giving him mints.

— I called Andy because I hadn't talked to him for a year, and he said, "I'll be there." That's my definition of a good friend. You call him up. Tell him the situation. And he or she does not equivocate, does not hesitate. He or she says, "I'll be there."

— Susan and Sal were disrespectful of the race.

— They were pathetic in their lack of knowledge of the track. Sal didn't even know where the Annex was, or Oklahoma. Susan didn't know what it means for a horse to "break down."

"Pathetic? You're calling us pathetic!" Sal screamed.

Oh Lord, oh Lord, why couldn't I have stayed cool.

"Pathetic." That did it. We were off and running, one hell of a family fight.

Other tensions surfaced. Colin, Susan and Andy's oldest boy, my god-son, a bustling powerhouse of energy like his mother, bounced in and sat down. It was well past midnight. He was cheerful, wanted to chat. I love Colin. I told him we were having a serious discussion, it really wasn't the right time for him to be with us. That didn't go over well with his mother. She was offended. She couldn't believe I had said this to him. I was inconsiderate. I was rude. She wanted him to stay. Yet, she wanted to continue our conversation.

Then: "Well, you know Patrick, maybe we don't have the same feeling for the track that you have," said Susan, Colin now sitting with us.

"Maybe Pop didn't take us to the track every morning, didn't do things with us as he did with you," said Susan. "I was scared, frightened, uncomfortable whenever I was around the racetrack. Men, always talking about sex and women. I felt unsafe. I never got any attention. All those men stopping by our house, the drinking . . ."

They started in on their negative portrait of our youth: of Pop's drinking, of women chasing him, of his friends and owners stopping by our house and staying late, of the supposed lack of meals after the fall that paralyzed Pop, of the depressing atmosphere enveloping our farm after Pop's fall: the worrying about money, the worrying about Pop's health, Pop getting weaker and sicker. They never saw Pop, even when he was healthy.

I countered. I told of a friend of Sal's I'd just seen who said that as a child she loved spending time on our farm "more than any place in the world." To her, it had been "a paradise, riding the ponies, watching your mother on the horses, swimming the ponies in the pond, building forts in the hayloft, being bounced on your father's knee while your mother played the piano, and all the fun people stopping by." She remembered falling off a pony in the back field, lying there stunned, and Pop running across the lawn, jumping the board fence, sprinting out into the field, picking her up and carrying her back to the house.

Sal rolled her eyes and dismissed this friend as having some sort of psychological problem caused by her own "dysfunctional family." The friend was an "enabler," she was in "denial," she needed to join ACOA (Adult Children of Alcoholics). And perhaps I too was in "denial," had some of the same symptoms, and should see a therapist about them. While she was at it, I needed to do some work on "anger management." In fact, she had brought along a short printout (twenty pages, I soon discovered), the basis for a course in anger management that a friend of hers taught and that I would find very beneficial to read.

I disregarded Sal's barbs and told of the many people who came up to me at the races, confided in me about troubles they'd had, about Pop helping them out of these troubles, about his modesty and genuineness, and his treating every man as an equal, how they might not have known him that well but there was this one time . . . and then each would recount, with passion, his or her story. Just the other day, Jimmy Wyatt, Todd's father, approached me and asked about Mikey. "You know, I like your Uncle Mikey a great deal," he said, grinning, looking me in the eye, "but I loved your father." For the first time, I learned, step-by-step, about the fall Jimmy had had alongside my father. Pop was on the younger horse, Jimmy on the more experienced one, and they were schooling over hurdles head-and-head at Belmont Park. Jimmy's horse fell at the liverpool, a hurdle with a water-filled ditch in front of it. Jimmy almost died. He was unconscious for six weeks. His left side was partially paralyzed for three years. Laughing, he let me feel two holes in his skull. "I knew who your father was ever since I was ten," he said. "It was the greatest experience of my life to work with him. I wanted to be just like him. You know, he came and saw me every single day I was in that hospital. Of course, I don't remember, but that's what they told me."

Over and over this sort of thing happened to me. After I'd recently published a piece on foxhunting which contained sections on Mom and Pop, Pop's second grade teacher from Friends School in Baltimore had sent me a letter, along with a photograph of his class. She wrote what a wonderful boy he had been, how he always wanted to ride, and how he often wore his riding boots to school. She asked him one day what he was having for lunch. Just an apple he said; he had to stay light so he could be a jockey when he grew up. She had quietly followed his riding career, had been saddened by his early death, and just wanted me to know what a special boy he had been.

I told stories Mikey had related to me. When they were kids, during the war and gas rationing, on the weekends Pop would walk down to the end of the driveway at Hydes, stick out his thumb and hitchhike to the nearest pony show. He'd pick up rides, hitchhike back at the end of the day, and not mention a word to Mikey or his parents of what had happened. "We'd find out a few days later," Mikey said. "Someone would stop by the farm, go up to Paddy, congratulate him for winning so many classes, and ask if he'd like to come over and give their pony a school. 'Then, if you like her,' they'd say, 'you could ride her in the show this weekend.'" This is called modesty, I told my sisters. This is called passion for a sport. This is called character. This is why there is a race held in his honor.

Susan stood up, ready to hike up to the third-story garret where she was camping out while we were visiting. She had generously given Ansley and me her spacious room with the tall windows. We pleaded that she stay and we work this out. I had clearly hurt her feelings. I, the big brother, what sort of a son to my father was I now to have hurt my sister.

Sal asserted she was willing to stay up all night until we solved this problem. That was not what I wanted to hear.

Finally, I stood up and headed to bed. I had to have some rest for work in the morning. In bed, it occurred to me:

They did resent Pop's love of horses; it took him away from them.

They did not like the racetrack. It took Pop away from them. It was a frightening place to them.

They disliked his flirting and the women chasing him.

They did not have an appreciation or a feeling for what he had accomplished as an athlete, a horseman, or even understand what his attributes as a man were. They were not concerned with this; they were concerned with us all being here together now.

They did not feel that he had been an especially good father to them—this was the first time in my life I had ever considered this concept! He was either away at the track, or away riding or away training, or he was away with me.

I discussed the evening with Ansley before we went to sleep. Yes, she had seen it all building. Yes, she had seen my side. But she saw their side too. This was a facet of her personality that I did not appreciate. She was perfectly fair and balanced—too fair, too balanced—and went out of her way to look at a conflict involving me, or our children, from an objective point of view, often taking this to the extreme of looking at the issue from the other side's point of view and even voicing support for that viewpoint! I wanted her to be more like my childhood friends, my best friends, whom I knew, when the going got rough, would ask no questions, require no explanations, would stand behind me whether I was right or wrong.

We got into a bit of a tiff, and instead of getting angry or upset, I chuckled to myself as I felt an uncontrollable, ornery manifestation of satyriasis rise up in me. Being so wise and experienced, I decided the way to smooth this over was to make an advance on my sweetheart. Wasn't she the same woman with whom I spent that delightful and physically exhausting honeymoon?

My artfully executed plan backfired. I was informed that I was ridiculous. "Why can't you be serious?" she said, and pushed me away.

I lay on my back, shunned, my love unrequited, alone, waiting for my heart to stop pounding, listening to the cars whooshing by.

CHAPTER 8

Going Home Again

There's a temptation to relax going into the eighth fence. You've made it over the third and the sixth. The thirteenth and the sixteenth are a long way off. You have a breather. Everybody is just galloping along, not changing their order. Many are thinking how they will set up for the ninth. Will they be able to get the inside panel so that the second they land they can turn sharply to the left, save ground and let their horses open-gallop going down the hill? But as with every Hunt Cup fence, you need to focus on the eighth. It is not part of a natural fence line such as the first and the last, the third-thirteenth, the fourth-fourteenth, the fifth-fifteenth, the sixth-sixteenth; it rises steeply and unnaturally out of the ground in the middle of the field. Out hunting, you wouldn't jump such a fence. Walking toward it, Mikey says, "You know, one of the toughest things about this race is that it is so damn late in the afternoon. You can't just wake up at 5:30 and think about these fences right up until 4:00. You'd be a nervous wreck. You've got to get your mind off the race. Focus on something else. Keep busy — that's what I used to do. I'd ride. I'd school horses. I'd muck out stalls. Get my mind off it — and then, we'd drive over." He's quiet for a few strides. "Mom and I," he starts to choke up, takes a few strides, glances over, and continues, "Mom and I would drive over together. I'd drive and she'd bring her Bible." He high-steps through the grass, stops, catches his breath. "You know that Christian Science, that Christian Science really works. She'd read the Twenty-third Psalm, 'Yea, though I walk,' " he takes a few steps, " 'through the valley . . . of the shadow . . .' "

"Of death."

"Yes, 'through the valley of the shadow of death,' then what?"

"Then — I shall fear no evil for thy rod and thy staff, they comfort me."

"That's it. Mom would read that. There was more . . . 'my cup runneth over. . .' I can't remember it all. I would drive and Mom would read."

⌒〜

THE ALARM. Louder and louder. Eyes closed, I reached for it, fumbling through books, pocket change and pens on the bedside table. Found it. Pushed the button in. Where the hell was I? Opened my eyes and felt the guilt from the night before spread over me along with the worry of how to spend the morning that I had botched up, made so complicated, turned into a double-bind, no-win, lose-lose situation. Lord, I wished I hadn't called Andy. Oh Lord, I was tired.

I was in trouble. Tom didn't expect me at the barn. What to do?

I paced and fretted. I should stay. Show the sisters I cared.

At 6:15, worried about waking Andy's wife and daughter, I called his house, thinking of not going, of staying home. No one answered. I couldn't *not* go, after I'd told him to meet me there, and there was no way to get through to him. I was trapped. I had to make a decision. The first set would be going out in fifteen minutes.

I grabbed my helmet, hopped on my bike and pedaled to the track.

After galloping two, I saw Andy, but only from the back of a horse. He held Katelin, three years old, and drove with Tom over to the main track. They watched as I hacked a nervous horse, Hashid, owned by Tom's and my godfather Gary Winants, around the paddock. Then, they headed for Oklahoma training track, where I galloped Hashid. Back at the Annex, dripping sweat, I was off Hashid, shaking hands with Andy, feeling his bicep, complimenting his fitness, patting Katelin on the head, and on the bike, pedaling fast, and finally, at the house, relieved to see that Sal hadn't left.

Infused with energy, wanting to make up, I wolfed down some scrambled eggs and toast. "Pathetic," I had called them. I was ashamed I'd acted this way to my father's daughters. I was not being kind or considerate to my own sisters who had lost their father at an earlier age than I. Sal had been fourteen, the age of Andrew. She had not really been around during Pop's heyday. She had only been seven when he'd had the fall.

I was willing to do anything to make up, yet prepared for dissenting opinions. Bracing for disagreement, I said I'd drive Sal to the airport. They were amazingly passive and willing to cooperate.

I started the car. Sal was in the front, Susan in the back.

Out we drove. I was talking a mile a minute about horses and the track, wanting to show them some of the beauty of track life. While delivering my monologue, I realized with shocking clarity that Sal had been too young to remember the years I was describing. We drove down Union Avenue, past the National Museum of Racing on our left. I complimented Susan on the stunning sculpture of horse and jockey—which she had orchestrated the building of—in the main window of the museum.

We passed the entrance to the main track on our right. A Pinkerton held up his hand. We stopped and waited for a set of horses to cross Union Avenue. I pointed to the barn in Horse Haven to our left where Ridgely White, the father of Mike White, used to be stabled, and told how we'd gallop our ponies head-and-head, flying, around Horse Haven. We drove past the buildings which used to house the rec hall on our left, and where in the long, lazy, late afternoons, Willie Dixon and I would shoot pool and play Ping-Pong, and where Mike, Willie and I would watch the boxing matches at night, especially when Speedy Kiniel—tall, thin, black, fast—Mikey and Pop's top groom, my mentor on the ways of the world, was fighting.

Susan asked about Mike: when had he died, what had caused him to commit suicide? I gave her my theory. He had been a "pony boy" in New York—meeting horses before their races in the paddock, and then, once the jockey was up, bringing them to the post. He worked at Belmont Park, Aqueduct, Saratoga, and he was one of the best. But, he was never truly happy doing this. He'd always wanted to be a jumping rider, and then a trainer, and there were plenty of social pressures on him—being from an established Virginia family—pressures that he should be doing better. He started taking drugs, got caught up in the back-and-forth tug of war of kicking the drugs, and one day, turned off the switch. I missed him.

Before pulling onto Interstate 87 to head for Albany, we passed a sign for Yaddo on the right and I explained my connection to Yaddo, a haven, a beautiful park with a mansion and studios and gardens endowed by a wealthy family in the 1900s to provide time and space and quiet for artists to work. Earlier in the summer I had applied for a four-week artist's residency there. I had received a card back from Celia Banks, secretary of the program, who pointed out she'd met my father back in the good old days and had closely followed his career. In fact, she had rented us her house one or two Augusts. I told Susan and Sal how the day after we arrived in Saratoga from the Adirondacks, I decided to hand deliver my application to Celia. I hopped on my bike and rode over, just as I used to do as a child, except this time I didn't have a fishing pole in my hand. I'd pedaled all around the park. It was more formal and organized than when Mike and I used to sneak in to fish. There were signs saying you couldn't go here or there. I had noticed how much more subdued I was and was disappointed to witness myself being so compliant. I rode over toward the elaborate garden, and instead of continuing across the lawn and pedaling-rattling through the lanes and down the steps past the nude statues as we used to do, I got off the bike, leaned it against a tree and walked around—what an old bore—so as not to disturb the tourists. Then, into the Yaddo office I went. I met Celia and handed her my application. She mentioned that Mike Damsi, who used to ride flat races and now worked at the $50 window in the clubhouse, would love to meet me. She wrote his name on the back of a WHILE YOU WERE OUT pink slip, with the words, "wants to reconnect with your father through you." Handing it to me, she explained that Damsi had some good stories to tell about driving up and down the New Jersey Turnpike with my father in a hot car—heater blasting, sweat suits on, pulling weight. He wanted to talk to me. He wanted to touch bases with me. He wanted me to hear his stories.

Onto the highway, I was staging a filibuster, soliloquizing about when we'd been stabled in this or that barn when I finally quieted down, the concept sinking in that Susan and Sal had only made brief and sporadic visits to those barns.

We drove peacefully. We started to talk about the period preceding Pop's death.

Had we ever, in the years since his death, discussed this nightmarish time?

Had we ever even talked about him like this?

It rushed back, the feeling I had when he'd been alive: I wasn't off by myself as a young man; I was part of a team. I was going through life connected with my father; I would report back to him; I would tell him of the life of writing. He would tell me of his life as a trainer. I would return from my writing assignments, spend the night on the farm, arise at 5:00 a.m. on Sunday mornings in the early spring, help him throw on a load of straw and hay, drive to the track and gallop a few. His old friends would come around and after I'd gotten off the third or fourth horse, we'd step into the tack room, stamp our feet, rub our hands together, laugh and take "Pimlico Communion": a swig of chest-warming Early Times right out of the bottle. Now driving along, immersed in this reverie, I laughed out loud at the thought of divulging this scene to my sisters who had heartily castigated me that morning for drinking two mugs of unadulterated coffee.

Out of the blue, almost back at the house, Susan asked, "How's the book coming along?"

"The book? The book on Gilman you mean? Fine," I answered, not wanting to break out of my reverie. "Fine." Lord, I was compartmentalizing. I was in Saratoga, I was at the track, I was galloping horses. Astonishingly, I had forgotten all about this book that had taken up a great deal of the last five years of my life.

"When will it be published?" she asked.

"It's at the printer right now. I'll have the galleys when I get back," I said.

"You know, Sal," Susan said, "I'm the one who talked him into doing it."

"Yes, you are."

"He was thinking about not doing it."

"Yes, I was," I said, and related the telephone conversation I had had with Susan six years earlier. She'd heard I was being approached to write a centennial history of Gilman School and that I was shying away from it. "Pat," she'd said, calling late at night, "this sounds like a great opportunity." Ansley and the children were in bed. I was by myself down in our kitchen.

"I don't know. I have mixed feelings about Gilman. I haven't had anything to do with the place for a long time."

"*Pa*-trick, this could lead to something else. Just think of all the interesting people you'll meet. It could lead to another book."

"I'm overscheduled as it is," I whined. "I'm . . ."

"Who's been contacting you?"

"Walter Lord."

"Isn't he someone famous?"

"He wrote some very successful books—*A Night to Remember*, *Day of Infamy*, *A Time to Stand* . . ."

"*Pa*-trick! You can do it. You can write this book."

She had been right. Writing *Gilman Voices* led to being hired to teach English and to direct the publications at Gilman, and to becoming friends with Walter. The book would be out in just two months and there'd be parties, and signings, and talks all fall, and it would eventually lead to receiving a contract to write another institutional history.

Late that afternoon, Eliza hopped on her bike. I jogged alongside her as she rode over to the Vosses to see Pip and Otis, the Norwich terriers. After giving them a long walk, we had glasses of cranberry-orange juice with Mimi, who informed us that the Fasig-Tipton cocktail party, ushering in one of the world's most elite sales of Thoroughbred horses, was being held in the evening and I ought to get some of our group to go. Equine art, including a series of paintings by Tom's great-uncle and my cousin, Frank Voss, was hanging in the sales pavilion.

Back at Rocky's, I shared the information about the Fasig-Tipton party with Susan and Ansley and went for a jog around Congress Park. Susan had single-handedly produced a beautiful little book on the trees of Congress Park. She knew every single one of them and had planted half a dozen, each in honor of a deceased loved one—Pop, our grandmothers, and, I'm sorry to say, more to come. As I ran, using the mnemonic aids she had taught me over the years, I tried to identify the trees, especially the ones she'd planted, got a few, lost track. Her memory tricks started to spin in my head, and I switched to people watching. At the house, I stretched, took a shower and changed. I felt freed in that I'd decided, whether or not anyone else was interested in the Fasig-Tipton party, I was going. While ironing a shirt, dressing, pulling on a tie, I palavered away, telling Susan, Sal and Ansley they'd like the party. The equine art was up inside the pavilion, and the sales, one of Saratoga's most glamorous events, were about to begin. Frank Voss's paintings were on the walls. Individual horses would sell for over a million. I reminded Susan of how much fun she'd had at the sales a few years before, when she'd enjoyed befriending a well-dressed gentleman seated next to her during a break in the bidding, and then, when the next horse stepped into the ring, been stunned and fascinated to watch as this man kept raising his hand, and finally, with the slamming of the auctioneer's hammer, bought the horse for over $1 million, the highest bid of the night.

There were no takers to be my date at the sales. I strolled over alone, walked in the back way through a gate, past the barns. The gravel walking areas outside the outward-facing stall doors were perfectly raked Zen gardens. Pots overflowing with red and yellow flowers hung outside the stall doors.

Around one more barn, and there was the party, right out of *Gatsby*, the people, swatches of bright color, juxtaposed against the rich green of the grass. They were milling around between two long and well-attended bars set up in covered pavilions.

I stepped over a low fence and meandered into the crowd of several hundred. At first, I didn't know a soul, felt like an outsider, an intruder, but also relaxed, confident. Fresh out of an ice-cold shower, skin tingling, I was razor-fit from the riding and running and no-drinking all week, combined with the hiking and canoeing the week before. Excited to be immersed in this randy horsiness, I felt tall and on my toes and free.

I got a cranberry and tonic and soon was talking to old acquaintances. I met an old girlfriend, now a millionairess living in Virginia on a big farm. We'd had some wild times. Seemed she and I were always jumping, leaping, plunging off walls, out of cars, out of windows at the Diplomat Motel in D.C., when each fall Tom and I would drive down to watch the Washington, D.C. International Horse Show with Bobby Burke, just retired from his riding days. I met another woman, once a buxom galloping girl who rode in skimpy halter tops at Delaware Park in the heat of June and July, causing all the galloping boys to take their eyes off the upcoming terrain, drop their reins, and swivel their heads and torsos. It was a miracle they stayed on when she went flying by. She was married to an Argentinian bloodstock agent. I sipped my cranberry and tonic and played the game. A French trainer based in Paris invited me to sit in his box at Auteuil if I were ever over for the races. Money and luxury and cocktail hours and travel and being outside watching horses all day oozed from their exquisitely tailored clothes. Uncle Mikey was there. I approached him but he was in his work mode—searching for a new owner, looking for more horses to train— his focus at this moment on the scantily clad middle-aged woman with the new boob job (and without her millionaire husband, who would be flying up from their breeding farm in Kentucky in a few days) before him. "Those are just beautiful," he said, staring at her breasts, about to burst out of her low-cut blouse. "I really think you made the right decision. They just look wonderful."

Veteran amateur steeplechase jockey Sebastian Cromwell was standing outside the circle of Mikey, the potential owner and me, trying to slide into the conversation, taking occasional pulls of his cigarette. He was an inch or two shorter than I, had black slicked-back hair, was darkly tanned and was wearing a light-blue striped shirt with a rounded white collar and a blue and yellow tie that had horses jumping hurdles on it. Around his waist was a green canvas belt with "MARYLAND HUNT CUP" sewn in yellow onto one side and horses galloping over huge fences on the other side. That belt was just about on its last hole; he'd grown a paunch since putting away the tack last spring.

I eased myself away and was immediately introduced to a tan, blond, fit, outdoorsy woman, Kate. She'd been doing the triathlon route for five years in California. I heard nothing about her having a job or vocation. She looked very single. She'd heard I'd been galloping, asked me about it, and informed me she was moving to Virginia, planned to foxhunt all winter and ride steeplechase races in the spring. I stood there, sober and clearheaded and joked with her, as if I were back twenty-five years earlier winking at Mike White across the lawn playing the same game with another racetrack groupie. I felt like high-stepping out of there with her and on into a night of dancing and carousing. The horses, the money, the grass beneath my feet, the sky above my head—it bowled me over.

I toured the equine art in the pavilion, enjoying being by myself. My passions, art and horses, were united, and some of my blood was represented on these walls by the paintings of Frank Voss. On returning to the hubbub of the party, the mood had changed. Everyone had been stiff and business-oriented, like horses vying for position at the start of a race. Now, after a few drinks, they had cast off their mercantile demeanor. Suddenly, I was shaking hands with one of Pop's old friends after another. Waiting for me to be free, Jimmy Murphy patiently stood nearby as I chatted with an old female admirer of Pop's. Soon I was asking Jimmy about his stable, and his daughter Foxy. I told him that as a child, I had so loved going back to his place after the Middleburg races, and how Pop and I would go upstairs and I would pull off his racing boots.

Jimmy, in no rush—even with the hundreds of people milling around us, a few still having a nervous edge, preparing to sell their horses—Jimmy stated, "Not a day goes by that I don't think of your father."

"Really," I said, looking into his dark brown eyes. "What makes you think of him?"

"He was my friend, one of my best friends. I miss him. It's too bad he had to go so early."

We stood there. "I've got to go," he said. He put his hand out. I gripped his hand, we shook, and as I was getting ready to release my grip, he put his other hand over my right hand, squeezed and looked me directly in the eye. Then, he walked away.

I, too, turned and walked away from the party.

When I returned to our house, no one wanted to go out. I grabbed Sal's arm and asked her to go with me. We walked, skipped, flew side-by-side down the cracked sidewalks to Sperry's, where we had a good time talking to some racetrack friends. Sal had a glass of wine and I had a couple of virgin "madrasses," cranberry and orange juice, soda water, and skip the vodka. Sebastian Cromwell walked in with a few colleagues from his investment firm in Boston, introduced them to Sal and me, and bought us all a round. He congratulated me on an article I'd written that I never dreamed he would've seen, and then started talking about the Hunt Cup, explaining to his followers that I'd been hunting two great Hunt Cup horses and maybe this spring I should ride one of them. "After winning it twice," he added, "I might just hang it up." His followers sipped their drinks and politely kidded him—"Oh no, Sebastian, you can't do that. We're all coming down to tailgate and watch you win it this year."

Sal was polite and attempting to show interest. She put on her serious-listening face—the funniest expression, which I knew from childhood meant: you are an utter bore; I hope you go away, but no matter what, I would rather die than have you, or my brother, know I feel this way.

Sebastian pulled out a thin, handsome silver cigarette case and politely offered Sal and me one. I chuckled at the concept of offering Sal a cigarette. Sebastian noticed Sal's shocked expression. "I put six in every morning, and that's all I smoke for the entire day," he said, looking her in the eye. Then, he looked at me, "Paddy, we were at breakfast at the track and saw you galloping that big puller a couple of days ago. Looked like a handful."

"Yes, he was."

"Made me think I might gallop out on a few of Tom's. What time does the first set go out?"

"About 6:00," I lied. He must've put on twenty pounds since last spring and I seriously doubted, first, that he would arise early to ride, second, that Tom would want him at this weight on any of his horses.

"Too bad about that Brigade," he said.

"What do you mean?" I asked, a little louder and more aggressively than I had intended. His friends and Sal leaned toward us.

"Oh you know Paddy, the way he races off at the start and then spits out the bit when it comes time to run."

I took a deep breath through my nose and grit my teeth. Sal put her hand on my arm. "Patrick, didn't you say you wanted to hear that band up the street?" She hopped off her barstool. "You ready?"

We walked out onto the sidewalk, into the fresh night air, live music coming from both the left and the right. We took a right, walked past a movie-sized mural painted in vividly bright colors on the outside brick wall of a pizzeria. Ansley, Eliza, Andrew, Paddy and I had eaten a delicious pizza here on the sidewalk one summer while Susan and the whole gang of kids she was mentoring from Catholic Charities bustled around with ladders, buckets of paint, and paint brushes putting on the finishing touches. The result was magnificent.

Sal and I took a few steps, then stopped at an outdoor bar that had a band and a dance floor set up in a garden. A female jockey I used to gallop horses with asked me to dance, and that got the cobwebs out. I danced a few slow numbers with Sal; she was light and graceful and seemed to be able to predict exactly where I was going a split second before I made the step. We walked, bounced, floated up the busy sidewalks, hand in hand, as if we were out on a date, buoyed by the music and laughter flowing from all the pubs.

Sal brought me into a bar. Upon entering, there was a stairway and a long brick wall on the right. We walked up the stairs, admiring a Gauguin-styled mural of animals and trees and plants set in a Garden of Eden. It was a work of Susan's I'd never seen. We stopped at the top of the stairs. The owner approached us, gave a talk on the mural and informed us that "Susan Shanley—do you know of her?—and her students in the mentoring program" had completed this project. Sal and I remained incognito, fully aware that Susan was a combination of the Pied Piper and the mayor of Saratoga, running Catholic Charities, working as a family therapist, and devoting herself to the children of these families.

Back out on the crowded sidewalk, we long-stepped up the hill to the new kid on the block, the Parting Glass, the pub that has it all—darts, dancing and Smithwick's Ale (our family ale in Ireland "since 1710" until my Irish cousins sold it two decades ago). We entered and I was transported.

The band cranked up "My Maybellene" by Chuck Berry and it felt as if the music were pulsating through my veins, had taken possession of my legs, was a powerful and wonderful and upbeat elixir that made my mind click, my pulse tick, and my reactions quick. We started jitterbugging, twirling and dancing and spinning. I picked Sal up and spun her around. She was light, balanced, like holding a bird. I did a flying dive to the floor, balanced on my hands for a second with my feet straight in the air, rolled down onto my chest and did a backwards somersault to get back up. Sal was light as a feather, laughing and spinning. We started using more of the floor. We got down low, our butts on our heels, and strut/danced. The other couples took to the sides and watched as we spun and pirouetted and jigged. Sal twirled in my arms and then, it was ending, the song was coming to its conclusion and I didn't want to stop, I didn't want it to end. I danced up to the lead singer, asked if he could go right into "I Feel Good" by James Brown. He nodded and without missing a beat we continued spinning and holding one another and twirling, ending with a final dip, Sal in my arms, my back bent low, Sal's body languid and trusting, her hair brushing the floor. The room broke into a loud, raucous, cat-calling, whistling applause and every single partying habitué of the Parting Glass, whether drunk or sober, underage or overage, gambler or galloping boy, jockey or citizen of the non-racing world, stood up, clapping and cheering and hooting.

THE NEXT MORNING, Ansley, Andrew, Eliza and I were up early. We had packed our suitcases and duffle bags the day before, and all I had to do was muscle them up into the two luggage bubbles. Andrew helped. We hung the bikes on the rack and tied them down with the baling twine and bungee chords I kept in the tire well. Andrew checked and tightened the straps that held the bubbles to the roof and soon we were on the road. Ansley and I were in the front bucket seats, Andrew and Eliza in the back. Paddy had left us again, deciding to stay for another week to bus tables for .

Casually—no pressure, all this driving time to come—I let my thought patterns flow serendipitously, searching for ways in which I could be more involved, ways in which I could make a buck in the horse business. I'd had a glimmer of the life of a bloodstock agent through Kip Elser's explanation of "pin-hooking," a term that originated in the tobacco industry. A buyer would purchase leaves of tobacco at an auction, bring them back to his farm, pinhook them—hang them back up—wait for them to mature and the price to go up, and sell them later. In this case, it meant buying yearlings, training them for the fall and winter, and then selling them as two-year-olds in the spring. When pressed by me, Kip recounted trips he'd taken to France, India, Argentina, England and Ireland in search of high-quality horses to buy for his clients.

I thought of the riding, of race riding in the spring. Imagined dropping my morning carpool and being on a horse instead of in a car creeping along in a foggy traffic jam. Held the beauty of Saratoga in my mind, the white board fence encircling the paddock at the main track in the afternoon. Envisioned walking up the old worn wooden steps into the clubhouse, taking a left, and then walking down the narrow aisle, one row of boxes higher up to the left, and one row lower down, to the right. Felt the grainy texture of the wooden counter in the boxes on which you set your elbows so you can steady your field glasses, inhaled the fresh, sunlit air. Saw the brightly colored silks sweep around the clubhouse turn in a tight pack and stretch out going down the backside. And then they're heading around the last turn, positioning themselves. They're in the homestretch. The riders are whipping and driving and the horses are extending their strides. Down the stretch they come and the crowd is roaring and the riders and the horses are at one with themselves, driving, driving, driving. The front horse is under the wire, the jockey stands up, the pressure is released.

And I remembered the timelessness of the green sales barns in the early evening and the power and lift of the pavilion with its immaculately raked dirt epicenter, like a boxing ring floating up above the bidders, the focal point where the colts and fillies would be led that night and people would be tipping their hats, nodding, holding a few fingers up, and bidding millions of dollars as the auctioneer's voice echoed off the walls.

Driving down the highway, drifting in and out of conversations with Andrew and Eliza and Ansley, cruising along with the two bubbles on the roof and the three bikes hanging from the rack, it was there with me, a palpable presence, a way of life, a way of love.

PART TWO

Fern Hill

And as I was green and carefree, famous among the barns
About the happy yard and singing as the farm was home,
  In the sun that is young once only,
    Time let me play and be
  Golden in the mercy of his means,
And green and golden I was huntsman and herdsman, the calves
Sand to my horn, the foxes on the hills barked clear and cold,
  And the sabbath rang slowly
    In the pebbles of the holy streams.

All the sun long it was running, it was lovely, the hay
Fields high as the house, the tunes from the chimneys, it was air
  And playing, lovely and watery
    And fire green as grass.
  And nightly under the simple stars
As I rode to sleep the owls were bearing the farm away,
All the moon long I heard, blessed among the stables, the nightjars
  Flying with the ricks, and the horses
    Flashing into the dark.

And then to awake, and the farm, like a wanderer white
With the dew, come back, the cock on his shoulder: it was all
  Shining, it was Adam and maiden,
    The sky gathered again
  And the sun grew round that very day,

So it must have been after the birth of the simple light
In the first, spinning place, the spellbound horses walking warm
Out of the whinnying green stable
On to the fields of praise. . . .

— from "Fern Hill," by Dylan Thomas

Chapter 9

Time Let Me Play and Be Golden

The ninth is the last in a series of four fences running alongside the woods up the hill on your right. In a stroke of coincidence, the ninth, on the left, is connected to the panels of the nineteenth, on the right. In fact, all the fences from the third to the nineteenth are set up this way. This simplifying mnemonic device gives the course an unusual symmetry and is part of the reason why so many people know the exact number of every fence.

About ten horse lengths away, Mikey stops. "Now look Young-Blood. This can be a tricky fence. If you can, it'd be good to swing out just a little." He stops, takes two breaths, looks back at the eighth, then forward at the ninth, "and then cut in, jump this one on an angle." We swing up the hill a length or so and walk toward the inside panel. "You want to jump this panel, right here, on the inside," he says, climbing up. He sits on the top rail. "In the air, you can even be pulling on the inside rein, you know, like in the show ring." He is holding his hands up again, thumbs close together, gripping a set of imaginary reins. "You land, turn sharp and you can gain three or four lengths on the rest of them. The trouble comes when some riders are trying to angle the fence and some others are just planning to gallop straight into it." He looks me in the eye. I nod at him and turn, looking at the downward-sloping, ninety-degree turn the horses would be making. It seems too sharp, it seems the centrifugal force would swing the horses out too far. "It looks sharp," Mikey states, studying the turn, "but they do it every year, and when you come out of the turn, you'll be lined up just right for the tenth."

We walk down the hill, predicting the path the horses will be taking.

You want to let your horse take advantage of the downhill slope, relax, coast and at the same time encourage him to lengthen his stride and pick up some free speed.

⁓

I HAD ARISEN EARLY to say goodbye to Ansley—off she was going up the hill to more Oldfields School weekend duty—and had gone back to sleep. My throat and eustachian tubes were swollen, and I felt weak and dizzy. I had felt like this more and more often since returning from Saratoga. Moments later I was awakened by Eliza and her friend Annie Isaacs chasing Tidbit, our new dachshund puppy, and Sawyer, our youthful golden retriever, around their bedroom. Soon, I was sitting at the kitchen table in my pajamas, sipping coffee, while Eliza and Annie sat on the floor, roughhousing with the dogs. They stood, ready to go out the door and take Tidbit for a walk. Here was my chance. Annie Isaacs was Eliza's one friend who loved to ride. "We'll have scrambled eggs for breakfast," I cheerfully sang out. "Then, you can pull on your riding boots and we'll go over and ride Chim Chim."

Eliza slumped and let out a negative "Ohhhh" but at the exact same time Annie hopped up and down, grinning, and saying "Great! Great!" before realizing that Eliza had done the opposite. Annie looked at Eliza, wondering if she had done the wrong thing, and was about to switch her tune but at this split second I started chattering away about how after they rode they could race the old Subaru station wagon through the fields. Immediately, they were into it.

It was a beautiful Indian summer day and though I felt woozy, I was determined that Eliza would have a good ride. As soon as we arrived at the farm, Mom walked out and greeted us. I told her that I hadn't really liked the way Warfield, her chestnut Thoroughbred, was going with the pelham bit; the light chain under the chin made it too severe for him. When I cantered into a fence, he had his head pulled in against his chest, taking no hold of the bit, and it didn't feel right. On the other extreme, I showed her the rubber snaffle I'd been using. It was not severe enough. Warfield could grab ahold of it and just take off with me. As we talked, Mom found an old but clean and shiny twisted snaffle attached to a bridle with no reins. "Your father used to ride Crag in this," Mom said. "I liked something more severe, but it should work fine for you on Warfield."

I found some rubber-sheathed racetrack reins. "Isn't this incredible? These are the same reins I used on Pop's horses, thirty years ago."

"I have a nice set of long braided reins in this house. Do you want them?" Mom asked.

"That'd be great. I'll put the braided reins on this bridle, and the rubber reins on the bridle with the rubber snaffle." That way, I'd use the twisted snaffle on the cross-country rides I planned to soon be taking with Eliza, and I'd use the rubber snaffle, in which Warfield would pull harder, when I was riding him to get myself fit. Fit for what? Ha, I caught myself—there it was, in the back of my mind, the thousand-to-one-shot idea of riding races in the spring, the ten-thousand-to-one-shot of riding in the Hunt Cup. I had no horse, no owner who was out getting a horse for me, no trainer, no one urging me to go back to riding races, no money to get a horse, and not one member of my immediate family who was even the least bit interested in seeing me ride a race. In fact, Ansley had been dead-set against my riding races since our first day of marriage. I had no tack. There was no one who knew I had this glimmer of an idea. And, I had no money to keep the family going if I "took a tough spill."

I spent some time buckling the reins onto the bits and soon had both bridles ready to go, something I'd been meaning to do for two or three years but had always been in too big of a rush.

I WALKED OUT into the field with a bucket of oats and caught Chim Chim. He was a small gray pony, strong as a bull, with a thick crest in his neck, a round rump and a barrel chest. I led him to the barn. Eliza pulled out her plastic tool chest with all of the new equipment we'd gotten, including two brushes, one with hard and stiff bristles, the other with soft bristles; a green curry comb; a red mane comb; and a new hoof pick, a modern type we'd never had on the farm that had a bright red metal handle split into a silver prong for getting the worst of the mud out, going one direction, and a tuft of wart hog stiff bristles for brushing out the inside of the foot, going the other direction. She also had a box of biscuit-sized horse treats, a plastic bag of pink rubber bands for braiding Chim Chim's mane, and a pink bottle of horse shampoo.

Annie and Eliza brushed Chim Chim, one on each side. Annie, all business, got out the hoof pick, stood beside his near shoulder, picked up his "near" front foot, picked the mud out of the "frog" of the hoof with the prong of the hoof pick, flipped the pick, and brushed out any remaining mud; she walked around to his "off" side, raised his front off foot, and started picking. Eliza watched, and after Annie finished, she too had a go at hoof picking.

Soon I had this chubby pony tacked up and was leading him around the top paddock. First Annie. I led her several times around, unsnapped the shank, and let her follow me as I walked. Then, I gave Eliza a leg up. I gently held the toe of one boot, placed it in the stirrup, held the toe of the other boot, set it in the stirrup. I led her several times around, having her stand up in the stirrups and count ten "Mississippi's" out loud.

Not knowing that Annie would be spending the night, I had originally planned to take Eliza out on a long ride, leading her on foot through the countryside in preparation for riding Warfield with her. As I led her around the paddock, I had this on my mind. I explained to her and to Annie, who was sitting on the fence next to "Dee Dee" (what my children called Mom), how I might bring them out in the big field, behind the house. Annie was excited by the plan but Eliza told me she didn't want to do it. I was in a jam. I looked over at Mom.

"Why don't you let them ride in the front paddock with the tall grass," she said. A perfect compromise.

Into the front paddock. Years ago, Pop, Tiger Bennett and Jack Grabeal spent a long afternoon digging a grave and burying Nappy, my first pony, there, right where a large locust tree now stood, giving the paddock plenty of shade. Mom leaned on the fence, telling us how she might not cut the grass—

it was so pretty, long like this. Wildflowers had sprouted myriad purple and yellow blossoms, and the tall grasses swayed and leaned, weighed down by oats at the tips of their stems.

Everything was going well but I was concerned about all this grass. I didn't want Chim Chim to put his head down to eat and yank Eliza forward, causing her to almost come off and set us back a month. Eliza sat up on the pony, her back perfectly straight, and talked. I was leading Chim Chim around the perimeter of the field, watching every step when, as we started down a slight grade where the rider has to lean back, I heard, "You can let loose of that halter thing."

"What?" I asked, unsure of what she meant.

"You know, you can let loose of that halter thing."

"You mean the shank?"

"Yes."

I unsnapped the shank. This was a huge breakthrough. I walked on, looking ahead, every one of my senses concentrating on what Chim Chim was doing behind me. I strode ahead, around the perimeter of the paddock, where we'd been walking.

"Let's cut across," said Eliza.

I looked up at her.

She pulled the left rein and headed toward the center of the paddock. I subtly lengthened my stride and picked up my walking pace, to get ahead of her. "Hey, Dee Dee, look at this," I yelled. We headed across the center of the paddock. I was fully focused on what was happening behind me. This grass was long and green and luscious looking. I didn't want Chim Chim to stop and put his head down, start eating, and discourage Eliza.

I told her to give him a little snatch with a rein, pull his head to the side and give him a kick, if he started to put his head down. She wasn't the least bit concerned. We walked over to Mom and Annie, chatted with them, and decided to go one more time around. When we got to the upper corner of the paddock, Eliza pulled the left rein and headed across the field, away from me, to the far corner. I let her go off, this little bundle of burning love and energy and adventure atop the pony—this little girl whom I wanted to run up to and grab under her arms and twirl-toss into the air and kiss. Then smoothly, so I wouldn't scare the pony and Eliza wouldn't think there was anything to worry about, I lengthened and quickened my stride, caught up and got ahead of her again.

"This is like me being in a boat sailing over a sea of crabs and not being able to eat them," Eliza said.

It took a second for this to register. I was amazed. Hard-shell crabs were a favorite of Eliza's. One time, when she was very little, I was preparing her for bed after an evening of picking and eating crabs; it was my job to get her in the shower. Confident I had the perfect motivating factor in mind, I pointed out that she smelled like a big crab, must feel all sticky, and had better jump in the shower. "I love it, I love the smell of crab," she'd said, "I don't want to wash it off," and had happily dived in her bed smelling like a pot of Chesapeake Bay crabs steamed in heaps of Old Bay seasoning.

Still walking in front of her, I asked, "What'd you say?"

"For Chim Chim to have to walk across this tall grass is just what it would be like for me to be in a boat sailing over a sea of crabs and not be able to eat them."

I laughed and repeated what she had said to Mom.

We untacked Chim Chim and turned him out. Mom made each of us a tomato and cheese sandwich. She said her back had been hurting, and she thought it was from having to lift a heavy metal gate that had fallen off its hinges. I walked out into the bright sunshine in the top paddock and took a look. The gate was twelve feet long, made of steel piping. It was heavy, and it was off the top hinge. Both hinges were bent.

I walked back to the garage, got a hammer, Sawyer following. I returned to the gate, banged on the top hinge and straightened it. I tried to lift the whole gate so the bottom hinge would remain secured and I could slide the gudgeon of the top hinge over the pintle. But I couldn't budge the gate. I found an old piece of wood, propped up the latch side of the gate, pushed the gudgeon of the top hinge over the pintle and hammered. Sweating freely, I swung the gate back and forth.

I leaned against the gate post there in the top field with the sun strong on my back, twenty feet down from where, years ago, Mom had lowered two panels of the board fence and had had the top of the post in the middle sawed off, to make an "inset" for "schooling over," or jumping the fence. We'd had an outside course around the entire farm, panels in all the fences, and I would hop on my black, flashy show pony, Twinkle, and canter through the barnyards and fields, jumping in and out of all the paddocks. The thought occurred to me to come over one afternoon with a saw, hammer and nails, and rebuild these panels, recreate the course.

Mom, her dogs and the girls bustled off to the house, then they all jumped in her car and took off for Jacksonville to get ice cream cones. I caught Warfield, tacked him up. Soon I was in the saddle, Sawyer beside me, and we were galloping through the countryside.

WE WERE HACKING HOME, walking along a path just off the road, when a classic, two-door Jaguar XKE with historic plates—just the car I'd always wanted as a kid—slowed, passed us, then pulled over on the shoulder. Sebastian Cromwell, holding a large mug of steaming coffee, stepped out. "Top of the morning to you, Paddy! Who's that you're on?"

I told him it was Mom's old hunter. He complimented me on Warfield's good looks, reached into his car, pulled out his cigarette case, offered me one, and lit up. "I'm down to five a day now, Paddy."

He was in town for a party for his nephew the night before and was now on his way to a farm to check on his yearlings. Hair still wet, it looked like he'd just gotten out of the shower. He was in fresh blue jeans, a polo shirt, and a pair of polished paddock boots. His face was slightly fuller than at Saratoga—probably from the night's activities—but his weight looked about the same, maybe a pound or two less.

He wiped away a few beads of sweat from his forehead. "Just went for a six-mile run," he said, patting his stomach. "Didn't set any records."

"Really?"

"Yeah. I started running 5-K's in August and now I'm doing 10-K's."

We talked about running for a few minutes. Out in the sunlight, I noticed he had a few grays sprinkled through his black hair.

"Well Paddy, I've got to be going." He took a step back, then looked up. "Haven't decided if I'm going to ride next spring or not."

Warfield was hot—so I had to keep him walking around the car. Sebastian asked if I'd been "galloping out" at Tom's or at Pimlico with "R. W. Small" and I said no.

Opening his car door, he said, "Wonder who'll be running in the Hunt Cup this year." Off the top of his head, he reviewed a list of a dozen of "the usual suspects," concluding with Florida Law—"who I don't want to ride. He's such a bad jumper," and Welterweight—"who'll be ridden again by the inimitable master of the show ring, Mike Elmore."

"No," I said, "Mike told me last year at the barn after the race, that was it for him." What I didn't tell Sebastian was that ever since I'd heard that statement, the glimmer of a far-fetched idea to ride Wellie in the Hunt Cup had been flickering in my mind.

"Hmmm," Sebastian mused, "I might have to ring them up," referring to the owners of Welterweight. He ducked down low, slid into the Jag, and drove off.

I WAS HOSING OFF Warfield when Mom and the girls returned. Mom walked out to me, grinning. "How'd he go?"

"Fine, fine. He went well," I said.

"What's wrong with you?" she asked, checking me out.

"Nothing. Just had a long week, that's all."

She frowned at me, walked back to the house, into the coolness of the living room. The girls jogged toward the barn. Piano music wafted out of the open windows and over the farm. First, some warm-ups. Then, a classical piece. I scraped the water off Warfield, focusing on each movement. With each stroke across Warfield's shoulders, chest, rump, I rid myself of a shadowy malaise, a pressing pall, that had hung over me since talking to Sebastian. I gave Warfield a good hard rub-massage and threw one of Pop's old cotton "coolers," a light blanket, over him. Walked Warfield onto the lawn and listened as Mom moved to a favorite bossa nova, "The Girl from Ipanema," the Brazilian love song from the sixties, while Warfield enjoyed grazing on the lush lawn grass. I had heard this as a child, many a time, late at night, when Pop was away at the track. Finally, she moved into some jazz pieces. This was her new passion, jazz. And Spanish. She was already fluent in French and was now learning Spanish so she could communicate with the many Hispanics moving into the area. Brightly colored Spanish textbooks lay open here and there in the house, and the Spanish names for doors, lights, beds, pans, dishwasher, washing machine, table, couch and everything else were written on index cards and taped to the object being described.

The girls were calling from the barn for help. I closed the gate to the driveway, pulled the cooler off Warfield and turned him loose on the lawn. The piano decreasing in volume with each step, I broke into a nice jog headed for the barn. The girls were looking at an old rope ladder Paddy and I had made of baling twine, which hung down six feet from a hatch in the shed attached to the barn. "Can we go up there? Can we go up there?" they were asking. I helped them onto the ladder.

Up they went into the old clubhouse of the Coo-Coo Lilly Club, also known as the Scrooch Club. I stepped inside the vastness of the barn, climbed two or three stories up a ladder, and, still in my riding boots with the leather soles, walked sideways—sliding my left foot away from me, my right to catch up, my left foot away from me, my right to catch up—across a beam to the room over the adjacent shed, stepped up over a projecting four-by-four, swung out over the emptiness that used to house several truckloads of hay, and pulled myself into the Coo-Coo Lilly Club.

The girls had found a loose-leaf notebook on my childhood flip-top desk (How did I ever get that desk up there?) and were writing their names in it. "Look Dad, look," said Eliza. She pointed to the signatures of Paddy, Andrew and their cousins Colin and McLean in the book.

The room hadn't changed in forty years. It was twenty by thirty feet. The walls were of the same splintery boards as the rest of the barn, with an inch of space between each vertical board. Nailed to the walls were rusted real estate and traffic signs, which Tom Voss, Frank Iglehart, Tom Iglehart, Tom Whedbee, Stephen Small and I had accumulated by riding around the countryside on our bikes, dismantling signs from their posts, sliding them into old burlap feed bags, and bringing them back to the club. There was an old mattress, which the girls asked me to toss out, shelves, a nice bench that we needed to return to Mom, and hundreds of soda bottle tops nailed to a beam. I had had a thing for bottle tops. I collected shoe-boxes of them, stored them in the attic, positive that they would one day be worth millions.

Coiled on the boards was a thick escape rope made of hundreds of strands of knotted baling twine which we'd throw over one side of the Coo-Coo Lilly Club so we could make a fast exit down into the mow of the barn. And there was the door, which opened into thin air, above the shed. To become a member you had to go out this door, slide down and onto the shed roof, and then jump off the roof.

Stretching across the entire room, about eight feet up, was a twelve-foot-long, six-foot-wide platform I had started building back when I was club president in the 1960s and Andrew had finished during his term as president in the 1990s.

Time stood still as I climbed up onto the platform, eyed the baling twine I had wrapped around the main support boards, stretched up and nailed to the ceiling for added support, forty years ago. Snatches from a few lines of Dylan Thomas's "Fern Hill" came back to me: ". . . green and carefree, famous among the barns. . . . In the sun that is young once only, / Time let me play and be/Golden in the mercy of his means . . ."

Up on the platform, where a few of us might have looked over a *Play-boy* or two, I watched my daughter and her friend, like two elves, bus-ily straightening and organizing and sweeping the clubhouse. The dust whirled. My nose got more stuffed up; my throat swelled, ears popped. Allergies, I realized. I was having problems with allergies again after a twenty-year hiatus.

Eliza and Annie were making progress. The place was starting to look like a club again. Hell, I might come up here to do some writing at my old desk. I watched as Eliza stood up on a chair and swept dust out from behind a thick triangular slab of wood that had been nailed into the right angle formed by a horizontal beam meeting the vertical post. Standing on her toes, she was reaching back into the space between the triangular slab and the outer boards of the barn. "Dad, we need a little ladder," she said, stretching to reach into the space. Then, she pulled something out—a piece of wood? She shook the dust from it and I recognized it instantly. "Dad, Dad, what's this? Look at what I found! Annie look!" she called out, stepping off the chair and hurrying over to lay it on the desk.

I could see the pirate ship, the sails, the flag with the skull and crossbones, all painted onto a plank of plywood, and I could make out the squares of rubber I had nailed to the covers for hinges. The feel, the precise movements, and the satisfaction of carefully tap-tap-tapping the cabinet nails through the rubber into the plywood covers came back to me.

"Dad, Dad," Eliza said, opening the book.

I climbed down the wobbly ladder to the platform. They had opened the book to its first page. It had been stuck in that crevice between the triangular connecting plank and the outer boards of the barn for over thirty years, exposed to wind and rain and sun and snow in the inch-wide spacing between the vertical boards, and it had held up, the book I had made in the fourth grade.

The girls flipped through it fast.

First page: "*THE SCROOCH CLUB*" written in my fourth-grade "calligraphy," and beneath the ornately scrolled letters, a list of the officers, *Patrick, Jackie* (Voss), *Whedbee, Tom* (Iglehart) and of the members, *Rob* (Deford), *Stephen* (Small), *Tommy* (Voss), *Frank* (Iglehart).

Then: *I. TESTS* (fifteen in all)

1. *Run across beam and get out of barn P.D.Q.*
2. *Climb up rope ladder and jump into club in under ten seconds.*
3. *Swim around Turner's pond twice with no clothes on. If you see a snapping turtle, you have to keep swimming.*
4. *Eat a worm. . . ."*

Second page: *II. TAKING OATHS*

Cut your hand with a clean, sharp knife. Press it against the cut of a member's hand.

1. *Do you swere* (sic) *to be a loyal member of the Scrooch Club—also, for secrecy's sake, known as the Coo-Coo Lilly Club.*
2. *Do you swere not to tell anybody the password (playboy).*
3. *Do you swere not to tell anybody that we have those playboy magazines and their hiding place.*

If any of these oaths are broken you will write your name in blood and it will be voted on how we should punish you further.

Third page: *III. RULES* (ten in all)

1. *If somebody is on the telephone and the other guy wants to talk about the club but you can't say, "Go go flush."*
2. *Get a straw hat with a feather in it.*
3. *The president must have a picture of you . . .*

Eliza slapped the cover shut, looked at Annie, scanned the room, and said, "Dad, can you get us another broom?" I climbed out of the club. Gingerly, looking down at the tractor and mower and their sharp edges of metal, I crept across the chestnut beam to the so-soothingly familiar, thick, sturdy rungs built into the two thick posts. The feel, the round impression of each rung against the balls of my feet brought back lines from Frost's "After Apple Picking": "My instep arch not only keeps the ache, / It keeps the pressure of a ladder-round." I made a mental note to bring up this moment when I taught the poem again, and while I was at it, why not bring up the associations throughout this day with "Fern Hill," too. And for a second or two, high up on the ladder, my mind fogged up, I became dizzy, and I completely forgot where the hell I was in time and place and what I was doing.

"Remember, Dad, a ladder and a broom too!" Eliza called. I took my bearings. Focused on my hands gripping one set of rungs, my feet balancing on another, and climbed down, one rung at a time, to find a stepladder.

Outside, waves of music from the piano no longer floated over the lawn. Mom stepped out the back door of the house, her pack of dogs barking and yapping and running around her, and walked to the garage.

"My piano teacher is coming late this afternoon. I wish you could meet him," Mom said, laughing at the dogs. "He plays at a nightclub downtown. We could go hear him one night."

Spying a stepladder hanging horizontally from a line of huge rusty nails high up on the garage wall, I stood on my toes, grabbed it, lifted up, and pulled it off the nails. Cobwebs and dust showered over me. "Sounds great," I said, brushing off the debris. "If I don't meet him today, I could come over another time. I bet Ansley would like to go to the nightclub."

"What're you doing with that?" she asked, eyeing the ladder.

"The girls need it. They're cleaning up the Coo-Coo Lilly Club."

"All right. Be sure to put it back." I found a broom, the bristles worn to the stubs. Mom was examining the electrical cord that ran from the battery charger out to our old Subaru station wagon, rusty and battered now, which we'd given her for a farm car.

"Let's see if it'll start up," she said. "I put these on last night. Andrew likes to use it for a truck when he comes over to work."

She cranked up the engine. I pulled off the cables. The muffler was shot. The engine roared.

Warfield cantered across the front lawn, across the driveway, past us, up toward the Coo-Coo Lilly Club.

"Keep it running," I yelled.

I caught Warfield. Turned him out in the back field. Jogged to the car. Tossed the broom and stepladder in the back. Mom stepped out. I jumped in, drove it up to the barn. "Hey girls," I yelled over the roar, "Want to drive the Subaru?"

The top door to the Coo-Coo Lilly Club swung open. Dust poured out. Looking like Huck and Tom, their faces smeared with dirt and grime, Eliza and Annie yelled, "Yeah! Yeah!"

I handed them the broom, then the ladder, and helped them down the rope ladder.

Eliza sat in the passenger seat, Annie on my lap. We drove out into the back field and careened around as if in a Marx Brothers scene chasing the ponies and horses, hitting bumps and flying into the air, skidding around turns. Annie moved to the passenger seat and Eliza sat on my lap. "Let's go through the stream. Come on, let's go through the stream." Engine roaring, we hit the stone crossing of the stream at a good pace. Water shot up higher than the windows. The girls screamed and laughed.

Then we saw the red Farmall 140—1950s vintage—heading down from the gate. Mom was wearing her straw hat and a pair of dark glasses. She waved to us, put her hand down on the lever and lowered the belly mower. The tractor hesitated as the blades bit into the thick grass, and then pushed on, the mower shooting out the cuttings on both sides.

CHAPTER 10

A Pretty Nice Place for a Horse

In the air, over the ninth, you're pulling on your left rein, and on landing, you pull harder as you gather speed going down the hill. You can walk this part of the course over and over and no matter what, it always looks as if you are going to barrel down this hill, swing out too far to the right, and not be lined up correctly for the tenth. But you go ahead, hugging the pylons on your left, trying to save as much ground as possible, and then, the hill flattens out and you look up, and somehow, there you are, lined up just right for the tenth fence. You keep that downhill momentum and gallop on into the tenth without slowing, without losing any speed or rhythm, and jump it "in hand," as Uncle Mikey says, perched on the top rail, studying the eleventh.

IT's SATURDAY NIGHT, September 19, Tom's birthday. Due to a frustrating and confusing set of circumstances and miscommunications—often the scenario when I attempt to plan an outing with Tom—he and I are driving, just the two of us, to a restaurant on the night of his forty-eighth birthday. No wives along. No children. They've all deserted us.

I'm shocked to realize this is the first time we've seen each other since Saratoga—mainly because our sons are off at college and we are no longer meeting at their games. For over the past decade I've been meeting him at my godson Sam's ice hockey and lacrosse games and he's been meeting me at Paddy's soccer, ice hockey and lacrosse games. We'd have relaxed conversations, with a natural give and take. It was just a couple of springs ago that Tom and I met at a lacrosse game of Sam's, and Ansley stopped by, on her way to drive Andrew's carpool. After the game, Tom mentioned he had to pick up some clothes he'd had altered at a tailor's. I hadn't seen him since the Hunt Cup. "Let's have a beer at the bar next door," I said.

Tom walked into the tavern carrying three black wool hunting coats on hangers and wrapped in cellophane, beautifully made old English coats he'd found in his grandparents' closets. He'd recently been made MFH, Master of Fox Hounds of the Elkridge-Harford Hunt Club, and was up-grading his hunting attire.

"Here," he said, thrusting two of the coats on me. "Try 'em on."

We ordered a round. I pulled on one coat, lined with a soft and thick red-and-black checkered wool. It had unusual bronze buttons—"EHHC" imprinted on each. I buttoned it. Snug around my waist, it fit as if it had been made for me. The sleeves were long so that when your arms are out-stretched your wrists aren't exposed, and the tails longer—so they'll cover your thighs, warming your legs, when in the saddle—than the ones made nowadays. The value of such a coat I knew to be between $5,000 and $7,000.

"Take it," he said. "It's yours."

I looked at him.

"The tailor said there is nothing he can do. There's not enough fabric to let it out further."

I handed it to Ansley, her eyebrows raised high, and tried on the next one. It wasn't lined but was made of a thicker, more tightly woven outer wool. It was an even older coat, the tails longer and flaring out, dating to the 1920s or '30s. Tom thought it had been his Uncle Frank Voss's. The price tag for this coat would be $3,000 to $4,000. Many a historical soci-ety would like to have it.

"Take it," Tom said. "Neither of them are any good to me."

It was nice, sitting there, elbow on the bar, sharing this moment with Ansley. Then she had to leave to drive the carpool. Tom and I fell into dis-cussing the Hunt Cup of a few weeks earlier. Florida had galloped around, chipping in at every fence—slowing as he approached, putting in an extra stride, then cork-screwing over it—losing one or two lengths to the other horses at every fence.

"Man," I said leaning on the bar, out of the horse game, being able to look at it objectively, "you need to get one of these young tough riders on him, someone who can make him run and jump, not just sit there on him like a bump on a log."

Tom stubbed out his Pall Mall, took a sip of his beer, put it down, got off his bar stool, looked me in the eye. "How about you? Why don't you ride him?" he asked, and walked out.

HERE WE ARE AGAIN, just the two of us, driving along, and the conversation turns to horses. I ask him about Saratoga, tell him I'd seen he'd won some more races, had pulled out of the slump. In fact, he is back as leading steeplechase trainer of the country. "How about my horse, Brigade?" I ask.

"He's in Florida."

"Uh-oh, what's he doing there?"

"Recuperating from the bowed tendon he got running in Saratoga."

We discuss the race, Jonathan's riding style. We move fast through topics, each of which I would like to discuss at greater length: Jonathan's lack of experience in rating horses, his short hold, his dropping the stick, his switching hands. "He made that up," Tom states. "He didn't switch hands. He just dropped it."

We find the restaurant. Dark. Italian. Reminds me of the Long Island restaurants Pop used to take me to as a kid. Reservation for four—but there are only two of us. The maître d'hôtel gives us a funny look.

"Our wives left us at the last minute," I offer, keeping him at a distance.

"Yeah," Tom laughs, looking him in the eye and getting his attention. "They might've left us for good," he says in that way he has of immediately welcoming another man into our situation as an equal who understands what we are experiencing.

"Well, I'm so sorry," the maître d' says, sympathetically, and seriously, eyeing us questioningly, with a strong Italian accent that the women would think is sexy. "But that's all right. You'll have a good time."

It feels like the old days, back when our wives would kick us out and we'd drive off for a few more drinks, dinner and a hotel room. I feel impatient, ready to get the hell away from this unctuous man in his shiny black suit.

"Yes, we certainly will," Tom says, and then he grips my arm, pulls me toward him and gives me a lingering kiss on the cheek. "Won't we honey?"

Oh God. I sigh, roll my eyes.

We get a table by the bar: smoking section. Tom laughs and laughs at the maître d's remark, mimics it, complete with the Italian accent. He lights up, mimics the shocked expression on my face when he kissed me. The waiter says he will return to get our drinks. I tell Tom I'm not drinking. He orders a beer. I order a non-alcoholic beer. He asks why I'm not drinking. I attempt to explain that my body doesn't seem to process it well anymore, and I get these draining hangovers, but I don't get the explanation out as I'd like and before I know it he's changed the subject. We talk about horsey people, horses. I jokingly ask about his sex life at Saratoga. We compare notes. Laughing, I ask him if he's ever had a romantic time while out riding. He rocks back on this one, as I seem to intimate I have recently had such an experience. He tries to guess who it could be, but he's immediately thrown off the trail: "Well, Ansley doesn't ride, so it can't be her."

I tell how we'd had a fight on a recent night (I didn't tell him it had had to do with my mentioning, briefly, in passing, so delicately, that I sometimes had the urge to ride a race), and the next day I brought her out riding on Eliza's pony, Chim Chim. We were back in a deep valley, soybean field on one side, woods on another, and the rhythm of Warfield's fast walk combined with certain thoughts—the ultimate fantasy for a rider—caused me to break my sulking. My back facing her, I jumped off, dropped my jeans, turned around, at attention, and suggested we have a romantic interlude right there in the tall grass. And she had her riding cap on!

He tries to one up me with a story about seducing Mimi in an airplane, in the tiny bathroom, a pretty good one.

We have a peaceful drive back to his place. We walk into his kitchen and sit there. It is time to leave. The end of this glorious evening has arrived.

So many half-explained topics. But when can you really nail these things down? How close can minds get? Suddenly, I see. You just don't nail these things down perfectly. You tap all around them. There are always loose ends. You keep tapping for a lifetime.

It is 10:00, and he says he is going to give the horses carrots. Every night, he walks through his barns at 8:00, looking over the horses, feeding each two quarts of oats and watering off. At 10:30 he returns to give each horse two carrots. He can tell if a horse is healthy as long as he has eaten the two quarts and comes for the carrots.

He gets in his pickup. I follow him to the bottom barn, park by a van which has the ramp down and is set up for loading in the morning. We walk to the tack room. He flicks on a switch. The light bulb flickers, dimly brightening the room. He opens the door of the refrigerator, a bright light comes on and I watch his big-knuckled, battered hand—skin scraped off one knuckle, thumbnail black and blue, and running across his knuckles to his wrist are a series of scratches and cuts, all going in the same direction, probably acquired by riding through a hedgerow of thorny multiflora rose—grab fistfuls of thick, knotty carrots and toss them into a bucket.

We walk down the line of stalls in the "Pretty-Boy Barn," as my Uncle Mikey calls the L-shaped stable, the open-faced stalls looking out through a shallow shedrow to an asphalt walking ring with a grassy area and one large tree in the middle, and then out over the fields and valley to a woods on the far ridge. Mikey's nickname is disparaging: he's teasing that the barn isn't practical. Mikey likes an enclosed barn which can be cool in the summer and warm in the winter.

Tom flicks on the light to each stall. Some of the horses are lying down, asleep, some are drowsily standing. Tom stands in the doorway, says the horse's name, studies him as he approaches. Reaching into his pocket, he pulls out a mint, holds his hand out, lets the horse nibble the mint off his hand. Gives the horse a pat between his eyes, glances into the feed tub in the corner to make sure he's eaten the oats, tosses the carrots into the tub, and watches the horse walk to the carrots. Checks the hay net, checks the water bucket.

We finish the Pretty-Boy Barn, walk to the "Charlestown Barn," named, jokingly, after Charles Town Racetrack, a half-mile track in West Virginia that used to be rinky-dink before it got slot machines. We feed four horses in the Charlestown Barn—a tractor shed until Tom converted it into stalls a few years ago—and move to the heart of the operation, the old bank barn with its center aisle and six stalls on each side.

In the old barn, standing outside a stall, Tom sighs. He ducks under the webbing, runs his hand gently across the horse's back and strides through the deep straw toward the hay net hanging in the corner. The net is bulging with hay and is hanging low, too low, blocking the view through the horse's window. "How is the horse supposed to look out the window like this?" he says, in disgust. "Details, it's the details." He unties the slip-knot, yanks on the rope strung through a screw eye high on the wall; the hay net slings upward. He pulls a section of rope through a loop, creating a slipknot, and like a cowboy finishing off lashing a steer's ankles together, releases it with a flourish.

"Have you ever seen the top barn at night with the lights on?" he asks.

"No."

I follow his car out of the bottom barn area, up the hill an eighth of a mile, past his house and up another eighth of a mile on the tree-lined driveway, to the indoor track.

We walk across the dirt track, which Tom had watered and harrowed before picking me up for dinner, making him late, as usual. Inside the perimeter of the track, Tom has taken what was once a roofed-over shed for farm equipment, adjoining one side of the indoor track, and put in a dozen good-sized, airy stalls. It is dark. He flicks a switch, bringing the whole place to life. He walks down the line, calling each horse by name in a low voice, letting the horse nibble a mint off his hand, checking the feed tub, and tossing a few carrots into the tub.

We walk across the open area, through the other side of the indoor track, into the field. We high-step through twenty yards of knee-high grass. He opens a door, flicks on a light, and we are in his new office—once, back in the heyday of the farm, the blacksmith's shop. It's a compact room, sixteen by twelve feet, with a desk running lengthwise in the center, and directly in front of it, an old wooden bar, its open doors revealing a glistening assemblage of bottles. There are leather chairs with matching footstools in two of the corners, and the walls are covered with "win" photos: recent and in color. In each, Tom is standing behind the owners, grinning, looking straight into the lens of the camera, but also appearing as if he's trying to be as inconspicuous as possible, to the point of hiding.

Tom sits at his desk and lights a cigarette. I slump down in a comfortable chair. We talk some more.

About the farm. About our first, second and third grades at St. James Academy—we'd both been invited to a reunion. About some of his owners. About the Maryland Hunt Cup. I mention that I've decided I might never go to the Hunt Cup again. It is a big pain. I dreaded going there, standing around, and everyone asking if I missed riding races, or, did I wish I were riding in it. We talk about Florida Law—yes, he would probably run again. I tease him, "I remember when we were galloping around the finish line field last spring," pointing to the other side of the indoor track, "and you were saying, 'You know, he's not that old. He hasn't run that many times,' and I knew you'd be thinking of running him again. Thirteen!"

"He's run four times a year since he was six. Seven times four, twenty-eight times. He's only run twenty-eight times in his life. Anyway, we can just hunt him, see how he goes. Run him in a couple of early races, see what he does."

My adrenalin kicks in. Oh no, I had thought this would be over. Another winter of foxhunting and wondering about race riding in the spring. I had thought I'd be free of it. I don't reveal any of these feelings to Tom. I stay cool. I shall stay cool, hunt, see what happens, I think. I am not under any obligation to ride this horse, or any horse, in the Maryland Hunt Cup. I am a free man. Florida will run again, perhaps. And do I try to get the ride? That is a small ball of nervousness inside my stomach: the same old debate. And that horse is getting old. I'd better say the hell with any such thoughts, focus on my job at Gilman, my writing, and my family, and let some young kid have the honors.

Tom keeps smoking, makes no move to leave. We discuss putting in a chimney so he can have a fire in the winter. He loves having a fire. On winter nights, he pads sock-footed around his and Mimi's sprawling house, up and down the stairways, making a fire in the den, one in the living room, one in Mimi's bedroom, one in Elizabeth's bedroom and returning throughout the night to replenish them. I rise from the leather chair and footrest. We walk out into the thick grass, through the dirt of the track, and across the island of mowed grass inside the track, toward the line of well-lit stalls.

He turns the lights off. We walk across the damp dirt of the track, across the long and inviting furrows, and out to our cars. The moon hovers to our left, across the creek and over a field called "The Meadow," after a beautiful and timeless painting by Frank Voss. The sky is vast. Straight ahead, the Big Dipper hangs over the Finish Line Field, where early every April the horses and jockeys at the Elkridge-Harford Hunt Point-to-Point Races make their final sprint to the wire.

"A pretty nice place for a horse, don't you think?"

"Yes," I say, looking out at the open space and thinking of the horses crammed together at Saratoga in barn after barn. "A pretty nice place for a horse."

CHAPTER 11

A Dream Deferred

You glide into the tenth with the momentum from coming down the hill and on landing you're on the flat for ten strides and then you start going up a gradual hill. There is a thicket of trees on the right, and, again, on walking the course it seems you should hug this thicket, saving ground, turning, and head into the eleventh. But it never works out that way. Instead, you come up the hill, ease to the right, keeping the thicket a few horse lengths away, and then, there is the eleventh, which means things are getting serious now, because right after the eleventh is the twelfth, and, close again, the thirteenth. These three are a series. How you jump the eleventh sets you up for how you jump the next two. You come around a bend, pulling on the right rein, straighten and pick out a panel of the eleventh. You are going uphill and the tendency here is for horses and riders to ease up and put in an extra stride; if you let that happen, it can throw off your rhythm for all three fences. "This is where I fell one day," Mikey says to me in disgust, sitting up on the second panel from the right. "I was on Pine Pep. Jay Secor was in front of me. I was right behind and when he went down, it took us down. Jay Secor. It made me feel sick. We were just galloping."

O N A COOL October Tuesday afternoon, I pack up and leave the office early: 4:00. At 4:05, I'm on the highway, pushing the speed limit. By 4:30, I'm at home. Ten minutes later I'm running with Sawyer around and around the Oldfields soccer fields. Ah, the sun on my back, out of the office, a nice breeze, my bare legs on cruise control.

Home, she's there. Eliza. Eliza! I'm hopping on one foot, stepping into a pair of heavy sweatpants, tossing my sweaty T-shirt and pulling on a dry sweatshirt. Then, I'm sitting on the floor in the kitchen, so happy to be alive and out of the office and here with Eliza. I take the soft, leather chaps that had been Andrew's off a chair and place the leather strap against the small of Eliza's back. Straighten the fall of the chaps and wrap the fine, soft, ruddy-red leather around the right leg, fold the bottom up under itself where it is too long, place the zipper into its socket and zip the right leg, from the top beneath her fanny, down to her ankle. Place the zipper on the left leg in its socket and zip it down right to her ankle. I plop the new blue velvet-covered riding cap we'd just gotten onto her head. Unlike my frayed and battered childhood hunting caps stuffed with newspapers that the boys had used, this one was certified as a safety helmet. Eliza fiddles with the straps, trying to snap them together under her chin, and I tell her she doesn't need to buckle them just yet. She insists, and I help her, pulling the soft strap under her throat—careful not to pinch the skin beneath her jaw—and snapping the buckles together. Then, we are in the car and on the way up to the indoor riding ring. Mom's wonderful pony Blossom had died of old age. It tore me up inside that I couldn't bring Eliza out riding myself, as I had with the boys, but meanwhile she could learn the basics with some friends during these lessons while I worked on turning Chim Chim into a nice pony for her. It is getting dark.

The indoor ring is cavernous. Indoor rings are not my favorite places. I like to be on a horse outside. Also, a month ago, a helicopter from Shock Trauma with a blazing searchlight had circled low over the Oldfields campus one night, over and over, its blades cutting the air in the disorienting, terrifying *whoop! whoop! whoop! whoop!* of *Apocalypse Now* and had finally landed in the parking lot of the indoor ring. I had run up to see if I could help and had watched as the paramedics loaded an unmoving woman in boots and britches into the helicopter and whisked her away.

Eliza stands knowingly beside what looks more like a small horse than a large pony. Bernie, the instructor, is teaching, though you wouldn't know it; he is subtle. Eliza is holding the bridle and has the bit in her hands. Bernie, standing beside her, says, "OK, Liza, can you let me have the bridle?"

"Wait a minute, please," she says, "I'm warming the bit."

"That's all right Liza, you don't need to today. It's not cold."

She holds the bit for another moment anyway. Where did she learn this? I feel embarrassed! I'd never heard of this technique. She hands the bridle to Bernie. He is holding the bridle, teaching Eliza the parts, extending the top of the bridle to the pony's ears and is about to place the bit in the pony's mouth. Eliza says, "Wait, wait. Let me do it."

Bernie, not much taller than Eliza, lets the bit fall into her hand, and with his hand under hers, he gently stretches out and pinches the pony's mouth. She pushes the bit up into the pony's mouth and he pulls the brow band and top of the bridle over the pony's ears. This technique—pinching the pony's lips and sliding one's hand into the wet, slobbery mouth, and between the big teeth—is something Paddy picked up quickly but something I never could get Andrew to do. "Yuck!" he'd yell, grimacing, and I'd give in and slide the bit into the mouth myself.

Two other girls Eliza's age arrive. Annie Isaacs, pigtail down the middle of her back, is on a cute little Shetland, its withers the height of my hips. The other, Riley, is on a rangy roan.

Eliza takes Charger, a melancholy bay, by the reins and starts walking forcefully across the riding ring.

Following, stepping through the deep footing, I ask, "Where are we going?"

Without looking up, she says, "To the block." I have no idea what she means but here she is, four feet tall, under fifty pounds, leading this 1,200 pound pony-horse across the ring and I'm walking obediently alongside.

She's up on the mounting block, foot in stirrup, and pulling herself into the saddle. She's on the horse and the stirrup leathers are too long. I adjust one, Bernie the other and before I know it, she's in a line with the other two ponies. They are trotting around the ring and she is posting, up-down, up-down, around the ring—in her black cowboy boots, sandy-brown chaps, red sweater, and new blue hunting cap.

Laughing, laughing, she is laughing and inside I too am laughing, posting along with her. Up-down, up-down, up-down.

They pull up and stand in front of their teacher as if they are in the U.S. Cavalry. Bernie tells them to do their twirl-and-turn. The girls look at each other, and then, in unison, each throws her right leg over the saddle to the left, lifts herself with her hands on the pommel, and swivels completely around, landing back in the saddle. "That's great girls, you couldn't have done it any better. Now, ready, OK, let's do it going the other way." They look back and forth at each other and in unison twirl to the right, landing back in their saddles. "Annie, that's your best yet. That's nice, Liza, very graceful. Riley, your practicing has really paid off." This is something new! I haven't seen these twirls. Eliza hasn't told me about them. I think that she might glance over to me, give me a smile, but she is total concentration. I'm not sure if I could do one of these twirls. I must give it a try . . .

Bernie lays rails down for them to steer through, first one set, then turn sharp and steer through another set, all at a trot. They do a sitting-trot, which I remember disliking as a child, and the "two-point position," standing in the irons.

My God! Standing in the irons, perfectly balanced, a long hold on the reins, her feet directly beneath her, she looks like a little jockey.

Cute, her new blue riding cap fitting just right. Cute, her short legs in the chaps against the too-big flap of the saddle.

She is standing beside the horse. Bernie has pulled the bridle off and I reach for the bridle to carry it for her.

She looks up into my eyes. "No Daddy, I'll carry it."

So proud, she leads me across the riding ring. I feel short and chunky-having to step high as I walk through the deep sandy-clay of the ring.

"Eliza, where did you learn how to post like that?" I ask, looking down at her striding forthrightly, holding the bridle high to keep the reins from dragging.

"Dee Dee taught me."

"How about that twirl-and-turn. When did you learn that?"

She looks up at me while continuing her quick pace. "Dad, we've been doing that for a long time."

Into the tack room—so familiar, the soothing scent of recently cleaned, saddle-soaped and oiled saddles and bridles. The pungency of brass polish. Holding the top of the bridle, near the brow band, Eliza stands on her toes, reaching upward, trying to slip the top loop over the bridle rack. She flips it up but can't reach it.

"Let me help," I say.

I hang the bridle from the rack. Riley steps in, and I help her, but that's it.

Eliza gets out a sponge, soaps it up, and starts cleaning the reins. She soaps all of the bridle that she can reach, then wipes off the lather with another sponge. She moves to the saddle. It is rolling around to 6:45. I need to return to the house, hop in the shower, pull on a suit, and drive back in town for Parents' Night at Gilman. In one hour I'll be standing in my classroom, explaining the tenth grade curriculum to thirty adults, each of whom somewhat eerily and amazingly resembles and acts like one of the seventeen boys I had in the class eight hours earlier.

I walk to the other side of the saddle, pick up a sponge, rub some soap on it, begin to clean a stirrup leather.

"Da-*ad*?"

"Yes."

"What are you doing?"

"I thought I'd give you a hand because I need to get going. I have to go back in to work tonight."

"No Dad. I am going to clean the saddle."

I move aside. She steps forward, cleans the saddle.

"Eliza, where did you learn how to do all this, how to clean tack?"

"Dee Dee taught me."

A FEW WEEKS LATER, the three girls—Eliza, Annie, and Riley—are up on their ponies walking and trotting around the indoor ring. It had been cold. Parents dropped their daughters off and returned to watch the end of the lesson, or sat in their cars with the engines running, heaters on, and took a nap. On this night, I had thought about doing that sort of thing myself: going home and lying down for half an hour. I had strained my lower back on Sunday by going for a long ride on Warfield and then throwing heavy oak logs up into the bed of Mom's pickup. The muscles had seized up in the middle of tossing a log and I'd had to finish the work from a bent-over, cramped position. It was nothing serious. I had just overdone it, but my back was aching as I stood by the outside rail to the ring. I hadn't been able to go for a run, or bend over and pick up anything, or to fully straighten up, for two days. It had been improving on this day to the point that I had forgotten all about it, and, at the end of a stimulating English class, challenged one of my all-too-cocky students to a wrestling match. The match was proceeding as planned, with the entire class whooping and hollering and clapping as the student and I parried. Then, I dove for his legs, picked him up over my head in a fireman's carry and twirled him around. All was going well when suddenly the back muscles seized up, and I could not throw the student down and pin him, as I had intended, but instead had to gently, gingerly, achingly and disappointedly set him on his feet and call an end to the match. "That's enough, that's enough . . . you all had better get to your next class . . ."

Lying down would have felt good but something wouldn't let me go back to the house. There I was, leaning on the four-foot-high outside rail, or "wall" as Bernie called it, talking to Betsy Isaacs—rider, runner, teacher and parent, with whom I had much to discuss. I was getting into our conversation, feeling relaxed about how well the girls were doing when I heard *psssssfffffftttt . . . psssssfffffftttt . . . psssssfffffftttt . . . psssssfffffftttt . . .* I stopped talking, turned and spotted a sprinkler by the main door shooting streams of water. Betsy screamed "The kids! The kids!" The volume and speed of the *psssssfffffftttt! . . . psssssfffffftttt! . . . psssssfffffftttt!* increased. I turned back to see water gushing, streaming, jetting across the ring, coming from both sides, and two ponies charging riderless around the ring. Up and over the wall, I was sprinting to Eliza. What was this, a fire? Was there a fire? I was running through the streaming cold water, my eyes like laser beams focused on Eliza lying crumpled in the dirt. *Move, Eliza move.* I was running to Eliza lying in the dirt. *Let me see you move,* I was thinking. *Move, Eliza, move,* I was praying. Annie was standing, circling around, her arm shielding her face from the jetting water. I was running to Eliza and she was getting up. In her chaps and jacket and helmet getting up. The water was gushing. The water was hitting her in the face. She was caught in a crossfire. She was getting up, out of the dirt, crying and scared and stiff. I was there with her and the ponies were tearing around and she was limping. Keeping my back straight, I dropped to my knees, wrapped my arms around Eliza's and Annie's waists, lifted and carried them to the outside wall, slung one high and over, slung the other high and over. Bernie and Betsy caught the ponies and got Riley, still seated on her pony standing quietly at the other end of the ring with the water shooting on her full blast. I vaulted over the wall, picked Eliza and Annie up again, carried them out of the cold and into the sanctuary of the heated tack room as Bernie turned off the automatic sprinkler system. It had either been set incorrectly, going off at 6:00 p.m. instead of 6:00 a.m., or had malfunctioned.

I brushed the dirt off them, brushed my hands against the wet, dark dirt on my daughter's rawhide chaps, feeling the bone and muscle of her legs.

We went back into the ring. Riley was still riding around. Up went Annie onto her little pony. Eliza looked into my eyes. She trembled on each intake of breath. She did not want to get back on. Her eyes were huge and blue as they looked into mine. They pleaded with me. I was torn. There was the old, old law under which I'd been raised. A rule. The first commandment of riding. When you fall off, always get back on. I turned away and Betsy talked to Eliza. Bernie said a few words. She was not going to get back on. I dropped to my knees in the mud and explained to her that I would lead the pony, we could do whatever she wanted. It wasn't working. I stood up. Eliza stood before me, pleading, her blue eyes piercing my soul. I grabbed her under her arms and swung her high, over the saddle, dropped her into the saddle and off we went at a walk.

ELIZA RODE GAMELY the next two weeks. The third Tuesday after the fall, I had just gotten back from work and was making hot chocolate, pulling on a turtleneck and sweater, as Eliza and her mother pulled up. I watched her get out of the car. Little girl with slumped shoulders. Little girl with worries. Something was wrong.

I ran out into the cold, lifted her high and swung her around and around until she couldn't help but laugh. I raced her into the house, put on a British accent, and acted the part of a butler, her valet.

"Would you like your hot chocolate now Madame, or would you prefer to dress for riding first? And which would you prefer: a chocolate cookie to dip in the hot chocolate or a slice of toast with a dab of butter and a sprinkling of cinnamon?"

We flew around the house, tossing off school clothes, pulling on warm riding clothes, sipping hot chocolate. She stood on the kitchen floor, chaps belted around her waist, laughing, as I knelt at her feet, talking nonstop, and zipped up her chaps.

Out to the car we went and up to the riding ring. We were soon tacking up. She took interest, insisting that first she warm the bit, then place it in Blazer's mouth. We got a girth for her saddle, my old saddle, in which I rode Nappy and Queenie at her age. We tossed the cute little saddle up on Blazer's back, and soon Eliza was riding, around and around.

I walked over to the outside "wall," leaned on it, and watched. There were show fences set up throughout the ring. Four of them, two on each side, were close to the wall with just enough room for one horse to pass between the fence and the wall. I did not like this setup.

They were supposed to trot. Eliza was holding back. The other two, Riley and Annie, went ahead and Eliza was kicking Blazer on, but not with real meaning. Bernie kept repeating, "Kick him on *E*-liza. That's it, give him a little push. See if you can get him going." (I had told Bernie that her name was not "Liza," which he had at first called her, but rather—and just to make my point clear, I had stressed the "E"—"*E*-liza." Now, every time he said her name, he emphatically enunciated the "E.") Finally, she did begin to trot.

She was on her own, away from the other ponies. And she was picking up speed. I tried not to be alarmed. Blazer was big. Horse size. Hard to control. Eliza was forced to cut the corners. As she rounded each turn, headed for the gap between the fence and the outside wall, her angle of approaching the gap became sharper and sharper. Blazer was pulling and I was worried, worried he might jump one of the fences.

Eliza's shoulders were heavy and she was leaning back against the reins. Her shoulders were heaving, I could just make it out, up and down. When she swept by me, her face was tensed up, she was sniffling, she was imploding, she wanted to be anywhere but on that pony in that riding ring.

Blazer's stride was lengthening. He was pulling her harder and she was coming around the ring, toward me, and she was crying. Blazer was trotting so strongly he was popping her out of the saddle. I held back, held back, not wanting to interfere with the teacher. Then, I said something to Bernie.

"Pull on the reins, *E*-liza. Pull on the reins *E*-liza," he said.

Up and down, she was posting faster, and leaning back against the reins. It was as if the pony were posting her. To hell with it. As quietly, as agilely, as quickly as I could, I climbed over the wall, glided into the ring.

Bernie got to her first. She was crying. She sat high up on the pony and said to me with pleading blue eyes, "I want to get off, I want to get off."

Oh Lord, how I wanted to grab her under the arms, lift her free of the pony, hug and kiss her, tell her she was safe. I wanted to get on that damn pony, reach back and knock the hell out of him, let him gallop around and around that ring until he would never pull again.

OK, you can get off, I wanted to say.

OK, jump into my arms, I wanted to say, holding out my arms for her to leap into.

Eliza, I want to gallop across fields head-and-head with you. I want to walk through the woods on snowy afternoons with you, your blond hair falling from your blue hunting helmet, my gray hair springing out of my old Caliente.

Eliza, I've so enjoyed watching you ride. The terror of the gushing water never occurred. It never occurred. Let's erase, expunge, eradicate that memory.

"Good job Eliza. Really good job the way you pulled that pony up!" I said.

"*E*-liza," Bernie said, "if you want Blazer to slow down, you just have to pull back on the reins, pull back until he's going the speed you want."

He was the teacher; I didn't want to override him, but I did want to take a rein, snatch the pony. "Look," I wanted to tell my daughter, "he starts pulling you, starts going the least bit too fast, you grab one rein—like this—and *bam*, snatch it. Then you go right to the other rein, *bam*, and snatch it. Then, you lean your whole body back, pull on both as hard as you can, and make him come to a complete halt."

She walked. Annie and Riley trotted—sit-down trot, posting trot, standing-up-in-the-irons trot. They did some dressage. I watched, listened and learned. Eliza turned Blazer "on the forehand from a standstill" up against the wall. Bernie was slowing the pace.

Finally, Bernie held each pony in the center of the ring. Eliza grinned as she did a full spin-around in the saddle without her feet touching the pony's neck or rump.

A WEEK LATER, I don't flinch in my decision to forego a late-afternoon meeting at work. I inform my colleagues that I have a conflict. I drive home purposefully. No radio: no news, no music. I'm concerned about the cold. Not an autumn chill, but a winter cold. It might be time to hang it up. I'd like to end on a good note. The ponies are getting too frisky. I don't want anything else to go wrong. I don't want Eliza to have a memory of being stiff and achy in the cold. One more night, tonight, and then we could have a treat, go out for some ice cream, celebrate all that she has accomplished.

Seated at the kitchen table, pulling on thick wool socks, I see Ansley's car pull up. I watch Ansley and Eliza get out. Eliza's shoulders are slumped, her head down. She is wearing her new red wool hat and her hip-length red wool jacket. In my socks, I run out the kitchen door, over the hard, cold ground, grab her, lift her high, ask, "What's wrong?" I twirl her around and around. She hangs from my arms, listless, head drooping. Won't meet my eyes. Shrugs away from me. I set her down.

"Ask Mom. Ask Mom." She runs into the house. Her mother walks in, sits on the big couch by the fireplace. Eliza snuggles up beside her.

"Eliza, you can just hop on the pony and walk around the indoor ring," I tell her. "I'll lead you," I say, knowing this won't work with the two friends being there.

She doesn't look up.

If I let this slide she may never again want to start back up. One more night. One more good night, that is all I want. It seems impossible that my dream of riding alongside Eliza as I had with the boys, may be ending.

Should I force her? Should I let this go? I rush upstairs to call my mother. No answer. I call Mikey.

I explain what had happened a few weeks before, and for the first time, sitting in my writing room, with a pile of cleaned, soaped and oiled saddles and bridles gathered on the floor, it hits me hard: how devastating this one event had been to Eliza, how much impact it could have on her riding, on our riding together, on our *lives*. It was not just the riding, it was the time and place the riding provided to talk, to go through experiences together, to get to know one another, to relax, let down and have easy, flowing, serendipitous conversations that would not take place any other time or place. It hits me in the gut: there may be nothing I can do to correct this situation.

Mikey says to let it slide. Not to force her. Wait till it warms up in the spring. Bring her down to his barn. Let her sit on Petunia. Let her ride Petunia into the house. I could hop on Waldo, the half-pony half-Thoroughbred, and she could get on the donkey and we could ride bareback right into his first-floor bedroom, through the kitchen, into the living room, and out the front door onto the front porch. He tells me a story about his father, Alfred. It was in the summer and Mikey, a little boy, had had a fall and was afraid to jump. His father never said a word about it. Every morning, Mikey would ride with his father and watch as Alfred checked on the horses and cattle turned out in the pastures surrounding the Elkridge-

Harford Hunt Club. Every morning, toward the end of their ride, they'd canter through a big field that was divided by a stone wall. Alfred would pull his horse up, say, "I'll be right back." He'd jump the stone wall, jog up a hill, out of Mikey's sight, around the perimeter of the field, check on the horses and the fencing, and then come back into Mikey's sight on the ridge, jog down the hill, and jump back over the stone wall. "Day after day, I sat there on Spotty, watching Dad go out of my sight, waiting for him to return. One morning, Dad jumped the stone wall," Mikey stops. He is choking up. He takes a deep breath, "and started . . . to trot . . . away from me. He was headed up the hill. I kicked Spotty in the sides, jumped the wall, and galloped up the hill to Dad. I was never afraid to jump anything again."

I sit there, slumped over, at my writing table. It is hard to let this go. It is difficult to comprehend that there is nothing more to do. I feel deflated. Cheated. Defeated. I force myself up, march downstairs and hug Eliza, hug her tightly to me, tell her it is too cold, we'll wait and ride in the spring. "How about a nice fire?" I ask her and Ansley, as I gather kindling, newspaper and matches. "Let's have a warm fire."

CHAPTER 12

Knocking the Dust off and Getting Back On

After the eleventh, the course flattens and before you know it, there is the twelfth looming ahead. It sits up on the crest of a hill. It's big and it's out there in the open, one of the most visible fences for the distant specta-tors. There is only a small gathering there to watch the horses close-up. Several inches lower than the upcoming thirteenth, it is well positioned. Mikey leans on a top rail. "You've got to really ride into this fence," he says. "Everyone talks and makes a fuss about the thirteenth but if you pay attention to this one, go on and stand off and jump it well, you'll be set up for the thirteenth. You want your horse to feel confident gallop-ing down into the thirteenth." Not many horses fall at the twelfth. Many more fall at the thirteenth and that's where the crowd on this side of Tuf-ton Avenue congregates.

⌒

A T GILMAN ON MONDAY, I am distracted. I am having one of those hor-rible days where it suddenly and viscerally seems that what I do for a living, all my activities and decisions throughout the day, is utterly without significance. I should be doing something far more important; I should be far more successful; I am a flop.

At 3:00 I call our church, speak to Claudia, the rector's assistant, and a member of our class, Education for Ministry (EFM). It is my third year. I have missed the last couple of classes. "I'll be there tonight," I tell Claudia. "But I haven't done any homework, I haven't even looked at the assign-ments. I'm not prepared to give a talk on the meaning of the Eucharist."

"O.K., Patrick," she says in her soothing voice. "It'll all work out. We're looking forward to seeing you." I hang up feeling better and even a little relaxed.

Twenty minutes later, the phone rings. I am on deadline, proofreading a printout of the school's magazine. It's Claudia. "Deetzie just called and mentioned she was looking forward to your reflection tonight."

"Oh Lord, I have a reflection tonight?"

"Yes, good driving work Patrick, good driving meditation."

I think of all the driving I have to do, plus the commute home. Yes, I'll do it then.

Pushing it, going through the five gears in my old Volvo as if it is a sports car, I rush into Baltimore, leave off the changes for the magazine with our designer and drive to Boys' Latin School to watch ten minutes of Andrew's soccer game and say hello to Ansley and Eliza, who are there for the entire game. Guiltily, I hop back in the car, drive to Pimlico where Jennifer, the acupuncturist I'd begun seeing in an effort to get rid of the whiplash headaches, happens to live. For a second, I wonder why the hell I am putting myself through this schedule. Many others, half the EFM class, have dropped out. I don't have to take this class. I don't have to earn another degree. I don't have to be away from the family every single Monday night all fall, winter and spring.

JENNIFER ASKS how I am doing. I tell her I'd felt great immediately after our last session; however, a depressing and nagging sort of distraction had afflicted me since. I explain that I have been flirting with the idea of riding some races in the spring. *It has been years. Decades. Three decades. I feel like I am backsliding . . . regressing . . . retrogressing . . .*

"This is good. It's good that this has happened. There may be a reason. Let it go. Let it run its course," she says. "Don't punish yourself for having these thoughts. Fantasize about it. Follow these thoughts. This is important to you. It connects you to your father. Maybe you'll ride some races. Why not? You're fit. You could still do it. What would your children think? I think they'd get a kick out of it."

I lie on the raised cot. She lights the moxa, an herb, applies it to the skin of my wrists. I tell her when it feels hot and she withdraws it. She slides needles into both my wrists. She applies moxa to the skin of my neck, and then slides a needle into one side of my neck, withdraws it, walks around my feet, slides a needle into that side of my neck, withdraws it.

I lie there feeling like I have been in a boat in a stormy sea. Closing my eyes, the rocking and plunging of the boat subsides and I drift into a half-sleep. I am floating in saltwater, out, far off the shore, the salt in the water buoying me up. There is a gentle roll to the waves, my body is immersed in the water and the hot rays of the sun are massaging me. The rays of the sun, flickering as they reflect off the ripples across the top of the water, dance across the red-speckled blackness of my eyelids.

Leaving Jennifer's, instead of going the way I usually do, I head down a side street to Northern Parkway, not paying much attention, wondering why the car is taking me this way. I come to a complete halt at the stop sign. Before me are two lanes headed east, two lanes headed west, and beyond them, the turn of Pimlico Racetrack between the three-eighths' pole with its black stripes and the quarter pole with its red and white stripes. I am directly across from the gap in the median strip through which my father, at 5:30 a.m., headed west toward Pimlico Racetrack, would pull his truck, roar along for twenty yards headed west in the east-bound lane—lights from oncoming vehicles coming straight at us—before ducking into a side street that took us directly to the back gate.

I drive through that gap, legally, going the correct direction for the first time in my life. I head down Northern Parkway to a stoplight. In the sky, above the stoplight, is the moon, a full moon—symbol of love and nature and Dionysian behavior. It hangs there, appearing as if a layer of whipped cream had been smoothed across the top of its pie-surface.

Then, a silver sliver, a jet: fast, sleek, impersonal, computerized, powerful, in a rush, never resting unless an engine is blown out or a computer malfunctions or the air traffic controller doesn't know its whereabouts and we read about the explosion, the catastrophe, in the paper the next morning. The jet speeds across the faded blue sky. Its path bisects the moon.

Like the blade of a knife slicing through whipped cream, it leaves a crease, and the dichotomy is there no longer, of jet here, moon there: they—modern man, ancient man; technology, nature—are joined.

I could integrate my interests. Writing and riding.

ARRIVING HOME, I go to my writing room, jot down notes on my post-acupuncture epiphany for my EFM reflection. I have twenty-five minutes, plenty of time before class.

Andrew and Eliza run into the house, the door slamming, the whole house reverberating. Ansley follows, the door slamming again, the reverberations going up through the walls, into the floor of my room. They've been grocery shopping and they are noisy as they unload, setting bags down, opening and closing the refrigerator, opening and closing cabinet doors. Eliza lets loose a scream upon finding a dead mouse in a mousetrap I'd set the night before.

Andrew calls out, "Yuk, look at all the blood, look at how his head is smashed. The poor mouse."

"Andrew, come on, help me unpack this bag. We can't have mice running around our cabinets, getting into our food and leaving their poop everywhere," Ansley says. "Dad will get it out."

And what am I doing? I feel awkward, my body in the wrong place doing the wrong thing. I should be helping them but I forge ahead. Finally, the slamming of doors and the bustling dies down. Ansley and Eliza have gone to Oldfields for dinner. It is quiet. I am focused, on a roll. Then the television. Loud. I step out of my monk's cell. "Andrew, can you please turn off the television. I'm getting ready for my class."

"Hi Dad, nice to talk to you."

In fifteen minutes I have to leave for class. I would normally give him holy hell, but since I am working on EFM material and am focused on Christian behavior, I don't. Besides, he has a point.

I gather up my Bible and EFM workbooks, walk downstairs. I sit at the counter beside Andrew as he digs into a huge plate of pasta.

I ask how the game went.

He hadn't played much. They lost. He's tired. He has a lot of homework.

I remind him of how much he played in some earlier games in the season, all four quarters in some cases. He has forgotten this. It never happened.

"How much longer is the season?"

"Two weeks. One more game."

"Well, basketball is around the corner."

"I'm thinking of quitting basketball."

"Andrew, why would you do that?"

Too much pressure. Not enough time to do his homework. Too many good players. Doesn't want to be a benchwarmer. These other guys are going to be incredible this year. Tired of having the coach yell at him. All the practices, all the work.

It takes me out of myself. He *is* myself. I would do anything for him.

I remind him of how he had loved basketball. After the summer camp two years ago, it was all he could think about. It had been his favorite sport. And I think of myself and horses.

I glance at my watch. Lately, more and more in these recent years, I've had to compress time. I had already passed through periods in my life that I'd thought had been the busiest and hardest working I would ever experience. But the ante kept rising. I'd been checking my watch the entire day, and now, I was going to race away from Andrew and up to the EFM class?

Planting my elbows on the counter, I let my body settle into the barstool. I tell Andrew he has to learn to not allow the coach's yelling to bother him. On the other hand, the pressure might be good; he could learn how to handle it, so that when more serious situations in sports, in life, come along, he wouldn't be rattled by them. And indeed, these more serious situations would come along soon. In just a few years, Andrew would breeze through the toughest physical-psychological military training program in the world and become a U.S. Marine. He would do two tours in war-torn Iraq, where he would see it all.

I kid him. Glad no one else is there, such as a sister or my wife, I take the following tack: I ask if he were going to become a nerd and play intramural sports and then go to the mall and sit around. I rib him, actually poking my fingers in his ribs, and he laughs. I tell him he doesn't want to quit now, this is great preparation for a few years from now when he will be going out for the varsity team. Doesn't he remember, after the first few soccer practices in the fall when he learned that he wouldn't be a starter, he wanted to quit? And isn't he glad he stuck with the team and stayed in the game? Overall, hadn't he had a good season?

And as for basketball, he is bigger and stronger this year. He has grown three inches. His height will serve him well. And what has happened to our playing after dinner? Why don't we go back to our schedule of eating in the dining hall, getting his friends together, and going to the school gym to play? He and I can play one-on-one some nights. I picture the two of us going one-on-one, our tennis shoes squeaking on the wooden floorboards, Andrew laughing as he steals the ball from me, fakes one way—all my attention and weight going that direction—and then suddenly shifts, dribbles behind me, jumps and shoots: another two points for Andrew.

Ansley and I have a close friend whose son had started quitting things at this age. He quit trying at school, quit sports teams, would quit in the middle of a touch football game if everything was not going just right, later quit the Marines, quit a marriage, quit college, quit job after job—and there was always a rationale. Now this friend's son is trying to quit an addiction to drugs and alcohol and sex and not working. I don't want this psychological trend to find a cozy dwelling place in my son's psyche. One little opening and it could snowball. The way to handle this had been taught to me by my mother. When you a fall off a pony, what do you do? You knock the dust off your blue jeans and get back on.

It's time to go. I like to walk up to church. I am five minutes late and walking takes a few minutes longer but this doesn't worry me. It is a time to settle my mind, when no one knows where I am because I am actually not anywhere. I am between one place and time, and another.

I walk to the kitchen door, holding books against hip, "Andrew."

Sitting at the counter, he turns and squints at me.

"See you on the court," I say and high-step it out of there.

PART THREE

To Dare

Far better it is to dare mighty things, to win glorious triumphs, even though checkered by failure, than to take rank with those poor spirits who neither enjoy much nor suffer much, because they live in the gray twilight that knows not victory nor defeat.

— Theodore Roosevelt

CHAPTER 13

"You Only Live Once"

Approaching the thirteenth is like approaching the sister of the third. The third, a few panels down from the thirteenth, is the first big fence in the race and it comes early. The thirteenth is difficult for different reasons: You make it over the twelfth, and then go down a hill into the thirteenth. It is tricky to meet a big fence correctly and jump it gracefully when it is approached at a gallop going down a hill. The rider has to be both bold — encouraging the horse to gallop on and open up his stride, and precise — controlling the length of the stride so that the horse will meet the fence right. The tendency when galloping down a hill into a fence is for the horse and rider to either check too much, shorten their stride, and then "get under," or get too close to the fence, which means the horse has to do an awkward, straight-up-and-twist, elevator-jump, in order to clear the top rail, or the horse and rider attempt to take off from a spot too far away from the fence, which means the horse has to fold his knees up perfectly, stretch his body to its limit, kick off from the ground with everything he has in order to get over that top rail and not be sent crashing and somersaulting to the ground. "Send him down this hill," says Mikey. "Horses jump this better if you let them run down this hill. But you've got to watch out. Everyone is starting to race ride. You've got to send him down this hill and hold him together at the same time." I'd seen a clip of Mikey jumping this fence in a documentary. It took your breath away. He was in front. The pack was pushing, trying to catch him. Holding his horse together, he galloped full speed down the hill. A few strides away, he dug in, squeezed with his legs, made the horse extend his stride, asked him to stand off, and the horse flew in a perfect arc over the fence, and then the camera stayed

*on the fence for a few seconds as the rest of them propped and slowed
nearing the fence, the horses popping and twisting over it, and the riders
and horses either falling or landing in a clump on the other side and losing all their momentum. You didn't see that kind of riding anymore — the
incredible nerve combined with the extreme talent.*

O N A BEAUTIFUL weekend morning in November, I arose early, grabbed
my satchel, a thermos of coffee and a handful of bagels, rode my bike
up the trail along Gunpowder Falls to my garret—or "bolt hole," as Willie
Dixon calls it—in the old "Monkton Hotel" and graded tests on the poems
of Robert Frost for four hours. Leaving the hotel, walking to my bike, I
bumped into Stephanie, a publications designer I often used, who was
stepping off her bicycle. She rushed up to me, gave me a hug, and said, "Oh
my Lord, did you read about Devon? Did you hear what happened?"

I had a student named Devin. I pictured him, hoping nothing had happened to him. I knew that his parents had just been divorced and he was
going through a tough time. Not a car accident, not a car accident, I chant-
prayed to myself. And then I thought of the show, Devon, the big-time
horse show, and I knew what she was going to say.

Not waiting for me to answer, Stephanie said, "A rider died there, at
Devon. A rider got killed."

She gave me the details of the rider's fall, then told me about the day's
biking she had ahead of her. I threw a leg over the seat of my bike, arrived
home at noon, the deadline I'd written in a note to Ansley. No one there.
I had lunch, changed into blue jeans and riding boots, called Sawyer and
headed over to Mom's.

As soon as I pulled in the driveway, Mom came out of the house and
started talking about an issue she had with my sisters. I walked out into
the front paddock to catch Warfield. He trotted away. I brought Chim
Chim in, brushed him off, picked out his feet, and tacked him up as Mom
continued to talk.

I hopped on Chim Chim, planning to take him out for a school, get him ready for Eliza to ride cross-country, but Mom mentioned she'd like to sit out on the lawn and watch him go. I rode him into the big field out back, stepped off him and was putting the fences up to two feet when I heard a roaring engine and looked up to see Mom in the Subaru, bumping and splashing across the stream. In the back seat, competing for space to stick their heads out the windows, were Becky, Willie and Wiggles (named after Bill Clinton, whom Mom could not stand and "who could wiggle his way out of anything"). The dogs were wearing electric collars and Mom had driven inside the perimeter of the electric fence, loaded them up, and then driven back out. Each of these dogs honored and obeyed Mom, especially when she casually held the hunting crop in her hand and motioned with her wrist, flicking it up and down. And each dog would not listen to one thing anyone else told him or her to do.

Jogging Chim Chim around, Mom in the middle, I was reminded of the years of working with ponies, cantering them around this same circle. I trotted Chim Chim in a tight figure eight, weaving between the fences, focusing on switching to the correct diagonal each time we crossed through the center. Instinctively, going back to my days in the show ring, I pulled Chim Chim up, patted him, let him relax and eased back on the reins to get him to back up. No way. He was as mule-headed as can be. His head went up so that his jaw was higher than his ears. I pulled his head, mouth outstretched, to one side, and then the other. His front feet remained cemented to the ground.

I stepped off, slapped him on the shins with my stick. One shin, then the other. He wouldn't budge. Mom drove the noisy Subaru up close to us, turned off the engine and told me of a technique she'd used on a tough horse called Roman Market, who, one winter, "savaged" her—knocking her down on the ice—and broke her back. "I used to walk him straight into the barn. Your father told me to do it. I'd walk him straight into the wall, keep pushing him, and then he had no choice but to back up."

I rode Chim Chim into the back of Mom's car. He backed up a step. Mom cheered. I pulled on the reins, trying to make him take another step back. His feet were glued to the ground. I pushed him forward. We were practically on top of the car. Worried, as I kicked and squeezed him, that he might panic and jump onto the car, I experienced a little of that old sensation I'd had so many times on horses of my father's, of pushing a horse to do something he didn't want to do, Pop behind me with the buggy whip. I'd feel oddly vulnerable to the danger of it, relaxed but prepared to move, letting all the tension drain from my body, and having confidence that the split second the horse reacted my instincts would kick in and I would do the right thing, keep my balance, win this contest whether the horse reared up or charged forward.

Chim Chim would not back up. I pulled him away from the car, trotted him around, schooled him over the course I'd set up over two-foot fences. Let him rest. Schooled him again. Soon, Eliza could be jumping him over these same fences.

Back at the barn, Mom mentioned getting on the tractor and driving it into him. I was astonished, as I'd been making an effort to be calm and gentle with the horses since the recent afternoon I had attempted to muscle Warfield into doing something and Mom had said, "Why do you always have to do it the rough way?" I couldn't imagine how you could use a tractor to push him back. It would be playing that game of chicken which we had played with so many racehorses: calling his bluff. And if he called our bluff?

"There's got to be a better way," I said.

"I know!" Mom said. "Just pick his feet up, one at a time, and place them back."

So obvious! She held Chim Chim. I bent over, pinched his near leg (the leg on the left side) between the tendon and the ankle, pulled his foot up, placed it back six inches. I reached across and tried to pick up his off-foot but he wouldn't give it to me. Instead of getting in a fight, I walked around his head, bent over, picked up the foot and placed it back four inches.

What would he do now? He was standing there like a circus animal balancing on a ball, his front feet close to his hind feet, looking like he might tip over. How stubborn can you be! Mom nudged him and he shuffled backwards. I patted him.

"You were right," Mom said. "You were right not to make him do it by force."

Pleased with these positive remarks, I caught and tacked up Warfield. Hopping onto his back, I felt my spirits lift and the worries and concerns wash away as my legs wrapped around his torso.

Mom asked if there were some place I could school where she could watch. I told her I'd meet her over at Joey Gillet's, a little house on his parents' place where you crossed Hess Road. She could follow us up the driveway to the back field. Joey's mother had said I could school in that field any time I wanted.

My adrenalin was pumping. We hadn't done anything like this together for years. Just the two of us. Out of the back paddock, I walked Warfield down the tractor path, warmed up into a jog, Sawyer, nose to the ground, sprinting off. It was a different feeling. I wasn't heading out to ride who knows where. I was riding to a specific place for a specific reason, and I wanted to get there by taking the most direct route. Trotting along, it felt natural, traveling by horse to get to a destination, eating up the distance with Warfield's long strides, my posting synchronized to the long-legged rhythm of his trot.

We jogged down the hard-packed tractor path that curved through an uncut golden soybean field to the east and an uncut brown cornfield to the west. Sawyer knew this route and shot ahead of us. We popped over a log in a hedgerow, landing in a fifty-acre nursery with row upon irrigated row of saplings glistening in the sunlight, the grass green and lush between the rows. We jogged down the grassy swath between two rows—the late afternoon sun behind my left shoulder, casting a long shadow—over another log and through another gap in a hedgerow, down a tractor path, the dry, brittle, about-to-be harvested stalks of corn shimmering and rustling in the breeze, the woods exploding with leaves of rust and bright yellow and deep burgundy. There was a big log at the bottom of the hill. I laughed to myself. Here I was trotting along, getting Warfield warmed up for schooling, and now I was going to give him a pre-school to prep him for the exhibition to be put on for my mother. Just like being a twelve-year-old again.

We trotted down the hill—the movement of it, up-down, up-down, up-down, felt good, timeless, simple—popped over the log. Landing, Warfield broke into a canter, let out a fart and a buck and took off, down the path into the woods, passing Sawyer who ducked out of our way. Laughing, I pulled him up at the stream, kicked my feet out of the stirrups, encouraged him to take a sip of water. He put his nose down, sniffed the moving current, acted as if he were on the verge of taking a drink, but didn't. We stood in the water and watched Sawyer find the deepest spot in the stream and flop down in it. Looking up at us in delight, he let the water roil over his back. He leapt out of the stream, shook out his thick coat and sprinted down the path. We jogged to a log fence near the road across from the long tree-lined driveway. I jogged up to the fence, one log on top of another. We were headed away from home and Warfield felt sticky going into it. I squeezed him with the spurs and gave him a whack with the whip. He popped over it. I turned him around. We were facing home now and he took off cantering into the logs. I was sitting there relaxed, not far forward, with a long hold, and he took off a full stride from where I thought he would. I didn't catch him in the mouth but going over that log jump I felt like one of those geezers in an old English hunting print: riding long, sitting back too far, this God-awful stiffness, creakiness, in my back. My feet were both up off the bottom crosspieces of the stirrups and we hit the ground with a thud, my weight slamming down into the stirrups. I laughed at the absolutely terrible form but I also wondered about my riding *and I was very glad Mom hadn't seen that!*

Realizing I was riding too loose, emulating my father's deep seat and long hold but at this moment lacking his exquisite timing, I decided to get more forward and "ride the roll," as he used to say.

Sawyer gallivanting off ahead, we cantered toward a chicken coop leading out of the field. I shortened my hold on the reins, shifted my weight forward, and he jumped it just right. We pulled up to a walk. We began to descend a steep slope between the thick hedgerow of thorny multiflora rose on either side, pulled to a stop, and listened for cars, our view of the road blocked by the hedgerow. Two or three zipped by, without slowing, four feet from Warfield's nose. It was quiet for a second. I called out, "Sawyer,

Sawyer," and pointed to the area to the right of Warfield's shoulder. Sawyer stood perfectly still and looked up at me; he paid little attention to my commands when I was on the ground, but when I was on a horse, he was obedient. We walked down the rest of the slope onto the shoulder of the road. I heard a car approaching fast. Nothing to do now but continue out into the middle of the road and make the car stop. Warfield, Sawyer and I stepped out into the road as if we owned it. We calmly clip-clopped across as the cell-phone-talking driver of the big SUV—all darkly tinted windows rolled up tight—slowed, slowed, and the second we reached the other side, roared past.

I waved to Mom who was driving toward us from the other direction. It seemed like yesterday I was riding down this road on Queenie, Mom on her favorite hunter, Fini. We were ambling along, on the way back from hunting. Two or three cars passed us. The driver of each slowed, gave us a wide birth, waved or called out, "Hey Susie." One stopped his car, got out in the middle of the road and chatted.

Mom pulled into the driveway. I walked alongside her car. Wiggles was standing on her lap, his paws on the door. Becky and Willie were whirling around in the back seat. There was a new, dark blue, two-door Mercedes there by the little yellow house, but I told Mom I was sure Joey was in California. "Hey Joey," I called out, to prove it, and there was no answer. We walked down toward the log jump which headed into the large paddock. Mom pulled up in her car.

I walked Warfield up to the fence and relaxed, feeling at home, my legs loosely wrapped around him. There were a half-dozen horses in the twenty-acre field; they galloped as a herd to the fence beside us, jammed on the brakes, crowded the fence, pushed up against the top rail trying to get a sniff of Warfield, snorted and stamped their feet and had a good time. Mom said I shouldn't go in the paddock. "That's how Dot got hurt, schooling in a paddock with loose horses." Dot was Mikey's wife, who trained horses on her two-thousand-acre family farm, Sunny Bank, in Middleburg, Virginia. Although Dot and Mikey had not lived together for twenty-five years, they were still married and stayed in close touch.

We talked some more. The horses in the field were quieting down. I wheeled Warfield around, gigged him with my spurs, took a short hold of the bit, got my weight forward, and jumped the fence into the field.

The loose horses swarmed around us. We jogged through the herd toward the series of board fences and post-and-rails, pulling up at the first jump in a row of six at the crown of the hill. "You can see all the fences from here," I yelled. Mom climbed over the paddock fence, walked out with the loose horses bucking and galloping around her, and stood at the crown of the hill.

I jogged Warfield conservatively down over the six fences. Keeping up our rhythm, our momentum, we jumped out of the field over a trappy log fence, took a sharp right, jogged down a line of trees, and jumped back into the field over a new triple telephone pole fence with a shiny plaque on the top pole somewhat hauntingly dedicating the jump to a teenage girl who loved to ride and who had been killed in a school van crash.

I had told Mom I would jump the fences over which I'd just gone and then head out through the countryside and home, but after I jumped the log I thought I'd better shorten the ride. The sun was low, there was a chill in the air and Warfield hadn't had much exercise in a while. I eased into a canter and then a gallop, headed up the hill and over the fences, this time over the larger panels. We were headed toward home so Warfield was taking a strong hold. Showing off a bit, testing myself—could I ride at full speed over fences?—I felt my timing returning. On landing after each fence, Warfield ratcheted his speed up a notch and by the time we reached the last fence we were moving right along. I squeezed with my legs, asking for a big one. Warfield stood off like an old pro and we sailed through the air, landing victoriously. I looked up at the crown of the hill, expecting approval and maybe even applause, but it was oddly vacant. I glanced in the direction of the barn. Mom's car was gone. Thinking we would not be coming back this way, she'd already driven off.

We galloped over to some spooky-looking jumps, barrels painted red and white arranged in odd formations. We cantered over those and called it a day, jogged across the paddock through the loose horses, grazing and bored with us, jumped out, walked, with Sawyer alongside, toward Joey's house. An old tree trunk, wide and about three feet high, lay in his backyard. I nonchalantly jogged Warfield up to it. Headed for home, he held his head high up and rushed it. We jumped, landed, but I wasn't satisfied. We took two steps upon landing. I saw Joey step out on the back porch.

"Hey Joseph!" I said. "Hold on a minute."

I turned Warfield. I could feel the disappointment in my legs; he wanted to go home. I poked him with the spurs; over the log we flew.

We walked to the back porch where Joey stood. I told him I wished I'd known he'd been there; Mom would've enjoyed seeing him. He asked about her and Warfield, and I explained that she had stopped riding. She'd been out last spring one morning and had wondered about her nerve.

"Who doesn't do that every day?" he said laughing.

Out came a young woman, her thick dark hair wet, her skin glowing, in a fur-lined leather vest, and tight slacks. French. I spoke a little French with her. We joked about Joey always being late.

Warfield was starting to get his winter coat, and was hot, so I kept walking him back and forth on the lawn. I asked where they were headed. Joey sheepishly answered, "We're going to look at the thirteenth fence," meaning the thirteenth fence of the Hunt Cup. He talked about the Hunt Cup and then gave me the scoop on the "Mink and Manure Set." He had flown home to ride in a flat race at the Pennsylvania Hunt Cup, where he'd learned that Tom's star rider Jonathan had been out late at night, run his car into something and broken his hand. He'd had a shot at being leading rider of the year. Ann Moran, who rode for Charlie Fenwick, had had a bad fall and broken something out on a two-year-old. Jack Fisher—that fun character who had kept us laughing every morning at Saratoga (suddenly I pictured the life-size, inflatable, half-naked Playboy bunny doll he had propped outside Tom's tack room one morning)—had almost lost his leg in some crazy accident involving a tractor. Another friend of Joey's, who was just starting to ride amateur races, had fallen in a race, broken his collarbone, cracked three or four ribs and punctured his lung.

I rode on. They got in the car and watched as Sawyer, Warfield and I crossed the road, jogged up the steep rise and over the double-log. Landing in a field of uncut alfalfa, I pulled Warfield off to the tractor path alongside the hedgerow, settled in for the mile walk home, and it hit.

It sprung up through the iron crosspieces of the stirrups. It bolted down from the sky as if my helmet were a lightning rod. It flowed like an electrical current from the flaps and pommel of my saddle through the inside of my calves and thighs. It progressed from Warfield's mouth, down the long, thirty-year-old, rubber-sheathed reins of my father's into my hands and heart and soul. It came from the wonderful, peaceful, reassuring, old-as-man-on-a-horse rhythm of Warfield's stride into my body.

Ride Ride Ride, it whispered.

Why didn't you win the Hunt Cup last year, it whispered. *Why didn't you win it and a hundred other races back when you were in your twenties*, it whipped.

Guilt fluttered down over me, a black cloak of shame, smothering me, blacking out all non-riding accomplishments. It dripped like oily black ink down my blue-jeaned legs, through my boots onto the parched, sun-beaten, wind-blown, hard-as-a-brick earth.

It nagged me the rest of the weekend. Saturday night at a friend's, it was in the back of my mind, and I wanted to drink, to break my run of six months without a drop. Sunday, during a ride, it was in the front of my mind and I pushed Warfield too hard, testing myself, and he didn't go well.

Sunday night, I was tired, frazzled. We had a beautiful fire, the music was on, Eliza wanted to dance. We were swinging and flying and doing pirouettes. We were ice skaters doing ballet, but I managed to save a little spot in the back of my brain to keep me from fully entering the moment, to keep me wondering, should I risk all this to ride. Though it was getting late, I asked Andrew and Eliza to walk the dogs. They complained, then pulled on their coats. I gave myself a kick, got up and pulled on a coat.

We walked up the Oldfields driveway, Andrew being dragged by Sawyer on a leash, Eliza stopping and starting as Tidbit sniffed and examined every other blade of grass. I was going to cut the walk short at the first school building. Andrew, to my surprise, said, "No, we have to at least go up to the show ring." I was still poking at the race riding idea when Andrew made another comment. I asked him to repeat it.

"You only live once," he said, as the three of us now glided, flew up the hill through the dark tunnel of trees that led to the ring. "You only live once," he repeated. "You need to do the good, you need to do the bad, you only live once so you might as well do it all the way."

CHAPTER 14

Opposing Views

In the air over the thirteenth, you can't believe you're up so high. You hang, and then you start coming down, continue descending, and finally are on the ground. You sigh, gather the reins — with the horse's neck outstretched so far, and his back arched to such a degree, they have slid through your fingers — and gallop across a long, flat section before reaching the fourteenth, which is a letdown, a letdown for which you are grateful. You gallop into the fourteenth without letting your horse prop.

Sitting on the inside panel, left hand on the pole to the red flag, Mikey points to the fifteenth — an eighth of a mile away, to our left, and perpendicular to the fourteenth. "It's best if you can jump this one right here," he says, slapping the rail beneath him, "on a slight angle. Then you land and you're headed for the inside panel of the fifteenth," he snaps his blue-blackened hand like a huntsman cracking his whip and points to the panel. "They won't be running yet. They'll hold back until after the sixteenth."

I STOPPED BY MOM'S every time I hunted. It was a ritual, a way of including her. It made it seem as if we were going out together. I'd bustle into the kitchen and she'd be standing there, waiting. Her first words: "Who are you hunting?" or "Who's Tommy have going out today?" A few times, the moment she'd asked, that very second, the phone had rung. I knew it'd be Tom. She'd pick it up. "It's Tommy," she'd say, handing me the receiver.

Without any introductory remarks, he'd say, "We're taking out Mickey, Florida and Welterweight. Who do you want your tack on?"

Three of the best foxhunters in the country. Two of the best timber horses. I'd pick one. "See you in twenty minutes," he'd say. He always cut it close so we'd pull in to the meet the moment the hounds were leaving and unload in an adrenalin-kicking rush.

"So you decided to hunt Welterweight. Why'd you pick him instead of Florida?" Mom would ask and we'd discuss the two as I stood there bolt upright in my father's black leather hunting boots, which had been his father—Alfred's—boots. I was wearing my father's spurs, Alfred's wool britches, Alfred's checkered yellow wool vest with the gold buttons, Pop's cowboy belt, a red long-sleeved undershirt tapered at the waist and arms, so that it fit perfectly, given me by Ansley when we'd first gotten married, and an old white Oxford shirt with the collar turned in, given me by Mom. In my left front pocket was a penknife Andrew had given me, and in my right rear pocket was a red bandana. I was ready.

Mom would grab the ends of my just-ironed stock hanging from my neck. My grandmother, Suzanne Voss White Whitman (Tom and I had the same great-grandmother) had made this stock. It consisted of a soft white cotton cloth six feet long and sixteen inches wide. Early that morning I had laid it out flat on an ironing board, run the steaming iron down the three creases of its length, one crease in the middle and one four inches out on either side. I had folded both sides inward so that the outer seams Granny had sewn ran straight down the center crease. I sprayed starch down the length of the stock, ironed a section, pulled the stock to me, ironed another section and folded the two lengthwise halves in on themselves. I pushed the steam button on the iron, slid the stock toward me, pressed the iron down on the four thin layers, reached the end, draped the stock around my neck, not to be touched again until Mom stood in front of me gripping the ends of the stock, shimmied the stock back and forth a few times—the way you buff a shoe—pulled one end lower than the other, flipped this end up, around my neck and to the front, whipped it beneath and then over the other end and gave it an extra tug. A stock had to be tight. Mom and Granny were purists about this. Granny had taught us that the purpose of a stock was two-fold: first, it was to keep your neck straight and your posture erect as well as to support and strengthen your neck in case you "came a cropper," as she put it. Second, it was essential to wear a stock so that if you were out in the woods and needed a bandage for your horse or yourself, you had one.

Mom would then finish it off by looping the ends of the stock through each other, forming a square knot. "Does it feel all right?" she'd ask, her lips unmoving, holding a line of safety pins.

"Yes, yes, a little tight," I'd say. I'd hook my finger under the stock, loosen it a notch. Mom would pull down on each end, retightening it. She'd unfold the longer-hanging end, drape it over the knot, smooth it out over my chest. My neck outstretched and chin up, I'd reach into my pocket and pull out one of two pins, either the gold pin of a fox, handed down through Mom's side of the family from Granny and the Voss line, or the more delicate pin of a horseshoe studded with tiny diamonds and emeralds, handed down from the Smithwick line, through Pop, Alfred, and Alfred's mother. Mom hadn't given the Smithwick pin to me until my fortieth birthday, when she thought I was mature enough to take care of it. Her eyes at the level of my chin, safety pins in her mouth, she would stick the pin through the smooth overlap of the stock at my Adam's apple, and lock it.

On a Saturday in December, I arrived at Mom's earlier than usual. She tied my stock. I buckled the straps to my spurs. Sipping a cup of coffee by the wood stove, I said, "I'm thinking about trying to get the ride on Welterweight this spring."

"Oh Patrick . . ."

"Well," I said awkwardly, "I've been hunting him all winter. I feel good on him and . . ."

"Patrick—that's ridiculous. You've got a wife, a family—your children to think of."

"He's an open ride. Mike doesn't want to ride him any more."

"Come on Patrick. Look, Mike's a professional show rider. He's riding indoors all winter long, competing. His timing is perfect. If he's decided he doesn't want to ride the horse, then why should you?"

I felt awkward, not myself, like a kid with his mother. "Look," Mom said, "when your father and Mikey were riding races, they rode all day, every day, throughout the winter. When the races came around, their timing was razor sharp and they were fit. It was a natural transition from the program they put the horses through over the winter to the races in the spring. They knew their horses inside and out."

Yes, yes, yes. "I know that, but . . ."

"You think you can go hunting once every couple of weekends over the winter and be prepared to ride in the Hunt Cup? That's ridiculous."

"I can ride on Sundays, school Warfield. I can run every day . . ."

"Why do you want to do it? Why can't you just go out and have fun hunting with Tommy. Look at what happened to your father. You have a good job, a wonderful wife, three beautiful children. Mikey had the best horses in the country to ride in the Hunt Cup. Everyone forgets about all the falls he had on other horses in Virginia. Look at him now. He can barely walk."

"Yes, but Wellie —" I pictured him. I felt what it was to be on him; it was to be transported, transformed from a run-of-the-mill, aging jogger, rider, skier, canoeist, tennis player, bicyclist to a world-class athlete; from an older guy who could still step out on the dance floor and show these kids a thing or two at the Parting Glass to a youthful ballet dancer spinning out into the center of the Mariinsky Theater in St. Petersburg.

"You've told me he's risky. You've told me how he takes hold of the bit and bolts for a fence. Oh, Patrick, you've worked so hard to get your writing going and now you have this good job at Gilman. Look at how everyone loved your history of Gilman."

"I can write *and* ride." This is what I had been working on—integrating my interests, my passions, *myself.*

"You can't compete with these millionaires who don't have to worry about making a living and who have all the time in the world. It's just crazy. You have more important things to do."

She was getting to me. The bright colors of my dream were fading into a dull gray. I was starting to feel guilt.

"Have you told Ansley?"

What answer could I come up with for that one? And why hadn't I told her? "No."

"What do you think she's going to say?"

FIVE-THIRTY ON THE DOT the next morning, Sunday, the phone rang. I knew who it would be. "Morning Young-Blood, you're up aren't you?" Mikey asked.

"Yes, good morning Mikey," I'd replied, extricating myself from my dreams, reaching over Ansley, trying to pull the cord to the receiver across her shoulders without awakening her.

"How's Andrew's riding going?" Mikey asked. Ansley, Andrew and I had hooked up the trailer, loaded up Warfield for me to ride, and gone down to Hydes to try out a pony for Andrew a week earlier.

I explained that it was getting difficult to pull Andrew away from his friends and video games and movies. One day Andrew had even said he was tired of riding "a little old pony" and why didn't he have a horse to ride, like the cowboys had. Also, now that he was involved in all these sports—soccer, basketball, lacrosse, karate—he was starting to lose interest.

"Well," Mikey said, his voice filled with confidence. "Sometimes you need to change things. Make it more fun. You've got to surprise a young-blood to keep his interest. Just like you would a young colt. When do you ride?" he asked.

"We go at one o'clock on Sundays."

"All right. Just remember to make it fun."

It was a cold, dreary winter day—and I'd told Andrew after church that we'd be leaving for Mom's at quarter of one. I wanted him to get on Chim Chim and "straighten him out for Eliza." He replied that Chim Chim was too small for him, and he was probably right about that. At 12:30, I pulled on a layer of long underwear, wool socks, blue jeans, turtleneck, and a long, roomy, wide-necked sweater of soft blue-green wool I'd brought back from a tour of Ireland with my British literature students in my first year of teaching. Mom had knit it. I had never washed it; you could still smell and feel the lanolin from the sheep, and you did not get cold or wet in this sweater. I began to look for Andrew. Made a few calls. Couldn't locate him. Looked for his chaps, then remembered he'd outgrown them and they were in Eliza's room. Grabbed his old holster and "Colt 45s"—just in case they might inspire him. Threw his boots and holster in the pick-up, fired it up, drove up to James Jewitt's house, snow flakes beginning to fall. By the time I reached the house, the sky was white with snow, and I couldn't wait to get Andrew out into it on his pony. I walked in without knocking. There they were, Andrew and three friends, lying around in the middle of the day eating potato chips and drinking sodas and watching some damn Arnold Schwarzenegger movie—guns blazing, explosions going off, buildings collapsing, flames shooting up. Terminator Totally Tedious. I stepped into the living room. Andrew was lying on the couch.

"What are you doing, Andrew?"

"Watching a movie Dad."

"You were supposed to be at the house by this time, ready to go to Dee Dee's."

Andrew glanced over at James, made eye contact, smirked and looked back at the television. "I'm good," he said. "You go ride. We're in the middle of a movie."

I crossed the room in three long steps, hooked my hands under Andrew's armpits, yanked him up off the couch, let him come down across my shoulder, and carried him yelling and kicking out to the truck. I unloaded him on the passenger's side, walked around, pushed Sawyer over toward Andrew, hopped in, and we took off, Andrew kicking the glove compartment and thrashing and yelling as we accelerated out of James' driveway and approached James' gentle, kind mother who was leaning into the wind and snow, returning from a walk. As soon as Andrew spotted her on the edge of the driveway, he picked up the tempo—the yelling, the kicking—as if she might save him. I turned on the windshield wipers. They thwopped back and forth, back and forth. I grinned and waved at Cathy. She gave us a startled stare as we roared by. I jammed on the brakes at the Oldfields barn and looked over at Andrew. He stopped his thrashing, stared back, questioningly, nervously, at me.

"Come on. You need to learn how to drive," I said. The frown disappeared from his face. The tangled barbed-wire rage of his body language unraveled. I spread my hands around his rib cage, lifted him up and over Sawyer and eased him down onto my lap, trying to find room under the steering wheel for his long legs. I revved the engine, popped the clutch. Andrew grabbed the steering wheel tightly, leaned forward, "Dad! Dad!" And we took off, a little faster than the proper speed limit for the Oldfields School driveways.

The wind was picking up and the snow was angling down fast. "Where're we going? Where're we going?" Andrew asked.

I had a light load of firewood in the bed and a set of snow tires on the back wheels. "Wherever you want."

We drove down the hill, the six-cylinder roaring, backfiring and sputtering, and the exhaust bluttering out of the muffler peppered with rust holes. Lord help us if a cute little girl comes riding around the corner on her spooky $50,000 show horse.

We passed the barns on our left. "Go on down to the tennis courts," I said.

Leaning into the steering wheel, he muscled it sharply to the left. We coasted down the steep hill past the tennis courts to the soccer fields. I set his hand on the stick shift as I pushed in the clutch, and then, with my hand cupped over his fist, we pulled the stick shift back into second. We sped down the hill, no one around.

At the bottom, we stopped, backed up, and turned around, moving our right hands back and forth from the steering wheel to the stick shift. Then, we were in first going up the hill, in second going along on the flat and descending down past the school buildings. We passed the pond where Paddy, Andrew and I had shoveled a foot of snow off the ice and skated the night before. It looked like we'd be doing some more shoveling.

"Dad! Dad!" Andrew yelled, his hands in a death grip on the steering wheel, Glencoe Road coming up fast. My hands remained at my sides.

"What?" I asked.

"Where are we going?"

"You know. We're going to Dee Dee's. Now drive this truck like you own it."

With all his strength he spun the wheel—no power steering—to the left to keep us from running straight into the high bank across the road. We headed up the twisting, turning steep hill, the snowflakes white against the black of the tree trunks. I turned the dial to the radio, put on some rock'n roll and cranked it up. Andrew was laughing and bouncing. Heading into a dip and then a big lip before crossing a bridge, I accelerated. We went down into the dip, then up, hit the lip of the bridge and the body of the truck was airborne, the load of wood in the back felt as if it had floated up off the bed of the truck, and Andrew was yelling, "Dad! Dad!" We were both up out of the seat. The truck flew over the short bridge, then landed, front wheels first, going full tilt, with a big thump at the end of the bridge, diving into the dip, and rattling and banging up out of it. "Dad! Dad! This is just like in the movies!"

We took a "wrong" turn.

"Where're you going? Where're you going now?" Andrew yelled.

We pulled into the parking lot of the Manor Tavern, roared to the middle of the empty lot, the snow billowing down, already three inches of fluffiness untouched by man, vehicle or animal.

"Dad, what are you doing?"

I built up momentum, yanked the wheel as hard as I could to the left, popped the clutch and floored the accelerator. The front wheels remained in place and the rear of the truck kicked up and spun around behind us spiraling the snow up high. We went into a spin, the rear of the truck wildly bucking and spinning and roaring around and around, faster and faster, in the exact same pattern, Andrew holding his hands over mine on the steering wheel in a vise-like grip, then taking his hands off the steering wheel and squeezing my thighs, yelling *DadDadDad!* as we looked out the windshield at the world gone crazy until it seemed we were still and the world was wildly revolving around us.

We left the tavern, eased down Manor Road, turned into Mom's and rumbled over the potholes, our breath forming cottony puffs in the cold of the cab.

Willie, Wiggles, and Becky came slipping and sliding down the snow-covered stairs of the back porch, across the back lawn, barking and yapping. Sawyer was up, across our laps, wagging and banging his tail against us, trying to get out. I turned off the engine, didn't give Andrew time to think. These weren't the big flakes of a warm day that would soon die out; these were small flakes and the sky was gray and the flakes were thickening, choking the air.

The engine was off. The rock'n roll was off. Mom's dogs barked and leaped against the doors of the truck. I opened the door, lifted Sawyer off my lap, let him slide to the ground. Handed Andrew his boots and guns.

"Check on Dee Dee and get dressed," I told him. He gratefully jogged through the dogs to the back porch no doubt looking forward to Dee Dee setting up a spot for him by the wood stove, fixing him a hot chocolate and perhaps telling him that yes, his dad was a little crazy riding in this cold and snow—after all, the weather channels said this was to be a blizzard and the temperature was predicted to drop to dangerous levels.

I scooped some feed into a bucket, headed out into the big back field, caught Warfield and Chim Chim, led them back to the barn. Tacked up the two of them, noticing that the cold was immediately penetrating my glove-less hands, my nose, and was even creeping into my toes. Concerned that Andrew might get a little too comfortable in there by the wood stove, I trudged back to the house through the fresh powder, thinking I might like to do some cross-country skiing later that night.

Into the kitchen. I tried to keep Sawyer outside but he forced his nose between the door and the doorjamb, pushed hard and barged in, creating a fracas, Mom's dogs rising and wagging their tails and bumping into each other and us. Andrew and Mom had their chairs pulled up to the black cast-iron wood stove, the door of the stove open, the fire blazing. I grabbed Sawyer by the collar and dragged him toward the door. "That's all right. Let him stay in," Mom said, looking up and giving me a smile. "Have a hot chocolate before you go out." She slapped her hand a couple of times against her thigh, "Sawyer, Sawyer," she called. He barreled through the kitchen pushing chairs out of the way, bumping against the legs of the table and knocking salt and pepper shakers down, until he had his head on her knee and was having his face gently stroked.

Mom was in a gray sweater she'd knitted, worn corduroys, and sheepskin slippers. She stood and scooped three brimming spoonfuls of chocolate into a mug, poured steaming milk into it, stirred, and handed me the mug. She moved with certainty, stepping in and out and over the dogs without looking at them. Mom was not a big woman; in fact, she came up to just a little above my shoulder, but I always thought of her as my size. She stretched over Willie—lying exactly in the way—grabbed a split log of locust with one hand, opened the wood stove door with the other, and tossed it in. She wore glasses now, and her hair was light brown—no longer the thick, wavy, dark brown of my childhood years—and that was it. Otherwise, she was as fit, as strong, as quick, as volatile, as in my senior year at Gilman when on Sunday afternoons after we'd finished galloping and schooling the racehorses she'd roast a leg of lamb with potatoes and onions and carrots, and we'd make buckets of Bloody Marys. My horsey as well as non-horsey friends would come over and have the best time talking and partying with my mother, though there was the one time they all insist on remembering when the living room couch caught fire and I apparently, nonchalantly—so they say—doused the flames with my Bloody Mary and Mom apparently, not so nonchalantly, chased me through the entire house and outside with the same riding crop that she used to spank me with years earlier and that at the age of ten or eleven Sue Sue and I had buried, thinking we'd never see it again.

Andrew was seated by the stove, his legs crossed as a sixty-year-old English gentleman in a smoking jacket might do while enjoying a cigar and an after-dinner brandy in the library of his club. I listened to them plotting a night to have a lobster dinner.

I sat down, the hot mug bringing life to my numb hands, leaned in toward the wood stove, and sipped the rich soothing chocolate. Now they were planning how to get in a day of skiing if school were called off as well as time for Andrew to stack four wheelbarrow loads of firewood on the back porch and throw a dozen bales of hay down from the hayloft to the bottom shed. The flames fluttered and licked the logs, and the bark and jagged edges of the locust popped and sizzled. The heat, tangible and seductive, billowed out of the open door, warming my knees and chest and face, and I leaned back in the chair, tilted my head, closed my eyes and listened to them discuss how Andrew could spend the night. They could get up early, feed the horses, straighten the barn, stack the wood and then head up for a day of skiing at Roundtop, Irv Naylor's ski area in Pennsylvania. I drifted off, drifted off, picturing Mom driving around in the big Ford station wagon with the wood sides in the middle of a blizzard picking up all of Sue Sue and my friends, tossing their poles and wooden skis in the back, driving us up to "Mt. Bennett" on Tiger Bennett's farm. We'd secure our rat-trap bindings around the notches in the heels of our leather boots, and then we'd push and strain and lean forward, trying unsuccessfully to snap the binding lever down without catching our fingers. Mom would glide over on her impossibly long skis, effortlessly secure our bindings, and off we'd go, skating and falling and walking to the hill. She'd teach a newcomer or two how to do the snowplow, show us how to pack the hill, how best to walk back up, and she'd set up poles on the hill, creating a slalom course through which we'd race. Some afternoons back at home, she'd harness her childhood toboggan to a horse, pack us onto the toboggan, hop on the horse bareback, and gallop through the backfields while we yelled and screamed and fell off. Or, she'd tie the toboggan to the trailer hitch of her station wagon and take us flying and screaming, the snow from the car tires stinging our faces—down the Manor Road, onto the Jarrettsville Pike, right into Jacksonville to Carroll's Store to pick up a few groceries, and then back to the house where Pop would have a fire of oak logs throwing heat into the living room. We'd peel off our outer layers, hang sweaters, jackets and pants from chairs close to the fireplace and stand barefoot in our long underwear by the flames, juggling and jockeying for position, turning our bodies one way then the other. Just when we started to warm up Mom would walk into the room carrying a big silver tray Pop had won at a hunt meet, and on it would be a full tea set: matching delicate tea cups, plump pot, a little pitcher of cream, a bowl of brown sugar, and slice after slice of hot cinnamon toast, the cinnamon—mixed with a touch of white sugar—visibly melting on the butter. We'd drink the tea and eat the toast, balance on the Bongo Board, play some checkers and a new ice hockey game and make the biggest mess. There was never the I'm-better-than-you, down-talk of a boss-bag adult ordering "the children" "to clean up first, then you can go outside." Mom treated us like equals; we *were* equals; she was one of us. We'd warm up, pull on our wool sweaters, jam our arms into our soggy down parkas, head back out again, and keep going until dark. My mother did not get tired. In fact, my grandmother had banned the use of that word through one of her many parables. If, as children, Sue Sue, Sal or I ever lowered ourselves to the state of whining that we were "tired," the brisk, simple, amazingly effective reply from Mom was, "that's tough, isn't it," and after being slapped with that, it seemed we were refreshed and energized, ready to toss off whatever malaise had attempted to bring us down, and to carry on.

A RUMBLING SOUND at first, then the wide-awake, hard-at-work roar of a big engine, the engine of a truck, coming closer, entering the driveway, passing the house, entered my warmth-induced, sleepy-headed state followed by a crisply enunciated, "Oh Sugar,"—one of Mom's expressions—and "Patrick, can you see who that is?"

I hopped up, putting on a show of being awake, waded through the dogs, tripped over Mom's rubber-bottom, leather-topped L. L. Bean boots drying on several layers of newspaper, reached the door and looked out through the snow slanting down at a forty-five degree angle. A three-horse van rolled into the driveway.

"It's a van, Mom. Is someone delivering a horse?"

"No, who could that be?" She got up and started to bustle around, reaching for her coat and boots.

I squinted at the writing on the side of the van. "D. M. Smithwick Stables," I read aloud.

"It's Mikey," Mom said, putting her coat down and sitting back in her chair. "What in the world could he be doing?"

Andrew hadn't budged. He took a small bite out of a slice of cinnamon toast. His legs crossed, he leaned forward, picked up his mug of hot chocolate by the handle, took a sip and set it down. He then dabbed, so properly, his lips with a napkin. "Come on Andrew, let's get going."

He looked up at me without moving. Keeping his legs gracefully crossed, he slowly, casually, set his mug of hot chocolate on the wood stove. Having accomplished this task, he reached down and began stroking Willie's back. He glanced up at me, right eyebrow raised as if I had just disrupted his meditation on his upcoming cricket match and I'd better watch my step.

"Come on. Let's roll."

Looking straight into my eyes, he ran his hand, again, down Willie's back, and maintained the exact same position.

"Andrew," Mom said, stroking Sawyer's face. "You'd better do what your father says."

Andrew reached forward, finished his hot chocolate, set it on the table. He took the empty plate off his lap, set it beside the mug. He stood, stretched. The snow had stopped. The wind was picking up. I knew this trick of his, enlisting Dee Dee's sympathy and support so he wouldn't have to go on yet another crazy adventure with his father.

"All right, stand up here," I said.

I glanced out the door window and saw Mikey, Irish wool cap pulled down over his eyes as if it were sunny out, and in his full tan Carthartt one-piece work suit, pulling the heavy, two-man ramp to the van out onto the side of the hill. Immediately, I recalled his words from 5:30 that morning: "You need to change things around, do something different, catch that young-blood by surprise."

Andrew had on his cowboy boots, blue jeans, and a couple of turtlenecks. "Arms up," I said to him. He shot his arms straight up and I dropped a rugged brown sweater Mom had knit around his torso. Over that, I zipped a bulbous down vest of Mom's and now Andrew was about as wide as he was tall. Thinking it was too cold to be fooling around with metal pistols, and besides, he was probably getting too old for them, I left the six-shooters in their holster slung over a chair. I was relieved that Andrew hadn't noticed. Recently, he'd wanted to shoot the guns while on Chim Chim. I'd said no, and that instead, we could shoot some cans with the new pellet gun I'd gotten him. These pistols didn't just go *click-click* as did my old guns; they were heavy duty and made a loud *clacking* every time you pulled the trigger.

Out we went. Approaching the van, we heard horse footsteps, the hollow, echoing sound they make on the wooden floor of a van, but they weren't loud. Almost to the van, we saw Mikey step out onto the ramp, holding a shank behind him. There was a three-foot-high plywood partition up on either side of the ramp and you could only see Mikey from the waist up.

We were prepared to view a big, good-looking, nervous Thoroughbred stepping out onto the ramp behind Mikey. My line of vision was set for the height of Mikey's shoulders. I didn't see anything walking behind Mikey, and then, I lowered my eyes a notch, and a pair of big ears appeared just above the top of the partition, or at the level of Mikey's waist. It looked as if a puppeteer were behind the partition holding up the ears, preparing to perform a skit. The ears stopped. A head strained to raise its eyes to see over the partition.

As Andrew and I walked up to the van, we could see the thick neck, and then, Andrew and I were up on the knoll. We could see Mikey's mount for the afternoon: this was no horse, it was no pony, it was Petunia, the donkey.

Petunia stood on the ramp. Andrew had ridden her before at Mikey's. In fact, we'd ridden her together, and then I'd gotten off, and Mikey had led Andrew on Petunia, into his house, through his bedroom, through the living room, into the kitchen for a treat, then out onto the front porch and down the steps.

Andrew stepped onto the ramp, walked up to Petunia, ruffled her furry face, gave her a hug, and patted the bulbous, wobbly thick tube of fat that ran along the ridge of her neck just under her mane. He grabbed the mane and pulled the balloon of fat back and forth, laughing. "Still has her sandwiches. Still has her sandwiches, Dad." Mikey told all kids that the packet of fat was actually a compartment where Petunia kept her emergency sandwiches and sodas. "Like the hump on a camel," he said. This enabled her to trek hundreds of miles across the desert or scale steep mountain passes for days without stopping. Petunia, in other words, was ready at any moment to climb the Himalayas in a blizzard or high-step it across the Sahara in a sandstorm.

Andrew ran back into the house to get something.

"I'll get Chim Chim," I said to Mikey.

"Hold on," he said, handing me Petunia and walking back into the van. I heard some chain ties slap against the walls, and there Mikey was standing beside a large pony with black and brown spots—a "paint."

"Who's that pony?" I asked.

"This is a horse, not a pony, and it is Andrew's mount," Mikey asserted.

Andrew walked out with the holster buckled around his waist, a six-gun on each side, saw the "paint pony" and jogged to us. I walked the pony up to the exact spot on the knoll where Pop, forty years earlier, had thrown me up onto Queenie, Mikey standing by our trailer watching. I gripped Andrew around his rib cage and tossed him up into the tack, Mikey standing by the van watching.

"What's his name?" Andrew asked me.

"I don't know, maybe we can give him one," I said, tightening his girth.

"His name," Mikey said, looking at us, hesitating, and then, his voice slightly breaking, "is Spotty."

I grabbed an old hunting cap, my childhood hunting cap with the frayed visor, off the aisle-way wall, jammed it down over Andrew's ski cap, untacked Chim Chim and then hopped up on Warfield. Mikey was on Petunia, bareback, his feet almost dragging on the ground. Andrew and I were both looking down at him, as we milled around in the back field, adjusting our stirrups and tightening our girths. Mikey looked up at Andrew, "You look good on that horse Andrew. You look like a cowboy on Spotty." Andrew was sitting up tall, his back straight. When he walked around the house, Andrew slouched. But when he was on a horse, he had perfect form, a natural seat. He had his stirrups adjusted to the correct length, and he sat in just the right spot, with his hands down low, his heels down, and his back ramrod straight.

Soon we were out in the woods and splashing through creeks with ice forming on their edges. The wind was picking up and drifts were building up along hedgerows. Whenever we saw one, we headed for it and cantered through its deepest part, our hooves making a muffled sound and the snow spraying up on either side of us. We found a series of logs in a field, each log having a four-inch layer of snow on top. Mikey schooled Petunia down through the series, his feet knocking the snow off the top of the logs. Then I went on Warfield with Spotty right behind. "You got Spotty going right Andrew. That's one hell of a good horse," Mikey called out. Andrew beamed and suddenly all he wanted to do was jump. Off we went looking for more logs.

Jogging through the woods, Mikey pointed out that a gang of outlaws and bank robbers had a hideout near here when he was a kid, and a small group still remained. There was a reward out for each of them, dead or alive. It made no sense for me to be in front. The man with the guns should be first in line. With that, Andrew gave Spotty a kick or two, passed Mikey and me, and took the lead. We didn't find any outlaws. Mikey said they must be off robbing a bank but that Andrew should practice.

"These guns are louder than you'd think they'd be," I told Mikey, hinting that Spotty might spook at the shots.

"Oh come on, Dad," Andrew said, his right hand leaving the reins and going for his Colt 45.

"SON," Mikey said to me, "Spotty's a cowboy horse! He knows how to do this. Andrew, you just say 'bang bang bang' a couple of times in a low voice, ride along quietly, then say it a couple of times in a louder voice, ride along quietly, and then take the pistol out and shoot it."

Andrew followed Mikey's directions as if he were 007 receiving them from Q. Everything worked out fine. Afterwards, he turned around, holding his pistol pointed toward the sky, the imaginary smoke spiraling out the barrel, and glared at me. "See, Dad."

We rode along, Mikey calling out, "To the right behind the tree," and Andrew would reach for his right six-shooter, pull it out, shoot at the tree, and then calmly, serenely, ever so professionally, slip it back into its holster. Mikey pointed out that he didn't have one horse on his entire farm that you could shoot a gun off without the horse spooking and throwing the rider; maybe Andrew could come down to Hydes and teach his other horses how to do this; it'd be good for the horses and Mikey's riders might learn something watching Andrew.

Andrew kicked Spotty on, led us at a jog through the woods and popped over logs without asking me if it were OK to jump them. When he pulled up to a walk, he reached up and patted Spotty's neck. By this time, Mikey was relating childhood pony-riding stories to Andrew—adventures Andrew would be emulating for the next six months—especially, when summer came, the ones about spending an entire month camping out with Pop, Gary, Peter Winants, and three ponies in a field not far from the Elkridge-Harford Club, riding the ponies to the club and up to "Spotless" Joe Flanagan's where Pop and Mikey would break yearlings throughout the morning, then, returning to the campsite, taking off their clothes and spending the rest of the day swimming the ponies in the pond and swinging from a Tarzan rope into the nearby quarry.

WHEN WE GOT BACK, Mikey loaded up and took off. I went out to the barn, gave Warfield a good rub and some feed, mucked out the shed, and returned to the kitchen.

Mom had asked Andrew to stay over for the night. It was fine with me. Either school would be called off in the morning, or, if it weren't, he had my permission to play hooky and go skiing. I left them sitting by the wood stove, planning their morning's work, day of skiing, and then—dinner at Red Lobster on the way back.

Sawyer and I climbed in the truck, bounced out the driveway, and at its end, instead of turning right and heading home to the Pond House at Oldfields, we took a left, heading for Hydes. I had something on my mind, something that I could ask only one person, one man, one horseman.

First, I stopped by the grocery store in Jacksonville, picked up a Sunday paper, some coffee, eggs and milk. Then, patting Sawyer's head, I drove to Mikey's at a peaceful pace, the snow falling gently now, lackadaisically, spinning and parachuting to the ground. I too would probably have the day off from school and I felt a twinge of guilt for not going skiing with Mom and Andrew. Instead, I was planning on going to the Monkton Hotel to put in a good morning's work on my book. I knew that if I made a certain decision, then not only for the rest of the winter and spring would I be giving up opportunities to write, I would also be wiping out time to spend with Andrew and Eliza, whether skiing, or playing lacrosse, or bicycling, or skating, or riding, and I would miss many of their weekend lacrosse games.

I turned into Mikey's entrance off Hydes Road, crossed the narrow bridge and drove up the crunching pea-gravel driveway, Sawyer sensing where we were, looking out the window, panting and wagging his tail. The big brown barn came up suddenly in the headlights, looking black juxtaposed against the vortex of snowflakes funneling toward us. To the right was one of Mikey's many innovations. He'd built what looked like a dock against the side of the hill. At the end of the dock, a manure spreader, hooked up to a tractor, was parked. A groom could push his or her wheelbarrow out to the end of the dock, flip it over, the manure falling into the spreader.

We took a sharp left, parked beside Mikey's Subaru, his *new* Subaru station wagon. This was the replacement he'd gotten after our collision the February before, his former car being declared a total loss.

The floodlight on the barn clicked on illuminating the snowflakes cascading down as Sawyer and I walked past Mikey's car. Strands of baling twine clung to the roof rack. Speedy Kiniel, Mikey's top man, could get six bales up on that rack. In the back of the station wagon, covered with a layer of hay stalks and chaff, were beaten black rubber feed tubs, a pile of rope shanks, two exercise saddles and a clump of bridles. Up a step, Sawyer jumping on me, urging me forward, I looked into the next compartment. Sprawled across the back seats were old-timey wool and canvas New Zealand horse blankets encrusted with layers of dog hair—black, brown, white, chestnut. On the passenger seat were piled a dozen hand-sized condition books, each containing detailed descriptions of every race at that track's current meet, *Daily Racing Forms*, white paper bags from the pharmacy that had held prescription medicine, and a beautiful, well-oiled leather case for binoculars. Two Irish wool caps hung from the mirror along with a National Steeplechase Association tag, and spread across the dashboard was a clutter of tags for hospital parking garages. The only open space was the driver's seat. One of the dogs had been working like a beaver on its corner so that the upholstery was ripped and the stuffing poking out.

I walked up six slippery stone steps, carefully proceeded down the mossy and snow-sprinkled brick path to the door. How in the world did Mikey navigate over such terrain every day? This was a three-story log cabin that I had loved as a child. It was packed with small low-ceilinged rooms that had plenty of windows, a mysterious catacomb-like cellar with a stone-walled apartment, and up in the attic a more spacious apartment that had its own entrance, a steel fire escape built around the huge, thick, chimney that led to the fireplace in the living room below. The horizontal tongue-and-groove pine paneling of the attic room, varnished to a deep, glossy brown, started at the floor, went up the three-foot walls, and then, gradually, no sharp corners, continued to the peak of the ceiling in a sort of Romanesque arch. Two beds were set up perpendicular to the north wall, and life was magical, filled with God and goodness and wonder, when forty years ago my grandmother Um would come up to the attic, kneel down with me beside one of the beds, and we'd recite the Twenty-Third Psalm and the Lord's Prayer together.

Many a groom, galloping boy or jockey who Mikey and Pop hired and inspired, and who then went on to have a good life, started their careers in one of these apartments. I'd met them all over the country: a rock star, an investment banker, a leading steeplechase jockey, a Kentucky Derby winning trainer, a Triple Crown winning trainer, a television producer, and they all told me how thankful they were for what Pop and Mikey had done for them. Two said their lives had been saved at Hydes.

I knocked. Sawyer wagged his tail, slammed his body against my legs. I cracked the door open. The big TV, up high on a platform, blared and shot its flickering colors across the dark room. Sawyer burst through, took a few steps and was swept back outside by a wave of dogs barking and yelping and smacking their tails against my legs. Mikey was in his big chair, tilted back, at the foot of his bed. He still had his Irish cap on and his full-body insulated canvas Carhartt suit. Awakening, he looked up, over the scratched dime-store glasses.

"Paddy, Paddy?" he said.

I didn't say anything.

"Is that you, Paddy?" He squinted in my direction. The television blared and shot its flickering light at him.

"Can you do the weight? *Can you make the weight tomorrow*? Mrs. Phipps called and wants you to ride the horse. She said he won't jump for anyone else. *Paddy, can you make the weight*?"

"Mikey," I said. "It's Patrick."

"*Pa*-trick . . . ?"

"Yes."

"I must've fallen asleep." He studied me. "You sure you're not Paddy."

"Mikey, wake up. I'm Patrick, Paddy's son." I stepped into the room.

On my left was a tall coat rack on which hung numerous sheepskin coats, down jackets, down vests, and Irish wool caps. Taking another step, I heard the dogs scratching against the door, turned, opened it and in they burst, Sawyer in the lead, the low-slung Basset hound close behind.

"Sawyer!" Mikey called. He slapped his leg. Sawyer lumbered in, rubbed up against him, beat against his legs with his tail, put his head in his lap. "That's a good boy. That'a boy, Sawyer," Mikey chanted, stroking his face.

"*Pa*-trick," he said. "I was just dreaming about Paddy." He peered at me. "Paddy?"

"Mikey—I'm Patrick—that's Sawyer. Paddy's not here. I have a son Paddy but your brother Paddy is not here any more."

"Not here." He looked disappointed. "I know. I know. I wish he *were* here. I wish Paddy were here. I miss him. I miss him every single day. I was dreaming I was trying to find him, that he had to ride a horse tomorrow that got in light. I wanted to warn him about losing the weight. Do you have dreams like that?"

"Yes, I do."

"He could really lose weight you know. No one could reduce like Paddy. He'd stop eating. He'd get in that hot car with all those clothes on. First, he'd go for a run. Sometimes I'd drive the car across the big field, and he'd jog behind me, a mile or two, get his heart beating. Then I'd get out, he'd jump in and drive around the countryside sweating off the pounds. He never complained. Think how much that must have taken out of him, year after year, for twenty years. It must have killed him some days. I could see it in his eyes."

We thought about that. The reducing in many ways was exactly what killed him. The smoking. The smoking of Pall Malls to replace eating. Cancer of the lungs. I hate Pall Malls, and yet the sight and smell and feel of a small, soft, red pack brings back a peaceful, pleasant feeling, a state of being from my youth, of life being the way it should be.

Mikey pulled himself up and looked me over. "Let's have a glass of poor man's port."

"Good idea." I stepped through the dogs to the dry sink filled with dust-covered bottles of liquor, picked up a half-gallon of port, pulled the cork. No glasses. I opened the door beside the dry-sink, stepped into the hallway. To the left was the steep climbing spiral staircase my grandmother Emma Smithwick used right up until she was ninety-seven. There was no banister. Instead a worn pole was set at the center of the stairs.

I took a few steps forward. On the left was a bookshelf-covered wall, lots on Churchill and Lincoln. To my right was the door to the living room, its walls covered with photos of Alfred and Emma on horses, Mikey and Pop on ponies, and then of Mikey soaring over timber fences and Pop over brush and hurdles.

I walked into the long, narrow kitchen with a bank of windows facing the driveway, searched in a cupboard for a couple of glasses, rinsed them out and returned. I poured the dark, syrupy port and set the glasses down on the table beside Mikey.

"Come on, Mikey, why don't you get out of this outfit."

He patted Sawyer, gently pushed him away, and stood up. I stepped behind him, pulled the heavily lined canvas down off his shoulders, pushed it off one arm, then the other, reminding me of sliding snowsuits off my children. We pushed the canvas down to his feet. He stepped out, now in turtleneck, sweater, corduroys. I adjusted the chair so that it was no longer reclining, Mikey sat back down and we discussed the afternoon's ride. Sawyer lay down beside Mikey, placed his head on Mikey's foot. We sipped our port. At first, I had to hold back a grimace. I'd been after him for years to purchase a better brand but he insisted on getting this "poor man's port" which was certain to take a year off our lives. I took a full drink. Its effect was instantaneous. I could feel it settle me, take me from my swirling questioning thoughts and memories, slow my thinking, put me right here, in the now, in the present, in this room smelling of wet wool and dogs and cats and hay and a horse's thick, dusty, winter coat, with my uncle.

"Mikey?"

"Yes, Young-Blood." He still had his cap on. His scratched and dusty glasses were balancing on the end of his nose. He looked seriously at me.

"I'm thinking of trying to get the ride on Welterweight this spring."

He furrowed his eyebrows, continuing to look me in the eye through the narrow space created by the down-tipped visor of his cap and the upper edge of his glasses.

"That's good," he said, totally, absolutely clearheaded and in the present, stretching out the word *good* and stressing, lengthening the vowel sound so that it was "*g-o-o-o-o-d*."

"That's *good.*"

"I don't think Mike wants to ride him again. I've been hunting him all winter and I've gotten to know him. What do you think?"

"*Do it.*"

"I thought I'd talk to Tom first, not the owners."

"That's right. Talk to Tom. Talk to the trainer first. He might know something you don't. And what if they talk Mike into riding Welterweight? You know they're going to try."

"Then I'll try to get the ride on Florida."

"You've got a good plan. Talk to Tom. Tell him you're interested in both horses."

"Do you think I can do it?"

"Course you can do it. You've been hunting them. You know them. They jump well for you."

"Mom's not so high on the idea. She doesn't think I can get my timing down, get fit enough . . ."

"Don't you run every day?"

"Yes."

"Run during the week. Hunt on the weekends. Let's have some more of that poor man's port."

I poured the port.

"Pick up some outside rides. Ride in the early point-to-points down in Virginia, that's how you'll sharpen up. Get used to standing in the paddock, talking to owners, going to the post. That's what I used to do. You can get an edge on these other guys. They won't ride a race until late spring." A big, fat gray cat slinked through the door, left ajar, to the kitchen porch, tiptoed long-striding across the room, jumped up on the bed, stealthily walked the length of the bed, around the languid basset hound now sound asleep, up behind Mikey and gently placed her front paws on Mikey's shoulder. Without looking, Mikey reached across his chest, stroked the cat's neck and shoulders. The cat climbed across his shoulder, down his chest and curled up in his lap.

"It's been thirty years since I've ridden in the Hunt Cup."

"That makes no difference. What matters is now, and right now you can put yourself in training. Don't worry about your mother. Once you make up your mind, she'll support you one hundred percent. She was the same way with Paddy."

We each had a sip of poor-man's port. "How's Andrew?" Mikey loved Andrew and was excited to hear that Andrew was on the basketball team at school. He couldn't wait to see a game. We'd gone to a few soccer games in the fall, and once, due to standing still out in the cold too long, had been forced to leave at halftime, drive across the county line (it was Sunday and no package goods stores were open in Baltimore County), to a store Mikey knew of, buy a half gallon of poor man's port, and return to finish watching the game from the car, engine and heater running. This game was played on the field of a school that Mikey and Pop had attended, to which they used to ride their bikes, and from which they were once suspended for leaving home with the good intention of attending classes, but along the way, they had gone off course, their bikes making a wrong turn which took them to a quarry where they spent the day skinny-dipping.

We discussed Andrew's Sunday riding and that led to Eliza and her riding. Mikey said to wait until it warmed up and then bring her down to the farm. He'd have some good ponies she could try out.

We had some more port. Mikey stood up. I pulled off his cashmere sweater, turtleneck, corduroys, and left him in two silk long underwear tops and a waffle-patterned bottom. He walked to the bathroom and brushed his teeth. I helped him get into the bed without disturbing the basset hound and the cat. He slid under the covers. On his bedside table was a small copy of a well-known photograph of Pop and him walking back after a race. Pop is wearing Mrs. Phipp's colors, Old Rose. He's light, very light. He's looking straight ahead, listening. Mikey's walking beside him, bending forward, looking into Pop's eyes. It is 1957 and Pop has just won the Grand National Handicap on Neji, their favorite. Fifty years later, this framed photo is set on top of a copy of *Gilman Voices*, published in 1997, the history I'd written. It has a tear in its cover and a racing program inserted into the pages where I'd written a section on Pop and Mikey commuting to Gilman on the Ma and Pa Railroad during the gas rationing of

World War II, and how in the afternoon, they'd drive the conductor crazy. There was an uphill grade leaving the school and the conductor preferred, if possible, not to fully stop. Pop and Mikey would throw a ball back and forth, back and forth, pretending not to notice the train. The conductor would slow, and slow. They'd run over, hop on at the last minute. The conductor would pull back on the throttle and the wheels would spin—due to the soap and cabbage weeds they'd rubbed on the tracks—before finally speeding back out to the countryside, to the station at Hydes.

CHAPTER 15

From Here to Reality

On landing after the fourteenth, you tighten the left rein, keep your horse pulling by squeezing with your legs and simultaneously slow a notch, depending on the going — for if it has been raining, this stretch can be bog-like. You want to keep your horse's momentum up, he's no longer fresh, and you feel badly for him if he has to labor going through the muck. You don't want to knock him out in this deep going and you don't want him to realize he is getting tired. You may be in wonder that your horse has done all that he has thus far — galloped three miles at a two-minute lick, jumped fourteen fences — and is still pulling against the bit. You take a breather, look where everyone is. This is the last time.

W E'D BEEN HAVING a good hunt and I'd felt like a million dollars from the moment I had swung up on Welterweight. It was a beautiful, clear, sunny January morning. It was great to see Tom. We were on time for once. There we were, the three of us, Tom, Jonathan, and I, jogging out the long entrance to Atlanta Hall Farm on the way to the Elkridge-Harford Hunt Club a mile away. We were talking and I was whooping and hollering, feeling freed, out of the office, away from the phone, the computer, e-mail beeps, notepads filled with to-do lists, stacks of photographs to sort, dozens of articles to write, designers to call, printers to hound, and Tom was asking what the hell was wrong with me—was I scared? (One of his negative takes on a situation. Can't he ever feel good? Can't he ever feel so good that his soul is about to pop out of his skin and merge with the blue

sky above, the thick turf below, the horse beneath his legs?) And, it was
Welter between my legs—slender, powerful, fit, confident, dancing and jigging and never taking a wrong step.

Tom looked better. He had recuperated from the grueling schedule of
shipping his horses as well as himself to the hunt meets up and down the
East Coast over the fall. He had color back in his face; he had dropped a
few pounds; he had a grin. He was back; we were back; let'em roll, let the
fox run, let the hounds bay, let the horses run and jump.

Welter was going perfectly. So he'd behave, I was hanging around in
the back of "the field," away from Johnny Garland, his stable mate, whom
Tom was riding when suddenly, just inches away from me, someone on a
big gray horse I didn't recognize, appeared. It was Sebastian. He had his
irons jacked up, and—was he losing his "seat"?—his rear was way back
in the saddle like some old-timer. Looking as if he were almost at riding
weight, he started right off, rapid fire, "Paddy, me boy, I really think I ought
to ride that horse," looking over Welterweight. "What do you say, Paddy?
Why don't you ride Florida Law and I ride Welterweight. I think you'd suit
Florida. You know Welter, what's it going to be like rolling down that hill
into the thirteenth on him?"

I didn't reply. I had decided this would be the day I'd talk to Tom, tell
him I was interested in riding Welter in the spring races. I allowed Welter
to jig away.

As we jogged through a swampy lowland, Joey Gillet rode up alongside me
and delivered a rather interesting soliloquy on all the problems with his
stepfather's scrap-metal recycling business in California, how a land giant
wanted to shut it down, the environmentalists were on his ass, and here he
was doing the environmentally correct thing: recycling! He was forced to
go door-to-door, drafting hundreds of people to show up at hearings.

We have a run, charge around, jump a few fences. I'm focused on this
incredible horse beneath me dancing and jigging and galloping and jumping and pulling—this bastard can pull when he wants—and then we slow
down. We're walking single file through a deep, muddy path in the woods.

Joey's in front of me. He's twisting around in his saddle, facing me, as only he can do—he can perform this stunt at a gallop—one hand on the horse's rump; he's practically riding backwards, and now he's switched to his love life. He really likes the woman he's taking out, but she's not his usual, preferred body type! I can't stop laughing. I have to concentrate on this horse between my legs. Joey just doesn't feel in love with this one woman, but should he go ahead and marry her? He is getting older, he's thirty-seven now. He wants to have kids. Would he grow into being in love, or do you have to have that feeling from the start?

We'd gone from a lecture on problems plaguing the scrap-metal business to pinpointing the meaning of love. He had my head spinning. "You need the fire and passion from the start," I said.

We milled around in a valley, a farm up on one side of a hill, a woods—in foxhunting parlance, the "covert," on the other hill where the hounds searched for a scent. We were on one side of a long hedgerow of multiflora rose. There was just one place where you could get through, a broken-down gate with a board, a "rider," nailed across the top, making it a foot higher. We bunched up near the gate. I wondered if we were going to jump it. The hounds had caught the scent of a fox and were going away from us on the other side. Wellie and I were ready to jump the gate. Then, someone got off and yanked the top board out. Irv Naylor, who usually hunted with the Green Spring Hounds, was out with us today. He announced, "In the Green Spring, we would have gone on and jumped that with the rider on it."

A few minutes later, Sebastian rode up to me, face twisted. "Did it, Paddy. Made the pitch." He pulled a flask out of his coat pocket, unscrewed the top, took a swig, offered me a taste.

"No thanks," I said.

He had told Welterweight's owners, who were out hunting, that he wanted the ride on Wellie in the upcoming spring races. There they were walking around on their horses twenty yards away—and I felt this horrible, yawning vacuum open up before me.

It sucked the energy out of me, he had snatched the horse out from between my legs. I rode on but felt jilted—a cuckold. What should I do? I needed to talk to Tom. Should I ride up and talk to the owners? Tell them of my interest? No, I wouldn't go behind Tom's back. I'd talk to Tom first.

We break out of the path in the woods and we're in a meadow, still near the creek, with the mist rising off it. Most of our horses have quieted down after the three runs, and I'm off by myself, enjoying having Welter relax when I overhear Joey telling someone a story about schooling around the Grand National course early that morning and the trainer of his horse, a woman we all know, having a fall. He rides up alongside me and relates this tale. They'd been schooling around the course and his trainer had taken off ahead of him, flying. Her horse had clobbered a fence. She had lain on the ground. He had jumped off, put her head in his lap; blood poured from orifices. She was out. He held her head and thought, "This is it." Finally, she came to but was not making much sense. They got an ambulance. Away she went, chanting, "I don't want to lose my nerve! I don't want to lose my nerve! I'm going to be all right and I'm not going to lose my nerve!"

Tom and I hacked home alongside Wellie's owners. I thought about blurting out to them that I wanted to ride Wellie, but it did not seem to be the right thing to do.

We walked side-by-side, discussing how his training was progressing: his coat was slightly dull, was there something wrong with his kidneys? Tom planned to have some tests taken. Last spring his back had been sore. This spring, Tom had researched the effects of magnets on soreness and had purchased a blanket with embedded magnets that we tossed over Welter's back as soon as he was put in the stall every morning after his gallop. Tom had also lined up a massage therapist to work on Wellie's back twice a week; he had bought a special gel pad which was always put under the saddle; and, he had proclaimed to all in the barn that I was no longer allowed to use my old hunting saddle on him, stating, "That ancient saddle, that's probably what's doing it to him." During the Saratoga meet, he had purchased a special exercise saddle with a stiff, supportive seat, that was supposed to be good for sore backs, and it was now the only saddle anyone was allowed to use on Wellie.

Back at the barn, Tom and I straightened up. We sat in his pine-panelled tack room, he with his feet up on the old army desk, me on the sofa. I explained what Sebastian had done. Tom was quiet. I mentioned that I was interested in riding Welter. Tom said he thought that Elmore would probably ride him again this spring and advised me to get the ride on Florida.

"What amazes me, is that to Sebastian, the horse doesn't matter in the least. It is simply a means to an end. The horse might as well be a VW Bug—or a BMW," I said.

"That's it," said Tom. "It's just a way for him to raise his social status."

I stumbled across Jonathan's racing saddles overflowing out of a duffle bag in a corner of the tack room. Tom laughed, pointing out that it had been there since the last hunt meet of the fall, and it would remain there until the first hunt meet of the spring.

We relaxed, talked about race riding and race riders. Brian Hickey came up. "The toughest man who ever lived," as Hall of Fame trainer Sidney Watters put it. Worked for my father off and on. Rode for Sidney. Had a career going as a steeplechase jockey but loved to drink and fight and raise hell. Left horses. Continued drinking. Got into drugs. Became purposeless. Was planning a comeback. Then said the hell with it. Pulled the trigger. Great admirer and friend of my father's. Had everything going for him. Could be so gentle, thoughtful. I told Tom how every time I drove by a small concrete island between the two lanes going east and two going west on Northern Parkway, I thought of Brian: I pictured Pop, Brian, Emmett Grayson and me jammed into the cab of the old Ford pickup, driving to Pimlico at 5:30 on a weekday morning, a full load of hay in the back, cars shooting up and down the parkway, and suddenly Brian yelling, "Stop!" We looked at him. "Stop!" Pop maneuvered over to the side, cars honking. Brian jumped out, ran across the traffic to the concrete island, got down low, put his hands out, approached a big German shepherd that was stuck there, picked the dog up, carried him across to the residential area, ran back to us and hopped back in the truck, letting loose a stream of colorful epithets describing all the commuters who had driven past this dog without doing anything.

We discussed Tommy Smith, the best timber rider in the country after

Mikey retired, winner of five Hunt Cups, and the first American to win the English Grand National. I told Tom how Tommy had been thoughtful and encouraging to me after the Wild Goose Chase. Tommy had grown up riding for Pop and Mikey, becoming one of their great friends, and had always been modest about his accomplishments. He was back in Maryland, training a few horses, losing that extra weight he'd packed on, and was, as he told me, for the first time in years enjoying riding again, enjoying it for the riding itself, not as a way to compete. Neither Tom nor I could've imagined that one day in the not-too-distant future Tommy would have a freak fall out riding and be forced into a wheelchair.

We stepped out of the warmth of the tack room. I helped Tom feed and hay, drove home through the dark, drank two bottles of Smithwick's Ale a friend had just brought back from Ireland. I whined to Ansley about what had happened with Sebastian and Welterweight and was struck by an unexpected onslaught, a crashing wave of rebuke. "Why in the world do you want to do it? Haven't you grown out of this yet? Don't you have more important things to do? What is the point? What if something happened to you? Really? Well, look at what happened to your father, and wasn't he one of the best riders ever? Then if you really think this is something you have to do, you'd better make it very clear to Tom. How is Tom supposed to know you want to ride Welterweight? This happens every single spring. . . . For God's sake, you need to make up your mind. Sebastian wants to ride the horse. So he is out to get the horse! That's the way he is. He's always been that way. It's nothing new. If you want to ride the horse, you'll have to go after him."

"WELL," I SAID to Tom, as we rode out to the meet the following weekend, "Who are you going to get to ride Florida this spring? Are you going to ride him?" I had learned that Mike Elmore had decided to ride Wellie.

Tom did this thing he does when you catch him by surprise. He flinched, tightened his shoulders and looked straight ahead.

We rode along. I was on Welterweight, he on Johnny. Florida was turned out, rolling around in the mud. Tom had hunted him on Wednesday.

"What do you mean?" he asked.

"I called Sebastian in his Boston office and asked what was up with his rides for the spring, knowing he would be trying to get the ride on Welter."

"No," said Tom. "Ben went down and had lunch with Elmore and talked him into riding Welter."

"That's what Sebastian told me. And he said he doesn't want to ride Florida."

"Really?" said Tom, still looking straight ahead.

" 'I don't want to ride him around that course,' " he told me.

" 'Are you sure?' " I asked.

" 'Yes,' he said, and he added, 'I don't know if I want to ride any horse around that course again. I might just hang it up.' "

We had a great hunt—sunny, not too cold, jumped some good fences. During a lull, Jay Griswold walked up to Tom. "Mister Voss," he paused, waiting for Tom to look over at him. "Master," he said, teasing Tom, referring to Tom's title as Master of Foxhounds, "Looks to me like you ought to let Patrick ride that horse this spring." Greg Ryan, an amateur rider from Virginia who was close to breaking the record for the number of steeple-chase races won by an amateur, drifted over to me. "He's right, Smithwick. You suit Florida. The last Saturday in April, you should be found in the tack headed across Tufton Avenue."

We headed in, cooled the horses out, rubbed them down, washed the mud off their legs, chests and stomachs with hot water. Tom made them a steaming, hot mash which smelled so good—like oatmeal but with more scents—that I felt like eating it myself.

Then, there we were in the pine-paneled tack room again, Tom at his desk, me on the sofa, blue, red, and yellow show ring ribbons dating back to the 1920s and 1930s and dusty old hunting saddles and photographs of winning horses lining the walls around us.

"Well," I said, "if Sebastian doesn't want to ride Florida, who will?"

"He'd be an open ride."

I took a deep breath. What I wanted was to be asked to ride him, and after being asked, to let it soak in, to think about it, to make my decision and then to give an answer. But if I wanted this ride, if I did not want this opportunity to slip away, I had to take the leap. "Put me down on your list. I'd like to ride him."

WALKING INTO OUR KITCHEN, my leather boot heels clacking loudly on the tile floor, I heard the phone. No one was home. In a good mood, I took a chance and picked it up. It was Sal, just checking in. I told her about the hunt and the people urging me to ride Florida.

"When I'm old and gray," she said slowly, in a deep voice—one Mom sometimes uses, "I didn't think they'd still be calling me to ride races. . . ." She hesitated. What was she up to? I wondered and waited.

"It just sounds like a neat way to start a book, a book about being torn. You could go back and forth, have flashbacks to your childhood on the racetrack and then come back to your current life." We chatted and I told her I had to go, had to get ready to go to a party at Tom Whedbee's.

Not a bad idea, I thought, flopping down on the couch, boots, britches, coat still on. Tidbit jumped up on my stomach, Tiger-Lilly, my marmalade cat, slinked and purred her way onto my chest. Sawyer laid his jaw across my hipbone, and I was out.

WE WENT TO THE Whedbees' party and got home late. The light was blinking on the message machine in the kitchen. Ansley pushed the button. I continued past her and started up the stairs. "Patrick," she called, not "Sweetheart"—she'd wanted to leave the party earlier but I just couldn't stop talking first to J.B., then to Reed and Rob and Tom and their wives— "it's for you."

"No thanks." I continued up.

"It's Sal."

"OK."

I pushed the button. The tape started over, "Hey!" It sounded like she was right in the room. Her voice was clear as a bell, after all, she is a singer as well as a pianist. "I didn't mean you *are* old and gray," she said excitedly. "It's just that to me it's fascinating to see that pull in your life and how you resolve it. There's an archetypal theme there! Following your father's steps versus your own steps. There's something fun about meeting you. It's humorous—you're still being tempted! As a reader, I want to know what lures you: The beauty of the horses? Being the son of a famous person? It's a cross you've had to bear, Pop's dying. It could be an honest book. Let it all hang out. . . ."

Standing there, alone, exhausted, tipsy, I hung up and was immediately reminded of a conversation in the same exact spot . . . , a similar conversation . . . one with Susan six years earlier when she had given me that push I had needed to go ahead, and to *go after*, to actively, *aggressively* go all-out: writing proposals, being interviewed by committees, by the headmaster, by the director of development, by alumni, driving with Ansley to New York to meet Walter Lord at his legendary apartment filled with *Titanic* memorabilia—in getting the contract to do the book on Gilman.

MONDAY MORNING AT GILMAN, I opened the door to the Health Center run by Peggy Classen, who as a youth galloped and schooled horses for Mikey and Pop, and was devoted to us Smithwicks. I was there to get an allergy shot. "Did you hear what happened?" Peggy immediately asked. I knew what it would be but not whom. "No, what happened?" "Erskine died, Erskine died out hunting. He was on an old favorite, and the horse had a heart attack, collapsed, threw him down on the hard ground." I pictured Erskine, fun-loving friend of my parents. I felt his hands cupped around my lower shin as he tossed me up on Crag after I'd had a fall at a fence way out of view of the judges of a hunter trial class. I heard him telling me not to worry, he wouldn't tell a soul, "Just get up there and ride the hell out of this old horse." Erskine, Master of the Piedmont Hounds in Virginia, son of Dean and Louise Bedford, both Masters of Foxhounds and founders of the U.S. Pony Club. "The funeral's next week in Middleburg . . . going to be a big one." My class was in half an hour. I walked to the library with my copy of *Huck Finn* and a legal pad under my arm, prepared to head downriver.

After class, I went for a quick run and returned to my office. The red light was blinking on my telephone. I knew it was Tom. I can sense when he's called. He'd left a message at home saying something about a student at Oldfields who was looking for a horse to buy and he thought he had one for her. Did I know anything about her? Could she ride? I sensed that he was not really calling about this horse. I had called back, trying his house, the tack room, the upper barn, his office, his car, and hadn't gotten him.

I picked up the receiver and waited for the message: there was a long pause and then a fed-up-with-the-situation sigh, a Tom sigh, and a click.

An hour earlier, while going for a run around Roland Park before lunch—enjoying running for the sheer love of it, not as a means to an end—I'd come to the realization that I didn't need to direct my life toward accomplishing this or that feat, winning this steeplechase race or writing that book. I felt good inside about myself, confident, self-sufficient, solid; I had no need for that attention, that recognition, that renown. I came to the conclusion that riding this spring was not going to change my life. *If I do it, if I don't do it, I will end up in the same spot!* I had written in my journal after the run. *Thinking about riding this race is what has brought me to this moment of insight: I can draw the strength and willpower and desire to live and to flourish from inside and not be dependent on the potential applause from the outside.*

THAT NIGHT, I am sitting at the dining room table, having pizza, salad and an ale with Ansley, Andrew and Eliza, and the phone rings. Usually, surreptitiously, before dinner I pull the receiver off the hook and stick it in the refrigerator so you can't hear it go *beep-beep-beep*, but not on this night. When it rings, I want to pick it up, yet here I am the one always giving everyone hell for answering the phone at dinner. Andrew answers it. Under orders from Ansley, he tells Tom I will call him back after dinner.

We finish dinner. I dial Tom's car phone. He's on Pocock Road, headed home from a workout, in a rush. He asks about the Oldfields girl who's looking for a point-to-point horse. I can tell he's not really calling about the girl or the horse.

"I hunted your horse yesterday . . ."

Your horse . . . your horse . . . your horse . . . He was saying it but he was not saying it.

"Oh yeah?"

"I was galloping into this big post-and-rail with a rider on top, and he was all set to stand off and jump." The signal faded and I couldn't hear him very well. He was going down into the valley. ". . . a car went by. He spooked and put in an extra stride . . ."

"Oh God, did you smash your balls?" I ask.

"What?" he said gruffly, doing his best imitation of Scrooge at his worst.

"Did you smack your balls?" Where the hell was this crazy question coming from? That's just what I didn't want the horse to do, put in that short one, put in an extra stride. There's static on the line. Damn, this is always what it is like trying to communicate with Tom.

"Wha-a-a-a-t?" he asks, now having fun, dragging out the word, taking his time, giving it a strong nasal and negative twist, tantalizing me.

"What do you mean, '*Your horse*'?" I ask.

He explains that as part owner, he talked to the other two owners and it was OK with them for me to ride Florida. They had decided I wasn't too old.

"Ha, well, what about you?" I ask. "What do you think?"

"I don't know . . . I thought it was fine and then you drank that whole bottle of hundred-dollar port the other night and I started to wonder. I got to go. Hunting Saturday. Meet's here at twelve."

"Oh yeah, you got something for me?"

"We'll have something."

"Eleven-thirty?"

"Yes," he whispered, serious now, "eleven-thirty."

"YOUR HORSE." The irony of it: this call coming on the day of the run during which I had shed myself of the craving for attention and applause and awards.

I call Tidbit and Sawyer while pulling on a jacket. I need to get outside, to think this over outside in the cloud-covered, rainy February evening. Andrew has his red ski parka on and is preparing to take them. Ansley says I could wash the dishes—let Andrew take the dogs.

"I'll take them anyway. I'll go with Andrew and wash the dishes when we get back."

Andrew snaps a leash on Tidbit. I give Sawyer a pat. Out we go. We walk and he talks about his friends, his upcoming weekend trip to the beach, the party he'll be missing, how he's decided to go to the beach and not the party in Roland Park. He's resolved that for this weekend he will turn down the opportunity of being the "reckless Andrew of girls and parties and dancing" with his in-town Roland Park friends and classmates, and will instead focus on being the "more youthful Andrew of taking it easy and shooting the new pellet gun and watching videos" with his life-long friend and neighbor and fellow country-boy, Jed, who has invited him to the beach. I am happy to hear this. He still has to call the in-town friend to tell him he can't make the party. I ask if he needs any help—if there is anything I can do to get him out of this bind. "No Dad. Don't patronize me. I have it under control."

Patronize him? Where the hell did he get *that* from? It zapped me between the eyes as if it were a pellet shot out of his new gun.

We return and bounce around the house. While the kids and Ansley are in the living room, I pull a parka on top of the jacket I am wearing, slap my leg and motion to Sawyer that I'm going outside again. We sneak out the door and head at a brisk pace up the hill, past the dormitories, past the barns, down to the tennis courts and out onto the soccer field.

A weight has descended on me. I have gone from the ecstasy and laughter of drinking the bottle of port Saturday night with Tom and Mimi—Tom would not let me forget that it was a "hundred dollar bottle of port"—after telling Tom to put me on the list of riders for Florida, to this: reality.

What am I doing? How have I gotten into this? Those fences are huge. I will have to be preparing all spring. It will be hanging over me.

On the soccer field, I have a private conversation with the Almighty, ask some questions, and am told, *"Ride!"* But I still am not absolutely positive. Under the influence of my EFM class, I whisper, "Show me a sign." I stare up into the sky, knowing there will be no sign, and at that split second, a bright, astonishingly fast-moving shooting star arcs, like a liquid bullet, through the firmament.

CHAPTER 16

Doing Light

At almost five feet, the sixteenth fence is the biggest on the course. Horses jump it well, but those that are exhausted collapse over it. They don't have spectacular falls. They gallop slowly up the hill; the jockey half-heartedly rides them into the fence; up they go, hit the top rail, and fall in a pile of legs and neck and torso and tail on the other side, lying there, breathing heavily, too fatigued to move for a few seconds as the rider disengages himself from the stirrups and reins, jumps up, brushes himself off and lives to ride another day. But for the horses that still have some zip left, the sixteenth sets up just right. "Look Young-Blood, you do this the same as with the sixth, only here you don't have to cut the turn as sharp," Mikey says standing by the pylon where you begin to turn to the left. "I like this sort of fence, horses jump a fence better, don't you think, when you come around a turn, and, bam, there it is. You're not staring at it for the longest time, watching it get bigger and bigger." We are walking up an incline, turning to the left. "Now some riders are a little careful going into this one. Their horses get in close, hit the top rail and down they go." He grabs the top rail of the first panel, the highest panel, just to the right of the red flag. "If you gallop on into it, and jump this panel, you can gain a few lengths on the field." We climb up and sit on the top rail of the highest panel of the sixteenth, envisioning the straightest path possible over the seventeenth, eighteenth and nineteenth.

～

THE NEXT DAY at work we had a long-range planning session, a "retreat," off campus. I was distracted, nervous. Drank too much coffee. Sweating, needing to take a leak every thirty minutes. Stuck. Felt claustrophobic. Had experienced more freedom in jail cells into which I'd been tossed during my teenage years. Sitting around a large table, we spent hours writing lists of schedules and deadlines, as we did every year, that no one ever paid any attention to. We began reviewing my publications. We were five miles from the campus and my class began at 12:40. We sprinted through my plans, everybody adding plenty of ideas and projects to an already overflowing list.

At 12:15 I stood up. Announced I had to leave. Stretched it, said my class had already begun. Still, the director would not give me the go ahead. She wanted me there when we reviewed the plans for the upcoming website.

She eyed me ever so seriously. "You really need to be here."

The other four directors stared at me.

The seconds ticked by as color-coded purple, red and green sheets of website material were passed around. I could sense the unbounding energy of my students as, bustling into the classroom, they laughed and bumped into one another and argued over chairs. I could hear and picture them starting to raise holy hell, the space behind my big wooden desk empty. One boy would be at the blackboard, drawing who knows what— but something these directors certainly didn't want to see. Another would have flung the huge window open, have one leg hanging halfway out the three-story window, and would be stiff-arming a smaller classmate with one hand while dangling his books out the window with the other, threatening to drop them unless the smaller boy performed some humiliating task. I stood up from the dining room table. The director passed out the final sheet of paper—the two-year website timetable containing more deadlines, ones that could never be met. Standing there, knowing I was doing the right thing by my school, my alma mater, I stated, "I'm sorry," they were all looking up at me, "but I have to go to my class."

And then, I was out of there. I was Henry Miller in *Tropic of Cancer* when he escapes Serge, the Russian: "When we get to the Place Péreire I jump out. No particular reason for getting off here. No particular reason for anything. I'm free—that's the main thing.

"Light as a bird I flit about from one quarter to another. It's as though I had been released from prison. I look at the world with new eyes. Everything interests me profoundly. Even trifles."

Sunny, blue sky, warm February day. I escape from the retreat. Drive to school. We have a spectacularly inspiring, fun, rollicking class on "Macbeth." After class, I walk slowly, meditatively, down the stairs, one flight, two flights, three flights—outside. to the car, get in, and away I drive— "Free . . . Light as a bird . . ."

AT HOME, I CHANGE clothes, help Sawyer up onto the seat of the pickup and hop in. Sawyer sets his jaw on my leg. He is tentative, not sure if this is allowed. I crank the engine, look down at Sawyer. His eyes are looking directly into mine. He wants to be closer. I reach over, pull him up against me. His brawny, fur-protected body is warm and I feel drool escape his lips and dampen my blue jeans. I pop the clutch and off we go.

On arriving at Mom's, I walk up to the paddock where Warfield and Chim Chim are standing by the gate. Looking down at the ground, I approach Warfield from an angle on the near side, quietly place my hand on his rump, run it up his spine.

Mom comes out of the house in a long, light-blue down overcoat. Deciding to ride Chim Chim so I can talk to Mom, I lead Warfield into a stall, return outside, and chase Chim Chim until I trap him in a corner. Soon, I'm jogging and cantering him around the paddock as we talk. I'm determined to get him ready for Eliza. Absolutely *will* get him ready for Eliza. Whatever it takes.

Then, I'm getting Warfield ready. Since Mom's first point of observation when I hop on Warfield is always how his mane looks—she has been working on getting his mane, which is thick and golden, to lay over on the correct side, the "far side," or right side, of his neck, ever since she bought him—I am diligent in brushing out his mane until every strand is lying perfectly on the correct side and there is not one knot or burr or clump of dirt in it. All the while I'm listening to Mom, the light blue of her coat accentuating the fierce dark blue of her eyes. Outside, I open the gate. Mom is going on about President Clinton and his sex life and the disgracefulness of his behavior and the behavior of all liberals in general and in fact of my whole permissive socialistic let-the-kids-do-whatever-they-want generation. She's relentless. I try not to take the bait. Finally, I can't stand it any longer. I disagree on a point or two and she heats up. She's done her homework. She's been watching CNN and she reads all the conservative columnists through the Internet—often e-mailing me the ones that strike hardest at Clinton. I try to turn it into a joke and, pushing it to the absurd, make an outlandish comment about the sexual habits of Republicans. She takes it seriously. Oh, Lord, I'll hear about this later. But I am about to make another escape. I close the gate behind me and hop up on Warfield. Mom leans on the fence, continuing the argument. I say something about Republicans being jealous of Clinton's sex life and multi-tasking abilities. Stoking the fires, jabbing the embers, laughing, I spur Warfield in the sides and away we go.

Down the tractor path between the cornfield and soybean field, along the edge of the woods with the sun at an angle but still bright over my left shoulder. Trot into the big log, jump it just right, canter back out over the log, jump it gracefully. Canter up to the road, over the inset. Cross the road.

Sawyer beside us, golden coat flashing in the slanting rays of sunlight, we jog down over the line of fences and out over the double log with the drop, then down the steep incline. I'm leaning back, having full confidence in Warfield, as, digging in his front toes, and keeping his hind end beneath him, he jogs down toward the creek. The moment the ground flattens he breaks into a canter. We gallop up over a series of new telephone-pole fences alongside the creek, Sawyer dashing in front of us, jumping some and running around others. Then we're standing in the creek, Sawyer splashing and rolling and crouching, panting and looking up at me, the frigid water ruffling and flowing over the long wavy hair of his back. Warfield stretches his neck, lowers his mouth, sniffs, touches his lips to the rippling current but won't drink a drop. We head home.

We're jogging up a hill, a yellow mansion to our right. It has a vast lawn, bordered by a post-and-rail fence. We jog along the spine of the hill, outside the post-and-rail, looking out over a field of winter wheat to the left and down to the wooded creek and valley, then back up to the pastures and yellow outbuildings and nine hundred acres of Atlanta Hall Farm. The rolling lawn is on our right. Stationed like sentries running the length of the post-and-rail are three long, straight rows of hundred-year-old oaks. They have shed their leaves and the leaves have blown off the lawn and over to our side of the fence, piled there like a long snowdrift, providing a swath of soft footing ten yards wide and stretching two hundred yards up the hill.

I loosen my hold on the reins, "drop" Warfield's head, and we canter up the incline. The chill is penetrating the wool of my sweater. We splash through the leaves, Sawyer ahead and then coming alongside us as we pick up speed. Warfield is pulling hard against me. I release him. We're flying. Sawyer is beside us fully stretched out, his golden coat blowing straight back. He's taking long, fast strides and Warfield's head is down, he's going all out, and I'm down low, Warfield's long golden mane blowing in my face. We're sprinting, it feels as if we are all about to lift off the ground as we reach the crest of the hill, and then I stand, catch the wind on my chest and lean back on the reins. We ease up. I laugh and pat Warfield—blowing hard but still pulling at the bit—gently slapping my right hand and then left on his neck. "Way to go buddy, way to go." Sawyer is deliriously circling us, looking up at me, wagging his tail, not paying attention to what he is doing and about to get stepped on. "Good boy Sawyer, that'a boy, that's a good boy," I say, looking down, getting eye contact with him. He settles. I sit up. "That's it for today, boys."

OUT HUNTING the next day, Tom takes the field—he's on Johnny Garland. I'm on Welterweight. We've been out for three hours and we're hunting around Atlanta Hall. The hounds suddenly pick up a scent and we're over a good-sized coop and galloping full-bore across a field. I see Tom on Johnny Garland four horse lengths over to my right and a stride ahead as we approach a big chicken coop going up a hill, right on the Elkridge-Harford race course. I goose Wellie and now we're moving right along and Tom and

I approach the coop and take off together, airing over the coop head-and-head in perfect synchronization, just as we used to do on our ponies, and later, as teenagers, on Mom's horses at the Hunter Trials.

We head in. M.J., not so tall, face flushed from the cold and in enough clothes to go to the North Pole, and Michael, tall, coffee-colored skin and in a slimmer winter outfit, are standing by the barn waiting for us. M.J. gives me a scolding look, taps her foot, her thick red hair shaking. "Thought you'd stopped off at the Manor Tavern on the way home," she jokes, shaking her head at us getting in so late and grabbing the reins as I slide off Wellie. Michael takes Johnny's reins and Tom slides off, slowly, landing carefully so as not to sting his feet.

"What's Florida been up to?" I ask Michael.

"Oh Patrick, Florida has been having a ball," Michael, who is from Trinidad, says, enunciating each word crisply and clearly. "He was out rolling in the field when you all galloped by and he started raising so much hell I had to bring him in."

"Poor Wellie," M.J. says, "Out until dark. He'll have to have a couple of days off after this." She rubs him between his eyes and he nudges her. We wash their legs and underbellies with hot water, rub down their backs, and rub them dry.

I put Wellie in his stall. "What will I do with you?" M.J. jokes, brushing by me. She shakes her head at my forgetfulness, grabs the magnetic blanket outside Wellie's stall, steps into the stall and tosses it on his back. M.J. and Michael rub down their front legs with alcohol and wrap them with bandages. They pack black clay-like mud inside the feet of both horses and then slap a hand-sized page from a racetrack condition book over the mud.

Tom mixes sweet feed, oats, molasses, electrolytes, vitamins, and boiling water in a tub. He stirs the mash with an old scraper. We feed and head up to the house for bowls of steaming kidney pie.

Last week, I drank the bottle of port after announcing that I wanted to ride Florida. This week I have a cold beer. We talk with my godson Sam and then Mimi. We watch last year's Hunt Cup—Tom draws shapes on a piece of paper as we sit at the counter. He points to the scrap of paper. I pull on a pair of Mimi's reading glasses and look at his thick, battered fingertips. His thumbnail is black. His fingernails are lined with dirt and need to be cut. The skin is scraped off the top of one knuckle which is bigger, knobbier than the others. A forefinger points to his sketches, and then to his scribbling after them:

Two vertical lines. Three connecting horizontal lines—"Elkridge-Harford."

Two vertical lines. Four connecting horizontal lines—"Grand National."

Two vertical lines. Five connecting horizontal lines—"Hunt Cup."

That is an accurate summary of the differences between the three races in which Florida Law will be running in April: from three-foot fences, to four-foot fences, to five-foot fences. They also go from a three-mile race, to a three-and-a-half-mile race, to a four-mile race. The Hunt Cup, the finale, is on the last weekend of April.

Monday, I leave my office for lunch, walk to the gym, pull on my sweats and run around Roland Park—out of Gilman, across Stoney Run, up past the cathedral, down to Spring Lake Drive, along the ponds, past the graveyard. (The graveyard is the one and only "common denominator"—a phrase used often during my student years at Gilman—of the terrain of every long run I have ever taken, whether in Baltimore, New York, Paris, London, Dublin, or Eatontown, near Monmouth Park, New Jersey, whether up mountains in New Mexico, through gorges in West Virginia, or along lakes in the Adirondacks, whether in the back fields behind my mother's farm, along the Gunpowder River near Oldfields School, or on golf courses in Florida, North Carolina, and Maryland. The graveyard—it is always there to remind you. "Run," it hisses. "Run, and live this very second, this moment, even though your knee hurts or you have a hangover or your tendonitis is acting up or your side is aching—because in the not-too-distant future, and for a very long time, you will be joining us.") I continue running along the perimeter of the leafy relaxed beauty of the College of Notre Dame, through the heart of Loyola College right as classes have been dismissed, through mobs of students, males and females, long hair and short hair, some laughing and joking, others seriously debating, all energetic, upbeat, exuberant, out of their classes, back to their dorms, free, and what's that? What the hell is that familiar college smell from years ago? Is it the sharp scent of marijuana lingering in the Catholic air? I laugh out loud, exhilarated, as it takes me back to lunchtime at Johns Hopkins circa 1972. I jog down a sidewalk to Stoney Run, passing more students, enter the fresh, water-cooled air of the tree-lined creek and run up a path on the old bed of the Ma and Pa Railroad—the line Mikey and Pop used to take from Hydes to Gilman during the war years—back to school. I love this path. It twists and turns, goes up and down. I pick up speed and sprint over to Gilman. Onto the green grass of the football field where I used to play as a kid. Push-ups. Sit-ups. Stretches.

Take a delightful shower—the water pressure is strong and beats on my back, neck, chest, face.

Step out of the shower, wrap a towel around my waist, walk up to the wrestling locker room, step on the familiar, heavy-duty Toledo scales, wonder if these are the same scales I used as a wrestler, watch as the needle sweeps like the speeded-up minute hand of a clock, time flying, up into the 160s, wavers back and forth, drops below 160, rises back up, and finally settles on 159 and a half. I dance off the scales.

CHAPTER 17

Hunting

Once you get over the sixteenth, every rider will be following his or her plan on how to gallop down over the straightaway of the seventeenth, eighteenth and nineteenth with the horses picking up speed, barreling into the fences head-and-head, some falling, some losing their riders, a loose horse galloping alongside you jumping magnificently.

⁓

TOM AND I HUNT every Saturday. Sometimes Jonathan comes. Sometimes Elizabeth. We have the best season of hunting in our lives. Florida and Wellie are getting fitter and stronger and tougher to handle and we're jumping bigger fences, going for longer runs. One day, I am galloping Florida into a solid board fence that leads to a path in the woods. There is no spacing between the boards. It is like galloping into a wall. Trees are on both sides. Someone has built this fence big and solid and spooky looking. We're on a run. Some horses refuse and run out at the fence. I keep Florida galloping through the melee, into the fence. We are two strides away from taking off when a hound shoots out of the woods and dashes between us and the fence. Any other horse would stop, smack into the hound, crash into the fence, making a horrible noise and sending the rider flying headfirst into a tree on the other side. I sit still and hold my breath. In disbelief, I feel Florida lift off—two strides early—soar over the terrified hound—land on the other side, and continue galloping down the path. All in a day's work. Florida takes care of me. Another day, Jonathan is on a young timber prospect, Iron Fist, Tom is on Johnny and I am on

Wellie. We are having a hell of a run, but are stuck behind a development. Jonathan has been sipping on his flask and has a fall. I wait for him to get back on. Tom isn't pleased and takes off, leaving us. Jonathan and I jump a board fence into a barnyard and jog down a driveway, jump into a plowed field. Everyone is galloping full tilt across this deeply plowed field. I watch the horses labor and struggle through the heavy, deep dirt. "Come on!" Jonathan yells at me, as he heads into the field. I'm not about to gallop Wellie through that and risk straining his tendons. I'm preparing him for one thing, to win the Hunt Cup. "No, this way, this way," I yell back, and we gallop around the field on a thin strip of grass alongside a wire fence. Before us are several acres planted in Christmas trees but never harvested. The hounds go right through. Members of the hunt ride into the thicket, the branches and limbs swishing and slapping across their horses' faces. Jonathan ducks his head and follows them. "Come on! Come on!" he yells. The hounds are baying and people are galloping all around the perimeter of the trees trying to find a path. Dozens of them are ducking down and entering the thicket. The sharp-pointed branches swing into the faces of the horses, dangerously close to their eyes. I hop off Wellie, lead him through the trees, fending off every swinging branch with my left hand and whip, protecting his eyes, as he pushes against me with his shoulder, flings his head back and forth, wanting to get the hell out of the dark, claustrophobic space.

Inevitably, or, as Mom says, "without fail," after an hour run like this, I have to water the wood pile. This presents problems. You are five feet off the ground, one leg on either side of a horse, fifty chatting, excited, wide-awake, hyper-observant riders all around you, and your horse has just galloped four miles cross-country and is so excited he can't even think of standing still—especially if during a lull you try to steal away by yourself, get away from the "field," hop off and relieve yourself.

Florida is the worst. He is so "herd bound" that if you ride him away from Wellie or Johnny or Iron Fist or Sam Sullivan and hop off, he'll behave miserably. If Jonathan is out with us, he'll see me start to steal away from the field. "Need some company?" he'll ask. We'll both jog away, put a hillside or a grove of trees between us and the others. I'll hop off. He'll stand his horse beside mine. Like clockwork.

On one clear and cold day, hunting around the Elkridge-Harford Club, we perform this ritual late in the afternoon after starting the hunt on a peculiarly positive note. At the meet we discover we both watched the same movie the night before, "Tombstone," starring Val Kilmer as Doc Holliday, an erudite Southerner and deadly pistoleer who drinks and gambles his way through bouts of tuberculosis-induced coughing that would incapacitate any other man. In the end, Doc rises heroically, incredibly, from his sick bed, and still feverish, shows up early at the meeting place for a scheduled shoot-out between Johnny Ringo, the evil hired gun, and Wyatt Earp, the exemplar of all good Western values and skills but one—he is not spectacularly fast on the draw. Ringo watches his adversary walk out of the shadows and prepares for certain victory. The target steps into the sunlight. It is not Earp.

A confident Doc Holliday grins, "I'm your Huckleberry."

We love this scene. Jonathan identifies with the hard-drinking, daring, willing-to-risk-all gunslinger who breaks the rules but is a loyal friend who will save your life at any moment and who is planning to die with his boots on, which is exactly how Jonathan, tragically, will go in just a year or two. From time to time, during the early part of the hunt, Jonathan rides up alongside me, looks me in the eye and blurts out, "I'm your Huckleberry."

Late in the day, the wind picking up, my body worn down, the cold piercing my wool hunting coat, I am ready to go in. Jonathan had told Tom he had "things to do" on this day and couldn't stay out late, but Tom—who is impervious to the cold when on a horse—seems to have forgotten. We are staying out, and the sun is going down, and I have given in, have had a few chest-warming slugs of a bourbon-and-port mixture out of Jonathan's flask. After a short run, we ride away from the "field." The second my feet hit the ground, the urge to go wells up so strong inside me I can barely control it. I pull off my right glove and unbutton the front flap to my britches. At that moment, the hounds catch the scent of a fox and take off.

Jonathan starts laughing. The whole field, including Tom on Johnny and Elizabeth on Sam Sullivan, gallops past, eight horse lengths away, Florida stomping and banging against me, as the stream shoots wildly from me. Florida swings around, leaving me on the side where the horses are passing, everyone getting just the view they were looking forward to. Jonathan grabs my reins. I finish. Now Jeff, the huntsman, is blowing his horn, the hounds are baying, the file has reversed and is coming back into the pasture at a gallop. Jonathan hands me the reins. I go to jump on. Florida leaps forward. I try again. He sidesteps away. I look up at Jonathan. Iron Fist is backing into the briars. We both start laughing at the absurdity of the situation, and at that, I have no zip left in the legs. The laughter drains all my kick from me. "Give me your leg," Jonathan yells, Iron Fist thrashing in the brush.

"How the hell . . . ?"

"Just cock your damn leg!"

I cock my damn leg, Jonathan rides up beside me, bends down, grabs my ankle. Both horses break into a jog, my left hand on the mane, my right on the pommel of the saddle, and then we are cantering! Jonathan is laughing, cantering right alongside, holding most of my body weight up by my ankle, and not letting loose. I'm hanging in mid-air between the two horses, looking like something out of the western we'd just seen. "Let loose!" I yell. Jonathan laughs and gives me a fling. I land in the saddle, grab one flapping stirrup, stick my foot in, grab the other stirrup, stick my foot in, gather the reins, and by now we are tearing across the field headed for a post-and-rail with a wave of horses jumping it, a few running out, their riders circling around to give it another try, some hitting the top rail—sounding like shotgun blasts—and one or two suddenly stopping at the moment of take-off, throwing their passengers over. Jonathan is in his race-riding position, down low, back flat, fully concentrated. Out of my peripheral vision, I sense him glancing at me. I know what he is doing: he is Doc Holliday, calling my bluff, waiting for me to stand up in the stirrups, slow Florida, and pull in behind him. But I have full confidence in Florida, and the horses and the sky and the trees and the fence and the speed and the bourbon/port and Florida beneath me—his power, his strength—it is all one, I am part of it, I am not I, I am *we* and we are Florida and Iron Fist and Jonathan and the upcoming fence. Ten strides from the fence, Jonathan grins and calls out, "I'm your Huckleberry!" He steadies Iron Fist, doesn't try to get the best of me, we stand off at the same time, fly over the fence, and land with our forward momentum carrying us up the hill past Tom—who eyes us suspiciously—to the front of the pack.

MANY DAYS, TOM AND I hunt until dark, rub and cool out the horses, go up to the house and have kidney pie. Sometimes, we're so cold and stiff and tired when we get back, Tom breaks open a fresh bottle of port in the tack room, and we take a slug out of the bottle before going outside to finish rubbing the horses. Some hunts, Tom takes the field—he's the Field Master determining where the field of twenty to sixty of us goes, how we follow the hounds—and I love his technique. He keeps us hovering right on the red line of disturbing the hounds' performance, of interrupting their ability to find the scent of the fox and to stay on it. His style is to lead us through the countryside so that we are positioned right behind the hounds where we can watch them work. On a few late afternoons, the field becomes smaller and smaller, until on one occasion, the sun dipping down behind the snowcapped hills, I hop off Wellie to give his back a rest and to stretch my legs. Letting him relax and sniff the hounds, I lead him around the fox's hole as the hounds scramble and wrestle and dig. The fox, which we'd "run to ground," was safely ensconced deep in his den. I watch Geoff, the Huntsman in charge of the hounds, on foot, talking to the hounds, letting them know they have succeeded, patting and congratulating them and pulling a few back that are digging too far into the hole. As Wellie places his forehead in the small of my back, rubs against me and nudges me forward, I glance at Tom in his Pink coat (actually a bright red, Pink being the name of the English tailor who designed the coats, which are worn only by the huntsmen, the masters, and honored members of the hunt), contrasting with the white of Florida's coat, and at the hounds and Jeff and the sun setting and I realize we are it. Tom and I are the entire field. We've been hunting on our own, and have had our own private pack for the last hour. I loosen Wellie's girth, let him take a few deep breaths, lift the saddle, pull it forward onto his withers, tighten the girth, hop back on, and Tom and I follow Geoff and the "Whippers-In" and the pack of hounds back to Atlanta Hall, no one talking, the fields and forests and the snow-swept hilltops turning crimson, the hounds jogging, wagging their tails, sniffing the carcass of something here, picking up a deer bone there, proud of what they've accomplished, the valleys going from scarlet to purple to gray to black, the stars coming out as we pull away from the hounds and walk down the long Atlanta Hall driveway to the barn, the steel hunting shoes of our horses rhythmically clacking on the asphalt.

AFTER A HUNT OVER Christmas vacation, a rider I don't know—he usually hunts with the Green Spring Hounds—jogs up alongside me and introduces himself as a great admirer of Ronnie Maher. He had not only practiced law with Ronnie but had also played polo with him. I ask him questions about Ronnie's law practice and polo playing, hoping to fend off questions about Ronnie's last hunt, but inevitably, he asks me to relate exactly what happened.

Having spent the entire Thanksgiving hunt of the previous year with Ronnie, I'd often been asked to describe that day. Every time I told the story, I liked telling it less. It was as if I couldn't do it justice, in the same way that I did not like relating the story of visiting my father in the hospital when I was a fifteen-year-old, after he'd had the fall that left him paralyzed for ten weeks before he began to recuperate.

The Thanksgiving meet was at St. James Church, a mile up Monkton Road from Mom's. The Huntsman, the "whips," and the three Masters of Foxhounds, all in their "Pink" coats, stood with the hounds in the middle of the show ring below the church. Members of "the field" dressed in black coats, white britches and black boots walked around and around the ring. Hundreds of spectators waited outside the ring, watching us, drinking out of the backs of their cars, waving and talking to us. It was like being in the paddock before a race. The rector stood on the hill above us in his flowing robes, speaking into a microphone hooked up to two raspy speakers. Our horses stood still for this primordial rite. Facing the rector, relaxed in our saddles, we held our hats in our hands. He blessed the hounds. Then, we were out of the ring, released.

I was on Mickey Free, whom I knew extremely well. I had galloped Mickey when he was a racehorse. I had schooled him over hurdles the day before he won the A. P. Smithwick Memorial in a stunning finish. He was getting a touch of age on him but was a real character and a wonderful mover. If you rode him strongly, he was a great jumper. Being an old hurdle horse, he was never bothered by what others were doing. You could gallop into a fence with people falling and stopping and hollering all around you and he'd keep his eye on the spot where you pointed him, gallop into the fence straight as an arrow, and fly over it.

The hounds caught the scent and we had a half-hour run, galloping through woods and fields, and then there I was on Mickey, jogging up alongside Ronnie, and the whole field of steaming horses was walking along the edge of the woods behind Mom's. I knew Ronnie like an uncle. He had driven me to school every morning from fourth to ninth grade, and had been my parents' lawyer for years.

Ronnie was tall, thin and had a "nice seat" on a horse. His back was ramrod straight and he looked well balanced but on this day during the run, when Ronnie had to pull hard on the reins as we slowed to cross a stream or came to a sudden halt in the woods, I noticed he was leaning to the left. Ronnie was over seventy. He had some crazy-looking sign, "Pass on Right," sewn with red thread into the back of his coat. For years I'd thought it was a joke. I asked him about it; he explained he wore it because his horse was blind in his left eye. I asked if he'd ever read Henry Taylor's "Riding a One-Eyed Horse." He hadn't and I told him I'd drop off a copy of the poem at his house. I could remember two lines that had stayed with me: "Your legs will tell him not to be afraid / if you learn never to lie . . ." I had thought about that line—not lying to the horse. It was just right.

The poem continues:

> *Do not forget*
> *to turn his head and let what comes come seen:*
> *he will jump the fences he has to if you swing*
> *toward them from the side that he can see*
> *and hold his good eye straight . . .*

We walked and talked and laughed and joked. This was a man who had picked me up in a black Volkswagen Beetle with no heater every morning for six years and driven me to Gilman and his son and two daughters to a Catholic school nearby. We'd had wild raucous drives, taking shortcuts, racing other car pools, using our small car (it was one of the first VWs off the boat) to our advantage, beating the competition—Christmases, Igleharts, Constables, Secors, Vosses, Smalls. After his children had unloaded, we'd have serious conversations: I asked what he did as a lawyer; he asked what I was studying at Gilman.

The field of foxhunters went over a trappy board panel into the back field beside Mom's, down along a creek, through a woods, over our first chicken coop—a small jump made by connecting the tops of two panels of boards and spreading out the bottoms, forming what looks like a gabled "coop" for chickens. We jogged though a paddock, out over another coop and onto the Manor Road. Riding alongside Ronnie, three rituals from past hunts of four decades came to mind:

First, after a run, if you cantered up to Ronnie, he would offer you a throat-clearing, forehead-popping sip out of his flask. His horse would be jigging, stamping his feet, yours would be sidling back and forth, and you'd both navigate the two ships so they were bumping together and you could pass the rescue-flask from one to the other. A blend of Irish whiskey and port.

Second—later in the day, he'd pull a sandwich wrapped in wax paper out of the leather case attached to his saddle, unwrap it, and give you half. One hand on the reins to control the horse, the other tightly gripping the sandwich to keep the thick slices of Virginia-baked ham from falling out, the woods and fields and steaming horses swirling around. Nothing ever tasted so good.

Third—at any time during a hunt, if anybody was being the least bit snooty or putting on airs, two minutes of conversation with Ronnie would cure all concerns, purge all recently heard hoity-toity, pathogen-fueled gibes from your mind, and you'd laugh so hard that with one final inhalation you'd feel a stream of energy jet through your nostrils into your brain cells, making it seem as if the top of your head were going to fly off.

We were two veteran members of the cavalry riding along together in a long line of horses headed down the shoulder of Manor Road. Hundreds of people were out; interesting men, women and children, passionate about hunting, most of them having come around the last ten or fifteen years. I could go back forty and Ronnie sixty; we made up a century of hunting. When we were out together we jumped head-and-head. We'd coast gradually into a fence side-by-side, steady our horses, keep them parallel and going the same speed, and then jump it as a team.

As we walked down the road and leaned back, pulling on the reins, Ronnie was not putting any weight on his right foot. I asked why and he informed me that he had broken his foot late in the summer playing polo. He'd been waiting all fall for it to heal but just had to get out on this day of the Thanksgiving Hunt. He had calculated the exact number of potential hunts he had left (and gave me that precise number) before he turned eighty—which was when he planned to give it up—and he wanted to get as many of them in as possible. Then we got into polo: the summer before he had traveled to California, played in half a dozen matches. Amazed and impressed at how he pursued his passions, I peppered him with questions. He was still working full time as a lawyer. "Have to, to be able to afford the hunting and the polo," he said, laughing.

The road steepened. We leaned back in our saddles. Mickey had shoes on all four, and "knuckles" of borium, which grabbed into the asphalt, welded onto each shoe. The road wound down a hill, angling to the left, and at the bottom turned to the right, crossing a concrete bridge, the length of two cars. This is the bridge my father and I were crossing on the way back from work at the racing farm in Hydes when he'd told me, "I'll ride my last race the day you ride your first."

On the left, leading into a big field before you got to the bridge, was a chicken coop. Pulled over on the shoulder, between the coop and the bridge were four cars—hunt followers, car-driving "hill toppers." The hill toppers had stepped out and were crowding the coop to watch as the horses clattered off the road, took three strides and jumped into the field. The riders of the first horses walked and jigged all the way down the road to a spot where you could turn and get straight at the coop. As the horses behind saw where we were going, more and more of them were slipping and sliding off the road early, and to the left, taking the shortest route to the coop. The horses' bodies were going to the left while the riders pulled on the right rein, forcing their heads to the right, where the horses' eyes were already directed. Upon reaching the grass, most horses directed their eyes to the upcoming coop, took three strides, and scooted over the coop on an angle. "Want to jump it head-and-head?" I hear myself ask with confidence, sitting easy on Mickey.

"Might as well," Ronnie replied.

He was on my left, just off Mickey's shoulder as we jigged down the road, off the road onto the grass. Mickey was giving the gaggle of cars and people a look and spooking away from them in a way I wouldn't have predicted, going to the left. I had to give him a slap with the stick, poke him with my left spur, and let Ronnie fend for himself. Ronnie was no longer alongside; I had drifted over so that I was headed for the middle of the coop, not the right-hand side. There was still room on my left for Ronnie to jump and as Mickey stood off and jumped the coop in show-ring form, I thought Ronnie was behind me and in good shape. Mickey and I landed, and I focused on what was straight ahead. We had built up some speed and had to lace through the horses and riders milling around too close to the coop.

I heard a loud and yet, somehow, muffled yell-grunt. I turned and saw Ronnie's horse galloping off, reins over its head, stirrups flapping. Ronnie was crumpled up, face-down, in the slick, cold mud. I stared: Move Ronnie, move. You can move, you can move. Please move, Ronnie.

I focused on catching his horse. Up and down a hill I galloped, finally trapping him in a corner. Once I had the reins, I rode around trying to settle the horse. One of the foxhunters, a doctor, dismounted, administered CPR and stuck a tube down Ronnie's throat.

Cold, I was getting cold. The damp cold was penetrating my wool-lined hunting coat, my Irish long johns, my father's leather boots. My body was becoming numb. Someone, Carol Fenwick, rode up and looked at me, "Are you all right Patrick? Are you all right? You look terrible." I felt as if all the blood had drained out of my face and I was white as a sheet.

The "field" galloped off. I walked the horse to the top of a hill and circled. I circled and waited. The helicopter arrived, flew Ronnie to Shock Trauma. Sick to my stomach, I prepared to hack back to Ronnie's house, and put the horse away, but then decided to leave the horse at a closer barn.

After untacking Ronnie's horse and putting him in a stall, I caught up with the hunt. They were continuing. It seemed like something out of the deepest forest of the blackest year of the Dark Ages. Tom and I finally hacked back to Atlanta Hall. He was quiet. I was quiet.

I rushed home, showered, fixed a Scotch on the rocks and hesitated. I was already late to a big family Thanksgiving dinner being hosted by my sister-in-law, Allison, and I had received a lecture from Ansley about being on time. I had been late to other Thanksgiving dinners . . . I fixed another drink, walked outside, got in the car, and headed not for the dinner, but for Baltimore. Once on the highway, feeling the Scotch calming, soothing, blunting the red-hot, fast-firing synapses of my brain cells in that seductively familiar way, I raced to Shock Trauma.

"Yes, I am a member of the family," I told the receptionist, and walked right in to the Critical Care Unit with its many beds and its bustling nurses and doctors and its patients hooked up to tubes and hoses. I took a few steps, and there Ronnie was, his wife Nancy and his daughter Jamie by his side. My eyes went to the crown of metal tubes on his head and I felt a jolt, a blow, as I remembered walking around the pulled curtain in the New York hospital and seeing my father, pale, thin and weak, lying flat on his back, his face pointing up to the ceiling so that he could not see me, and a crown of metal tubes screwed into his skull.

I stepped forward into Ronnie's line of vision. He couldn't talk. He could just barely crack a smile and nod. He looked me in the eyes, nodded yes to my questions. Nancy interpreted his nods. He was saying, "Yes, I am going to fight it!"

I wanted to know what had happened. I wanted to know why he'd had the fall. I wanted to know if I had contributed to his fall. I thought Ronnie might say something about the fall, about what had caused it. But he didn't mention it. What a man. His spirit was incredible. His bravery was amazing. He fought it. He did come home, but six months, eight months later something went wrong and he caught pneumonia. He soon died.

THE SATURDAY MORNING before Christmas, Tom calls to tell me to get to the barn early. There is a joint meet at 11:00 with the Green Spring Hounds and we have to van over for the hunt. He's in a rush and is pleased with the battle plan he's mapped out. Jonathan and I are taking the van over. He's taking his car. We're going to hunt for two hours, then he and Jonathan are going to hop off their horses, hand them to me, jump in the car (he'll change into corduroys, coat and tie while Jonathan drives) and dash the hour and a half down the highway to Laurel Racetrack to run a horse, who should win, in the seventh race. Tom will drive home right after the race. Jonathan will stay, cool the horse out, and return in the back of the van with the horse that's just run, and another one a Laurel trainer is sending the Voss stable to turn into a jumper. Meanwhile, I'll get someone to help me load up the three hunters. I'll drive them back to Atlanta Hall where M.J. and Michael will meet me.

Tom's been working at the barn since 6:00 a.m. At 6:00 p.m., Mimi will be throwing their annual Christmas party to which hundreds will come and will stay late. She's told him he'd better be on time. That's an impossibility. The challenge of such a day gets his adrenalin going.

"Have you done your Christmas shopping?" I ask.

"No," he whispers. "See you at 10:15. Horses will be tacked up." He hesitates. "There's a bottle of port under the seat, not to be touched until after the hunt. Do not tell Jonathan."

The two clubs meet by a series of silos and cattle barns, and the hounds catch a scent the moment we are in the tack. Welterweight is pulling my arms out of their sockets as we gallop up and down steep hills in the woods at breakneck speed. Like a regiment of Confederate cavalry, we form a line of two hundred in the woods, all of us in black knee-high boots, tan or gray britches, thick, black long-tailed wool hunting coats, and either hunting caps or racing helmets with black caps pulled over them. Just a few riders—the Huntsman, the Field Master, the Masters—are in Pink coats.

The horses in front tear down a steep path, splash through a rock-strewn stream and gallop up another hill, only to pile up on top of one another, coming to a rear-end banging stop at the top of the hill. I am taking care of Welter. I slow him going down the hill, make him walk through the stream, and let him canter up the hill.

Reddy Finney, the past headmaster of Gilman School, the man on whom I'd spent the most time and thought and energy while editing and writing the history of Gilman, is directly behind me on a former Hunt Cup winner, Ivory Poacher. Reddy's body is more streamlined than when he had been an All-American football and lacrosse player in the same academic year at Princeton, the only athlete in the history of American college sports to pull off such a feat—with the one exception of the great running back, Jim Brown. Reddy is forty pounds lighter than when he was knocking opponents off the field, but his body still exudes a rawboned strength, not the type you usually see seated on a horse. It starts at that thick neck and continues down his erect torso, his veiny arms to his big-boned hands, and into his steely legs.

At the top of the hill, we slow to a walk. Right behind me, Reddy speaks in a whisper, asking if I've gotten his letter. Yes, I have. It is about a factual error in a piece about the history of the school that had appeared in the centennial issue of the school magazine. Stopping and starting, we talk about Gilman and horses and hunting; he thanks me in his low voice for slowing while going down the hills and through the creeks.

Meanwhile, I have my hands full keeping Welterweight in control. A tall, athletic bay, he is exceedingly quick. He doesn't like you to take hold of his mouth—you ride him on the yoke. Holding the reins with both hands, you grip the yoke, the leather strap encircling his lower neck, with two fingers of your right hand. You try to control his forward surging by leaning back on this leather strap. Going into a fence, out hunting—where you're often waiting for those in front to jump—Welter will put his head up high, "in your lap," if you so much as touch his mouth, and he also might start going sideways. So you ride him into the fences standing in your stirrups, a couple of fingers through the yoke, steering him with a light touch toward the correct panel, and not slowing.

All has been going well. I am behind Tom, on Florida Law, and Jonathan, on Ironfist (it would not be long before the two would team up to win the Virginia Gold Cup, making it look so easy). We are scrambling/cantering up a steep path, erosion having ripped a scar right down the middle of it, and the scar having filled with leaves and rocks so that the horses are slipping and sliding and straining. A sapling is down to the left and a bare limb, its end jagged and pointed, is projecting into our path. Each rider is walking his horse into the limb, bending it forward, and then, once past, catapulting it—the pointed end scraping across the horse's neck, shoulder, the rider's leg, the horse's rib cage, rump—into the oncoming horse and rider. I don't want Welterweight getting mixed up in this trap, and I don't see how each rider out of the long line behind us can safely get past. I slide off Welterweight. Holding the reins with my right hand while Welter jigs and dances around, I grab the limb and pull it toward me, trying to break it but it is too green and strong. I grip it as tightly as I can, lean into it with all my weight, and wedge it behind a stump.

Hundreds of riders are piling up behind me and the horses in front have taken off. I put my hands on the pommel of the saddle, leap-pull myself onto Wellie.

We gallop through the woods, Welter not paying any attention to where he's going. He stretches his neck way out and thrusts his head down low. I'm forced to let the reins slide through my fingers. As we pick up speed, I reel him back in, taking a hold of his mouth, and he snaps his head back creating a slackness in the reins. I shorten my hold on the reins to take up the slack and he lunges again, thrusting his head forward and down and low, pulling the reins through my fingers.

Coming around a turn in the woods, we crest a hill and hesitate at its peak. I look down the steep slope, not unlike the way you analyze an up-coming slalom course. Reddy is right behind me. Twenty yards down is a large log lying diagonally across a seldom-used path. It is overgrown with maple tree shoots and tentacles of multiflora rose and continues for forty yards to the bottom of the hill where it meets a path washed out by erosion. The path jackknifes to the right and rips up into another hill. The horses ahead are leaning back on their haunches, scrambling down, and then we are on our way down. I'm leaning back, my feet braced out in front of me, the reins sliding through my fingers—how the hell can I jump something when I'm leaning so far back before taking off? We're skidding and shuffling down through the loose leaves and sticks and through the saplings and brambles and thorns and Welter is going faster and I'm leaning back farther and Welter takes off three strides away from this damn log. He stands way off and we're in the air, flying, picking up speed. His head low, the reins slide all the way through my fingers, my left hand whips back and I am barely grasping the reins with the tips of the fingers of my right. I'm gripping the reins at the buckle and my feet are up around Welter's shoulders as we land. I get both hands on the reins and Welter has no thought of slowing down. We skid and gallop full tilt down this hill, my back banging against his rump. I attempt to steer Welter to the right, following the old path, while the centrifugal force is pulling my body out of the saddle and farther and farther to the left. I'm almost off . . . , almost off . . . , my torso swinging out to the left, my legs gripping tightly, but at the bottom I regain my balance, pull myself back onto the center of Wellie's back, gather up the reins, and we head up into the deeply eroded path.

I turn back to see Reddy barreling down the hill and starting to turn to the right. His right hand is gripping the yoke tightly and he looks as if he is secure. Ivory leans in, starting to make the sharp right turn, and Reddy's body is pulled more and more to his left. Then, snap, something breaks. Reddy looks as if he's been released, jettisoned, as he flies off to the left of Ivory, who immediately stops. "Reddy's had a fall!" I yell. "Reddy's had a fall!" I hesitate for a split second—what to do?—then turn around and gallop back down the path, pull up at Reddy's side and hop off. "Go on, go on, I'll be all right," Reddy calls to me. His helmet is all cockeyed. He has so many leaves sticking to his coat, they look like they were glued on for camouflage. The yoke of the martingale is broken, the straps hanging down between Ivory's legs. "The martingale's broken," he says in a doomed and disappointed tone I have never heard from him before.

I hop off Welterweight, throw the reins over his head, loop them through my left arm. "It's all right," I say, untangling the leather straps of the yoke beneath Ivory's legs, tying them in a square knot. Wellie leaps and jigs and pulls against me. We are creating an incredible bottleneck. Horses are scrambling down the hill and banging up against the ones nearest us. "I'll give you a leg up." Reddy Finney, one of the greatest headmasters in the history of independent schools, cocks his leg. I brush some leaves off his back and wonder about his weight. I grab the shank of his leg; it feels as if I am gripping a just-split half-log of hickory. My shoulder bumps his thigh—muscles flexed, ready to spring—and up onto the horse the seventy-year-old man of steel goes, Wellie banging into me. I grab Reddy's foot, put it in the stirrup—the exact way I do Eliza's—turn Wellie away from Ivory, vault into my saddle, and without taking the time to put my feet in the stirrups, fly up the hill at a full gallop.

CHAPTER 18

Into Thin Air

You're running now. You're down low, pushing your horse, squeez-ing him, increasing his speed. You want him to think he's doing this on his own. You're setting up for the nineteenth, the all-important nineteenth, but — no you're not! You must focus on one fence at a time, you must fo-cus on this upcoming fence, the eighteenth. "I've seen a lot of good jump-ers go down at this fence," Mikey says, leaning on the top rail, looking ahead, eyeing the path he would take to the nineteenth. "This may be the first fence in the race where they're pushing themselves beyond what they're normally capable of. Some of the young jocks might start race riding here. You've got to stay away from them. One falls and he could take you down." He starts to climb up the five rails, stops halfway, scans the course — the nineteenth, the water jump, the last fence, the wire. "Re-member, you still have a good three quarters of a mile to go." He climbs up the remaining rails and down on the other side. It begins to drizzle, a chilly drizzle. The long, thick grass soaks up the water. Our feet become wet and heavy. Mikey picks up the pace, his breathing quicker, his limp more pronounced.

～

I AWAKE ALONE. Ansley, Andrew and Eliza have driven to Florida for spring break. My students are on spring break, and I have taken the week off from the Development Office. It is the thirteenth of March.

You really are forty-eight now, I think, lying on my back in the big bed all my myself. *Your father never lived to be forty-eight. You are be-*

yond his age. You are in new territory. Going off into thin air, alone. This is extra, an added blessing. This is the gravy. Your father was gone at this point and here you are with three wonderful children and a beautiful wife and a job and you're riding. Thank you Lord, oh thank you. Thank you Lord for this blessing.

The house feels empty. I rise, fighting off the temptation to let the emptiness invade my soul. I could be in Florida on the beach with my family. Ansley had pulled no punches in criticizing my decision to stay home and ride. I walk the dogs, sip my coffee, pull on my riding boots, shift into gear. Yes, I am forty-eight, alive and well and have three wonderful children and my wife and a job and *I am riding.*

At the barn I keep putting things down and losing them. Spurs. My father's old dime spurs which I love. Whip. Pop's old whip which I love. I am all wound up. I'm forty-eight. I've made it to forty-eight! Beyond Pop's age. It's a new birth, a fresh launching. To be alive is a miracle. I am tingling. Everything my eyes fall upon is shimmering, bright, alive, buzzing with energy.

Finally tacked up, we hack to the club to breeze the horses on Tom's three-quarter mile "gallop." Jonathan has generously lent me the Australian saddle he uses for timber races. A full leather saddle. He's made all his tack available to me. I'm up on Florida—big, gray, powerful, feeling good—heading out the driveway at a trot. Tom is at the head of our posse and jogging fast. I am posting, up and down, up and down, have most of my weight in one stirrup and am trying to lengthen the other—difficult to do in this unfamiliar racing saddle—and I drop my stick, my father's old stick, with which he won hundreds of races. I wonder what the hell I will do now as the posse continues on at a fast and furious trot. Easing his horse into a slow trot, Jonathan hops out of the saddle, lands beside my stick, scoops it up, jogs two steps and vaults back onto his horse. He sticks his toes in both stirrups simultaneously and hands me the stick—without saying a word, without anyone ahead of us knowing—and we continue on without missing a beat.

Soon Jonathan, Todd, Becky, Celeste, Tom and I are jogging down Pocock Road to the club. *Clock, clock, clock, clock*—the shoes go as the horses jig and skid down the asphalt. I hear each step, clearly, perfectly, and the *clock, clock* of the steps, the posting movement in the saddle, the energy of our posse heading down the hill, is all there is, is everything. *Clock, clock, clock, clock.*

I am being given the treatment. Tom is calling me "Lord Smithwick." Spring is here. It feels free not to be wearing a jacket. Thin gloves. Spurs. Stick.

The incline of Pocock Road steepens, and Tom—who has always been able to jog his horse faster than anyone else, and who is not fazed by the most shiny, slippery, slick asphalt, even going downhill with the horse's hooves sliding forward an inch or two upon each foot-planting—finally slows to a walk. We all walk and *clop-clop* down Pocock, talking and joking, past the Elkridge-Harford Clubhouse, past the Alfred J. Smithwick Kennels, named in honor of my grandfather, and then we're cantering back to the woods, and I'm in racing boots and the leather of the boots feels good against the leather of the saddle flaps.

We turn, Jonathan leading Becky and me, and we break off on the only flat part of the course, galloping the quarter-mile back toward the road, with the line of trees and stream on our right, and a steep grassy hill, Tom and Todd at the top of it watching, to our left. We gallop through the bottom, easy, steady, single file, eating up the ground, keeping the orange pylons (which Tom had recently "borrowed" from the county maintenance crew one night on our way back from dinner) to our left, and then there's the sharp turn after the last pylon: swing onto the left lead, turn to the left, and Florida extends his stride galloping up and around the side of the steeply sloping hill that breaks away from us. Florida's big hooves are skidding, shooting out to the right, and the horse's hooves in front of us are catapulting high-flying divots into the air, one slapping me in the eyebrow. I pull down my goggles. We crest the hill and suddenly, as if on a rollercoaster, we're flying down a short, steep slope. We gallop near the post-and-rail where, as a kid, I'd had a fall in a horse show, and Erskine Bedford, the fence judge, had helped me back on. The downward slope flattens and we start up. I empathize with Florida now. I feel him stretch out, lengthen his stride, dig in. He knows this hill. We power through the first steep part, then start turning to the left, and we're going easy, one-two-three, up a gradual rise to where it almost flattens. I relax on Florida, let him relax for one . . . two . . . three seconds. I feel his chest swell—he takes a deep breath, exhales—and then I bow down lower and ask him to run down this last stretch. The three of us pull up, jog and walk down the hill, back to where we started before, turn, and go.

THIS TIME WE GO FASTER through the bottom. Around the last cone—Jonathan is on a little hurdle horse with a lot of zip and he's accelerating. I don't think he'd mind in the least losing us. I keep him in my sights, divots flying and twirling back hitting me in the face, on my goggles. We go up the steep hill that breaks away from us. Jonathan's compact horse is handling this turn perfectly. He's picking up speed, turning to the left, his hooves shooting out to the right. I hold Florida steady. We lose a length or two. Tall and lanky with a long stride, Florida does not excel at sharp turns. Jonathan reaches the peak, and is over it, going downhill and swinging wide. Florida and I reach the peak. I send him hard down the hill and up on the inside of Jonathan, as Tom had instructed. Jonathan, thinking he'd left us behind, looks at me with a startled expression. We're turning to the left most of the way up the hill, so Wellie, the third horse out, has the most ground to cover. He's a head back, not quite up with Jonathan and me, and then as we reach the top of the hill he is with us, "going easy," Becky, with her long red hair flying, sitting against him. I urge Florida on, trying to do so without his knowing I am doing it. The three of us gallop out the last quarter of a mile head-and-head, the horses' noses even.

Off Florida, onto the little gray, Sam Sullivan. Breeze him, going just once, this time with Todd on my outside on Iron Fist.

Back to the barn, up onto another gray at the indoor track. Sir George. A quiet horse. Soon we are cantering around Tom and his car in the big polo field and Becky and I are jumping a hurdle head-and-head. And then we're letting them gallop over three hurdles head-and-head, Jonathan following close behind. I'm pumping Sir George, asking him to jump and he jumps all three well. We gallop back to the first hurdle.

I slow, let Jonathan come up alongside Becky, and then we head into the first of the three, Jonathan and Becky in the lead, with me following as Tom had directed. They take off fast into the first and are speeding into the second. I let them open up too far on us. Sir George gets in all wrong at the second hurdle and dives over it, landing in a heap. The lead horses gain ground. I gather Sir George together—squeeze with my legs, get him back under me, and on the bit—and ride him into the last fence and he jumps it fine. This is the first time I have schooled over hurdles in company in over twenty-five years—since I worked for Bobby and Jill Davis in Camden, South Carolina.

Off and on, throughout the morning, Becky, M.J., Michael, Jonathan and Louis keep asking how old I am. Tom tells them that I am forty-nine (which is what *he'll* be in six months!), to which I reply that I am thirty-eight. Suddenly the number forty-eight itself sounds so high. Out here doing this with Jonathan, twenty-one, and Becky, in her twenties, and Todd, maybe twenty-eight, thirty, and here I am, forty-eight. They are checking me out, eyeing me, measuring me, wondering: can he really do this?

THAT NIGHT, Tom and Mimi have me over for dinner and a birthday cake. As soon as I arrive, Tom walks me into the den, picks up the remote control, points it at the television screen and pushes the ON button. It's a movie on Johnny Francome, the great English steeplechase jockey. We watch Francome ride quietly into fence after fence. He sets his horses from way out. The narrator explains that most riders set their horses three strides from a fence but that Francome sets them six or seven strides out and his horses seem to meet every fence just right. He has the lowest percentage of falls of any English jockey. Mimi steps into the room, gives "Thomas" hell for showing me, the second I arrive, "some horse movie," and tells us to come on to dinner. We finish the movie. There is a method to his madness.

Next morning, I breeze Sir George at the club. Down along the pylons, up the steep hill, and let him run, really run, going up the long stretch. Feels great.

The days blend together. A few mornings later, I'm down at the Lower Barn and get a phone call. Sir George has just died. Jonathan was galloping him around the polo field and he dropped dead. Must've had a heart attack. No one talks about it. A gloom descends on the farm.

Later, riding out on a set with Jonathan, I ask him how he managed to get off before Sir George hit the ground.

"When he started to bobble I just stepped off. It helped that my irons were short." I glance at his legs, his heels practically touching his rear end.

"I'm a professional," he says. "I know what to do."

Oh Lord.

On St. Patrick's Day, I have dinner at Tom and Mimi's. We have Smithwick's Ale, corned beef and cabbage. Tom mentions that he read somewhere that older athletes need to train at least two hours a day, or, depending on the sport, twice as much as younger athletes. This gets in my head. Sounds like a good formula.

The week alone is winding down. After riding all morning, I take a hot bath in Epsom salts, collapse on the bed, fall asleep, arise, dress, make a cup of coffee and take some vitamins and Advil before either schooling Warfield or riding my bike. I have my ups and downs. Suddenly, it's Thursday and I am not near to completing my To Do list, which includes finishing a draft of the book on my father. In fact, I haven't even pulled out the manuscript to give it a look.

One morning, I get on Florida and he isn't sound. Becky is up on Welterweight. We tell Tom Florida isn't sound and he says to go on and breeze him. Becky and I jog out the driveway. With every step he is off in the left front. Instead of a nice even *clock, clock, clock, clock* of his heavy hunting shoes on the asphalt, it's a clock-*click*, clock-*click*, clock-*click*. This worries me and a terrible thought runs through my mind. I entertain the idea that he is unsound, that he will have to pull out of training, that he will not be able to run this spring, and it pleases me. Then I would be out of this entire imbroglio. I'd be free. But it doesn't please me that the thought pleases me. I end up back where I started: I want to ride him in the Hunt Cup. No! I don't want to just "ride him in the Hunt Cup." I want to ride him to victory in the Hunt Cup. I know that this year Welterweight is the horse to beat. I love Welterweight. Everything is in his favor. I want Wellie to win. And yet I want Florida to win. I want both of my hunters to win.

We jog over to "Pocock Hill." We are in a cow field that has one sharp and steep hill, about a half-mile climb. We jog down the hill, circling around for the gallop, break into a canter and when we face the hill, let them go at a good "two-minute lick"—the equivalent of galloping one mile in two minutes. We are going straight into a strong March wind blasting over the top of the hill. We gallop up head-and-head and then ease up at the top. We two-minute-lick up again, jog back down. The third time, we let'em run, flat out, the wind making a deafening noise in our ears, Becky's red hair flying straight out behind her, both horses going great. I manipulate Florida so that we remain even, head-and-head, and I am trying to do this without straining him, without seeming to push him, putting as little pressure as possible on his off-leg, but Wellie has more left at the end. Becky can barely pull him up. Wellie, Wellie, he always has a little more gas, a little more acceleration. The turbo-chargers can be opened up at any time.

Walking back, my head and lungs are cleared out. The gloomy feeling—partially brought on from too much wine the night before—almost a guilty conscience, a feeling of shame to have given in, regressed, come back, yet again, after all these years, this self-doubt, this questioning of why the hell am I back here, on horse after horse, four generations of riders later, all these old memories of years past sweeping through my mind, back here doing something I'd clicked up my heels and said fine-and-dandy and goodbye to a lifetime ago—this gloomy, guilty whipping of myself is wiped out, obliterated. Becky is cheerful and laughing and sweet, and her long red hair is sweeping back and forth across her sharp shoulder blades, and although I am still wearing a turtleneck and sweater, she is in a tight half T-shirt that shows off her belly button, and tight blue jeans, and she is sitting up straight, her back arched. As Welterweight jigs, she bounces around in the saddle, her coccyx exposed to the chilly air. I notice a barely perceptible whirl of fine wispy hair and a bolt of electricity shoots up my spine, igniting me, making me laugh, giving back to me the wildness I feel when I am with my free-spirited friend Hank Slauson, restoring to me the what-the-hell "I'm your Huckleberry" spark of Jonathan. Let's enjoy this moment—the unreality of it, the craziness of it, this riding, this run at the Hunt Cup!

I PUSH IT the rest of the week. Arise early, brew coffee, write in journal. Drive to Atlanta Hall. Ride—eight, nine, ten horses. Am making ten dollars a horse. Return home. Have lunch. Go to Mom's. Ride. Come back. Go for a run with the dogs or a bike ride by myself. Long beautiful bike rides. Sprint. Ride that finish. Back to the house. Push-ups. Sit-ups. Lift weights. Put the weights across my back and get down in a squat position and move up and down, up and down as if riding a finish until thighs are burning, scorching, on fire. Shower. Make a big fire, turn on the CD player, crank up the Celtic music. Have an ale. Play Enya. Have another ale. Eat by the fire. Why not some wine with the dinner? Have lost weight. Liquor hits me fast. Am eating no fat, no salt, no sugar. Listen to the bagpipes. Pull the chair up to the fireplace. Stare into the fire. Listen to the bagpipes rising, rising. Philosophize into the fire. Dream into the fire. Turn up the music. Lie back, close my eyes, let the call to arms of the bagpipes and the release of the harp wash over me. Throw more wood on the fire. At peace. Kitchen a huge mess. Den a mess. Chair pulled up to fire. Sawyer lying beside me. One hand on Sawyer. Tidbit up in my lap. Tiger Lilly jealous, wanting to be in my lap. Working it out: Tidbit across my thighs, Tiger Lilly across my chest, Sawyer by my side. Smothered by animals. Horses all day, dogs and cats all night.

I have finally figured out that my allergy problems made a comeback during Saratoga, the catalyst being the hay, straw, dust, heat and the relentless smoke from cigarettes out at dinner and in bars. Tobacco is my worst allergen. My continued work around horses has exacerbated the condition. I am now on allergy pills. The ear canals are swelling, clogging up, creating pressure. If they get any worse, the doctor says, I'll have to have tubes put in. After being away from shots and pills and steroids for fifteen years, I'm now on steroids. Powerful stuff, the doctor tells me. Watch the mood shifts. It might bring you way up. It might send you way down.

Up in the morning. *Ride*. Feeling limber and as if I can predict every move of the horse. Get on as many of the tough ones as I can. Feet in the stirrups. Irons jacked up. Hands on the reins. The horse is an extension of me. We are one. We gallop up hills, down hills, around turns. Slow for dips. I tighten my legs and squeeze as we canter toward spooky spots. Keep my hands down and settle the high-headed ones. We breeze. Go head-and-head with other horses. School over hurdles. I am used to the hurdles now. We go around and around the indoor track. My hands, a part of the reins, which are a part of the horse's mouth, which is a part of me. Feet, a part of the stirrups, which are a part of the saddle, which is a part of the horse's back, which is a part of me. Could do it blindfolded. Can jog along with all my weight in one stirrup and adjust the holes in the leather of the other stirrup. Can check my girth at a canter. The muscles across my shoulder blades no longer ache from galloping the pullers. My hands and arms feel stronger every day.

I am fit.

PART FOUR

Taking the Leap

"I had to arrive at the brink and then take a leap into the dark."
— Henry Miller

CHAPTER 19

Guardian Angel

The nineteenth is everything. It is here you either have it or you don't. It is here that the highest percentage of falls occur. It is here that you really start to run. You have to push your horse going into this one. It seems impossible that the horse beneath you can jump this fence well, for he has not only galloped three and a half miles at a two-minute lick, he has also propelled his 1,200 pounds plus your 160 over eighteen fences, every one of them bigger than anything anyone with any common sense would jump if out for a ride through the countryside. Nevertheless, you mash down on the accelerator for you know that if you drive him into this fence, holding him together with your hands and legs, he will jump it well. This is the miracle of the Thoroughbred — he can do the impossible. "Now listen, Young-Blood," Mikey says, gaining his breath, standing before the inside panel. Water is dripping off the tip of his cap and his glasses are fogging up. "If you were riding with professionals in this race . . ." He stops and takes another breath. I am starting to worry about the length of time we've been out here, about the three miles Mikey has walked, about this cold drizzle. "Back in your father's day, if he were riding with Riles or Schulhoffer, with Dooley or Joe, with Tommy Walsh or Bobby MacDonald, they'd all know how to approach this fence." He points away from the fence. "They'd swing out as a group." He turns back toward the fence, "and then they'd drop in, jumping it on an angle. It'd look like it'd been rehearsed." He eyes me. "But you have to remember, these are amateurs you're riding with. They're from all over. They haven't ridden together. Some will gallop straight into it. Others might want to angle it. The point is, you don't want to get caught in the middle." He climbs up

on the top rail of the inside panel, the highest panel, and surveys the path
of mowed grass leading downwards in a gradual curve to the twentieth.
Some riders make an effort, on approaching the nineteenth, to jump one
of the smaller panels to our right. "It's best if you jump it right here, on
an angle, and then you'll land headed in the right direction, down the hill,
and not swing way out there to jump it," he points to the right, away from
the course, "like some do, and lose five lengths."

⌒

SATURDAY MORNING, Mom picks me up to drive to the Howard County race meet—a small point-to-point, unimportant in itself, but the first of three for many horses and riders headed for the Hunt Cup. Howard County in late March, skip a weekend, then the Elkridge-Harford races in early April, skip a weekend, then the Grand National in mid-April, and then—although most trainers would like their horses to have a weekend off after the National—just seven days later, on the last weekend of April, the Maryland Hunt Cup.

I haven't been to the Howard County races since I was seventeen. Thirty-one years ago. I can remember winning the Green Spring Old Fashioned and then racing over to Howard County and winning a timber race on a horse trained by the Fenwicks. So easy and natural it was then. I took it all for granted.

I'm riding a flat race, on a horse of Uncle Mikey's. No worries. The sun is out. It's a beautiful, brisk day. Mom and I have a great drive over. We pull in behind a line of vans and trailers.

I ask some of the young riders where the flat race goes. Jonathan and a couple of other professionals are there and they're all joking and kidding. Jonathan is in high spirits. The week before, he'd flown to a hunt meet where a top trainer's jockey took "a spill." Jonathan picked up those three rides and also rode a horse of Tom's. He swept the card, winning on all four. He'd flown home, stayed up late shooting pool, smoking and whatever, and the following day went out and won two more races at a local hunt meet. The turf writers were calling him a "boy wonder." He *is* a boy wonder. And I can't get a straight answer from the boy wonder or anybody else about where the flat race goes. Sebastian Cromwell, cigarette dangling from his lower lip and fedora cocked on his head, is walking the timber course with a group—including girl friends and sycophants. Sebastian has transformed his body, yet again, into that of a jockey's. He has lost the paunch. His skin is stretched tight across his face—no full cheeks—and the bulk has been honed from his shoulders and legs.

The fences seem to be in odd positions. I can't remember the old timber course. Apparently it is now a figure-eight course. I'm not concerned. I walk the flat course, part of it with young Charlie Fenwick—son of the Charlie with whom I used to ride. Charlie helps me out, looks me in the eye when he speaks, answers my questions, points out the eccentricities of the course.

We're in the paddock. The horses are circling. I meet the owners for the first time. They are delighted I am riding the horse and make me feel that they are honored. I get a leg up onto the gray. Mikey is on the pony beside me as we leave the paddock. The announcer sings out the horse's name and then the phrase "trained by D. M. Smithwick and ridden by A. P. Smithwick, Jr." Mikey is grinning. He's in his element. He's up on his pony, holding one of the reins of my horse. I feel good. I feel relaxed.

Back at the van with all the female assistants, Mikey had said the horse would probably get tired. He'd only been galloping for a couple of weeks at Hydes. Before that, in order to not put any pressure on an old bowed tendon, Mikey had him stabled at a farm on the Eastern Shore where he swam every day. Now, away from the women, Mikey points at a timber fence, half a mile from the wire, looks fiercely into my eyes, and states, "Keep him in contention until you get to that fence. When you reach that fence, make your move. *Send him down the hill as hard as he'll go.*"

We break off from the start, and we are moving right along. It is taking all my strength to hold this horse back. I am leaning against him as hard as I can and we're flying down a hill, the timber fences to our left, and then we're cutting sharp to the left and the hill is breaking steeply away from us and I am right on someone's outside. I drop back behind this other horse and we're turning to the left and skidding around the turn, "hugging" the red barrel, the hill steeply breaking away from us, my horse feeling like he could go out from under me. My arms are shot and we are around the turn and heading past the paddock and the steward's stand. We sweep around another turn, completing a figure eight, and we head past the spot where Mikey said to make my move. The other jockeys are pushing and humping on their horses, clods of turf are flying, hitting me in the face, and I'm winded. They are winging it around the sharp turn again, the horses' heels flying out to the right as their bodies lean sharply to the left with the hill breaking away from them and they're pulling away, pulling away from us. I ride, staying low, pushing him hard, up the stretch, hitting him only a few times, feeling that my whipping is synchronized with his gallop.

Drained, I pull up, catch my breath, amazed at how strenuous the race has been, pleased with the overall performance. Mikey appears from nowhere on the pony, grinning, "Good job, good job, nephew. Want to ride another one?"

I'm a little washed out, sitting back, legs loose, "What?"

"Want to ride another race?"

"Sure," is what I hear come out of my mouth.

We ride together back to the paddock. I had thought that the race would be later on in the day. First, I discover it is the next race. Then, I learn that it is a timber race. What have I gotten into? I worry about the fitness of my legs but I stay calm. I hop off the gray, weigh in. Feeling short, as if it takes so many steps to cover any distance, I walk fast, carrying my tack, back to Mikey's van. People are congratulating me. Childhood friend John Bosley, "J.B.," Secor bounces up to me with a huge grin. Broad shoulders, a head shorter than me, beginnings of a belly hanging comfortably over his belt, J.B. carries himself with a hearty assurance, radiating positive energy and a playful, fun-loving, bawdy approach to life. He's in a tweed jacket that fit him perfectly ten years ago, a pair of sixty-year-old tassel loafers he picked up at an estate sale, and an Irish cap that is a bit threadbare at the brim and probably belonged to his uncle, Jackie

Bosley. I stop moving and am still for the first time since I'd gotten on Mikey's horse. "A.P.," J.B. says, "I got to hand it to you. You looked great out there. Great. You brought a touch of class to that group." Others approach and tell me I haven't lost a step. They ask what I'm doing. I tell them I'm riding in the next race, as if this is a normal turn of events for me. I pass by our car, see Mom. She asks. I feel oddly calm. I tell her I am riding Mikey's horse in the timber race. Showing no surprise, she calmly supports me. She knows this is no time to ask a lot of questions or put any doubt in my mind. I can count on Mom.

At the van, Mikey says, "My nephew is riding the horse. Take that tack off and put Patrick's on." The women who work for Mikey are arguing. They're taking some other rider's tack off the horse. It's rider called Jody. Who the hell is Jody—a woman or a man? These girls clearly think Jody is the latest hotshot. Mikey walks away.

The horse is on the van. Off comes a heavy saddle with thick pads and girths. On goes my new three-pound saddle. Feeling light—must've lost a couple of pounds in the flat race—I sit in the shade as they rush around looking for silks, giving me one set which is apparently the wrong one and then exchanging it for another. I have no idea what the timber course is. You go through the central point of the figure eight three or four times. Barrels to go around. Which the hell direction are you headed at the finish? The opposite of the direction in the flat race? There is no time to look at the course. I'll just have to gallop around behind a few horses, let someone else lead the way. The die is cast. I am riding the race. Mikey has been training the horse. He may not be fast and he may not be fit, but one thing is for sure: he will know how to jump.

I walk into the paddock and sit down on the grass against the red snow fence beside Jonathan and Jack, both in their racing boots, britches and silks. I ask Jonathan if he has any chewing gum. He doesn't. Dying of thirst, I find a plastic bottle of water over by the scales, sit back down and take a sip. One of the owners of Florida Law offers me an Altoid. Jonathan snaps, "Don't take that! It's bad luck." I withdraw my hand.

Charlie Fenwick the elder throws me up on the horse. I get "tied on" and we circle around. Mikey is on the pony, leading me out of the paddock again. We are a team. This couldn't be more fun. He's having a ball. I plan to just "hunt around" behind the field. Mikey lets me loose. Not having ridden a Maryland timber race in thirty years, never having been on this horse in my life, not having a clue of where the course goes, and I feel calm. *"Go on with 'em A. P.!"*—that's J.B. Perfect timing. Puts a little fire in my belly. He's my only friend who calls me A.P., going back to the days of our youth when we were riding races and I would be listed as "A. P. Smithwick, Jr." in the program.

There's Irv Naylor, one of my inspirations for being here. He gallops past and yells out, "Does your horse jump straight, Patrick?"

"Yes."

We canter to the start. We are walking our horses up to the third-to-the-last timber fence. This horse is on the bit, leaning hard against me. To get his attention I walk him up to the post-and-rail from the wrong side, so that the fence is leaning into us and looks tougher to jump than it really is. We walk, one, two, three strides, and the horse prepares to take off. Mikey's training. I have to hold him on the ground. This is good. Gives me confidence.

The starter calls us over and we circle. He tells us to prepare to walk up to the tape. Jonathan and another professional rider, J.W., both riding with their irons very short, commence telling the starter how to do his job. Meanwhile, Jack, Irv and a few other riders circle their horses and pay no attention to the ruckus. J.W. and Jonathan inform the starter he should start us by walking us head-to-tail around a circle, then call us in and have us file out to the end of the tape.

They are blabbing away as we approach the tape. The starter pays them no attention, releases the elastic tape and it goes slinging past our horses. Their horses both spook at it, duck out, and they barely hang on. Irv and I are the only ones left up in front. We take off. Irv is ahead going into the first and my horse is pulling like a train. I can't hold one side of him. He stands off at the first fence and surges past Irv. We fly into the second fence which is on the crest of a hill lined with spectators and, goddamn!—

we are moving right along. Long striding. Flying. Headed straight for this board fence. Three and a half feet high. The horse's mouth feels like iron. We approach and I goose him *one . . . two . . . three . . .* and we sail over it, opening up a few more lengths on the pack and now going even faster. We head down a slope, cross through the center of the figure eight, and then *one . . . two . . . three . . .* we hurdle the next fence.

We're accelerating down the hill, turning to the left, and around the turn with the barrels on the inside and the hill breaking away from us, turning, turning, turning and then we're straight, coming up the hill and I don't know which way to go. I aim straight ahead for a barrel in a dip. "To the left Patrick!" someone yells from behind. "To the left Patrick!" It's Jack. And he has saved me.

To the left. Up the hill. Feeling better now. Have more control over him. Can feel all the horses behind me. Over one fence. Over another. Circle around, turning to the right, four or five more fences, over the one in front of the spectators. Am more sure of him now. But just in case, I'm taking a deep seat and a long hold like Pop used to do. Down, around that sharp turn again, leaning in to the left, and up the final steep hill. Now they are coming to us. They're pressing us.

Jack passes me on my right going into the last fence down the backside. He starts drifting over to his left, in front of me, so he can jump the far outside panel to set himself up to then cut to the right around the upcoming extremely sharp turn. "Hey, give me some room!" I yell, as he pulls his horse directly in front of mine, blocking our view of the fence. I sit still. Incredibly, my horse jumps it fine. Now they are all flying by and my horse and I are tiring. My legs don't have any strength left in them. My arms are like lead. I'm blowing. I watch as they ride into the last two fences. Jonathan and J.W. have Irv between them and they are giving him the squeeze. They are bouncing off one another and Irv is pushing and fighting them off. They are whipping and driving over the last fences. I am astonished by the violence of it. There's a loud crack-crashing sound and fragments of a rail twirl through the air. They've taken the top rail out of a panel of the third-to-last fence. I head for it. Actually, they have broken the top two rails, leaving one rail a foot off the ground. I ask my horse to stand off and hurdle this tiny one-foot jump and damn if he doesn't put in another stride, hit the rail, and get discombobulated on landing. The only fence he hasn't jumped well. One foot high.

We jump the last two fine and finish O.K. I ease him up and all the tension rushes out of me. Pull him up to a walk. Thump down into the saddle. Give him a good pat on the neck. It's over. I've done it. First timber race in thirty years and we jumped every full fence like an open jumper in the show ring. I feel united with Pop, at one with my father. Having my wind and my legs back, I nudge the horse with my heels and we trot up to where the riders are dismounting.

Mikey is there beaming.

Walking back to the car everyone is stopping me and telling me how well we did. An older woman, leading two Norwich terriers, is suddenly standing six inches from my face. She explains how it made her cry seeing me ride, it reminded her so much of my father. She starts to cry as she talks to me. J.B. is there—"That a'way A.P. That a'way. You haven't missed a beat. Your timing was right there. Every fence." George Mahoney stops me and stares at me wide-eyed, "Good job Irishman, good job, they'd be plenty proud of you across the pond," and delivers a monologue about an Irish horse he has that he wants to run over timber. I am dying of thirst and still holding my tack and wanting to put it down. George tells me that the horse has won over brush in England and he's offering me a ride on him in the maiden timber race at the Gold Cup, the big race meet the week after the Hunt Cup. Charlie Fenwick the elder rushes past and yells out, "Well done. Well done A.P. You're like Mike Mussina's fastball. Your timing's on and you haven't lost a split second." I bump into the owners of Florida Law, and they are ecstatic and amazed that this old guy, the rider of their horse Florida Law, has done so well. One of them pats me on the shoulder. "You did good. You did good. The horse jumped great." Standing within earshot is Sebastian. He saunters over, frowning, looking down at his feet. "Yeah, but what happened up on the hill at the third from last?" he asks, throwing his cigarette on the ground and stepping on it. "That looked terrible! " He shakes his head, chuckles and walks away, dismissing the whole trip around the course with this one comment.

Finally, I find Mom. "You rode him beautifully, just beautifully," she says.

At the car, I pull off boots and britches, step into khakis. I unzip the chest protector, snatch off the sweaty T-shirt and pull on a dry turtleneck.

On the drive home, Mom and I have a wonderful time talking about the old days, race riding, Pop. Mom tells me how she had the best riding years of her life in her forties when hunting with the Elkridge-Harford.

At home, still on a high, I walk the dogs. Intermittently, uncontrollably, I start crying. I think of Pop and start crying. It will be dark soon. After not knowing the timber course that afternoon, I decide I'll never be that unprepared again. We pile into the pick-up and roar up to Madonna, where the Old Fashioned race will be held the next morning.

We park at the start. Leading Tidbit, and with Sawyer jogging along beside me, I decide to do something crazy; it is dusk and I resolve to walk the entire course, my course. The Old Fashioned is just that, an old-fashioned, cross-country race. There are three checkpoints. Other than that, each rider picks his own route.

The dogs and I take off, walking fast, over the first fence, a chicken coop. I walk toward it, imagining how Florida will stand off and fly over it. We're walking down the hill to the next fence, through a cow field, woods on either side of us, and I am thinking of Pop, thinking how he would have been proud. I am picturing Pop, talking to him, he is there walking along beside me. He is leaning to the left and covering the ground fast and gracefully so that it doesn't look like he is hurrying. We are talking about his grandchildren, his namesake Paddy and his grandson Andrew and his granddaughter Eliza, the cigarette hanging out of his mouth, the tip of it glowing.

The sun is sinking behind the hill and a chill is sliding down into the valley. A blood-red glow streams across the sky, refracting through the strands of cirrostratus, and I am the little human so close to the ground, so small and inconsequential with this huge sky above and the fields and the woods stretching out before me, with the miniature dachshund on a leash and the big, rangy Golden retriever having the time of his life scouting the woods for deer and flopping down in streams. There is not a sign of human habitation. No houses. No cars. No barns. No lights. Just the quiet, the muck, the woods, the trees, the dogs and the sky, vast, powerful, infinite.

I imagine myself at a gallop on Florida with Tom's other horses following behind. Crossing streams, tiptoeing sideways through thick patches of multiflora rose, I carry Tidbit through the tough spots. Houses on hills now, rectangles of light punched through their walls. A stomach ache coming on. Two more miles to go. This is no planned course. You pick your own course. Through barnyards. Over a post-and-rail. On the other side, I pull down my pants and squat—ten yards from where I would be jumping the fence.

It is darker now and colder. We have a difficult time finding a way across a creek. We trudge up and down the thick hedgerow choked with multiflora rose until discovering a narrow path through the thicket to the edge of the creek. Holding Tidbit like a football against my left armpit, I leap to a rock in the middle of the water, land and skid off the rock. Clutching Tidbit tightly, I shoot my right arm out as if stiff-arming a tackler. My free hand punctures the surface of the swift current and goes a foot deep up in freezing water before it strikes a rock, forcing my wrist to snap back toward my arm. Keeping my forward momentum, I step into the river bottom, then up the steep bank. The sun is down. The red glow has gone. No flashlight. My hand throbs. My legs have lost their spring. Only a few stars out. We march on, picking panels to jump, memorizing which way to turn after jumping a fence, what path to take across a field. We climb up a steep hill straight into a herd of sleeping cattle. Sawyer charges into their midst, barking and darting from one to the next. They scramble to their feet and start closing in on us, following us, sniffing us. They are big and black. They become huge as they gain their group nerve and press in on us and we are over a board fence, out of there, free for an instant, then tangled in a mass of multiflora. We come to a halt, the cattle on the other side of the fence walking up, forming a line, and staring at us, the thorns finding their way into my pants, into my jacket, into my hair, across my hands. I cannot move. Trying to keep the thorns away from my face and eyes, I pull one strand of the barbed wire-like vine off at a time, slowly unwinding myself without letting Tidbit get tangled or pricked. On we march. The last fence: I decide to jump it on an angle, and then, I linger, memorizing the exact location of three closely grouped fox holes before us that could break a horse's leg. Finally, we are in the pickup, heater blasting, Tidbit huddled in my lap, Sawyer merrily flapping his tail, smearing mud and cow manure all over the seat.

We stop at a little country store. I march up and down the aisles searching for Epsom salts. The cold has seeped into my bones. My feet are wet and frozen. Hand is swollen, looking like an old-time baseball glove. I'm craving a hot bath.

At home, I make a fire, crank up Celtic music, pour brown frothy ale into a glass. Slosh ice and water into a pot. The kitchen phone rings. It's Sal. She has been praying for me and thinking about me all day. I stick my hand in the ice water, tell her of riding the two races for Mikey, of the walk and the communing with our father.

Sal has gone to a psychic. "He said you are a late bloomer."

"A late bloomer?"

"Yes, a late bloomer, and he said that Pop is your guardian angel."

THE DEEP, SOUL-REACHING Celtic music—the bagpipes along with the rising, going-to-war drums—sends fire through my veins. Thinking how in the morning I would rise, energized and invigorated and ride the hell out of Florida—we would put on a show going around that Old Fashioned—I am about to relax with the dogs and the ale and the pot of ice water by the fire, but first, one call.

I dial Tom.

"Hello."

"Thank you," I say, and wait.

"What for?" he asks, gruffly, yet with a hint of curiosity.

"For schooling the horses over hurdles."

"Yes," he says, voice low.

I tell him about getting the timber ride and that I just wouldn't have been prepared for going that fast if I hadn't been schooling over hurdles all week. And I tell him Sal had just been to a psychic who said I was a late bloomer and that Pop was my guardian angel.

"Guardian angel?" he repeats.

"Yes, she said Pop was my guardian angel."

CHAPTER 20

An Old-Fashioned Day

The twentieth comes up fast. The horses gallop down the hill toward the twentieth faster than they should. They're being run off their feet, the downward slope enabling them to build up speed they wouldn't be able to reach on the flat. You have to let your horse go full blast down this hill if you want to stay in contention. It's a board fence, a black fence made of thick oak boards, the top stiffened with an extra board. "First time I rode in the Hunt Cup, I got all excited and carried away here," Mikey says, leaning on the fence, chuckling. "I made my move too early and fell ass-over-tin-cups. Hit the deck. I was just a kid — didn't know what I was doing. Your father would have known better. I had to learn the hard way." He starts to climb over the fence, hesitates. "They wanted to take me to the hospital. The ambulance was here and they were going to take me, but Mom wouldn't let them. She raised hell with that ambulance crew, took me home and worked the Christian Science on me." He starts to choke up. "I might've had a broken collarbone or a few cracked ribs. There was nothing a doctor could do, but Mom had me healed in no time." He takes his fogged up dime-store reading glasses off, jams them in his jacket pocket, rubs his eyes. Water drips from his nose. He looks up at me, "Remember, you still have half a mile to go."

⤳

SUNDAY MORNING. The Old Fashioned. Florida Law—big, rangy, gray, can jump the moon—I can't wait to get on him, I can feel myself on him. Wellie—lithe, graceful, fine boned. I wish I could ride him too. Well,

263

you can't ride two horses in one race, and anyway, Tom said he called
Mike Elmore, and that Elmore would be there. Wellie would be ready. I'd
been hunting him all winter, and he was definitely ready. Both my boys
were ready for the day. And it would be Florida on the lead.

I eat, feed the dogs, walk the dogs, pull on my hunting clothes. I pop
three Advil, ice my wrist and hand, find an Ace bandage, wrap the wrist,
pull my sleeve down over it. Toss an extra turtleneck and my Irish wool
sweater in the back.

We load the horses onto the van as soon as I reach the barn. Jonathan
is driving and I am in the back with the horses snorting all over me. It reminds me of years ago when I used to travel in vans as a kid. As we pull out
of the driveway, I think of Welterweight and holler to Tom, "Hey, where's
Elmore?"

"Eah—he couldn't make it."

Halfway up the road, the top hatch to the forward compartment above
the cab comes unlatched. The hatch swings out, bangs Iron Fist in the rump,
slides across his rump and bangs into the side of the van, then swings back.
Iron Fist's eyes light up and he starts jumping around. I whoop and holler
above the roar of the engine—Jonathan guns it faster than most of us—and
get Jonathan to slow.

He yells out the window, "What's wrong *now*?"

"The hatch is unlocked and hitting Iron Fist in the ass."

"Well, put it back!" he hollers, as if I hadn't thought of that, and drives
on. I squeeze sideways between Iron Fist and the side of the van, sidestep-
ping forward. Jonathan goes around a turn too fast; Iron Fist loses his
balance and all his weight shifts toward me. I yell a few Jonathan-aimed
epithets I wouldn't want my Gilman students to hear, hold both hands up,
and push against Iron Fist's shoulder and chest. Both hands bend backwards and a howling pain shoots up the tendons of my right hand and arm.
I catch the swinging hatch and snap it to the wall.

On we speed. We arrive at the start. Cars and vans are parked around
the field. Sebastian is smoking in his Jag. He gets out and limps around
with one shoulder hanging down and an arm in a sling. He'd had a fall yes-

terday on his most recent Hunt Cup prospect, in a late race. He jokes about it, says he might've broken a collarbone. I am standing in the van, holding Florida. Jonathan unsnaps the tie-chains to Iron Fist's halter. Sebastian limps up the ramp, cigarette in mouth.

"Hold it, hold on," Jonathan calls out, staring at Sebastian, and making the gesture of raising his hand to his mouth, grabbing a cigarette, and tossing it.

"Okay, okay," Sebastian says, flinging it down on the ramp and stepping on it. He enters the van, kiddingly tries to take the shank, and Florida, from me. He thinks it's funny but I know that his joking betrays his real intent. I push him away, toward the horse he's riding, the young gray, Sam Sullivan. He limps across the floor of the van, grabs Sam's shank with one hand, stands there with his other arm still in a sling. Jonathan unsnaps the tie chains. Sebastian leads the horse down the ramp, tosses his sling in the Jag.

Soon we're circling up on the hill where the pups and I had just been ten hours earlier. A few other riders have latched on to us and not one of them has the slightest idea where the course goes. Tom has told Jonathan and Sebastian to follow me.

There are about twenty of us on this hill and Geoff, the Huntsman, is there. He's the starter. Holding a red flag, he calls us forward. We're a motley group. Jonathan has his irons jacked up as if he's riding on the flat at Belmont Park. Sebastian is sitting back a little farther than usual. Anna McKnight, fifteen years old, looks calm and confident on her pony. We all know that she has found the shortest route and will win. We are walking up and Jonathan begins telling Geoff how to start us. "Why don't you have us all get in a line and file in one behind the other . . ."

"Oh go on, Geoff, don't pay any attention to him. Let's go!" I say. Geoff drops the flag and we're off, galloping into the first fence on top of the hill.

Florida meets it just right and jet-propels an extra foot over it, as he loves to do when he's feeling good and playful. Reaching the peak of our arc, the power of his take-off sends his rump kicking up behind me, soaring even higher. As Mom would say, "He could jump the moon." We land, headed down a steep hill. Sebastian gallops off, following someone else. I turn to the left toward a big log fence, "Come on boys! This way!" Florida is pulling and I can feel the pressure on the tendons in the right wrist. I decide to make this soreness a plus, an advantage: to not rely on the reins but to ride him with my legs, and to think ahead, make this as smooth a trip around a course as Florida has ever had.

We jump the log fence, going steady, in a straight line. We land and I can see Sebastian out of the corner of my eye winging off in one direction, then swinging back toward us. We jog across a road, gallop across a field headed into a big log fence. Sebastian and Jonathan let their horses gallop on, past me. I call them back. I slow, we jump the log fence. Florida has too much momentum built up. We miss making the path on the left. We pass it, pull up, turn around. Sebastian and Jonathan go flying by. I jog back to the entrance of the path in the woods and then down the steep path to the stream. Sebastian and Jonathan, along with a dozen others, pull their horses up, turn around. Florida leaps over the stream and plunges powerfully up the bank. And now we're galloping toward the long line fence, a post-and-rail, the tails of my coat flapping behind me. Old Florida opens up his stride and we fly over the post-and-rail where I'd made the pit stop the night before.

Up along the edge of a tractor path in the field, then along the edge of a clover field—we have had strict orders from Geoff not to gallop across any planted fields. Slow, jump a log fence, cross a creek, trot between two flags where some officials cross us off a list—I miss picking up the poker chips as we used to do—and then we gallop into a full-sized post-and-rail. Some others are cantering down the fence line and jumping a chicken coop. My group hesitates behind me. Sebastian goes off toward the coop and then comes back.

"Come on boys," I sing out, galloping into this big post-and-rail, picking the panel I had climbed over the night before. Florida stands off and sails over it, swishing his tail high. He's having a ball. The tails of my black coat are flying. We are galloping across the flat bottom of an open field now. I hear, "Go on Patrick. Go on Patrick!" and glance up at a group of spectators gathered on the hill. "*Let 'em roll, A.P.!*" one bellows, louder than the rest. That hoarse Bosley voice—it's J.B. I laugh to myself and feel my spirits rise. I bow down, Florida extends his stride and we eat up this ground. Over coops, across rivers, through cow pastures. Entering a marshy area, I pull up to a jig, almost to a walk, my group banging into me from behind, Florida's feet sinking deep into the mush. "Go on, why don't you go on!" Jonathan yells. I'm not going to strain Florida, to endanger his tendons trudging through this deep muck. Also, he hates deep going, doesn't move well in it. I don't say a word and continue trotting through the marsh, Jonathan on my tail. And then we are out of the marsh. I release my hold on Florida, allow him to fully extend his stride, and we take off up a steep hill, the hill I remember well from the night before, leaving Jonathan and the rest half a dozen lengths behind.

Right where I want to go is the same damn herd of cattle that was there the night before, and here I am on the spookiest horse in the barn. Most riders would slow him here, maybe trot through the herd, and Florida would prop and snort and spook and ricochet through the herd like a ball in a pinball machine. Riding as if there is nothing in front of us but a bare hill, I stay down low, squeezing with my legs, keeping Florida on the bit. We maintain our speed. Approaching the herd, Jonathan yells, "Are you crazy! Where the hell are you going?" We blaze through the middle of the herd.

Trot down the road. Through fields, over jumps. It begins to drizzle. Sebastian gallops up alongside, passes me, then has to turn around and come back after he misses a turn. We are nearing the finish. The rain is coming down hard now, making it difficult to see. We splash through the last creek. There are two ways to go. One, straight up a steep hill and over a small post-and-rail at its peak, then sprint on the flat to the finish. I had decided the night before that I did not want to force Florida to strain himself scrambling up this hill. Sebastian and Jonathan have pulled away from us and are pushing their horses up the steep hill, to my left. I go the other way, slightly longer but not as steep. It suits my long-legged, long-backed horse better. He can build up speed that we can carry through to the finish. We gallop along the bottom of the hill, along the creek. When we turn and head uphill, we have plenty of momentum. The chicken coop is coming up. It is on a forty-five degree angle but we're not going to slow and swing out to get straight at it, as you would out hunting. I drive Florida into the coop, crack him on the rump with my whip. We hurdle it without breaking our stride, land moving right along and tear across the ridge, the flags of the finish a quarter of a mile away. Jonathan and Sebastian are fifty yards off to my left, jumping their last fence. We are on converging paths. In seconds, Jonathan is on my left and he is down low and driving, and he is coming closer, and *wham*, he slams into us. He is riding all out as if he is at the track. He hits Iron Fist, once, twice. Florida is a neck ahead and we hold it. I don't hit Florida, I don't over-push him. He knows what the hell he's doing, and he gets the best of Iron Fist at the finish. Sebastian is ten lengths behind us. Florida had jumped great. He had been the master.

Anna McKnight is sitting there, relaxed in the saddle, on her pony, politely waiting for us. She is the winner. I jog Florida away from the crowd, loosen the girth, take both hands off the reins and pat him on both sides of his long, strong neck, "That'a boy Florida, that'a boy."

BACK AT THE BARN, Welterweight is being tacked up. Sleek. Lighter boned than Florida. Built more for speed. Tom has cured whatever the problem was that caused his coat to be dull and listless a month ago. It is now a resonant, deep bay, the color coming from inside as if there were a light within him.

It is Sunday and everybody wants the morning to come to an end. Jonathan is supposed to breeze Welter. The cold rain is coming down. Jonathan, stripped down to T-shirt and britches, is rushing around, rubbing off horses, putting away tack, sweeping the shedrow one minute, hanging a hay net the next, trying to get finished, doing the work of two men, grumbling about still having a horse to go out—especially in the cold rain. I'll ride him, I say. I'll ride him.

Out by my car, I pull off my hunting coat, weighed down with water, and then, all in one clammy clump, my undershirt, turtleneck and vest. I unwrap the bandage. The cold rain beats against my naked torso. The stinging and pinging of the pellets against my skin reinvigorates me. I grab the turtleneck and sweater in the back, pull them on, then the saturated black hunting coat.

The temperature is dropping and the rain is relentless. Jonathan, wearing no hat, pulls Wellie out of the barn, leads him up to me as if I am Eddie Arcaro or Laffit Pincay, or Jonathan's Saratoga mentor, Mike Smith. He has thrown a thin wool blanket over Wellie's back. I lift the blanket and check the tack. It's perfect, exactly how a rider likes it. Jonathan heads Wellie away from the barn, walks him in a big circle and pushes the blanket back behind the stirrups so that it lies across the cantle of the saddle and Wellie's rump. There is a surge of rain, a cloudburst of fat drops. Jonathan's T-shirt is instantly soaked. The rain blasts his bare head, flattens his hair, pours down his face. A funnel of water jets off the end of his nose, a nose that is a little on the large side and that he has told me is part of the package that completes his aristocratic sex appeal, causing chicks to flock to him, something I have seen little evidence of and which must be, I had kidded him, a behind-the-scenes and very quiet flocking of chicks. I approach Wellie. Jonathan continues walking him. I stretch my hands out, grip the mane with the left, the pommel of the saddle with the right.

"Christ, what happened to your hand?" Jonathan asks.

"Banged it up last night," I say, hopping alongside Wellie.

"You going to be able to hold this horse?"

"Yes, yes. I'll be fine."

"I can get on him, right now, just like this," he says.

I look at him in disbelief, standing there, drenched, no hat, in a flimsy T-shirt clinging to the striated muscles of a gymnast.

"Thanks, but I'm ready to go."

Gripping the rein with his left hand, he grabs my upraised foot with his right, flings me up onto Wellie without breaking stride, lets loose of the rein and sets my foot in the stirrup as we pass. "Listen Young-Blood," he says, "when you get back, I'll have some DMSO and Bute set out on the trunk in the tack room. Rub that DMSO on right away, swig down a couple of Butes and you'll be good to go."

I chuckle and point Wellie toward the house. Bute—phenylbutazone tablets—and DMSO (on the bottle is written: "For Industrial Solvent Use Only—Not for Drug Use"), two drugs that worked miracles on swelling and inflammation in horses, and even on humans, but that had been discovered to have serious side effects on humans. I had used them in younger years, but for now, no thanks.

I jack up my stirrups, lean into the rain, and jog up the driveway, past the house, past the indoor track, around the edge of the plowed field, to the big, wide-open, rolling hills of the "polo field," as we call it, polo having been played there for a few seasons back when Tom had taken it up. I had wished I could have ridden Florida *and* Welter in the Old Fashioned. This is close to that wish.

Tom's battered pickup is parked in the middle of the field. I ride over to him; the windows are completely fogged up. He rolls his window down. Smoke billows out; he has a cigarette hanging from his mouth and two Norwich terriers on his lap. They jump up, setting their feet on the window sill, panting and staring at me. Behind them is a chocolate lab and a yellow lab, both bumping up against the terriers, pushing against Tom's right side, attempting to get a better look at whatever is so exciting. The terriers are scrambling, pawing Tom, smearing mud all over him. He pays them no attention, takes another pull from his cigarette, and gives me my orders. I've warmed up jogging the half mile over and feel top-heavy, constrained in all the clothes. I take off my gloves—they are soaked—and stuff them in a back pocket. Tom steps out of the truck. He lifts the wool blanket off Wellie's rump and tosses it in the cab. He holds Wellie while I release both hands from the reins and try to peel off the hunting coat. I fumble around. Tom reaches up, grabs the back of the coat and snatches it off as Wellie jigs away.

There is no one else in sight. No riders. No cars. No owners. No spectators. Just the rolling mountains of black clouds overhead—the sky huge, right out of a Munnings, the lush green grass below, and Tom, Wellie and me. The pellets of rain sting my face and shoot nonstop against the skin over my knuckles, dulling and deadening the feeling in my hands. The wind is picking up.

Fully focused, I jog Welter down to the far corner, pull up to a walk, do a mental check, or rather, a visualization, of our gallop. Then, with a sense of release, with a feeling of saying "so long" to the world of everyday worries and mundane concerns, we jog off a few steps, my hands down low, and break into a canter. I don't touch Wellie's mouth, I stay relaxed and he eases into a gallop.

The feel is different from riding Florida in the Old Fashioned. On Florida, I had my irons down long, only a few holes shorter than foxhunting length. On Wellie, I have my irons up short like a jockey. Welter is smooth, smooth as silk. He moves with no wasted motion. He glides over the ground. He doesn't eat the ground up with long, hungry strides like Florida. He floats over the ground, light, agile. It's just the two of us, Wellie and me, out there, and we are connected, as if by an invisible thread, to Tom's intense, squinting stare.

As usual with Tom, the directions had been complicated and he had been mumbling. It is possible he was chewing a chicklet of Nicoret gum at the same time as smoking the Pall Mall. I had directly, at the risk of annoying him—and at the moment when any other rider would have turned his horse away and headed out—repeated the directions back to him, and then asked, "Right?" Without showing any sign of exasperation or impatience, he had taken the cigarette out of his mouth, flicked it into the grass, and replied in a sigh-whisper, "That's right."

Wellie and I gallop one loop around the outside perimeter of the polo field, three quarters of a mile, up and down hills. My eyes are focused on the dips and rises and changes in the terrain before me, my peripheral vision keeping Tom, now standing in the pouring rain outside his truck, within sight. The thick turf is absorbing the rain. The going is not deep or muddy, but the relentless downdraft of rain is sucking the speed out of it. Wellie has to expend more energy. The pellets beat against my face, sting my eyes. Welter is pulling and the cold rain is numbing my outer palms, but I have a nice grip on the reins and a good long hold that has him relaxed. He tries to put his head up. Feeling the tension in my stomach muscles and triceps, I stay low and force my hands to remain just above his withers. Around we go, Welter's stride long and smooth and easy.

Reaching the bottom of the hill, we've been three-quarters of a mile and I let him pick up speed. Up the hill again. Galloping past the three hurdles, I wish we could be schooling over them, and I think—that's a good sign: wanting, craving, desiring to jump. Welter is relaxed. All his nervousness, flightiness is gone. His head is lower. Up the hill, moving right along now, across the top. Down the long gradual hill, maintaining our pace, the bumps and the dips jarring us. I am keeping a good hold of his head so he won't stumble. The going is getting deeper by the second. He is dropping the bit. The sharpness, the brilliance of his stride is leaving him. We prepare to go up the hill, past the hurdle, one more time.

Before asking him to run, I ease up, as Pop taught me to do when riding a race. On cue, the old pro takes a deep breath. I feel the inhalation, his chest between my legs swelling outward, and then the exhalation. Shortening my hold of the reins and squeezing with my legs, I ease myself down low in the saddle, put my face in his flying mane in order to dodge the pellets blinding my vision, and urge him on. Glancing once to my right to make sure Tom isn't signalling me to slow down, I push him, within what feels comfortable, up the hill. At the peak, the rain gusting at us, I rise up slightly and lean back. He pulls up quickly. It caught him. The breeze caught him just right. After five or six steps, he regains his composure. I take my hands off the reins, give him a strong pat on both sides of the neck.

We jog back to Tom, standing outside the truck. I give a brief report. Tom listens. He holds my coat up, offering it to me for the ride back. Wellie won't stand still. He's rooting, extending his head and neck down and away from me, snatching the reins out of my hands. I turn down the coat and head back toward the barn, holding the reins with my left hand and letting the wind and rain work on my right.

CHAPTER 21

The Elkridge-Harford Races

On landing after the twentieth, you keep riding without any hesitation. You gallop in a pack, each rider maintaining his position, across the mulch on Tufton Avenue, which on weekdays is a heavily traveled rush-hour artery to and from Baltimore. Cars zip along at forty to fifty miles per hour.

"You go straight across this mulch," says Mikey, standing in the middle of Tufton, pointing down at the double yellow line he's standing on. *The drizzle is hitting the asphalt and then ping-bouncing like something out of* Alice in Wonderland. *Thousands of drops are dancing on the asphalt and a line of cars is rounding the nearby turn, picking up speed as they come into the straight-away where we are standing.* "I've seen riders try to turn to the left, crossing here, and the horses have slipped, their feet going right out from under them." *The line of cars now slows, the drivers staring at us. Mikey pays them no attention. One line passes us on one side as another line of cars slows and begins to pass on the other. He stands in the drizzle on the double yellow line, turns, nods to the driver of a car who comes to a complete halt. I brace for a nasty remark from the driver who opens his window all the way — middle-aged, white shirt, red tie, gray suit — leans toward Mikey, staring at him.* "How you doing?" *Mikey asks.* "Fine, fine. Mr. Smithwick?" "Yes." "You won't remember me. I worked for you years ago as a kid. Long hair, pony tail, played in a band — smoking too much pot and going nowhere. You saved my life. This your son?" "My nephew, Patrick." "Well, I wish you both luck. Hope you win it Saturday!" *He speeds off. The car behind him waits as we walk across the road back onto the grass.* "As soon as

273

you cross the mulch," Mikey says, "You pull on that left rein and get lined up. Everybody's going to be bumping and race riding, not paying much attention to this little jump." We stand before a small board fence, about hip height. It leans away from us, over a little stream out in the middle of the field. "This fence looks completely different from anything on the course. Horses will spook at it." He looks me in the eye. "You've got to ride into this fence like your father going into the last fence of a hurdle race. You might crack him with the whip nearing it. You've got to make your horse pay attention to this funny looking thing."

⌒

THE ELKRIDGE-HARFORD races, held on the grounds of Atlanta Hall Farm, are a week after the Old Fashioned. The day before the race, I am nervous at work. What have I gotten into? I have seen Tom look me over a few times. He's thinking.

I gallop two around the polo field, one in the indoor track. After the third horse, Sebastian shows up with his amateur rider friend from England. They parade around the barn area. Sebastian jokes about having lost a million dollars in a business venture with this friend. I dodge them both. Then Sebastian is standing outside the stall door as I tack up Florida. His friend has a video camera and he's interviewing me. Sebastian's standing behind him, asking me all sorts of ridiculous questions—what did I think of this, what did I think of that, was I sure I wanted to gallop full tilt into the third fence, after all, didn't I have a wife and three children, what did my wife think about this, how old was I, you know they say when you hit the ground when you're older it does more damage. I'm trying to be polite, after all I am on camera—I'm trapped—while attempting to not allow his questions and silliness to affect my focus or to invade my thoughts. I dread the possibility of Sebastian and his friend going out with us to gallop. And then I'm up on Florida, Becky is on Welter, we're leaving the barn, we're leaving Sebastian still talking a mile a minute on the ground and I am relieved. We go for a long beautiful gallop over at Andor Farm. We pull up.

I think that's it. The next day—the race, the fences, the speed. My heart pounds. For a split second, I think, what the hell am I doing here? We jog back to Tom in his pickup; we quietly circle the truck as he squints at each of us, studying our horses. I feel his eyes settle on me for a few extra seconds. Then he tells us to pop over a coop leading out of the field, cross the gravel road, pop over the next coop, canter over across the field, jump the "hog fence," let them roll headed for Pocock Hill, jump the log fence going into the field, gallop in hand up Pocock Hill, then ease them up and jump out over the big coop near the top entrance to the farm. I never would have dreamed of having the horses do all that the day before the race. We do it, and it is just what Florida and I need. I needed to school Florida one more time. I needed to loosen up. Tom sensed it. Both Florida and Wellie are perfectly prepared.

THE NIGHT BEFORE my first planned timber race in thirty years, I don't sleep well. I think back on an old headline about Pop in the *New York Times*: "Smithwick Frets Before Race." The article was about his sleepwalking.

In the morning, both boys are home (Paddy having gotten in late the night before), Eliza is home, Ansley is home. I feel guilty running off and leaving them. Ansley is grumpy and doesn't want me to leave before the kids wake up. I have to leave. I have to go.

Driving to Tom's, I feel spaced out, tired, nervous, rushed.

Tom has me school a horse over hurdles. I gallop him over the one hurdle three times, each a little faster than the one before, following Jonathan. Jonathan gives me the perfect lead each time, and after jumping, asks, "How was that? Was that fast enough?" He's been doing everything he can to encourage me throughout the morning. I am appreciative, and I am aware that this attention is partly a backlash against Sebastian.

Sebastian is there on a horse of Tom's, joking and making comments but doesn't school. I learn that he has decided not to ride the horse that fell at Howard County (a no-brainer), and thus, that he now has no ride today. Only Jonathan realizes that Tom has me school to loosen me up for the race. Then I hear that Sebastian will ride a horse I'd hoped to ride in an amateur race next weekend. That knocks me back a stride or two. As soon as Sebastian is out of earshot, Jonathan lets loose with a whopper of a diatribe on Sebastian and pronounces that so and so, Roger somebody, an amateur friend of his, an Irish jockey, should ride the horse. No one mentions the possibility of my riding him. Also on my mind is the fact that the overnight—a sheet listing all the horses running, and their riders—had come out a few days earlier, and Tom had not named me on Florida Law in the Elkridge-Harford race. There was just a blank beside Florida's name. Meanwhile, Jonathan had informed me that Sebastian was criticizing my riding and trying to get back the ride on Florida.

After galloping a few more, I want to leave but Tom hands me a damn horse to graze. It's getting later and later. The race is soon. They are putting up the jocks' tent. Setting up the scales. Preparing the paddock, all just yards from where I'm grazing the horse. Jocks are pulling up in their cars and walking the course. Charlie Fenwick is out walking the course with young Charlie. I think back on walking the course with my father. I can't shake loose. This is ridiculous. I want to get the hell out of there, get my head together. Finally I escape. I have just enough time left to rush home, shower, cook and eat some scrambled eggs, get my tack bag and return. Not how I'd planned it.

DRIVING IN TO THE RACES, I buy a program, looking forward to seeing "A. P. Smithwick, Jr." down as the rider of Florida Law. I pull into a line of cars in the finish line field, turn off the engine, open the program, and there it is again. A blank. White space. No name. Just "Florida Law." Every other horse has a rider named beside it. And this at the Elkridge-Harford. In the Elkridge-Harford program. At the point-to-point that Tom completely controls. Is he thinking of taking me off Florida at the last minute? Was Sebastian's bad-mouthing paying off? Or does Tom just not bother to "name" jocks at the point-to-points?

I have to think clearly. I have to control my feelings. That is their business. If the owners and Tom are doing something strange, some funny business, well, then, that's their business. I can do nothing about it. If Sebastian is running around criticizing me, then I have nothing to do with that either. I am the rider. I will get on Florida and ride.

Ansley runs up to me—her eyebrows furrowed, her deep-blue eyes looking directly into mine. Asks me about the program. Looks up into my face and asks. She is angry. She knows I am hurt. I could easily slip into that. I could be there. I choose not to. I tell her I don't know why. I don't know why Tom has done this. And then I focus on the race. I focus on deep breathing. I focus on the here and now. I trust Tom.

Mobs of people. People in the way everywhere! They ask me this, they ask me that, they want to chat. I feel claustrophobic. I just want to get my tack out and be alone. I carry my tack bag into the jocks' tent, set it up in the corner. Other riders come in. Irv Naylor, self-made millionaire, avatar of the American Dream, asks us all how we're doing. He's organized. He's happy. He's excited. Carefree, exhibiting no inhibition whatsoever, he snatches off his pants and boxers, his equipment bouncing all over the place, pulls his shirt off revealing his tough, wrestler's torso, and thrusts his arms into his silks. He reaches into his tack bag and pulls out his tack: the saddle, pads, and yoke are all wrapped up in a perfectly organized package, as neat as can be, ready to be carried to the scales. How does he do that? Snapping the bands of his jockstrap under his legs, he jokes about how he feels like going out and finding a woman at that very moment. Pulling on his boots, he recites a bawdy poem that has a great Kiplingesque range and rhythm to it.

I hide out in the tent, a few people stopping by to say hello. It is a big roomy canvas tent, the scent of the oiled canvas reminding me of my father's old army tent that I used for camping as a kid, and I have a chair to sit on. Oh Lord, Joey Gillet has control of the loudspeaker. His voice echoes over the grounds. He's going "to call" the races and he is talking nonstop.

Finally, it's time to weigh out for the race. No more Ronnie Maher at the scales. Some new foxhunting type dressed up as if he were at Ascot. I take off my helmet and flak jacket. Holding my saddle, pads and girths, I step onto the scales, hoping to hit 165, the weight listed in the program beside every horse in the race. I'm light, might've lost too much. I need two more pounds. I slide two slivers of lead into the pockets of my father's old leather lead pad. Start walking toward the paddock, threading my way through the crowd.

I see Rob and Julie Deford with my goddaughter Lillian and her brother Ben. They are all smiles and full of interest and wishing me good luck. Rob is here, my most non-horsey friend—has come to watch the race. I am flattered. Lillian—how I love her!

I stop to talk to Tom Whedbee and Hilles and my goddaughter Claire and her sister Rosalie. Tom has come to watch the race. He is full of interest. I can feel his intensity, his support, his understanding of what I am going through. Claire—how I love her!

I bump into Reed Huppman, one old friend after another, friends who rarely go to the races but who are here to support me, and I am astonished.

I hang back as Tom and Todd put my tack on Florida. Tom adjusts the yoke. They fuss with the girths. Sebastian arrives in the paddock with his video camera, explaining what's going on to the English friend with whom he lost a million. He starts filming me from a distance, then comes closer. All I am doing is standing there. I can't really wave him away, as I'd like. I ignore him and he finally moves on to another subject.

Florida is tacked up and Michael is leading him around. "Don't beat him up," Tom says. "You won't beat this bunch. You won't beat Welterweight." This is a three-mile race, Wellie's specialty. He's the favorite. Joey Gillet is talking away on the loud speakers, giving the horses, the riders, their past performances.

Tom throws Mike Elmore up on Welter. Florida is acting up. He is jigging and dancing all over the damn place like some three-year-old. I hop on my right leg, the left cocked, alongside Florida as Tom jogs along, grabs my ankle and throws me up. He holds my foot with one hand, the stirrup with the other and slides my foot into the stirrup. We circle once around the perimeter of the snow fence, Michael leading Florida. Michael unsnaps the shank and we are free, free from the crowds, from the loudspeaker.

Some of the riders take off galloping over to the start. I jog and canter over, keeping a good hold of Florida's mouth and keeping my butt low to the saddle for he's being skittish. I am remembering that a couple of years ago here, his rider rode him into the first fence like a bump on a log and Florida refused, stopped dead right before the fence, and the rider had flown up onto his neck, just barely hung on, as the rest of the horses galloped past. This is Florida's back yard; he knows it a little too well.

Tom's the starter. The riders begin telling him how to do his job, how to line them up. I laugh to myself and look forward to what I know will be coming. He tells them to shut the hell up, and gives one of them a description of what he will do with the pole attached to the flag he is holding if that rider so much as opens his mouth again. I am quiet, feel loose and relaxed, totally in the moment. We all move forward. One rider is about to steal the start and it is not looking good for me. I don't like where I am. Tom's eye is on me. He calls us all back. We circle around, file forward, headed up the hill, toward the little hog fence. Tom drops the flag and we're off. I allow the horses to stream ahead of me, positioning myself so there is a horse on either side of me as we approach the hog fence and I'm sitting tight riding him into it. It's just like riding him through the herd of cattle. No problem. We're up and over, and one horse—it's a veteran professional, Arch Kingsley, in the tack—has taken the lead and he's accelerating.

We sail into the second fence. This is the fastest I've headed into a timber fence in thirty years! We meet it just right and we're up and over and we're headed into the stiff double-board fence with the log in front of it by the driveway. I feel a bit of discomfort with this speed as we gallop into this big, solid one, Florida pulling hard, leaning on me. Nearing the fence, I am not certain at this speed what Florida is going to do. It is possible he could try to put in an extra stride. I don't want him to do this. I hold him steady, sit still, keep him going the same speed with his natural extended stride, and he stands off. We soar over it.

We circle around the indoor track, the cow barn, head up a steep hill and then we're flying into a little board fence at the peak of the hill and I still just don't have the rhythm of jumping going this fast. I settle him, hold him together, keep him going the same speed, and he jumps it fine and then we go down a dip and they've opened up on us. The lead horse is twelve lengths ahead, and for a second I wonder just what the hell am I doing out here. Down the dip, up the hill, and over the airy post-and-rail fence.

We head down the long slope behind the paddocks and barns, slow going through a mucky part, turn to the right and head up toward the chicken coup. I have the feel back. Thirty years of rust. It is coming off. I can judge the fences. I feel in control. I ride him into the coop, seeing and feeling exactly where we'll take off and he jumps it great. Up the hill, turning, down the hill, turning to the right, we are circling around Tom's house. Across the driveway, and now we have three in a row, the third up by the paddock, where all the people are standing, and where the finish will be next time around. I have a long hold on the reins and up and over the log fence, up and over the board fence nearing the crowd we go. We are galloping into the post-and-rail. The crowd is lining the snow fence just a couple of feet from where we are headed. I ride Florida into the panel closest to the crowd and I don't let him chip in, put in an extra stride, as I have seen him do for years here, after which people have walked away, shaken their heads, called Florida "chicken," and I have felt like strangling them. I get down and squeeze and give a low hoarse yell and Florida stands off, jets over it without even having to try and I hear the crowd cheer. A deep voice calls out above the others, *"Go on with 'em A.P.!"* and I feel myself grin.

Around the turn we fly. Geoff the Huntsman is ahead of us. We jump the board fence by the driveway and then I ask Florida to "pick it up" going down the hill. I yell at Geoff to give me room and he lets us through on the inside. We're moving. We're reeling 'em in. We jump two more. We're flying down the hill back behind the barn. Irv is in front of us. He doesn't know we're coming and glances at us with a shocked expression. We whip by on his inside, moving now, focusing on the upcoming coop. We hurdle over the chicken coop, gallop up the hill, and then, when we reach the peak and we have half a mile to go, I ask him to run. He starts reeling them in, we're gaining on them.

We are galloping into the last fence and my stick is cocked and just for the pure bliss of it I reach back and crack him as we take off. We're in the air, gaining ground on the others, and I have that feel Pop experienced on jumping the last on King Commander, on Neji, on Crag. We land, fly up the last quarter of a mile, gaining, gaining, gaining on Welter, Welter not gaining on Arch Kingsley in front of him. This is the best Florida has ever run here.

I pull Florida up, turn, canter back. I see Tom over by Welterweight, frowning, down to business, talking to Mike, and then he's running toward me and he is yelling something, he is grinning wildly and he is yelling something to me. This is extremely unusual. Jogging Florida toward Tom, I stand up in the irons and pull Florida up. Tom grabs one of the reins and looks up at me with this huge smile and repeats, "You are sitting on the next winner of the Maryland Hunt Cup! You are sitting on the next winner of the Maryland Hunt Cup!"

Weighing in, I am approached by Johnny Bosley, J.B.'s first cousin, who had ridden Florida in many races. "Patrick," he says slowly and deliberately in the raspy yet languid Bosley cadence he shares with his brother Louis and his cousin J.B., "I've got to hand it to you. He never jumped like that for me. Good job, old-timer." He pats me on the back.

Not bad, I think. Not bad coming from Johnny, but, I brace myself for more.

"You do look like hell," he chuckles, saying it slowly, looking up and down at my physique. "Do you have AIDS or did you just have to lose a lot of weight?" I head for the scales.

Betty Bosley, Johnny's aunt, Pop's great lifelong friend, and one of the best and most natural riders who has ever lived, steps out of the scrum of people surrounding the scales. She is glowing. "He jumped beautifully for you Patrick. I've never seen him jump like that! You could take him to Madison Square Garden."

CHAPTER 22

Heading into the Starting Gate

A cruel hill awaits after you make it over the twenty-first. You're in a valley; you're at the same spot from which you started the race a lifetime ago, and you're headed up the same hill but this time the panels you're jumping are farther to the right, at the hill's peak, and if the others are pulling away from you or if your horse is tired, this hill can seem very long. Mikey puts both hands on the top rail of the water jump, leans into it. He squints up at the last fence. "You've got to watch yourself here, take the shortest route. I used to aim for the inside panel." He takes a deep breath. "I'd jump it right beside the flag." I climb up on the top rail, preparing to hop off the fence and across the stream. Mikey doesn't move. "You go on ahead, Young-Blood. I've been up that hill enough times." The cars are whooshing by on Tufton just a hundred yards away. Yet, there is a different sort of engine sound. A four-wheeler, two people in the front, bumps across the field toward us. Long blonde hair from the driver flies in the breeze. Collarbone length auburn hair flips and hops on the passenger side, and then they are beside us. They have pulled up inches from Mikey, and they're joking and smiling and good looking and young and asking, "Mikey, what are you doing out here in the rain? Who's riding in this Hunt Cup, you or Patrick? Come on Mikey, get in here with us." Mikey and I are in sweaters and oilskins. They're both in low-cut V-necks that show off a recently acquired, tanning salon glow on their chests. The passenger steps out, helps Mikey into the four-wheeler and then squeezes in beside him. Laughing and joking, "Mikey," they say, "Mikey" they repeat as if they are in love with the sound of his name. He gives me a parting glance, as if he is so helpless, and they zoom off. I vault over the stream, and start up the hill, alone.

Landing after the water jump, you gather your horse together and ride him steadily up this last hill. You do not ride frantically or wildly, for you have to save a little of that horsepower to get over the last fence. Your thighs will be on fire, your lungs exploding and your horse exhausted. Your body and soul will be crying out to stand up, that's enough, you can't take any more, and yet you must keep pushing. The spectators cannot see that your horse is wobbly; he has no coordinated power left. They can't see that he is running on willpower, on heart as you approach the last fence, a solid, four-foot black board fence, and he reaches down deep and takes off.

⌐

WE ROCKET INTO a chute; we are being poured into a funnel; I am speeding toward the Hunt Cup through the Grand National. I must put the Hunt Cup out of my mind. Focus solely on the Grand National. The Grand National races: where I had won my first timber race, the Benjamin Murray Memorial, when I was seventeen, on Moonlore. We had just galloped around, easy as could be, running and jumping, and I had made my move at the road, three fences from home, passed Tom Voss, passed Charlie Fenwick, and went on to win.

Rumors circulate. The latest horse Sebastian has procured to ride in the Hunt Cup is unsound and Tom informs me Sebastian is really down to business, trying to steal my ride. He's fit; he's light; he says this will be his last year, and he's going all out. He even wants to ride some hurdle races—where the weights are lighter. It's hectic at home. At work, the word is out and teachers constantly ask me about the races. One in particular, who had been at the races the day I had the spectacular fall on Moonlore thirty years earlier, makes a point of remarking on my riding prospects every time he passes me. "They say once you're over forty, when you hit the ground it feels like concrete," he says with a big grin as we pass in the hall. "You know your bones break a lot easier once you're nearing fifty," he adds, feigning serious concern, as we walk together into the faculty room. "Hope you don't make your wife a widow next weekend," he whispers, as we walk into the auditorium for the morning meeting with the Upper School. Leaning back in his chair and laughing heartily after we have discussed the schedule for an upcoming visit by Walter Lord, Class of 1935, who, having Parkinson's, I often pushed in a wheelchair, he chuckles and says, "You and Walter. Ha! If that horse of yours takes a wrong step going into the third, you and Walter will make a fine pair wheeling around together. Hell, maybe you can enter the Middle School chariot race."

Schadenfreude is a word I learn and then teach in English class while we are studying the *Odyssey. Joy in another's misfortune.* I have hundreds of friends, colleagues and even people I don't know cheering me on, wishing me luck. I am flabbergasted by their attention and interest. I never foresaw such an outpouring of support. And then, I do have these others. They eye me warily. They keep a distance. "Isn't that a dangerous sport?" they ask. "How's your wife feel about this?" Or, "Is that what Christopher Reeve was doing?" They stare at my newly gaunt frame, look me up and down. "What age are the other riders?" Or, "Is this really something you should be doing at your age?" In other words, they not only think I'm crazy, they are judging me, condemning me for being irresponsible to my wife and children, for risking too much, and I get the feeling that some of them, if things go wrong, will not be uncomfortable knowingly, sagely, shaking their heads and saying to their wives, and perhaps even to me, "I told you so." I get the feeling that a dose of self-righteous schadenfreude would pulsate through their veins.

My schedule is getting to me. I am riding at Tom's in the early morning, rushing home, showering and speeding to work. I am riding in the late afternoons on Warfield—schooling cross-country. I thought I'd get a ride or two at the Manor Races the previous weekend, but I didn't. I didn't even go. Suddenly the Grand National is around the corner. Mikey calls. "Hey Young-Blood, could you ride a horse for me in the Benjamin Murray?" I accept. I get on him the day before the race, pop him over a few tiny jumps. He feels completely different from the afternoon I had hunted him a year earlier. Then, he had pulled. My arms had been exhausted at the end of the day; he had stood off and flown every fence. Now, he feels like a pony. Mikey has been working on his mouth. He'd had a "hard" mouth and Mikey had softened it, and it seems had gotten it too damn soft. Untacking, when Mikey is not beside me, the female assistants tell me: watch out for his jumping. Watch out. I wonder what the hell has happened to this horse who once had felt like one of the best jumpers I'd ever been on!

On the evening after the Grand National, I am due to participate in a special dedication at Gilman and then attend a huge dinner under a tent. All week, I've been organizing a photo shoot of the deep pockets who have given $2 million to the school. I will have to rush from the paddock after the last race, leave the horsey scene, speed home, change, pull on dinner clothes, and drive to Gilman. I am dreading fulfilling this schedule. Monday at 6:30 a.m., I have to be at school to start setting up for the day-long photo shoot.

Our house has been a madhouse—friends calling, friends stopping by. It's been raining, and occasionally I feel doomed. Florida hates the deep going. The night before the Grand National, I drive over to Mom's. She's already in bed. I savor a cold beer by myself in the living room, walk upstairs and get a good night's sleep. In the morning, after galloping at Tom's, I speed back to our house, get my tack ready, bolt out the door to get to the races, and there, trooping toward the house, is a wall of old friends from the Oldfields School side of our lives who have flown in from out of town. The dogs start barking, barking loud, causing the whiplash headache to begin digging at my left temple. I don't have time to talk. I don't have the energy to explain, again, what I am doing. Without breaking stride, I say "Hi," and politely as I can, dodge around this cocktail-imbibing group.

We're in the jocks' tent. I don't know any of the other riders; they talk and banter and smoke and joke. I am left out. The jocks, in their twenties, do not acknowledge my existence. It is as if I am invisible. I feel in shock. As if in a dream. Is this really me, here, in the jocks' tent, needing to get my

tack ready to ride, first in the Grand National, then in the Benjamin Murray, after not having ridden a race here in thirty years?

Irv Naylor ducks his head under the entrance of the tent, surveys the
scene, steps in, finds a good spot to set up. He is filled with exuberance.
Unlike me, he walks up to whomever he doesn't know, shakes the jock's
hand and introduces himself. Laughing and joking, he pulls out his tack,
all perfectly organized, wrapped up in a bundle. I feel more comfortable
with Irv there. We're not close friends, but I have known him since I was
eighteen and Pop trained, and I rode, an ill-named horse—Crunchbird—
for him.

Finally, we're lined up at the start. In the back of my mind I am a little
worried about two fences. The Grand National fences are all normal height
and size, or perhaps a little higher than normal, except for two. Two are big
as hell. They are both on the peaks of hills. And I haven't jumped a fence
that big for a long, long time.

We break off and I ride Florida like I did at the Elkridge-Harford. He
is running and jumping well. I cut one turn very sharp to save ground, as
Mikey had advised me to do. Florida skids and slides and doesn't maneuver it well. We jump a few more. We are falling behind. The horses in front
are flying. Irv is on the lead.

We go down into a boggy area. Florida struggles to get through it. Another sharp turn is coming up. I turn Florida sharp as Mikey had directed
and Florida skids and slides again! I feel terrible for doing this to him. We
go up a hill and we are all by ourselves now. I have dropped too far out of
it and we are headed into this big son-of-a-bitch made of thick posts and
rails on the peak of a hill. I sit there like a muck-sack wondering what the
hell I am doing out there galloping into this fence. Florida gallops into
it and—without my holding him firmly together and encouraging him—
he shortens his stride, gets in close, and hop/twists over it, landing in a
clump, losing ground, jumping the way I had watched him do for years. I
feel ashamed.

We have a few more easy fences, and then there is the one other big
one, and we do better. The lead horses are twelve lengths ahead of us now.

On landing, my mind clears. Feeling a sense of release, I gather myself together. I spit out my chewing gum, drop down lower in the saddle, put the past the hell behind me and start riding. All or nothing. We have found our rhythm. We gain. We gain. Horses are falling all around us. Thick rails of timber make loud gunshot-like cracking sounds and go spinning into the air. Riders roll like bowling balls with flailing stick-like arms and legs across the ground, and horses slide upside down, their legs churning, grasping for the ground, the reins and stirrups whipping and snapping through the air. Florida gallops perfectly straight through the confusion. But I can't get him to ratchet up his speed. It is not like the Elkridge-Harford where he flew at the end. He is used up by my letting him pop awkwardly over the big one, by cutting that one turn too sharp, and by dropping too far out of it. I am on a horse who is giving out, but who is not giving up.

Eight lengths off the lead going into the third-to-last, the hog fence, I am whipping and driving, feeling that I can judge perfectly how to ride Florida into this fence, ask him to lengthen his stride and take off at the right spot. Ahead of me I see a horse go down hard, and another right behind. We continue our same path toward the hog fence. We don't suddenly pull out, change our rhythm, and jump a completely different panel to avoid the fallen horses. This is like galloping through the herd of cattle. Florida jumps it great. He isn't distracted by the scrambling horses. We pass a horse rolling on its back and a rider planted facedown in the turf. The rider is absolutely still. We jump the last two well and finish fourth.

Welter has won. That group is happy and celebrating. Back at the jocks' tent everyone is talking about the falls. I am glad not to have been one of those horses and to have made it around. I need to pull myself together, prepare to ride another race. I am getting my tack ready. Welter has won and they are all celebrating and now this, this is all I needed: Would I ride Florida in the Hunt Cup? What would happen? Sebastian will be like a vulture, like a hyena tearing at this. He'll be knocking me right and left . . .

The jocks are talking about Irv.

"Is he alive?"

"It didn't look like he was breathing . . ."

"He hasn't moved . . ."

He . . . has . . . not . . . moved.

There is no word on whether or not Irv is alive. I fool with my tack, existing in a bubble, getting ready for the next race, trying to focus, yet, in reality, feeling in shock, stunned, as if I had been shot with some strange serum, as if this had to be a nightmare, and soon the lights would click on, a cool breeze would flow in the windows, I would awaken, roll over, touch Ansley's shoulder, and it would be over. But it wasn't over. One young rider, acting self-important and as if he had control of all the horses headed into the hog fence, says it was his fault. Another tells him that is ridiculous. Someone steps into the tent and announces: "Irv is breathing. He's alive. He's just not moving."

I have another race to ride. Standing outside the tent, sliding a sliver of lead into my lead pad, I hear, "That's not what I told you to do."

I know this and feel guilty about it. Ashamed. Tom had wanted me up closer to the pace. I was wrong. Tom continues to talk. I focus on my tack. I slide another sliver of lead into my lead pad.

Mikey doesn't have his silks. I run around and borrow a pair. He has not named me on this horse, Bronze Angle. No one knows I am riding him. As we tack him up, the girls tell me how he hasn't been jumping well, he always chips in, puts in an extra stride. Mikey says not to listen.

Calling on everything I have learned over the spring, I try to get up for this race. Athletes experience this sort of emotional downturn often, and the great ones put the bad, the negative, the embarrassing, the humiliating performance behind them and go full tilt into the next downhill race, horse race, bicycle race, round of boxing, set of tennis, whatever it is.

At the start: Depressing. Quiet. No one is talking. I have never been to a start like this. I have never imagined a start like this.

It is what should have been a beautiful scene, something like Toulouse-Lautrec's *Jockeys* or Degas' *Caballos de carreras*. A dozen horses and jockeys are circling, late afternoon clouds are hovering above, filtered rays of light are beaming down. Lord Alfred J. Munnings could have had his easel set up under the tree by the second fence.

We are awaiting the helicopter.

Irv is still lying there in front of the fence. *He hasn't moved.*

The helicopter arrives. The sound of the whirling blades brings back that horrible cold day Ronnie was taken away after his fall. The helicopter hovers over us. Its pilot spots the waving arms of those circled around Irv, and it darts for the circle. Its engine slows, the heavy blades *thwoop-woop*, *thwoop-woop-woop*, and it touches down, out of our sight. Seconds later, it rises magically, terribly, into the sky and shoots off, angling through the air, rising, and then flattening out and speeding to Shock Trauma. We circle. No one says a word. The starter lines us up. He drops the flag. We are off and running.

Paying too much attention to what the girls said, I let Bronze Angle chip in—get too close to the fence and pop awkwardly over it—a few times early in the race. I try to keep him up with the pace. Toward the end, I make myself forget what the girls had told me and we are running and jumping. Again, horses are falling all over the place. We lace through them. I ride over the last three fences as though my life depends on it, whipping and driving and not letting up for a second, but we have too much ground to make up and finish back, fourth again. I am secretly pleased with myself for getting both horses through the melee of crashing timber and flying jockeys and rolling horses but I get no credit for this, and I feel down.

Ansley and I have to get in the car, head home to shower, dress in dinner clothes and rush to Gilman while Irv is fighting for his life at Shock Trauma. Ansley is not pleased that on this night we have yet another Gilman School function to attend. She is in no mood to make me feel any better. She has nothing positive to say about the races. She is horrified and shocked by what has happened to Irv, and she is giving me absolutely no positive feedback on my rides or on the concept of riding races in general. She does not say one word the whole way back to our house. I drive fast, waiting for her to scold me, to order me to slow down, but she never does.

Irv—joking, talking, kidding, tough-as-nails, with a torso like a twenty-year-old's, his chest and arms wrapped in sharply delineated, ropey muscle—is in my thoughts, in my prayers. Irv—uninhibited, belting out bawdy ballads while pulling off his clothes in the jocks' tent. Irv—who loves to ski, competitively ski—he'll race any eighteen-year-old down the mountain on a dare. Loves to scuba dive. Loves to run and jump out hunting.

At Gilman, we survive the dedication. I have a couple of drinks and we go to the tent for dinner, where I have quite a few glasses of wine. The news is out on Irv. He is paralyzed.

The next morning I feel awful. I awake with the full blackness of the day before me. I have coffee and drive over to Atlanta Hall. It is late. I hadn't intended on riding. I pull Tom away from his work, talk to him by my car.

"Well, what's up?" I ask. I am worried they will take me off Florida. I am worried Tom thinks I can't do it. I am worried the owners are pressuring him. I am worried that Sebastian has weaseled his way in there and gotten the ride.

"What do you mean?" Tom asks.

"I'll be riding him Saturday?"

"Yes, you'll be riding him Saturday."

We both stand there, and then Tom says, "One speed." He looks me in the eye. "Your horse only has one speed. You've got to keep him up there with the pace, keep him going that one speed for the whole race." I had thought I could come from out of it, as I had at the Elkridge-Harford. I had thought it might be good for Florida, as old as he is now, to gallop along behind saving himself, just like being out for a hunt, and then ask him to run like hell at the end.

I walk around, say good morning to everyone at the barn. They barely say hello; they glance at me as if I am a sinner and go back at their work. One week a hero, two weeks later, a pariah. Jonathan walks past me, studying the ground directly before him. I am worse than invisible.

I leave and I put the race out of my head.

Arriving home, walking into the kitchen, I pick up the ringing phone. It's Sal. She says she's had a bad dream about me and wants to know how the riding is going. We talk. I tell her what's been happening. She analyzes the situation, clarifies it and gives me her support. I hang up feeling up-

beat, ready to go. Sal can always tell if I am the slightest bit "off," as Mom
would say. In just a few years, when Ansley and I buy the sisters out and
move onto the farm, Sal will make a special trip to visit me the night of
my birthday while the family is in Florida on spring break. I'll be working
around the clock at three jobs, fighting a losing battle to keep up with what
has transmogrified into a Ponzi scheme, painstakingly and nerve-wrack-
ingly hidden from Ansley, of credit card debt and mortgage payments and
money owed veterinarians, blacksmiths, fence builders, carpenters, tree
trimmers, plumbers, painters, electricians, well diggers, Bobcat opera-
tors, roofers, the tractor maniac—not maniac, *mechanic*—the feed store,
the hay man, the bank—what the hell had I gotten into!—and it won't be
looking good. Sal will rush off at 4:30 a.m. the next morning to drive to
a conference and will leave behind three thin packages in bright green
wrapping paper, with, "Happy Birthday—enjoy the socks!" written on one.
Ridiculous, I'll think, a foot of snow still on the ground, just what I need,
lightweight dress socks. I'll leave them on the counter under a mounting
pile of bills, not opening them until I'm on cleanup duty the night before
the family returns. In one package of thin socks, ten $100 bills. In another
package, ten $100 bills. In the final package, ten brand-new, crisp $100
greenbacks and the note, "Hope you find some peace while the family is
away. Tell me if more would help."

MONDAY I HAVE the photo shoot at Gilman. There I am setting up shots of
all kinds of horsey types who have given generous amounts of money to
the school, and every single one of them asks about Irv. Have I heard more
about Irv? How is Irv? One family arrives. They all ask the questions. I
give brief answers. That family leaves. Another arrives. They ask the same
questions.

Tuesday, I am up and riding early in the drizzle. I step into the indoor track. Jonathan has my horse out, tacked up, and is walking him in
a circle. He's been winning races at the big hunt meets all spring, being
written up in the papers as the next Willie Shoemaker, and here he is tacking up my horse and about to give me a leg up. "Come on Young-Blood,"

he says, "Jog a mile, gallop a mile, and I'll have one waiting when you get back." Giving me a leg up, he asks, "How's it going? How's your weight? Don't worry about that son of a bitch trying to steal your ride. If he comes around here, I'll kick his ass. You can do it, Young-Blood. Florida is looking good and you can do it. Put that last race behind you. Tom has some good news for you."

As I walk out to the finish-line field, Tom drives up to me in his pickup, hops out and in an upbeat and uncharacteristic manner, tells me that Florida had a hematoma on his belly where the girth goes, and that might very well be why he wouldn't run, why he sulked and wouldn't pick it up at the end. He also says not to wear my father's old spurs, "those anachronistic spurs with the dimes that no one uses anymore," and to just wear a normal pair. The dime spurs might have made Florida sulk. He is training. He is figuring out all the angles. I let him have the training reins. I will do in this race whatever he says to do.

I meet Mikey at the Hunt Cup course in the afternoon and walk it with him. At the very end of the walk, after Mikey has left, I bump into Sebastian and a coterie of sycophants. He's laughing and in a good mood—he's gotten a ride he thinks "has a shot of surprising us"—and it rubs off on me. He gives his friends a flattering sketch of my career as a writer and rider. "Well Paddy, what are your plans?" he asks for the sake of his group, "Hanging back again?"

Letting down my guard, I say, "No. Might just go out on top."

Wednesday, I am up and riding early, again in the rain, and rush to Gilman. I ride that afternoon in the drizzle. All week, it rains. It seems every night I awake to hear thunder and rain. Florida hates the deep, muddy going; he flounders when he has to run in it, and here my dreams are getting murkier and less possible.

All week I do positive visualization. I ride. I run. I walk the course. "One thing I learned when I rode in the Hunt Cup," Jonathan says, "was that the more times I walked the course, the smaller the fences looked." He offers to walk the course with me. He lends me a video of the time he rode in the Hunt Cup.

I am disconnected from Ansley, from Paddy, from Andrew, from Eliza. I am doing what I have to do. Time speeds up. I will do anything to better prepare for the race: school the toughest horse over hurdles, jump Warfield over the largest of fences, jump rope, ride the bike, run, memorize the course, take the leap, the leap of faith.

Thursday, I ride early and rush to work at Gilman. In the afternoon, I walk the course with Tom and Todd Wyatt. It is getting deep. The section from the fourth fence to the sixth is like a bog. We slosh through it. Friday, we have houseguests coming in from all over. Hank and his new wife, Jeannie, are flying down from Vermont. Ansley's younger brother Graham, whom we had raised for two years and who is like a brother to me, is flying up from Florida. Willie Dixon—whose grandfather, the late Morris Dixon, a legendary trainer, had been my godfather—is driving down from Pennsylvania. Oldfields colleagues, with whom I'd taught twenty years ago and who had gone off to other boarding schools, are flying into town. The phone has been ringing: Bob Witham and Kip Elser call, wishing me luck, from South Carolina. My cousin Speedy, Mikey's son, calls from Kentucky. There'll be little sleep at our place. Ansley reserves a room for me at Embassy Suites, a hotel not far from the Hunt Cup. I ride all morning at Tom's, dodge incoming friends and relatives during the day, jog around the course at dusk in a thunder storm, and return to Embassy Suites.

Tom stops by. Into my room, water dripping from his jacket and wool cap. We watch movies of Florida in past Hunt Cups. "One speed; he has one speed—that's all he has. You've got to keep him up with the pace." We have a beer. Tom has to go. I think there might not be much pace, much early speed, in the race. If so, that would set up just right for Elmore who likes to hunt Wellie around, way off the pace, and then make a run at the leaders after jumping the nineteenth. Wellie is the odds-on favorite. I'd like to put as much distance between me and Wellie as possible. I ask Tom about being up in the front. "That's all right. You could do fine in front. Just keep him going that one speed."

CHAPTER 23

The Hunt Cup

*And now, this is it. You land after the last fence and you are grip-
ping your horse tightly with your legs, retaining a snug hold of the bit,
holding his head and neck and legs together in one coordinated forward-
thrusting athletic package of Thoroughbred genes and heart and lungs
and character as you fly down the stretch, thousands of spectators lining the snow fence, screaming and yelling and jumping up and down an
arm's reach away. "Your horse is tired!" Mikey had told me. "The spectators criticize the riders for their finishing styles, but they don't realize
you've got to hold your horse together, keep him going, some are about to
collapse. You've got to do as your father did for twenty years: ride from
that last fence to the wire as if your life depends on it."*

⸻

LYING FLAT ON MY BACK at the hotel the night before the Hunt Cup, unable
to fall sleep, I picture us at the start, then envision us leaving the start.
We fly into the first fence, air over it, down the hill, air over the second,
and then we're moving, we're moving, we're in front and we're crossing
Tufton Avenue and we're headed into the third fence and then, my positive
visualization breaks down, crumbles, implodes. We approach the third—
which most spectators thought had sent me to an early grave thirty years
ago when I had the crushing fall there on Moonlore—we are four strides
away, three, two and suddenly we are a crashing maelstrom of arms and
legs and broken rails.

Lying on my back, eyes closed, I take that image, pack it into a suitcase, pick up the suitcase, get on an airplane, fly far out over the Atlantic, drop the suitcase, swirling, twirling, picking up speed, into the ocean, and down it sinks until a great white shark hones in on it and swallows it in one bite.

I rewind the film in my head, begin back at the start. We're lined up. The starter is talking to us. He gets us just right, we're going into the first fence along with the rest of the field. We sail over the first fence and Billy Meister on the gray speeds out away from us, heading down the hill into the second. I'm behind him, steadying Florida. I steady him, sit still. We get in just right and sail over the second. We're crossing the hump of the mulch on Tufton, and we're heading down into the third. Billy is up and over it and I'm steadying Florida, though I'm not slowing him, and we're galloping into that big son-of-a-bitch and hundreds of people are all hanging over the snow fence watching and hollering and I ride Florida into it, one stride, two strides, three strides, four . . . just like Warfield that morning . . . and we are in the air, up and over, and the crowd is cheering and on we go. I visualize the entire race, every panel, every stride.

Now I am riled up and can't get to sleep. There's a party going on a few rooms down. My room is austere. No personality. Reminds me of a jail cell in Lexington, Virginia, I'd once spent the night in, and another in Denver I'd inhabited for an entire day, and in fact, it is similar to one in Roanoke, but it is different in that Hank had been in that cell with me and we actually had a good time singing and carrying on, and now that I think of it, most of all, it is like the cell in Orlando, modern, austere, prison-like, but then again, I hadn't been alone in that cell. Hank and Tom had been there after we'd taken on the Orlando City Police in a street brawl and had not come out the winning team. Here, I am alone. Yet, I think, I am free. I am not locked in. Or am I? What I am, is starting to go a little goofy. I worry that I will never get to sleep—I'll be out of it the next day, the one day I wanted to be right on. No Ansley to hug, to talk to. To make love with. She's back at the house with all the guests and confusion.

I start to pray. I lie there and I pray.

I elaborate on the prayer, amazed at how it develops on its own, with

rhyme and meter. I think of my father, my guardian angel. I pray repeti-
tively, trying to lull myself into sleep. I keep catching the edge of sleep, like
having my hand out and just about to touch the halter of Warfield in the
back field, but then, with incredible quickness, Warfield takes off bucking
and kicking and snorting and farting and, there I am awake again, heart
thumping in my chest, more awake than before.

I get out of the bed, have another beer, pace around the room as I had
done in the Orlando cell with Tom and Hank. I climb back into what is a
much more comfortable bed, start to count down from one thousand.

Soon I awake and it is oddly and amazingly late—the light is coming
through the shades. It is 7:30, and I am far from Tom's and riding. I am in
this hotel and all by myself with my tack.

I get up, shower, pull on blue jeans, walk down, have eggs, toast and
coffee at the buffet. I've been having a hard time keeping the weight on
me. Suddenly, it seems that my body is burning up fuel faster and faster
no matter what I eat. I have passed some sort of barrier, my body is used to
losing weight and wants to continue. It is on full-speed ahead at all times.

Though woozy from the late-night beer, I feel relaxed knowing I will
work it off. The drive to Atlanta Hall takes forever.

Childhood friend Tom Iglehart is at the indoor track with his video
camera. He's doing a documentary on Tom and me teaming up to make
this run for the Hunt Cup. He is incredibly sensitive to everything that is
going on; he is quiet, never gets in the way. He is there in the background,
waiting patiently, getting the shots and dialogue he wants. It has created
a little more pressure—for me, at least. I already have friends calling, the
newspaper calling, teachers as well as students at work asking about the
race, and now, here I have a man with a camera following me and thus
others staring and wondering what this is about, and a few, especially
around Tom's barn, perhaps thinking I was getting more attention than
I deserve. I would prefer to not see another human being besides Tom
Voss up until the second I get up on Florida in the paddock of the Hunt
Cup. Once up on Florida, my legs around his torso, my body feeling the
rhythm of his walk, the same rhythm I'd felt in the cold winter mornings

heading out to gallop, on the late weekend mornings heading out to hunt, I wouldn't care who was there or what they said or what they did. But that's not what comes with riding in the Hunt Cup after being away from it for thirty years.

Tom steps into the shedrow of the indoor track, pulls out Brigade of Guards. Betty Merck, Brigade's owner, is there. Out I go on Brigade, into the field between the lower and upper barns. Feels good. Jog down the hill. Mucky in the bottom. There is nothing I can do. The mud will be there in the afternoon and Florida will deal with it. I focus on the riding, on the present. Around the loop. Past the house. Hands down. Canter up the hill, past the airy timber fence in the Elkridge-Harford Point-to-Point, loop around toward the little fence with the drop, then back and ease up to a trot by the gate where Tom and Betty are watching. I glance at Tom to make sure he doesn't have a signal for me. Head around the downhill section at an easy trot, standing up in the stirrups, feeling a part of this horse, loving this horse whom I had hoped would win the A. P. Smithwick at Saratoga last August, loving the grass beneath him, the blue sky above. Swing to the left at the bottom of the hill and ease into a canter and on up the hill. Tom Iglehart is standing out in the field, filming us. I allow Brigade to let out a buck or two as we gallop past the man with the camera, ease to a trot passing the owner and do the circle again.

Pull up. Hop off. Talk to Betty. Tell her Brigade feels like he'll win the A. P. Smithwick this year.

A tractor pulling an empty hay wagon passes us. Tom Voss, now standing in the indoor track, yells out, grinning, "What're you going to do now?" The tractor and wagon pulls up in front of the loft of the cow barn. Tom nods toward the wagon, "Maybe go over and load up that wagon. Get you loosened up."

I hear the phone ring. Tom ducks into the barn.

"Hey Jumping Rider," he hollers. "You've got an important phone call."

I duck into the shedrow. Standing by the saddle horse, he hands me the old, black, grimy receiver attached to a phone on the wall and walks away.

"Pa-pa-patrick, good luck to you today." It's Bob Witham, now train-ing for one of the billionaire Arab sheiks.

"Bob, how are you?"

"Fine Patrick, fine. How are you?"

"Good Bob. Will you be up here soon galloping for Tom?"

"Never mind that Patrick. We want you to know we're all rooting for you down here. Show'em what an old-timer can do."

"OK, Bob, I'll let him roll today."

"Good luck Patrick. Good luck."

I walk away from the phone, laughing and filled with a sense of good-will. Bob is one of my oldest racetrack friends. Hasn't had a drink in twenty years. Has the absolute best sense of humor. Has the cushiest job on the track. His sheik gives him three months off, paid, every summer, when Bob comes to work for Tom. He loves to get fit, gallop eight to ten a day at Tom's. Everybody loves Bob. He'll continue this extremely active lifestyle until well into his sixties when, one morning in Camden, he'll have a fall off a two-year-old that will paralyze him and, a week later, he'll decide not to live like that.

I walk over to the hay wagon, talk to the tractor driver about the hay, decide against it. I don't want to get all tied up like I did before the Elkridge-Harford. Tom is good at tying me up, making me late.

Back to Tom. "I think I'll go over to Mom's and go for a school."

"A school?"

"Yes, get on my hunter and school him cross-country."

"Damn—you break your leg or something and then what? I'll have to ride the horse."

"So be it," I said. "So be it."

Feeling upbeat, I drive to Mom's barn, step out of the car, open the gate, step through the muck, walk directly to Warfield. With full confidence, I slowly raise my hand and gently grasp his halter.

Into the stall. Tack him up. Grab an old jacket out of the tack room, pull it on, and pull the zipper up tight. Ride out into the field. Hop on in a new way I've developed, without putting weight on my right hand. Safely on the horse, I call to the house. Mom steps out onto the back porch, followed by Susan and Rocky, who drove down for the race yesterday. Breaking into a jog, I wave to them.

Out I go. Feel loose, agile, limber, a part of Warfield, of the sun, of the grass, of the sky. Adjust my stirrups to the length they'll be that afternoon. It's noon. Four hours from now I'll be in the tack, at the start. Thousands of people milling around, picnicking, drinking, watching. Hard to believe. After all this time, it is now four hours away. Time. How could I be out here by myself, in turtleneck and sweater and ripped jacket, in blue jeans and old paddock boots—when four hours from now I'd be going to the start in boots and britches and silks before thousands of onlookers?

We school through the countryside. I ride calmly, breaking a nice sweat, not asking him to stand way off. Able to judge the approach of the fences from farther out than usual, I sit still as much as possible. He gets in just right and jumps each fence the same. We are in the zone. We could jump anything. This is the best Warfield has ever jumped in his life and the best I have ever ridden him. On the way home, I ride by Joey's to say hi. He too will be going to the post at 4:00, but nobody's there.

At home, Susan and Rocky come out. I have fun talking to them. Even more fun handing them Warfield to cool out. I'm in the car and Susan calls out, "Ride safely, ride slowly!" And I know it's time to go. I'd like to go into the house, give Mom a hug—she's too nervous to go to the race—but I don't want to get all tangled up.

"Remember to rub his saddle mark out," I call, grinning, from the moving car.

In the car. Crank up the heat. Pull up the zipper of my jacket. In the zone. Thinking about Pop. Sweating. Certainly don't need to lose any weight, but feel this is the right thing to do. In a hot car. Stay in the zone.

Rushing. Need something to eat. Go to a supermarket, get a ready-made ham and cheese, pick up some Gatorade. The line at the counter is long. Takes forever. Back to the hotel. Take a bath, turn the bathroom into a steam room, sweat. It's getting late. Check over my tack, organize it. Lord, got to get all this stuff into the car. Hard to organize. Tack, clothes.

Out of there. In the car. Forgot the damn car sticker to get past the state police and onto the Hunt Cup grounds. Have to go all the way back. Have to get the maid to let me in. Getting late. Damn, got to make this race. A little like one of those nightmares I sometimes have. Stay calm. Stay calm.

Finally, in the car. It's 2:30. Race at 4:00. Tack up at 3:30. Need to be in paddock weighing out at 3:00. Don't want to get there too early. Don't want to get there too late. Got to push it. Feel good driving. Have to drive way around to miss the traffic. God, did I forget my stick? Stop in Butler, get out, run around back, open up hatch, finger through tack until see the stick. I kiss it, my old stick that I bought at Saratoga from a man on the back side after a morning of galloping horses for my father. Back in car. Have a feeling in my core everything will be all right. Beautiful drive. Come around the back way. I have the tape from *Good Morning, Viet Nam* playing in the tape deck that Sal gave me. An old favorite is playing: "I Feel Good" by James Brown. I crank it up. It reminds me of Hank—which is always good for the spirit—and the night we drove to Roanoke to see James Brown perform. There's a long line of cars by the third fence. I'm going to have to blast by these cars like in the old days and then it comes on, an old favorite of my father's: Louie Armstrong singing "It's A Beautiful World." "I see children . . ." I feel Pop's presence there with me, we're doing this together. He's sitting beside me. Goddamn, let'em roll, goddamn boys, let's see what you got, because we're going to let'em roll today. I choke up at the miracle and wildness of the moment. Pushing the clutch in, I downshift into second gear, let the clutch out, roar by the line of fifty cars, three or four policemen waving frantically at me, and enter the gate through which I'll soon be galloping Florida, headed for the third fence. I park and walk by myself, carrying my tack bag—thinking back on walking along beside Pop, helping him carry his tack bag, wishing one of my children were there by my side but not minding because I know I will be with them soon—to the paddock.

Focused. Focused on weighing out. Everybody is coming up and talk-ing to me. There is a swirl of colors and brightness and excitement. Every-body is grinning and laughing and in love with the day. I duck into the tent. It's hot. It's small, cramped and hot, this sanctuary for the riders in a sea of hubbub. A couple of other riders are there. I go through the tack bag, gather my tack, walk to the scales, weigh out. Happy to see I don't need two pounds of lead, I pull two slivers of lead out of Pop's old lead pad, set them on the grass, stand on the scales, photographers snapping pictures. Got it: right weight, all gear is here.

There's still some hang-around time. I sit in the tent to get away from everybody. Check my goggles. I borrow a safety pin from Mike Elmore to connect the elastic strap of my goggles to my helmet cap. Sebastian walks in, lights a cigarette. He's found a horse to ride at the last minute. Smoke fills the tent. I don't want it to trigger my allergies, and yet I don't want to be outside with the crowd. "Well, what're we going to do?" he asks. "Does anyone know what he's going to do? You know, in England, the riders dis-cuss what they're going to do before the race . . . Paddy says he's going out, going out on top, setting the pace . . ." He looks at me, shuts up, but it's too late. Every jock in that tent gives me a look, registering what he said, and then goes back to shining his boots, buttoning his silks, cleaning his goggles. Joey Gillet steps in, casually starts undressing and immediately starts talking nonstop, lightening the mood with a few funny stories about past Hunt Cups.

The tent is in the center of a circular paddock enclosed by two con-centric blood-red snow fences that form a ring, like a miniature racetrack. We carry our tack out of the paddock crowded with owners, trainers and horsemen, into this ring—a ten-yard-wide donut swath of thick grass where no spectators are allowed. The horses are walking the gauntlet, spectators crowding on both sides, their hands on the old, jagged, wired-together staves, trying to get as close as they can to the horses. We're in an oasis. Tom tacks up Welterweight. Then, it's Florida, and Florida is giving them a hard time. Louis Bosley does most of my job. Florida jigs and dances to his right, to his left, pushes everybody forward. Michael patiently jiggles the bit, backs him up. Tom is on the near side. Louis is on the off side. Tom is holding the yoke. He slips it around Florida's neck. I hand Louis the black non-slip pad, then the old squashed foam pad Tom had used last year in the Wild Goose Chase, then the lead pad and number cloth—green and made of cotton, not a throw-away model. They set the saddle, Tom tightens the undergirth. It's not just right. Tom and Louis fool with it. I have fool confidence, damn—not fool confidence, *full confidence*. Here are the professionals. Tom is doing it. I'd stake my life on how he sets that saddle. Louis says he needs to stretch out the girth. It's on and it's tight, but with his tremendous strength and huge hands, he grabs a section, down low, slides his hands up, grabs another section, slides his hands up so that the pressure is distributed more evenly. On goes the overgirth. We're ready. I want to get on. I want to get on Florida. Get off the ground and away from all these people.

Around Florida goes. Around Welter goes. Tom is standing between Mike and me. "Well," he says to both of us, "you're locked in now." I laugh and grab Mike's arm.

"Dad, Dad!" I hear. It's Eliza. Where is she? "Sweetheart! Sweetheart, over here!" I spot Ansley waving an arm and pointing at Eliza, so cute, face so round, so beautiful. Her eyes can just barely see over the top of the fence. I run across the area where the horses are walking past, reach over the fence, pick Eliza up, give her a big kiss, and turn to go back. It's about time to get on, and Ansley is calling me, but I have to get back. I continue across, even as I hear her calling me, back to my spot with Tom and Mike Elmore and the owners.

They're having a hard time tacking up the horse beside us. He's holding up the works—raising hell, rearing and plunging. Finally, he's tacked up and we're about to get on. A senior steward walks by and pings me in the chest, hard, hitting my flak jacket. At first I'm bewildered at this out-of-character move and then I realize he's checking to see if I have the vest on. Here comes Welterweight. He's fairly quiet. Tom throws Mike up. Here comes Florida. He's giving Michael a hard time. I walk along beside him. Michael keeps him walking. I hop up and down on my right foot, while progressing forward alongside Florida. Tom walk-jog-skips, grabs my left ankle and tosses me up. Jogging, holding my foot with one hand and the stirrup with the other hand, he places my foot in the stirrup. I thank him.

We walk around the loop. My irons, set at last week's length, feel too long—a good sign. I pull each one up a hole, two holes, and goddamn I feel good. People all along the fence, on both sides are yelling to me, "Go for it Patrick," "Hey Patrick!" I can pick out their voices. J.B. sings out, with pride and confidence, "Go on with'em, A.P." Rossy Pearce sends encouragement, "Looking good, Paddy." Jay Griswold, with whom I'd last ridden in this race thirty years ago, "You can do it, Patrick!" Jodie Westerlund's voice is highly recognizable—I've heard him play and sing everything from Chuck Berry to the Beatles to Van Morrison at parties throughout Maryland—"We're rooting for you, Patrick!" reminding me of the late-night conversations we'd shared about galloping horses. A boy, determined for me to see him, yells, "Hey Mister Smithwick, Hey Mister Smithwick." I look into the crowd and can't pick him out. "Hey Mister Smithwick!" even louder. He's assertive. He's demanding. I look down and there is one of my students. It's Matt! Talks in class, doesn't do his homework, always has some excuse why his paper is late, and here he is. He said he'd be here. He is here. His grade will definitely be a notch higher this marking period. There's another student beside Matt—it's Tom, quiet, tall and thin Tom. They're waving and hollering, "Mister Smithwick, Mister Smithwick." I wave to them both, call out their names. Jumping up and down, they wish me good luck.

Walking around, approaching Louis and Tom, Tom waves to me to come over. He waves me in, as if we're going to have a chat, then he points at the ground. What the hell is this? I look at him again, and yes, he is motioning for me to get off. I hop off Florida. Michael continues walking him. Mike Elmore and I stand together. Tom tells us that the girth broke on the horse that was rearing and plunging beside us. We laugh. Not a great sign, we say. A girth breaking before the horse even leaves the paddock? I'm using two new girths, a new saddle, new stirrups made of space-age material, and heavy-duty, good old-fashioned leathers—the exact same type I had hunted in all winter. They're made of two strips of leather stitched together with a strip of nylon sandwiched in the middle, and the buckles are strong. You don't want to go out here, jump a fence poorly, come down with force, and have a stirrup leather break.

Standing there, I'm not the least bit nervous. Not overwhelmed by the crowd and the scene. Calmer than at the beginning of a tennis match with an old friend. Calmer than before giving a talk at Gilman. I see a horse and rider in the paddock; it's Mikey. He's wearing a wool riding jacket and tie, jodhpurs, polished boots and an Irish cap. He's on Waldo, a small half-Thoroughbred and he's sitting up perfectly straight, looking better than any of us had on our horses just a moment ago.

Around and around the riderless horses go. Finally, the rearing horse— what the hell have they done to that horse?—is tacked up, again. We get back on. We are down by the gate. The grooms are releasing the horses. "I'm O.K., Michael."

"You can do it Patrick," he says, enunciating each word, unsnapping the shank. "You can do it now."

Off we go, trotting. This is it, I feel good, not a worry in the world, totally in the present, sure of myself, sure of Florida. We are away from the crowd, released. We jog down to the start. No one is galloping off fast. We're all subdued. I'm trotting along, headed for the start, and I realize that Florida has sidled up alongside Welterweight as if we're going out for a hunt. The old pals! I laugh. "Hey Mike, look at this, the two old friends."

We let our horses walk up to the first fence, give it a look. I feel silly having Florida look at this little fence. Some of the other riders let their horses walk right up and press their chests against the fence. I let Florida look at it for a second and then we trot off.

We start to circle. I'm sizing things up, trying to figure out where we're going to break off. I want to get a good start. Am determined to get a good start. There's the starter, red flag in his hand, and it's Bill Wylie, great guy. I used to start these races with him a decade ago. Charlie Fenwick got me the job. "Patrick, I have a position for you. I think you could do well at it, and you might be able to make something of it. Could be a future in it."—and now here I am up on a horse, Charlie's been retired from race riding for a decade and Bill's starting me. I'm less nervous than when I was the starter, a position I never liked. Felt I was in the wrong place. Craved to be up on a horse. Bill knew. "Good afternoon, Mr. Smithwick," he says, very clearly, as I near him, a conspiratorial grin on his face.

Bill explains to us that we have more time, but he will soon ask us to line up, one behind the other, in a circle, and then we will file out toward the orange pylon. When we are all in a straight line, he'll let us go. "Hey Billy," I call out to Billy Meister, the only rider around whom I seem to know. "Have a good ride." It's incredible to me that I don't even know the names of quite a few of the riders, but that's the way it is. Not like it was thirty-one years ago at this spot.

"You too, Patrick."

Everything feels natural. This is where I'm supposed to be, a part of Florida, of the turf, of the course, of the fences, of the horses.

False start. We circle around again, line up. I'm staying relaxed but ready at a split second to get a jump on the field and go to the front. I'm on the inside. I'd rather be in the middle of the line of horses. But this is good. I'll just have to get off the starting block fast so the others don't cross over in front of me. I'm loose, about the second-to-last in the line as we file out. We turn, the starter drops the flag, and we're off. I let Florida go and after a few strides we are in the lead headed up the hill to the first fence of the Maryland Hunt Cup.

I sense Meister behind me and I think he'll come up on my inside, jump this one head-and-head, pass me, but I'm not really thinking about this. Florida flies into that first fence. I don't slow him. He takes off and soars over it, lands running, moving on down the hill, in front, to the second fence. We're moving right along down that hill and into the second. It's not a big fence. He jets over it, jumping slightly to the left. In the air I'm eyeing the Tufton Avenue crossing and the third fence.

I'm bent down low, leaning against him. We fly across the mulch on Tufton and we're headed in a straight path for the far right panel of the third fence, and we're moving into it, funneling down a chute. I don't slow him and start him propping—shortening his stride. The crowd on our right is just a few feet from where I plan to jump. Approaching the fence, I sit still, judging it from farther out than usual, just as I had with Warfield in the morning, and then I encourage him a bit, instinctively squeezing one ... two ... three ...

He stands off and it is amazing—we are up so high—this is the highest I've ever jumped over a fence. In the air, at the peak of our trajectory, I let out a whoop and the spectators lining, crowding, thronging around the third whoop along with me. I have this feeling they're all with me and I'm smiling inside and I can't get over how long we are in the air and then how steeply we are coming down.

We're over the fence, on the ground, galloping along and I assume the rest of the field is directly behind me. It feels just like in the Old Fashioned, leading the pack. Come on boys, I was yelling back.

We gallop along, the going gets deeper. Florida is the master, out front. We know the shortest route and they're going to have to come after us. One or two will start pressing us now. You can lose some control when a horse comes up from behind, presses you, and your horse starts to go out from under you, begins to feel unresponsive to your hands as he digs in, pulls harder, and speeds up in an attempt to stay ahead of the horse pressing from behind. I turn and look back and, goddamn, they are way back! I am shocked by the length of our lead. What are they doing? Have we sprinted off too fast? Nothing to do about it now, can't rewind this one, must make the most of it. We slow down, slow down. We must use this huge lead to our advantage. We must go easy now so Florida can recoup the energy he burned going over those first three fences. Easy now, easy. Let him catch his breath, settle down, and coast along, coast along.

Focus. Go straight. Save every inch of ground. Don't wander. Into the fourth. I'm disdainful of this little fence. Heading into it, it looks as if you are going nowhere in particular, or out into the abyss, since you turn to the left just five strides after jumping it. There's no crowd. Nothing to make us focus. I sit still. He acts as if he has just spotted the fence and is spooking at it, props, puts in a short one, and lightly hits it. I had let him do what he'd done for years and it was a good lesson.

We slow going through the muck, out to the pylon, turn to the left. Slow even more. But I don't want to give up my lead. We canter into the fifth. I run the bit through his mouth, wake him up, and he jumps it perfectly. Around the pylon. Turn and into the sixth, one of the biggest fences on the course. Totally focused, I do as Mikey said, ride him into it as if he were an open jumper. We get in just right, up and over.

Galloping along now. In the zone. Trying to float. Trying to make this as easy on him as possible. Out here in front. Ten lengths in front of the field in the Maryland Hunt Cup and it feels as everyday as taking the dogs for a walk up past the sycamore tree behind our house.

We head up a slight hill, the top of which blocks our view of the next fence. It feels like we're going so slowly. I space out a little. I realize I'm drifting, "wandering" as Mikey calls it. I'm wandering up toward the seventeenth. Jesus Christ! I had worried about this when I visualized the race. I quickly pull him in line for the seventh. The eyes of the riders behind me burn into my back. No one was going to yell, "To the left, Patrick, to the left!" as Jack did at Howard County. I am back on course but approaching the seventh I'm distracted and we get in a little close.

I put this lapse, this "wandering," behind me. Head for the eighth.

A long distance between the seventh and eighth. I glance back—they're still way back, but Florida is going easy. We slow another notch but I don't want to give up this ground we've gained. We're way out here by ourselves. I slap him twice, snapping my wrist, with the whip on his shoulder to make him pay attention, to keep him on the bit.

Seems like we're barely out of a hunting gallop.

Up over the ninth. Far left inside panel. We are racing now. We are racing. Turn sharp. We roll down the hill, around the first pylon, and then approaching the sharp turn marked by the second pylon, turning to the left, the turn feeling sharp, sharper than I like, the ground slippery beneath us, I hold my breath, Florida sliding. We can't turn as sharply as Mikey said to. I'm not going to make the same mistake I made at the Grand

National. Around the pylon, in order to avoid having our feet skid out from under us, we drift out farther than planned. We drift out in a smoothly carved arc and then gradually swing back into the line headed for the far left panel of the tenth, just as Mikey said we would. Not slowing as we approach the fence, we get in just right, continuing our exact same pace, and sail over it.

We head to the thicket of trees, up a hill, toward the eleventh. This one has me concerned. It is not early in the race, when your horse is fresh. It is not late in the race when you're pushing and driving and riding into the fences like they aren't there. We slow going up this hill and yet it feels like we are still really moving along and this fence is hard to judge, something to do with the way Florida is steering. I sit still, allow Florida to shorten his stride, give him a slight breather, and Florida handles it well. We land and we put it behind us. Picking up speed, as Mikey and Tom said to do, we head for the twelfth, for the panel on the far left. Twenty or thirty spectators are lined up on the left, along the snow fence, their cheering helping my focus. I head directly for the far left panel—*Come on boys*—the snow fence and spectators just yards away on my left helping me to judge the fence, increasing the three-dimensionality of it. I am thriving on jumping well when the people are there. We barrel into that bastard and Florida flies over it.

Now we're rolling down into the thirteenth. I'm galloping down a path clearly visible to me, straight into that inside panel, and I don't have a care in the world. I feel at home. We're dragging those bastards behind us. Let them come, let them come. We're going straight into this wall of a fence the height of a man. The spectators are three feet to our left, hundreds lining the snow fence. They're yelling and screaming and we're moving down that hill. It's like riding him through the herd of cattle in the Old Fashioned. I don't have the feeling we're going to stand off at this one. I sit still and let him continue at a steady pace. Going down this hill, it's hard to judge how many strides away from the fence we are. I sit still, don't take any chances, allow him to put in an extra half stride on this one and we're up, high, really high, and we're in the air and over it. I let out a whoop, hear the crowd whoop, and we're coming down, coming steeply down, very steeply down, and finally we're back on the ground.

Fourteenth, up and over. Slow around the pylon, slow through the marsh, thinking they will come and get us, but they don't. Have to gallop around a stick someone stuck in a hole so no one would step in it. This—at the Maryland Hunt Cup. I laugh.

Into the fifteenth, slowly. Up and over.

Land—out of the muck, head for the pylon. Next is the sixteenth. Jumping it while going uphill makes it the biggest on the course. But I don't think of that. Pick up a little speed. They haven't come to us yet. Up the incline, turn to the left, gradually, after passing the pylon, accelerating—headed for the third panel from the inside, where it leans away just a bit, meet it exactly how I want to meet it, squeeze, up and over we go. Perfect. We're over the last really big one now, and I hadn't even thought about its size. All that foxhunting, those wild hunts with Tom, have paid off.

Aiming for the seventeenth, I get down lower and ride him into it. I ask him and he stands off. This is it. I've been doing this every day of my life.

Put my sights on the tip of a limb hanging down outside of the woods and some ass is standing out in the field with a camera—right where I want to gallop. I continue to aim for the spot, yell at the photographer and a few others and they back up into the woods.

Over the eighteenth.

Florida is tiring. I can feel it. It's been a great ride, but I can feel him running out of gas. It happens suddenly. I get low and push.

They come to us. Someone, it's Jack, on our right. He's moving. He's passing me fast on our right. He passes and then cuts to his left directly in front of us, his horse's rump crossing under Florida's head, as we approach the nineteenth. I yell for him to give us some room. He continues to cut right in front of us, blocking Florida's view of the fence, and jumps the inside panel. I'm directly behind him, Florida's nose on his horse's rump, and I'm really having to push. At the same time, I sit back, get my feet out in front of me, bracing for what might happen, but Florida gamely stands off, jumps it great, with all these horses suddenly crowding around him.

Any other horse would've put in an extra stride there, clobbered the fence and turned ass-over-tin-cups. I trust you Florida. I thank you Florida. I love you Florida.

We barrel down the hill. Suddenly I'm tired. I've gotten a bad side ache. We're flying down the hill into the stiff board fence. I'm winded. I'm blowing. My legs are giving out and I've gotten this damn side ache. I pick up the stick and use it. We're running, running down into the twentieth. I'm driving Florida now, riding him into it like it's not there, and he starts to come on again, to catch them. What heart. What guts. He stands off and jumps it great and we're flying with the pack down to the Tufton Avenue crossing. My body is wrung out. Like a squadron of Blue Angels holding a pattern while diving, the tight group of us wings it straight across the mulch crossing. I pull on the left rein and we're heading into the water jump. I let my rump down into the saddle, giving my legs a rest. Rake up with my spurs and crack Florida hard on the ass, once, twice, galloping into the water jump as if it were a hurdle. As tired as he is, Florida hurdles it, gaining on the three in front of us. We start up the hill, we're not far back, we're still in contention, but then they start pulling away.

We have one more fence to go, the one where two years ago the rider let Florida chip in, Florida hit the top rail, and the rider not only fell off but also, on landing, picked up his stick and beat Florida across the face with it. The one where last year, the rider completely stopped riding, let Florida shorten his stride, shorten his stride even more, and then at the last second asked Florida to stand off from too far away. Florida put in an extra stride, twisted, popping the jock up into the air. There is no reason for him to jump this fence badly. The hill has taken away all our momentum. We are going slower and slower. I keep riding and pushing him steadily into it, getting him in just right, so that, as tired as he is, he is not put in the position of having to decide between standing way off or putting in another stride. I am taking care of my horse. I will do anything for my horse. I crack him once with the whip on our takeoff and he jumps it like a show horse.

I'm pumping and pushing. Three are ahead of us. Welter and two others. I ride down to the finish but I don't hit Florida again. I'll never hit him again. No one will ever reach back and hit Florida again. My lungs are blown out, the ache in my side is red-hot. I push and push but, sensing there are no other horses nearby, I don't push as hard as I could, not wanting to unnecessarily strain him. Under the wire. We're fourth. Florida pulls right up. None of this galloping out. He's exhausted too. Think how he must feel! Sebastian comes up from behind us—God, I won't have to deal with him anymore—and makes a show of galloping past before pulling up. Off to my side, I see Mikey on Waldo trying to ride through the crowd. He's coming toward us but the crowd thickens and then he's surrounded by a noose of women all looking up at him, calling out his name.

The crowd implodes on us. I wish I'd let Florida gallop out a little farther, to get away from the people, so I could catch my wind and let the sideache subside. A girl that works for Tom grabs a rein. "Are you all right? All you all right?"

"Fine, fine, I'm fine," I answer, trying to catch my breath, my side on fire. Michael appears, takes hold of the reins.

I wave my stick to the stewards. Duck Martin nods, giving me the OK to dismount. "Good job, Patrick," Michael says. "Good job. Florida has never jumped better."

I hop off. My legs give way for a split second when I hit the ground. I struggle to unbuckle the girths. There's no one on the other side of the horse. I scamper around, disengage the yoke from the girths, pull off the saddle and pads soaked with sweat, and off Florida goes, sucked into the vortex of people. It feels strange. He should be remaining with me. I feel hands patting me on the back. They should be patting Florida. I hear, *Well done, A.P.! You showed 'em something out there, A.P.!* I know who that is and I feel a swelling of thankfulness for his support all spring.

Wellie's won. My hunter has won. My efforts on him over the fall, winter and spring have paid off. Wellie's won, and I'm proud of him, happy for him and Elmore. And goddamn if Florida and I didn't go out in style. Everything's confusing and a whole group of people—the victors—are moving toward the old hay wagon for the presentation of the trophy and the photos. I carry my tack toward the scales. Charlie Fenwick helps me by pulling my helmet off as I step up onto the scales. "Exactly 165, didn't even lose a pound," I joke, knowing that actually, with the flak jacket on, I had weighed out at 167 and had thus lost two pounds.

Back I head, toward the tent, a group coming along with me—hugging me, praising me, congratulating me. "Beautiful ride." "Beautiful ride." "He jumped so well. How did you get him to jump so well?" "You rode beautifully." And off in what seemed like the distance, even though it was only twenty-five yards away, there they are up on the wagon. I can see Mike Elmore, Tom and Mimi, and the owners having their victory celebration and here I am back at the tent. We had gone out in style. We had done it.

In the tent, I fool with my tack, try to get it organized and into the old heavy leather tack bag that had belonged to my great-uncle Charlie White, who had won this race twice. I attempt to get out of my silks and britches. The other riders are in there—except for Mike Elmore, the winner—and people keep bending down low, stepping in, shaking my hand, slapping me on the back, asking how I'd gotten Florida to jump so well, and congratulating me. I'm slightly embarrassed. The riders don't say a damn thing. Sebastian has lit a cigarette and I want to get the hell out of there. One rider says how Florida had "kicked up behind over some fences," and I thought of that wild, go-to-hell, enjoying-himself feeling that Florida had given me over every fence on the course—as if he were feeling so good he couldn't help but jet his hind quarters up higher than they needed to go, celebrating, showing off, flinging his tail high, vaulting us over the fences. I am about to say something, after all, I am the one who had been on him. I am about to describe that joyful, ecstatic feeling when Sebastian takes the cigarette out of his mouth and says, "Oh, he always does that. Always gets in too close and twists." Nothing good from that bastard. Then friends, classmates, acquaintances I haven't seen for years are busting into the tent. I can't get undressed. Can't get dressed. "You did it, you did it!" they sing out. "It was Florida, it was Florida," I reply.

I step out of the tent and am interviewed by several reporters while a photographer with camera on shoulder films us. Friends take photos of Tom, Hank, and me. As we line up, a few call out, "the jailbirds." After Ansley's and my rehearsal dinner, the three of us had a disagreement with the Orlando City police and were soon spending the night in one of Orlando's most highly frequented centers of accommodations. Susan should be in this picture, I am thinking. Purely to defend and help her brother who was taking a beating from the police, she had dived in that night and been the toughest of us all.

Speak of the devil. As soon as Tom, Hank and I break up, Susan approaches and her arms are around me and are squeezing tight—reminding me of her preternatural strength as a child. I reflect back to that night long ago when the huge undercover cop had me down on the ground, his arm tighter and tighter around my neck until I was about to pass out and I heard, "You're strangling my brother!" and with that remark that poor bastard didn't know what hit him. She just tore him up and I was released. Hours later, in the Orlando City jail, I asked this same policeman, "Who, out of all of my ushers, had been the toughest to subdue?" Without blinking, he turned and pointed to Susan, who was entering the room in her new prison attire—a striped pajama prison suit right out of an old Cagney movie.

Standing there in the paddock of the Hunt Cup, Susan releases her hold on me and pats my shoulder: "Boy, I'm glad that's over. You've had a good time riding these races with Pop. Now he's telling you to get back to your writing," and walks back to Rocky.

The jocks are out of the tent. I duck back in, get my saddle, lead pad, undergirth, overgirth, yoke, nonslip rubber pad, thick sponge pad, boots, spurs, rubber bands, britches and silks together. It is taking me forever. I give up on organizing it, and just stuff it into Uncle Charlie's old tack bag.

Mimi waits for me and walks back with me toward my car. How much better this was than walking around after the race, not having ridden, as I had dejectedly done for so many recent years. But where is Paddy? Where is Andrew to help me carry the tack bag?

I am craving a cold beer. I turn down a fancy European ale. I rarely drink Budweiser. But that's what I want. A regular old American beer. Finally, out of the confusion of cars and coolers and tablecloth-covered card tables and lacrosse-playing kids and gin-and-tonic swilling spectators, someone hands me a cold American lager.

God it tastes good. Lord, it feels like I've earned it. The sun beats down on me. I weave through the thickets of picnicking drinkers toward my car, carrying the heavy tack bag. Mimi grabs the other side of the tack bag. It's like old times. Like carrying Pop's tack bag. But where is Paddy or Andrew or Eliza? I want one of them to be carrying the bag with me. Mimi is in a rush to get back to the barn. Women stop me and hug and kiss me. A couple of college-age girls, teetering this way and that, tripping over the tufts of grass, their clothes more or less falling off, their drinks splashing, stop me and ask for my autograph. I laugh and sign their program. Mimi breaks out laughing, rolls her big brown eyes, gives up on me, takes off for the barn. Four women in their mid-thirties surround me, congratulate me, tell me they loved a recently published magazine article of mine about steeplechasing in Maryland. They laugh and giggle, hold up their magazines for me to sign. I finally arrive at the car, coax Hank away from the large group of family and friends. Off to the stables just beyond the fifth and the fifteenth fences we go.

At the barn—how much better than recent years. I have ridden. And I am patting Florida. He is grazing and we have done it. I am patting Wellie—he is the winner. Hank has a ball talking to Nat Nat, an old-timer who drives Tom's van. Tom Iglehart films us all.

Hank and I head up to Duck Martin's, the house on top of the hill overlooking this beautiful racecourse. Tom Iglehart follows. We park, get out, head in. Find the bar. More congratulations. Into a crowded room. Watch the tape of the race. For over half of the race, the camera is just on Florida. I am astounded. I didn't know it would look like that. I didn't think we were that far ahead for that long. In fact, with the going as deep as it was, I realize we might've opened up too far on the field, gone too fast over those first three. I was used to the faster early pace of the three-mile races. But what the hell, I am pleased with our result. Fifty people are crammed into this den, cheering Florida and me on.

Watching Wellie pass us and win, I congratulate Mike Elmore, tell him he is the only one who could have ridden Wellie around the course like that. I stand to leave. Someone pushes the button to play the film again.

"It's going to be on again. Patrick, don't you want to watch it again? Come on, have another drink."

"No thanks." I high-step out of there.

We drive twenty minutes north and start down a long gravel driveway to the quintessential Hunt Cup party at the Colhoun-Fishers. These are real Maryland horse people. There'll be mint juleps, the best in the world, in huge polished silver loving cups, Hunt Cup trophies won by the great Mountain Dew. You grab one with two hands, tilt your head back, raise the big silver bowl and let crushed sugar and mint slide toward you till it tickles the skin beneath your nose and the bourbon seeps through the ice and mint and over the cup's silver lip with its bell-like taste and into your mouth.

We pass Ansley, Hank's wife Jeannie, and a pile of kids in a car going the other direction. They're leaving. "You can't go, Patrick. You can't go. We'll be late for the Hunt Ball! Come on, you have to turn around!"

On we go.

At the party: More congratulations. Old friends. Childhood friends. People shaking my hand, patting me on the shoulder, asking me what it was like, Tom Iglehart following with the video camera. Loving cup after loving cup is passed around. Isn't this so much better than last year? Don't I remember the depression of last year? Don't I remember sitting dejected in the car after everyone piled out and rushed to the party?

It is getting late. Hank and I grab a beer and head out. We drive the twenty minutes to Tom Whedbee's, where he and Jeannie are staying. Hank is in deep trouble with Jeannie. She's fed up with both of us and has been trying to catch a flight back to Vermont. Then, I suddenly realize I still have to drive all the way home, another twenty minutes. Thirty to be realistic.

Arriving home, I catch hell for being late. I catch hell for staying in the shower for too long. I catch hell for never having tried on my rented tails which are too tight, for taking too long to get the whole outfit on. I am one sorry hell-catching son-of-a-bitch!

The Hunt Ball. More congrats. Dancing and swirling, eating and drinking. But I'm not really as happy as I'm acting. After all, I wanted to win. I wanted to be the guy up there giving the toast. And there is that sliver of guilt, guilt for having gone out so far in front over the first three. I feel slightly anxious. About what, I am not sure. The music plays, I dance and dance, but I don't kick in full blast. Part of me hangs back, whispers that I am a phony. Dancing with Paddy's girlfriend, my legs become weary. I can't remember this ever happening. Dancing slowly with an owner of one of the horses in the race, she tells me that her husband may look young, but when he takes his clothes off he looks and acts old! Then she pulls away from me, raises an eyebrow and looks me in the eye. Goddamn, I know I'm going to get in trouble dancing with this crazy woman. I'm out on the floor with her for three dances, maybe four. "You're leading now." "What?" "You're leading now—do you *always* lead?" What have I gotten into? She congratulates me on my ride, tells me it must be so wonderful to ride in the Hunt Cup, that her husband is not fit, does not exercise, and while relating all this to me, her lips occasionally touching my ear, she continually rubs her thigh up high between my legs. She informs me that Sebastian (with whom I knew—but she didn't know that I knew—she'd been having an affair) had been backstabbing me for several weeks, trying to steal the ride on Florida. And thus, here she was backstabbing the backstabber with whom she'd been cuckholding her husband . . . Oh my! I get away, sit back at our table, and am met by neither warmth nor a smile from my wife. For the past few weeks, I had imagined that if Florida and I did well, then this would be the night, the celebration, one hell of a release, a night of romance to remember. Sitting at our table, dancers returning from the floor in a sweat, I picture Kip Elser, his playful grin, and hear an expression he uses when called upon to explain *what in the world happened?* "Fucked up again," he says, and moves on.

Alas, upon our late arrival home, my Penelope tests me strongly, but in the end, we return to our old rituals.

NEXT MORNING, up early for some crazy reason.

Don't know what to do.

The race is over.

I have made no plans on what to do after the race.

Everything feels different.

The race is no longer out there in front of me. It is no longer a purpose. I look out into the field of the future, and there is no Hunt Cup out there, no big fences out there; the field with the tall green grass blowing in the wind just goes on and on with all this space surrounding it, a void waiting to be filled, extending into the future.

Drive to Atlanta Hall.

Up on Brigade. Tom and Jonathan and I ride over to the Elkridge-Harford Hunt Club. Tom and I watch Jonathan breeze. I gallop Brigade. Tom doesn't say one word about the race. He's an old grump. It's business as usual. Or, business a little worse than usual. This silence is a letdown. What the hell is up?

For the first time, I think: What do I do now? Who do I ride now? Do I push for more rides? Do I try to get a ride next weekend in the Virginia Gold Cup, and the next, and the next, and next, and then at Saratoga—get really light, lose ten more pounds, and ride in the A. P. Smithwick Memorial?

Hanging around the barn, I ask Tom, "What next? What do I do next?"

"I don't know," he says. "I don't have any horses running for a while. I guess you get on the phone and hustle—just like anybody else."

PART FIVE

Flying Change

1.

*The canter has two stride patterns, one on the right
lead and one on the left, each a mirror image of the
other. The leading foreleg is the last to touch the
ground before the moment of suspension in the air.
On cantered curves, the horse tends to lead with the
inside leg. Turning at liberty, he can change leads
without effort during the moment of suspension, but
a rider's weight makes this more difficult. The aim of
teaching a horse to move beneath you is to remind
him how he moved when he was free.*

2.

*A single leaf turns sideways in the wind
in time to save a remnant of the day;
I am lifted like a whipcrack to the moves
I studied on that barbered stretch of ground,
before I schooled myself to drift away*

*from skills I still possess, but must outlive.
Sometimes when I cup water in my hands
and watch it slip away and disappear,
I see that age will make my hands a sieve;
but for a moment the shifting world suspends*

its flight and leans toward the sun once more,
as if to interrupt its mindless plunge
through works and days that will not come again.
I hold myself immobile in bright air,
sustained in time astride the flying change.

— "The Flying Change" *by Henry Taylor*

"Never give up. Never, never, never give up."

On a hot day, the hill going up the gray stone dust driveway from Mikey's barn to the top one-hundred-acre field can seem long, especially if you're worrying about your seventy-one-year-old uncle — who has weak lungs and has had a couple of seizures at work — hacking a young horse around for some prospective owners.

A big new SUV with Virginia tags is parked in the middle of the field. I walk toward it, looking forward to seeing Mikey. I haven't seen him since the operation on both his hernias a few days earlier.

Approaching a young, handsome couple, I introduce myself, shake hands and ask where Mikey is. They point to the far end of the field, half a mile away — where I see a horse and rider jogging. It is Mikey. He is riding very long, which he has to do because of his titanium hips. The dark bay is pulling hard against him but Mikey is keeping his hands low and giving one rein then the other a little tug, unnoticeable to most observers, to make it all look easy. I am too far away to hear, but in my mind, I can hear him chanting, "Wo-o-a boy, wo-o-a son, that's a boy, wo-o, wo-o-a boy" as he creates and releases tension on the reins in his inimitable style. He starts cantering in a circle. Why is he doing this so far away from the potential buyers, I wonder, but then notice the horse jerk and yank against the bit, trying to snatch his head up, and watch as Mikey takes it, keeping his hands down low, taking the snatches and yanks and jerks in his lower stomach muscles. Having had two separate hernia operations, I know what this would feel like, not to mention what it might do to the stitches.

Mikey canters around, the horse relaxing. I am waiting for him to canter over to us. Instead, he gradually opens up the size of the circle and then swings wide up the hill, cantering toward a hurdle at its crest, the horse increasing his pace, pulling hard. Riding so long, Mikey can't simply lean back, let the weight of his body pull against the reins as you do when you're riding shorter. He has to take the pulling with his hands and arms, which transfers the pressure to his stomach and groin.

The canter becoming a gallop, they near the wings, the bay lugging to the left, thinking about running out, but Mikey calmly pulls him back in line with his right rein and they're inside the wings. The horse flies recklessly over the hurdle and upon landing throws his head up in the air, trying to loosen Mikey's hold. Mikey slows the pace, gallops across the crest of the hill a quarter of a mile away, silhouetted against the late afternoon sky, and over another hurdle they go, "in hand," in control.

Now, they turn, coming toward us, going down the hill. The horse has gotten a touch of freedom and is rolling right along, picking up speed, turning to his left as he wanted, tossing his head side to side, trying to get away from the bit, really moving down the hill, into the dip, around a big log, swinging out a little wider than you'd like — stride fully extended — to get straight at the next hurdle, which is just thirty yards from us.

Mikey has the visor of his Irish cap down low, his heels down, his eyes focused on the upcoming hurdle, and now, finally, the horse has his head down, still pulling hard, still lugging to the left, but Mikey is in control, making it look easy, and they gallop into the hurdle, Mikey placing him perfectly, making him stand off for the buyers, brush through the top of the hurdle in classic form, increasing the horse's worth by five to ten thousand dollars with this one jump.

Later, Mikey's collapsed in his big chair in his bedroom. We're having a glass of "poor man's port." I give him a lecture about his health: what he's been eating, the seizures, his lungs, schooling a horse right after an operation. He finishes his glass of port, looks over his dusty dime-

store glasses into my eyes. "Young-Blood," he says, "I'm not afraid of my
health. Now let's have another glass."

I pour two more glasses and sit down.

"Tell me about the race," he says. "Let's see what you learned."

I review the race, fence by fence. He nods, comments, let's me keep
my rhythm. It's getting dark outside. We have one more glass of port. I
prepare to stand. He puts his right hand, the mottled, sun-seared, blue-
blackened hand, on my knee. The right side of his third finger, where the
rein had tightened, is raw, and the flesh on either side of the indented
raw area where the rein had been is puffed out. He squints, his brown
eyes boring into my eyes, his hand squeezing my knee. "Never give up,"
he says. "Never, never, never give up."

⟋⟋

Monday.

Early morning. I don't ride. I don't write. I drive the car pool. Andrew to
Boys' Latin, Jed and I to Gilman. Get to work early, first person in our
building, determined to make a big push on the magazine. I sort out the
notes, photographs, and partially written manuscripts for five major stories, set them in five neat stacks on the floor and start to work on the first
one. Receive a call from Ansley; she talks about Andrew, says he hasn't
been getting as much attention from me as Eliza and Paddy.

She brings up the moment right before I'd gotten on Florida in the
Hunt Cup, when either she or Eliza had called out to me. I thought back on
it, remembered glancing over, spotting Eliza standing in a sea of onlookers
on the other side of the snow fence, running over to her, reaching across
the fence, picking her up and giving her a big kiss. What could be wrong
with that?

Ansley says I should've given Andrew a kiss and I should've given her
a kiss.

I can't believe it. I explain to her it was hard enough running through
the path of horses and giving Eliza a kiss. I thought I'd done something

special, taking a moment out of the race concentration to kiss Eliza, and here I was being criticized for it. I explain I'd already given Andrew a hug just outside the jocks' tent earlier. (Susan had told me he had felt left out, which motivated my hug, but I didn't tell Ansley that. I also knew that Andrew had seemed worried about the race. He hadn't really been himself since witnessing all the falls, and the helicopter, at the Grand National.)

She says that as I was going back to my spot standing by Tom and the owners, awaiting Florida to circle around one more time, she had called out to me and I hadn't come back.

This—seconds before getting on the horse.

I am furious. This is ridiculous. I drag through the day at work with occasional lifts from people congratulating me on the ride. "You're an inspiration, Patrick. You're an inspiration to all of us," they tell me. "What's next?" they ask, looking questioningly, seriously, hopefully, into my eyes. "What're you going to do next?"

AT HOME. Sitting on the bed, having a glass of white wine, which totally disassembles my brain, I casually bring up to Ansley that I'd been having a difficult time that day, that I'd been wondering whether or not I wanted to keep riding races, that I hadn't been getting any writing accomplished lately, the manuscript I'd been working on had been "languishing, gathering dust . . ." To my surprise she starts crying and releases a litany of worries and criticisms:

"A difficult month? How do you think it's been for me? I can't keep living this life . . . The horse people are fickle, singing your praises one minute, cutting you down the next . . . It's dangerous . . . Look what happened to Irv . . . You've been absent for two months . . . You haven't even known I've existed for a month . . . I've had to do everything . . . You've missed almost all of Eliza's lacrosse games . . . When was the last time you threw the lacrosse ball with Andrew or even had a good talk with him? Everything in the house has been an unbelievable mess . . . So many things have been left undone: the bills, errands, chores, things that just have to be done . . . You thought you'd have fun with Tom, and instead it's been all nerves, all tension, all business . . . You've been rushing rushing rushing and you don't even realize it . . . You race in here, you race out, we've hardly seen each other . . . You look terrible, all skin and bones . . . You've been on edge . . . Sex, when was the last time we had sex?"

Oh my. I listen. I pay attention. Each statement feels like a punch in the gut. Each knocks me down another notch. Each has truth to it. Each makes me feel a little less positive about myself. I am shocked. I see it from her point of view. A déjà vu feeling strikes, the same jolting feeling as when Susan and Sal told me how they felt about their childhoods with Pop. It does not look good. And I also resent her for it. Couldn't she say one thing positive? Couldn't she be the least bit empathetic?

THROUGH OUR CLOSED DOOR, I hear, "Dad, Dad." I haven't told Eliza her bedtime story yet. I go into her room and lie down, hoping she hadn't heard our argument. I take a deep breath, summon my imaginative energies, and launch into a high-action adventure tale about "Plumpy the Bear." At the end of the story, instead of turning over, pulling up her covers, and acting like she is asleep, Eliza says, "Dad?"

"Yes."

"I liked it."

"Liked what?" I ask, thinking she means something about the story.

"Liked watching you and Mikey ride in the Hunt Cup."

She did overhear us arguing. "Mikey riding in the Hunt Cup?" I ask.

"Yes, I'm going to sleep now, Dad."

I let it go and give her a kiss. Get up and return to Ansley.

Tuesday.

I'd been planning to gallop at Tom's before work, but upon awakening, and feeling the new day, I decide to write. From a shelf, I pull down a beautiful journal, stitched and with a marbled blue-green cover, I'd been saving. Ansley had gotten it on her last trip to France. I open it. A note on a narrow sheet falls out.

Dearest Sweetheart,
  A new journal
    for you to write in . . .
      all the way from Paris –
        let's go
          together,
            and soon!
              — Je t'aime.
                  A.

I don't have the car pool to drive. I had set the morning up—with Jed's father to do the driving—so that I could gallop. I start the new journal, writing by hand across the purple-and-blue-checkered French pages. My hand is stiff. I write in large letters and skip lines.

Driving to Gilman, I hit a traffic jam. There's an accident. I'm near the photography lab, so I pull off the highway, drop off three rolls of film I'd shot the week before, look over four new contact sheets and order some prints. I arrive at work at 9:15.

There's a pink note on my chair. "Meet with Kate at 9:00." I call Kate, the director of development, whose office is directly below mine. Busy. I walk down to her office. Door shut.

Around 9:45, I try again. "Where've you been?" she asks, seated behind her desk, which has a writing surface that resembles the landing deck of an aircraft carrier.

"I've been right here. I called and your phone was busy. I stopped down and your door was shut. I assumed you were having a meeting."

"No, you weren't."

"What do you mean?"

"No you weren't here. I went upstairs and you weren't here. Hunt Cup's over now. Riding's over now. You need to get here at the normal time. You weren't riding, were you?"

"No, I wasn't riding. I got in a traffic jam on the way in, so instead of wasting time sitting there, I stopped at the photo lab." I struggle to remember just what it was I'd dropped off. I couldn't believe this. "Hunt Cup's over now . . ." It irked me when people said, "Hunt Cup this or Hunt Cup that," instead of "the Hunt Cup." "I dropped off some shots I took. A few rolls of film to be developed."

"Shots for what?"

I waver. Hesitate. My brain is locked. I can't remember what the hell was on the film. This lapse, this blank in the brain, had been happening to me more and more as the spring had progressed and my daily schedule had grown more hectic. It was as though my brain was overloaded, and a negative surge pulsated through the circuits, a black-cloaked ghost of guilt surreptitiously, stealthily patroling the pathways of my brain. This was the ghost that thought what I was doing—devoting all this time and energy at my age to race riding—was absolutely, irrevocably wrong, even stupid, and reeked of hubris, of selfishness, of self-centeredness, and, when I sometimes tried to reach deep into my mind, say for a complex explanation required in English class, or when, during a development department meeting, I was suddenly called upon to explain the overall design/writing/photography concept behind a publication, this ghost of guilt flapped its cloak like a big turkey buzzard, jostled any coherent thoughts I might have had, and caused me to stand there, stunned, a deer in the headlights, for a few seconds before I could drive the black flapping wings out of my mind.

On the film was something unusual. Something for admissions. It was not of people. I pictured myself holding the camera, pointing it, focusing it . . . "For the admissions view book. I took some color shots of the blossoming dogwoods for the designers. And while I was at the lab, I also . . ."

"OK, OK. Well, Hunt Cup's over now. Riding's over now, right?"

I don't reply.

I drag through another day. *Huis Clos. No Exit.* This is it. My existential nightmare. I've accomplished this feat. I've met my goal. I've pushed myself to do better than I ever could have imagined a year ago. I raised myself, my riding, to another level. I willed myself through the ups and downs of this experience and now what?

AT FIVE-THIRTY, the diabolic office phone rings yet again. In exasperation I snatch the handset off its receiver, thrust it to my ear, preparing to briskly and professionally and agitatedly blurt out, "Publications office, Patrick Smithwick speaking."

Before I say a word, I hear: "Dad?"

"Yes, Eliza!" I sing out.

"Guess what I did?"

"I don't know." I think hard, trying to get it. "Went for a swim?"

"No, Dad."

"I'm at Dee Dee's, Dad. I trotted today. I trotted on Chim Chim, all by myself, no one holding him."

On arriving home, I step out of the car, the kitchen door slams and Eliza comes sprinting out of the house, barefoot, across the lawn, arms pumping, hair bouncing up and down, legs churning. I take two steps, drop my satchel and jacket. She is almost to me, she is looking up into my eyes, she's close—blue eyes, blond hair pulled back off her forehead and held back by a green headband, long blond eyelashes, fair skin, big eyes, grinning—she jumps. I catch her and she's up, up, over my head. Suddenly serious, she is looking down into my eyes and she is making a pronouncement. "Dad, I trotted Chim Chim today all the way around the big field. Then I stopped, backed him up, and trotted the other direction, standing up the whole time just like you do." She looks into my eyes—I cannot get over this love, this connection, this nexus. I can't get over that she loves me. It amazes, bewilders, astounds me.

Wednesday.

I decide to do it. I'd felt selfish but I'd known in my bones I couldn't go before riding in the Hunt Cup.

I drive to the hospital at lunch. It's a hot, sunny day. I receive permission to go in. I am carrying the magazine in which I'd just published a story that included Irv and me riding in the Wild Goose Chase together. I thought I'd read it to him—he wins the race in the end. And I planned to give him hope by relating how Pop had been flat on his back on a hospital bed, paralyzed, when I had first seen him after his fall. We'd had little hope for his recovery, but then he had surprised the doctors by fighting his way out of the paralysis.

I walk down a long hall aware of every movement I am making—the way I swing my arms, the way my heel touches the floor and then my foot rolls, the length of my stride, longer than normal when I am on a mission.

I open the door to his room. It is large. He is in the bed. "Good afternoon, Irv," I say, striding in, keeping my momentum. I sit in the only chair; it is an oddly long distance from the bed.

He is stoic. He talks about the Hunt Cup as if nothing has happened to him, as though he had been there at the Hunt Cup. He analyzes the race and congratulates me on my ride, saying he thought my tactic of going to the front had been an excellent one, and he compliments me on the way Florida jumped. "How did you get him to jump like that?" he asks.

I give a brief explanation. Then I tell the story of Pop's recuperation from the paralysis, how he had recovered seventy-five percent of his strength and coordination. I try to give him hope. I pull the magazine out and read the section about the Wild Goose Chase. Halfway through, I realize I have started the passage too early and the reading of it is beginning to drag. I am feeling awkward and ineffective in cheering Irv up. I finish; Irv wins the race. Irv is polite and congratulates me on the article. He is tiring. I can see that he is tiring and here he is doing more to help me than I to help him. I shake Irv's hand, walk out of the room, down the long hallway, the *clack, clack, clack* of the leather heels of my loafers echoing off the walls.

He'd be able to fight his way back. He'd been in incredible shape and he'd wrestle his way out of this. I stride down the empty corridor. I walk out the door, my legs carrying me briskly, moving through space, through time, the sun's rays warming my bare arms.

Thursday.
Up early, I edit the first few pages of my book on Pop while everyone is still

asleep, then drive the car pool, which gets me to my office before the rest of the crew. I'm receiving e-mails from an alumnus who is a foreign correspondent reporting from Belgrade for the *Christian Science Monitor*—a position to which I had aspired during my last year at Johns Hopkins. The e-mails are Hemingway-esque and need almost no editing. This alumnus—two decades younger than his editor—is living on the edge. Witnessing people and animals being shot. Escaping bullets and explosions. Tired of being sequestered in his apartment, he takes a chance and sits out at a cafe with other journalists. They hear bombs explode a few blocks away, watch the building blow up, while having a drink. He's sending his e-mails to a friend, a teacher, in Los Angeles, who is then showing them to his students, who are then forwarding the e-mails to their friends. They are all writing him back. I am writing him back and am planning to publish his e-mails in the school magazine.

I have class at lunchtime. I feel love for my students and for the subject, Homer's *Odyssey*. I return a major paper on which they all did well. My hand is improving but writing the comments so they'll be legible had been difficult. I walk around the room, deciphering my marginalia.

After class, I go for a run, thinking of the feats of athleticism in *The Odyssey*: Odysseus challenging his opponents, throwing the javelin, whirling the discus, wrestling, swimming, fighting. We are getting to the end. After all these incredible adventures, after finally escaping Calypso, having been "cloaked" by this seductress (We did share a hearty, politically incorrect, all-male laugh about his half-hearted attempts to leave), he finally makes it home to Penelope, and at the very end, what does he do? Settle down? Stop? Become Calypsoed by his wife and home? No, he is movement. His name is Odysseus: trouble. Penelope tests him; he proves to Penelope who he is and then he sleeps with her, proving himself again. He does this in the bed that is rooted to the center of the earth by the olive tree which he had used for a bed post when he'd built it. He tells Penelope, "Dear wife, we have not yet come to the limit of all our trials . . ." The epic ends not with a conclusion but with Odysseus *setting out*.

I run and run. Ten, fifteen, twenty percent faster than usual. I am at my peak of fitness now, the fittest I have been in over twenty-five years. What to do with this fitness? I shower, stick my hand in a bucket of ice, eat a sandwich, and return to the office feeling fresh.

AT 5:45, I'M RUSHING. I'm proofreading the bluelines of a newsletter. The printer was supposed to pick it up at five. He'll be here any minute. The phone rings. I reach for the receiver planning to continue proofreading no matter who it is. Automaton-like, I say, "Hello, this is Patrick Smithwick."

"Guess what, Dad?"

"You patted Chim Chim today," I kid, looking up from the desk and out the window at the blue sky, the green fields, the varsity lacrosse team going through its drills. Maybe I'd go for a ride tonight.

"No, Dad!"

"You walked Chim Chim out of the barn and . . ."

"No, Dad. I jumped today! I jumped Chim Chim over an X. Dee Dee made an X and we jumped it."

Knowing immediately what she means, I picture two standards placed eight feet apart, and two rails, each set a foot or two up on a standard on one side and crossing over to the ground on the other side, forming an X.

"Really?"

"Yes, I trotted him over an X."

"Eliza, that's wonderful. What did it feel like?"

"It felt like we were flying."

Just as I felt in the Hunt Cup.

"Especially coming down. We were way high up and then his rear end was up high and we were coming down."

Exactly what it felt like on Florida jumping the third fence.

"When are you coming home, Dad?"

"Soon, Angel. Soon."

ON ARRIVING HOME, I have an iced tea. Eliza puts on an imaginary pony show. She trots, walks, backs up, canters. I teach her about leads: when going around a circle at a canter, the inside front foot should go down first.

She listens. She's attentive. She is soaking up this information. I get up out of my trainer's chair and canter around a circle, showing her. I sit down. She does it perfectly.

Ansley walks out, asks if I want to come with them. They have to shop for a confirmation present and then they're planning on having dinner.

"Sure, yes, can you wait for me to change," I say, but in the back of my mind I am thinking that the videotape of the Hunt Cup is being shown this night at the Manor Tavern, a mile from Mom's.

"Want to go to the Tavern for dinner?" I ask hesitantly. "I think they show the movies of the races there on Thursday nights."

"No. No. I want to get the present, have dinner, come home early and write my exams. I'm on duty all weekend."

Oh well. I feel let down in one way and relieved in another.

I change, make a cup of coffee, grab Sawyer under his front legs, help him scramble up into the cab of the pickup and off we go, hot coffee splashing across the dashboard.

WE ARRIVE AT MOM'S—this farm, Prospect Farm, my favorite spot on earth. My sanctuary. It is the soul of my family, rooted to the earth by the blood and sweat and talent of my father winning hundreds of races, riding thousands of horses, working seven days a week for twenty-five years to pay for it, by the perseverance and tenacity and even ferocity of my mother, working for three decades to hold onto it, and by my own, and my sons' work, mucking out sheds, shoveling snow, splitting wood, mowing fields, digging out the stream, nailing in boards, throwing bales of hay and straw down from the loft, riding and training and galloping horses and ponies. This ten-acre plot is my sanctuary to which one day, some day, Ansley and I, and our children, will move.

Mom is not home. I had looked forward to seeing her, to her seeing me enjoying myself—going for a ride on Warfield for the sake of riding him, not as a means to hone my race riding skills. I step out of the truck, help Sawyer down. He jogs off, wagging his tail, barking, looking for Mom and her dogs. I walk over toward the barn's white sliding door that opens into the main aisle way, tack room to the left, stalls on both sides. Take a few steps up the hill, toward the two twenty-foot-high red doors that slide across the entire side of the barn, leading into the barn's loft.

There is a breeze. Sunlight flickers through the trees onto a swatch of grass on the hillside. I flop down on the sun-lit blanket. Four horse lengths across the crusher-run, closest to me on the left side of the driveway, is the red-slatted corncrib. Then the compact, brown-shingled smoke house; the large, airy, brown-shingled garage with the old red Farmall barely visible; and the stone steps leading from the driveway, down and across the dip in the lawn, to the stairway up the back porch and to the kitchen door. Behind me, near a small gate, stand Warfield and Chim Chim, swishing their tails and staring at me. I turn and look at Warfield. He looks directly into my eyes, hopefully into my eyes, anticipatingly into my eyes, flicks his tail, moves his lips, releasing and regripping them, and then licking them with his tongue. I can hear the light chomping.

Sawyer runs up and slams himself against my torso. His wagging tail shoots pond water all over me. He puts his nose under my armpit and pushes his body into mine, stepping over me, straddling me. He's grinning and wagging his tail and pushing his wet, cold, black nose against my hands to get me to pat him. Laughing, I'm getting drenched and covered in the snaky, grassy, spermy, tadpole-smelling pond water. The feel and scent of the black mud and water bring back images of catching frogs and snapping turtles, of building dams and tadpole-harvesting pools, of swimming the ponies and going skinny dipping. I shove him off. He stands perfectly still in the sunlight, thinking what he will do next. He spreads all four legs out, braces himself and then shakes wildly, streamlets of water shooting into the air, his soaked, mashed-down coat loosening, freeing itself, airing itself out, becoming light and fluffy and full, enlarging his torso and neck. He has gone from being a sleek seal-like swimmer to a majestic lion with a thick and glowing mane. He freezes, staring out into the back field.

Two geese strut away from the stream. Between them is a gaggle of goslings. Pulling up the rear are two more pairs of geese. They head up into the pasture where they will graze, pulling the grass out by the roots.

Farther up the pasture, another dozen geese are venturing out to the rich grass. Sawyer is poised. His body tenses. He is ready. I grab him by the collar. I pull him back. He pulls against me. "Go get'em Sawyer, go get'em," I tell him in a raspy voice, holding him back, pulling him back, then releasing him. He catapults away, flying across the driveway, under the fence, down to the stream crossing, up the hill, into the geese. They run and wobble and flap their wings, rushing back to the pond.

HEADING OUT ON WARFIELD, I plan to hack around, not jump anything, but once I get loosened up, I think it'd be fun to do the same course we'd followed the morning of the Hunt Cup.

Relaxed, we walk, trot, canter and gallop over fence after fence, not a care in the world. Warfield is on the bit. He's pulling harder and harder and starting to put his head up, trying to get away from me. I lean back, pull him up, give him a breather. I look down at his neck—he is hot, sweating, but he's not tired. It creeps up on me. I start to wonder. What am I going to do? Am I going to get on the phone and get more rides? Am I going to continue race riding? Am I going to keep this level of fitness? Can I continue to pull myself away from Andrew and Eliza and Ansley? How can I give it up? And yet how can I continue to live like this while also fulfilling my duties as a husband to Ansley, as a father to my children, and as a man who is blessed with great, lifelong friends?

We jog to the edge of a creek and pull up. I kick my feet out of the stirrups. Warfield gingerly puts his feet out in front, stretches his long neck down, and drinks the quickly moving, clear water. I listen to the bubbling and gurgling and the hum and buzz of insects and watch the long-legged water striders dance on the water's surface.

Up and to our right is a steep bank, fifty yards long, built from the dirt dug out of the hillside to make the pond. The bank runs the length of the long, narrow pond and at the end there is a deep dip where the bank drops off, and then, a few strides up a steep incline, a board inset—two panels of the fence that are lower than the rest—that leans slightly toward you. It is a trappy jump. Beyond the inset, the thick grass rises in a long gradually steepening slope toward the half-melon of sun sinking behind the ridge and splashing the hillside with sharply angled yellow rays, leaving our side of the two panels dark in shadow.

I stand in the irons, stretch, look downstream at a bridge that leads to a path in the woods we could take, and then I look up at the pond. Warfield is leaning, literally, toward the pond, which he knows is on the most direct line home. Sawyer sidles away from us and takes a few steps toward the pond, which he knows holds cool, clear water. And I, drawn by the light and the memories of the hill above the pond, release my hold and let Warfield plunge up the bank.

Walking along the spine of the bank, I think back on galloping head-and-head with Paddy up this steep hill ahead of us on a late winter afternoon with the long red brush strokes of dusk dipping behind the crest and the last of the sun's rays angling straight into our eyes so that with the speed and wind and cold making our eyes water, and the red rays reflecting off the white snow, we could not look straight ahead. We could only see the flaming snow splashing high on either side of us, and we laughed and I yelled out "Hold on, Buddy, hold on," taking myself back to an early morning bareback ride with my father on a finger-numbing, toe-freezing morning at Hydes, my arms tight around my father's chest as we loped across a field, the snow spraying up around us, and I heard Pop cluck to the horse beneath us, and we took off at a speed that I had never imagined, and he called out to me, "Hold on Bud, hold on!" A sadness, a nostalgia passes like a cool breeze through my chest, but then I envision Eliza on Chim Chim, Eliza riding in my old saddle. I picture Eliza and me walking through the far woods, Chim Chim safely tucked in behind Warfield, Sawyer scouting ahead, and I hope and yearn for the rides and conversations and times to share with her.

Warfield and I walk along the bank of the pond, the fence twenty lengths ahead, daring us, taunting us, Sawyer on our right swimming powerfully across the pond, his jaw set in concentration. I have eyed this fence many times and have never jumped it. I shorten my hold on the reins and give Warfield a squeeze. Sawyer splashes and muscles his way out of the water and is sprinting beside us. We gallop down off the bank, across the dip and up an incline. I squeeze. Warfield keeps his stride, stands off and we are in the air over the fence in the blazingly angled sunlight, high up—reminding me of Florida over the third!—and coming down alongside Sawyer. Landing, I whoop and bow over and I know at this moment, my mind is made up that yes, I want to ride, that yes, this is wonderful, yes, it makes no difference whether it's now on Warfield, not a human in sight, or five days ago on Florida with thousands of dollars on the line and thousands of eyes on us, or, in a few weeks, riding across the countryside with Eliza. I envision us crossing the Hess Road stream after a strong rain. I see the water swirling up around Chim Chim's belly and Eliza—as Paddy used to do on Nappy and Andrew on Blossom and I on Queenie—lifting her feet high and laughing.

I HOSE OFF WARFIELD and head for the Manor Tavern. The bar is crowded. It is a cheerful throng, and everybody wants to buy me a drink. I get a beer, stand in the midst of the hurly-burly as the movie comes on and Florida and I go to the front and the crowd cheers us on as we fly over fence after fence, friends and people I don't know, some already thoroughly inebriated, slapping me on the back and calling out, "Go on with 'em, Paddy," "Let'em roll, Patrick," and then I see him. I see what Eliza was saying. There is Mikey on Waldo, the pony-sized half Thoroughbred. When I reach the eighth, he is just down the hill from me, riding in a straight line parallel to my line but a few horse lengths away from each fence. He is standing up high so he can see, galloping along, with his head turned to look at me as we gallop down over the eighth, ninth, tenth, eleventh and close to the twelfth. Then he picks me up again at the eighteenth, as the horses are coming to me, and he gallops down along the eighteenth, nineteenth and twentieth watching my every step, ten lengths away, and only pulls up, only leaves us when we reach Tufton Avenue. Eliza was right.

On leaving, I bump into an old friend of my father's, tall and strong, whose name I can't remember. "Times have changed," he says, grinning.

"Yes, they have," I reply without thinking. Then, sensing he is referring to something in particular, I stop and ask, "In what ways do you mean?"

Standing out by the front door to the Tavern, he says, "Remember the night the bouncers held you up against the wall right here and worked you over?"

"Yes," I laugh, not particularly pleased to be reminded of that twenty-year-ago memory. "I'd gotten in a fight with a guy in the band who kept making eyes at Ansley while she was dancing and he had a whole table of friends there."

"Who do you think it was that pulled them off you?"

"Well, thank you," I say, shaking his hand. "A belated thanks."

"And now you're an inspiration to half the people in there."

"I don't know about that," I say.

"Paddy," he says, "your father'd be proud of you."

Friday.

Up early. Feeling great. For the first time since the early mornings at the Ping Pong table in the boathouse at Camp Forest Craft, inspired by Eliza's enthusiasm, I take out a legal pad and write fresh material about my youth for the book, including a scene when Pop and Mikey bring me my first hunter-pony, Queenie, and Pop throws me up onto her bare back.

Work goes well at Gilman. The days are less hectic without driving to Tom's at 6:00, galloping a few, showering and changing, then racing to Gilman. It is amazing how much more time I have. My schedule now seems to be, as Walter Lord says, "a piece of cake." Home from work: Iced tea. Horse show. Race. Then, what can we do new?

Using my hands as a horse's front feet, I direct Eliza on how to canter in a figure eight. I explain how to stay on the inside lead going around the circle, to act for a split second as if you're going to continue around the circle, and then, instead, in the air, in mid-stride, to uplift and turn the horse the opposite direction. The horse, all four feet in the air, will do a flying change, switching from one lead to the other. Eliza listens attentively.

I stand up and skip/canter. Over and over, at the center of the figure eight, in mid-stride, I shift my weight and continue in a figure eight, galloping around a loop and cycling back to the center, to the focal point.

Eliza tries it. The skipping is tiring. I drop in behind her, grip her under her arms, lift her partially off the ground and guide her, cantering/skipping around the figure eight until I am exhausted. I stop, raise her high over my head, wheel her around and around and fall to the ground, laughing, as she calls out, "Dad! Dad!"

Saturday.

I arise early, write for a few hours, then go to Mom's where I am far behind in work on the farm. First, I school Chim Chim. I'm impatient. It's hot and the flies are out. He doesn't go well. The ground is now hard as a brick. Why couldn't it have been like this last Saturday—Florida wouldn't have had to labor through the deep going, he could've held his speed on the hard ground he loves. We would have had a chance at winning. I realize I'm rushing Chim Chim. I am not paying attention. I slow down, pay attention. Focus on the present. I ride Chim Chim, just as I rode Florida Law. I cannot simply be "a passenger."

We bump into two members of the Elkridge-Harford Hunt out exercising their hunters. They've been watching me school over some logs. They walk back to Mom's with me—laughing at my current mount, asking all about the Hunt Cup, praising Florida's jumping, asking if I am going to continue, urging me to do so.

I muck out the stalls, muck out the two sheds, push one wheelbarrow load after another filled with manure up to the top field, spread the manure with a pitchfork, clean up the barn. I'm still too thin, too light from the reducing and now I am working to regain some muscle.

On arriving home, I tell Eliza how well Chim Chim had gone. She looks me in the eye, tells me she wants to ride him the next day but first she wants to get "some of those riding pants." I ask what she means and she says, "You know, those riding pants like what you and Mikey wore in the races."

"Let's go," I say.

Eliza jumps in the car and we drive to a little tack store. I receive some compliments for the Hunt Cup ride from the thoughtful and patient woman who runs the store. We find a pair of dark, cream-colored jodhpurs. Eliza loves them. We spend an hour trying on new riding boots—I am gasping at the prices—but can't find a pair with which we're both happy.

We escape from the tack shop without buying anything but the jodhpurs, planning our ride the next morning. Meeting Andrew at home, all three of us pull on bathing suits, run up "Graduation Hill" and jump in the pool. We get dressed and prepare to go to a confirmation party for a boy we know well, whose parents are from the non-horsey side of my life, and who live over by Mikey's. Ansley can't go; she's on dorm duty. Finally, we are in the car, ready to go, air conditioner on, and Eliza says she wants her jodhpurs.

We are getting late. Andrew and I tell her she doesn't need them. I have already looked all around through the stifling heat of the third floor for them.

She has to have them.

I jump out of the car, run into the house and up the two flights of stairs to her room, search through a few piles of clothes and, miraculously, find them.

We're in the car—Ansley's "new" car, a secondhand station wagon we bought from a friend. The music is on, the AC is on, we're on our way, and Eliza is in the back quietly, determinedly, changing into the jodhpurs. She wants to wear them on the way over.

I drive slowly, luxuriating in the sound system, the air conditioning, and the car's powerful engine. I adjust the rearview mirror and watch as she maneuvers, getting one leg and then the next into the jodhpurs, pulling them over her shorts. I'm happy. She's into this, it's her thing, it's not as though she wants to show them off to anyone. She just wants, in her quiet way, to have them on.

As we near the party she changes back into her original outfit, neatly folding the jodhpurs and setting them on the back seat. We walk into the party. Andrew and Eliza join a group of friends on the trampoline. I am immediately surprised by the barrage of questions and compliments—spurred by the Wild Goose Chase magazine piece that had just hit the stands—about my writing.

What're you working on now? Who's your agent? I fumble and mumble replies to these questions. Instead of feeling good about the attention from these readers, I whip myself: What have I been doing?

The invitation for the confirmation party had mentioned rum punches and I had been looking forward to a drink or two, perhaps looking forward too much to the rum. I put down a couple of big ones and suddenly it is time to leave. Andrew stays, looking forward to spending the night at the party, sleeping with his friends on the trampoline. Eliza falls asleep in the back on the way home, her jodhpurs on.

In our driveway, I unbuckle Eliza's seat belt, pull her off the seat and sling her high, over my shoulders. She is getting so long. I carry her across the lawn to the kitchen door, imagining doing this forever—as she turns ten, eleven, thirteen, fifteen, eighteen—slinging her over my shoulder and carrying her into the house. I'll have to start lifting more weights, increase my strength, so I can keep up with her size and weight. I love carrying her; it reminds me of hiking down the Adirondack mountain with her lapped over my shoulders, pretending to be asleep, her arms hanging down on my left, her legs on my right, her breath against my neck.

We head up the two flights of narrow stairs. Three steps from the top, I slide her off my shoulders and set her on her feet. Holding her upright, I step up onto the floor and guide her into the bedroom, steady her in a semi-standing position beside the bed. Pretending she's asleep, she leans, trusting me, drifting one direction and I catch her, pull her back into an upright position. Then she leans, drifting the other direction, her eyes closed. I place one arm behind her knees, the other around her shoulder blades—lift her up, then gently set her down on the bed. I stand there, wondering if I should let her sleep in her jodphurs. She sits up, takes over. "Dad, can you get my pajamas?" I jog into her room, grab the pajamas, return, hand them to her. She holds them and stares at me. I turn away as she pulls off her shirt and jodhpurs, steps into the pajamas. I lie down beside her, as happy and peaceful and content as can be, my arm around my daughter, not a worry in the world, not another place I'd rather be. I whisper Yeat's "A Cradle Song," which she's heard many times, to her.

The angels are stooping
    Above your bed;
They weary of trooping
    With the whimpering dead.

God's laughing in Heaven
    To see you so good;
The Sailing Seven
    Are gay with His mood.

I sigh that kiss you,
    For I must own
That I shall miss you
    When you have grown.

I lie beside her, listening to her peaceful breathing as she falls asleep, and think about Ansley. She is still up at dorm duty but will be back soon. She is only half a mile away and I realize I have been away, miles away, off on a psychological as well as physical odyssey, from the conception of the race riding idea at Saratoga to the riding in the Hunt Cup, August to April, nine months, and now it is time to return. I quietly get out of the bed, pull the covers off Eliza, carry her to her room and tuck her in her bed. I return, flip on the fan, flop down on the big bed and wait, making plans for the night.

Sunday.
It is early. I'd had a late night, but I feel wide awake, fully reinvigorated. I tiptoe into Eliza's room and gently touch her shoulder. Unlike the boys, or

myself—more like her mother in this—she doesn't procrastinate; she can awaken, and at that exact moment step out of bed, into her clothes, and be on her way. I whisper to her, trying not to awaken Ansley on the other side of the wall, that we will ride before it gets hot. She sits up and slides out of bed. Pulls on her jodhpurs. She hasn't gone to the bathroom, brushed her teeth, washed her face, or brushed her hair. She is pulling on her jodhpurs, and then she is looking for a pair of riding boots, asking me what she can wear, then pulling on the old pair of worn black ones—once Paddy's, then Andrew's. She used to love them but now thinks they're far too small: she needs a new pair of brown ones like the ones she tried on at the tack shop. We are sitting on the floor. I am helping her lace up her boots. I am riding this wave, catching this current, gliding on this billowing surge of air. I ask, "What's gotten you interested in riding again?"

She looks into my eyes. She knows what it is. But she doesn't want to say it or doesn't know how to say it or is too shy to say it.

"It doesn't matter," I say, not wanting to create any pressure. "Don't worry about it."

"The races," she says.

"The races?"

"Watching you in the races. That's what it is."

She laces up one boot while I lace up the other, the two of us ready to have breakfast, get in the truck—she on my lap, steering, Sawyer by our sides—drive to Mom's, catch Chim Chim, brush him off, and *ride.*

A Note to the Reader

IN *FLYING CHANGE* I have striven to show my love for my children and my fierce dedication to giving them the best upbringing I possibly could. Thus, if *Racing My Father* was a son writing about his father, and then learning to live without his father, *Flying Change* is from the point of view of a father writing about his children, a father who will soon be learning how to live without them, as they leave home for college and careers in medicine and the military.

I wanted to complete *Flying Change* for my sons Andrew and Paddy, for my daughter Eliza, for my sisters Susan and Sallie, for my nephews Colin, McLean and Coston, and for my nieces Rachel, Abigail, Avah, Louisa and Annie. I also wrote it for those who have grown up indoors, in front of computer screens, on the internet, wired to earphones and headsets, sealed off from the textures and feelings and smells and sounds of life.

It's a travesty that in the wealthiest, most powerful nation on earth a generation is coming of age out of shape, overweight, with all kinds of health problems. So many high school students live much of their lives vicariously through television and computers, at a distance from the wonder of the out-of-doors—from the meaning of walking a horse to a stream and letting the reins slide through your fingers as the horse stops, paws the water, sniffs it, and then, bracing his front feet in the current, stretches down his neck and takes a long drink; from the importance of finding a canopy of trees under which to ride in the August heat, when you kick your feet out of the stirrups, loosen the girth and your horse lowers his head, relaxes his stride, his tail swishing away the flies; from the timeless peace of trotting along the ridge of a hill on a February afternoon, the wind lacing through your deerskin windbreaker, numbing your face, tearing at your ears—then pulling your horse up to a walk, pointing him down the south-side of the steep hill, and, leaning back with your feet braced in the stirrups out in front of you, heading one step at a time down the stony slope, out

343

of the relentless roar of the northwestern wind, and into a sun-warmed southern-facing bowl of unfrozen turf.

Many young men and women today may go through a lifetime without ever having experienced the exhilaration of making an instantaneous decision in a life-threatening situation and the ensuing rush from having survived by skill and quickness and nerve and training handed down through generation after generation from father and mother to son and daughter. Many have not worked alongside their parents and grandparents with interest and respect, as apprentices, as youths on a farm, or as fledgling horsemen. Many have never pushed themselves in their work to the point of complete physical exhaustion, even pain, and then had no choice but to continue pushing and working.

I wanted to convey for them what it is like to survive a near-disastrous, potentially bone-crushing situation with a horse between your legs—the horse being nature, the horse being the out-of-doors, the horse being part of the heat and the cold and the wind and the snow and the ice and the rain out in which you ride, the horse being the great equalizer. The horse doesn't know if you're a hotshot accountant, a wheeler-dealer investment banker, a "galloping boy" being paid ten dollars a head, an orthopedic surgeon just out of the operating room, a writer with his dreams of the purity of his art. The horse only knows that you are there on his back, and he is there between your legs, and this is it: the horse is living in the present, and you'd better follow his lead.

Acknowledgments

I'D ESPECIALLY LIKE to thank Harriet Iglehart, Mrs. G. W. "Betty" Merck, Ned and Rachel Owens, Frank Richardson, Hank Slauson, Mrs. Bruner H. Strawbridge, and George Strawbridge Jr. for being my patrons. Their generous grants gave me the time and confidence to finish the final editing of this memoir and enabled what was a typescript to finally bloom into a hardback book. Their excitement, interest and confidence in *Flying Change* spurred me down the homestretch.

I thank Harriet for being a lifelong supporter of my literary endeavors—both teaching and writing—ever since I got my first non-horse job as a reporter on the *Dorchester News* in Cambridge, Maryland, up to recently when she attended a day-long "Medieval Feast" at Harford Day School in Bel Air, Maryland, where I now teach Medieval History and English. Harriet is my patron-critic. I had a remarkable session with Harriet out on her porch one chilly March night as she went through a manuscript, page by page, providing me with clear, crisp, and sometimes sharp critical feedback on everything from using the incorrect "elegant nominative" to over-employing God's powers.

Ned Owens' enthusiasm for the book injected me with energy and a can-do attitude and directly led to finding my publisher, the Chesapeake Book Company, right here in Maryland. Ned's enlisting of the support of his wife Rachel, mother Mrs. Bruner Strawbridge, and brother George Strawbridge Jr. was critical to getting the book on press.

Mrs. G. W. "Betty" Merck—The Fields Stable—owned the horse Brigade of Guards, featured in the beginning and end of *Flying Change*. I was thrilled to hear of Betty's excitement and interest in the manuscript from my godson, Sam Voss, as we swam laps on a hot August day. Sam had read a chapter to her a few nights before. And I'll never forget the cheerful telephone message Betty later left me in her soft, mellifluous voice.

Frank Richardson sent me a letter—by coincidence at the time I was finishing *Flying Change*—about an excellent biography he'd just read, which, he wrote, "put me to thinking that we need a biography of D. Michael Smithwick." This former owner of Mikey's then urged me to write such a book. I wrote back explaining that Mikey played a major part in a book on which I was now working (which I enclosed), and soon Frank, who had seen every Hunt Cup Mikey had won, signed on as a patron.

There were many readers, test pilots and editors of *Flying Change*. First and foremost was Cary Woodward, retired master English teacher of Gilman School, passionate, insatiable reader of literature, and devoted believer in Mies van der Rohe's "less is more" theory of artistic composition. Cary provided invaluable insight and constant support. He also gave me the following quote, knowing it would strike a chord, since it is from one of my favorite authors: "A successful book is not made of what is in it, but of what is left out of it." Oh, the pain of cutting out those one hundred pages!

The late Peter Winants, brother of my godfather Gary, and a noted editor and writer of equestrian books, patiently made suggestions on early versions when he was in the grip of cancer and in his last days. Peter's expertise in writing, his familiarity with all the characters in the book, and his knowledge of steeplechasing made him a rare reader and invaluable critic.

My contemporary Bill Santoro, great friend since our teenage days, penned enthusiastic late-night opinions that sprang from his lifelong love of riding as well as his passion for the theater. He did this at an ironic and trying time. In his late fifties, Bill began to dedicate himself to the riding of steeplechase races and was enjoying remarkable success when he sustained an injury that prevented him from riding some fine horses during his last months of eligibility before turning sixty. It was during these last trying days of inactive eligibility that I handed him a typsecript.

Larry Haislip, Anglophile and bibliophile, cracked the whip on me after reading a first draft, lent me his rare copy of Siegfried Sassoon's *Memoirs of a Fox-Hunting Man*, and spurred me to read *Brideshead Revisited* and study Evelyn Waugh's novelistic use of time.

John Egan—Kentucky lawyer, avid foxhunter, Johns Hopkins class-mate, and an avid supporter of my return to race-riding—galloped head and head with me, line by line, through the manuscript, responding to scenes and passages with pithy and interesting remarks in the margins, and writing polished critiques at the end of most chapters. He also wrote a final letter of critical opinion so polished and provoking that I felt as if I were reading it in the *New Yorker*.

I had several readers whom I picked because they had no experience with horses. How well I remember my long session with Denny Clouse in my writing room—a converted cow shed with stone walls, cement trough, chestnut beams, and four big windows overlooking the back field. It was an Indian summer day. Windows open. Just the two of us on the ten-acre farm. I didn't even know this articulate woman, and here we were. She reviewed her helpful and inspiring comments. Reminded of Wallace Stegner's *Angle of Repose,* Denny urged me to read this great novel. I gave her a peck on the cheek as she left.

Carl Gold, not as "easy on the eyes" as Denny, but just as insightful, was a force of nature. I did not give him a kiss when he left, but his enthusiasm, insight and ability to pick out themes and motifs that I was unconsciously employing, his knowledgeable literary marginalia swirling up and down the sides of pages—stoked the engines of my work ethic.

Lawrence Shumacker urged me to make the book interesting and relevant to the non-horsey reader and gave me a copy of the novel *Any Human Heart: The Intimate Journals of Logan Mountstuart*, by William Boyd, to study.

Maureen Henderson—I hadn't seen her in fifteen years. She had once been a student in a creative writing class I taught at Johns Hopkins. Now, she was my critic from the Midwest, providing me with a mother's and a wife's point of view, and very concerned about the depiction of my wife Ansley in these pages as well as my treatment of her in life. Maureen sat before her fireplace in Minnesota after making her own writing deadlines, sipped wine, gave the book its last reading before going to the publisher, and sent me emails. Maureen gave me a recommendation about the sequencing of chapters that at first I thought was so preposterous, I laughed aloud, and that two weeks later I followed, reminding me of a certain pattern I often follow with my wife's suggestions.

The students of Harford Day School, the parents, especially John Horst, the teachers, especially Jennifer Dippel, encouraged my writing. Most of all Mrs. Margot Lazarony, grandmother of my high-achieving History and English student Philip, and the most international, cosmopolitan and beautiful grandmother I know, kept me going over the last cold winter of work on *Flying Change* by sending me bright, sun-charged tangerines and sweet notes from Fort Pierce, Florida, when I was devoting every school closing on "snow days" to the book. Also, a special thanks to History student extraordinaire, Justin Hawkins, graduate of 2011, who for three years inspired my teaching of History as well as English every day through his unabashed enthusiasm for history, giving me confidence, and making me feel as if I were accomplishing something worthwhile, during this turning point in my life.

Su Harris, head of HDS, and Katy Dallam, head of the Middle School, have allowed and even encouraged me to be myself. My CV does not fit the cookie-cutter teacher prototype, or any other occupational mold. Both Su and Katy have respected my desire to write and to ride and given me freedom to develop methods of teaching that best suit my interests, personality and background.

I have been blessed with a wonderful group of childhood friends. Tom Iglehart, member of the "Coo-Coo-Lilly Club," sacrificed many weekends over a long spring to chase after me with a camera, then spent many hours turning these tapes into the short documentary, "The Later Years," that goes with *Flying Change*.

Will Dixon provided his gifts of high energy, financial savvy and knowledge of the racing world. If it hadn't been for Willie's passion and business skills in drawing up a good publishing plan, *Flying Change* might still be three hundred typed pages held together by rubber bands and gathering dust in this writing room on a shelf above the old feed trough.

Chin strap unbuckled, feet kicked out of stirrups, girth loosened, speaking on a cell phone while hacking a horse home on a September Sunday, I told Hank Slauson about Willie's and my publication plan, said it was going well. "How about me Paddy?" Hank asked. "I sure as hell would like to be in on this." I sent him a manuscript. A week later, I received an inspiring note—not quotable here but taped to the window in front of me—and a contribution in the mail. I did shed a tear.

Through our bimonthly "geezer dinners," Reed Huppman, Tom Whedbee and Rob Deford kept me from taking myself seriously and made sure I was grounded and laughing and in love with the adventure that is being a father to our children, a lover to our wives, and a friend to each other at this stage in our lives.

Tom Voss not only provided the horses to ride in the past pages, he also keeps me directly connected to the world of horse racing, and especially to my father's memorial race, while, in his own way encouraging my writing, say, by giving me a box of seventy-two 100 percent premium cedar pencils for my birthday instead of a whip or pair of spurs, or by calling me one afternoon after I'd made a poor decision, at the age of "almost sixty," in accepting a last-minute invitation to ride an inexperienced horse for an inexperienced trainer in the Maryland Hunt Cup, and asking, "What the *hell* are you doing?"

My sister Sal. You read about one gift from her. There were others, and decades of notes and intense phone calls to tell me it is all right not to be a professional steeplechase jockey, it is a good thing to write and to teach.

My sister Susan has also been a lifelong, forceful proponent of my writing (and opponent of racetrack life) even though, to this day, she puts no trust in my maturity or what I might've learned over the past five decades. With no provocation, she will lecture me in front of her new friends, complete strangers to me—while even shaking her finger at me—to be sure not to say such and such (usually something about sex, which she exaggerates, something I might've said one time when I was sixteen), or to be sure not to do this or that wild act (usually something about driving a car, which she exaggerates, announcing that I used to drive 125 mph at midnight with no lights when I was eighteen), or something about drinking. (Usually she'll tell a series of stretchers about Tom and me drinking wine out of wineskins while skiing with Tiger Bennet, or about having an early morning drink at the track: Pop and Sal Tumenelli and Brian Hickey might've brought me to the Uptown Bar and Grill outside the front gate of Pimlico Racetrack for breakfast at 7:45 on a weekday morning or two after galloping horses in below-freezing temperatures around Old Hill Top and before rushing to class at Gilman School. Seated at the bar, out of the howling wind, they might've offered me a full breakfast—a strong screwdriver, a three-day-old hard-boiled egg, and a stiff-as-steel slice of beef jerky, followed, Brian would insist, by a shot of blackberry brandy "to warm the soul." Ah, those were the days of love and camaraderie and working for the family, for Pop, for Mom, for my sisters, for and with the grooms and riders and hotwalkers who worked and shared in any success with us). Susan will exaggerate aspects of those days as she scolds me—with a sly, wry grin, and a twinkle in her eye.

My publisher, Robert I. "Ric" Cottom of the Chesapeake Book Company, was calm and patient and professional. I am thankful to him for settling me down many a time, for his ability to gradually work through problems, and for his old-fashioned, painstaking work in laying out every page and creating an aesthetically pleasing flow of paragraphs, pages and chapters that make up this physical *book*. Likewise, I am appreciative of Donna Shear's precise and final editing.

Allison Dickinson struck like a bolt of lightning as the book headed for the printer, revving up and modernizing my musty marketing plans, spurring me into the computer age, injecting the whole process with pizzazz, and laughingly, but forcefully, poking me with a cow prod to make me creep outside my comfort zone.

I tip my cap to Jimmy Murphy, best friend of my father, well-known trainer who was even better known for being one of the most kind, giving and gentlemanly men on the racetrack. Cheerful, positive, telling me stories of my father and asking me questions about the progress of work on this book, Jimmy lay on his deathbed in a hospital room a couple of years ago. We both knew it would be our last meeting. I shook hands and walked to the door, but it wasn't right, not quite right. Jimmy sensed my feelings. Thinking of me, and not of himself, he pushed his torso up off the pillow with his strong arms, sat up, smiled, and said in his calm voice as I reached for the door handle, "Keep writing, Patrick. Keep writing."

Most of all, I thank my wife Ansley. Work on *Flying Change* has taken up countless early morning hours, weekends, and vacations, that could have been used in money-making ways or as love-making days. Writing and editing the book marched forward while bills went unpaid, fields needed mowing, cars had to be towed, the tractor needed oil, the stream cried out for weeding, piles of firewood waiting to be split and stacked clogged the driveway, invitations were left unanswered, dinners and parties with friends were skipped, fences went unrepaired and money owed was moved from one credit card account to another. I am glad Ansley didn't move her love account to another more available and less stress-inducing source.

Ansley is the stability in my life. I leap into projects, sign contracts, take new jobs, toss off old jobs, become enamored with multiple, diametrically opposed lifestyles at the same time, grow overwhelmed by devoting myself to too many competing "careers," make life-changing decisions based on love, loyalty and emotion rather than finances, common sense, and what others are doing, and throughout it all, she remains steady, constant—and usually right.

Patrick Smithwick
Prospect Farm
Monkton, Maryland
29 October 2011